State Power, Autarchy, and Political Conquest in Nigerian Federalism

State Power, Autarchy, and Political Conquest in Nigerian Federalism

Kalu N. Kalu

LEXINGTON BOOKS

A division of
ROWMAN & LITTLEFIELD PUBLISHERS, INC.
Lanham • Boulder • New York • Toronto • Plymouth, UK

LEXINGTON BOOKS

A division of Rowman & Littlefield Publishers, Inc.
A wholly owned subsidiary of The Rowman & Littlefield Publishing Group, Inc.
4501 Forbes Boulevard, Suite 200
Lanham, MD 20706

Estover Road
Plymouth PL6 7PY
United Kingdom

British Library Cataloguing in Publication Information Available

Library of Congress Cataloging-in-Publication Data

Kalu, Kalu Ndukwe.
   State power, autarchy, and political conquest in Nigerian federalism / Kalu N.
Kalu.
     p. cm.
   Includes bibliographical references and index.
   1. Federal government—Nigeria. 2. Nigeria—Politics and government.
I. Title.
JQ3086.S8K35 2008
320.4669'049—dc22   2008009970

ISBN: 978-0-7391-1955-6 (cloth : alk. paper)
ISBN: 978-0-7391-1956-3 (pbk. : alk. paper)
ISBN: 978-0-7391-2992-0 (electronic)

Printed in the United States of America

♾ ™ The paper used in this publication meets the minimum requirements of
American National Standard for Information Sciences—Permanence of Paper
for Printed Library Materials, ANSI/NISO Z39.48-1992.

For my daughter
Reneé Elizabeth Aluba Ndukwe Kalu

Contents

Figures and Tables

FIGURES

TABLES

List of Acronyms

AC	Action Congress
AFRICOM	Africa Command
AG	Action Group
ANPP	All Nigeria People Party
ASEAN	Association of Southeast Asian Nations
COR	Calabar-Ogoja-Rivers States
EFCC	Economic and Financial Crimes Commission
GNP	Gross National Product
IMF	International Monetary Fund
INEC	Independent National Electoral Commission
JDZ	Joint Development Zone
MAMSER	Mass Mobilization for Social Justice, Self Reliance, and Economic Recovery
MASSOB	Movement for the Actualization of the Sovereign State of Biafra
MEND	Movement for the Emancipation of the Niger Delta
MOSEIN	Movement for the Survival of Ijaw Ethnic Nationality
MOSOP	Movement for the Survival of the Ogoni People
MSM	Mid-West State Movement
MZL	Middle Zone League
NADECO	National Democratic Coalition
NCNC	National Council of Nigerian Citizens
NDC	Niger Delta Congress
NDDC	Niger Delta Development Commission
NDPVF	Niger Delta Peoples Volunteer Force

NDV	Niger Delta Vigilante
NDVS	Niger Delta Volunteer Force
NEPU	Nigerian Elements Progressive Union
NLC	Nigerian Labor Congress
NNA	Nigerian National Alliance
NNDP	Nigerian National Democratic Party
NNOC	Nigerian National Oil Corporation
NNPC	Nigerian National Petroleum Corporation
NPC	Northern People's Congress
NUPENG	National Union of Petroleum and Natural Gas Workers
OPC	Odua People's Congress
OPEC	Organization of Petroleum Exporting Countries
OGJ	Oil and Gas Journal
PDP	Peoples Democratic Party
PENGASSAN	Petroleum and Natural Gas Senior Staff Association of Nigeria
PPAC	Presidential Policy Advisory Committee
PSCs	Production Sharing Contracts
SDPC	Shell Petroleum Development Corporation
TRADOC	Training and Doctrine Command
UMBC	United Middle Belt Congress
UPGA	United Progressive Grand Alliance
WAI	War Against Indiscipline

Political Map of Nigeria

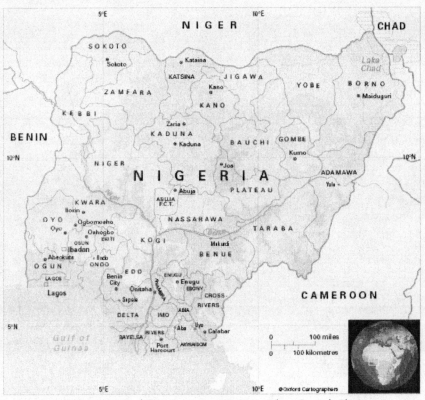

Political Map of Nigeria. Area: 923,766 sq. km. Capital: Abuja

Preface and Acknowledgments

The inspiration for this project began in 1997 while I was studying as a postdoctoral fellow in the Department of Political Science at Yale University and continued throughout my period as a research affiliate at the Council on African Studies/the MacMillan Center for International and Area Studies, Yale. The initial profile and structure began to develop over the course of several lectures in two courses that I audited: *Contemporary Political Theory*, which was taught by Vittorio Buffacci who was then a visiting professor in the Yale Department of Political Science, and *Comparative Politics*, which was taught by Yale Sterling Professor William Foltz, in the fall of 1997 and spring 1998, respectively. Out of these two courses, two important themes captured and sustained my preoccupation: *state power* and *military authoritarianism*—two constructs that apply equally to the Nigerian experience. But of utmost importance was how state power could become all-too-consuming and pervasive, and how the venality of its institutions can transcend as well as undermine its ability to maintain the constitutional and fiscal responsibility necessary to nurture a genuine political community and citizenship.

In order to understand how specific historical and social settings transcends the choices political leaders make in the course of a state's political development; it is also important to explore the nature of interest aggregation as well as the patterns of state intervention in matters dealing with secularism, distributive politics, security, autonomy and legitimacy. My objective thus is to draw from the different trajectories of the Nigerian experience, and to tie them as much as possible into a more organic concept of political development and the challenge of state building. To the extent that state power has a transformational effect on the inchoate sociopolitical structure, it can also be used to serve the instrumental objectives of political conquest and domination. As I began putting together various materials and archival information, and with a few additions and deletions here and there, the manuscript began to take the shape in which it has finally unfolded.

REFLECTIONS ON POWER, CONQUEST, AND POLITICAL OPPORTUNITY

Retracing ones steps has remained an age-old admonition. But it seems to me that the Chinese having once suffered the brutality of Imperial Japan, have become the custodians of this simple virtue. For the Chinese, the two steps forward and one step backwards ritual goes beyond mere prophecy and has, in fact, become a religion. The fable of the two Roman Decii who deliberately rode full speed to their deaths without pausing to contemplate the nature of the terrain ahead, offers an apt metaphor. The history of state power in Nigeria has been fraught with precipitous actions reminiscent of the two Decii. From the political activism of the First Republic, to the long trail of military coups and dictatorships, from a murderous civil war to the exigencies of flawed reconstruction, from electoral malpractices to corrupt administrative technocracy—and many more in between—the average Nigerian continues to wonder how far all this would go before things get better.

The moral problem of Nigeria has rarely changed since the time when it was a choice between colonialism and anticolonialism, from the time of the battle for secession and preservation; between an imperial feudal aristocracy and the natural imperative of self-determination, to the last few years when one chooses between ruthless authoritarianism and popular consensus. After many years, the post war history of Nigeria is still being written. Perennial shocks within the political space continue to draw blood and steel as citizens, now and then, set upon each other over issues ranging from territorial disputes, political competition, to religious intolerance, with the state as a central actor in the process. To the extent that it will be unnecessary for me to show in detail that the passing of time compensates for the unlikelihood of these events recurring, that very slight causes can be surprisingly very powerful when they act unceasingly, that there are hypothesis which cannot be destroyed even though they cannot be given the certainty of facts; I take solace in the fact that history is able to provide the connecting links and to reduce the facts to a much smaller number of cases that are not beyond one's imagination.

The issue of North-South dichotomy continues to bedevil the nation as the foremost obstacle to an honest political discourse and compromise. The geopolitical issues of governance that have always pitted the three major ethnic groups (the Yorubas, Igbos, and Hausa-Fulani) against each other continue to dominate center stage, even with the rising political ascendancy of the minority groups. But if there is any ethnic group that is better placed to do what it wants to do in Nigeria (at least today), it is most probably the Yorubas. And should events move in ways contrary to their expectations, they have the human and material resources to proceed in the direction dictated by their self-interest and cultural preservation. For they have mastered one principal axiom of Nigerian politics: "Even when you have enough, complain otherwise the one you already have will be taken from you." If we are told that complacency breeds weakness and weakness breeds defeat, how much more should we be surprised when Yoruba political elites often come out to challenge and berate the very system they have helped to construct.

During the Babangida and Abacha years, Yorubas complained that federal infrastructures including the law school were being moved from Lagos to Abuja. Much of this happened during the Abacha regime, and in an ironic way, sealed the fate of the relationship between the progressive Yoruba elite and the dictatorial regime. But in the midst of this outcry, it became evident that there were some people who saw it quite differently. It became evident that the Yorubas had nothing to lose but everything to gain as the federal government continued to extricate itself from Lagos to Abuja. Lagos used to be Nigeria's federal capital and was essentially built with federal funds. Federal investments in the state cannot be moved since many of these are fixed property and assets. In the same way, the private sector capital that is the hallmark of Lagos cannot be moved. Many of the international companies and banking houses in Lagos will never contemplate leaving the city; not only because of its proximity to the coast and international airport which provides a quick exit out of Nigeria, but also because of its cosmopolitan qualities and ease of assimilation.

To them, the hinterland of Abuja brought back the aura of the desert caravans and the perennial battles of the early European explorers with the tsetse fly. No matter what becomes of Abuja today, it can never replace Lagos both in terms of economic capacity and sensitivity to basic human instincts and inclinations. To that extent, instead of protesting the dismantling of federal presence from Lagos, some Yoruba leaders encouraged it, even if indirectly. As the federal government moved away from Lagos, Lagos moved closer to the Yorubas; as the amorphous culture of federal presence left Lagos, Lagos embraced authentic Yoruba culture. With prospects for oil resources along their southern shores and with their enviable industrial and commercial base in the Lagos-Ibadan axis, the Yoruba retains the potential to overcome most adverse consequences that might arise if "resource control" is ceded back to the states. And so with the economic muscle of Lagos and their newly acquired industrial and political astuteness; it is therefore more likely that they would emerge, even stronger, should the issue of decentralized federalism become a fait accompli.

Alternatively, the North maintains almost total hegemony and control over key institutions of the national government, be it military, economic, bureaucratic, or otherwise. And to cap it all, it continues to hold sway in all facets of Nigeria's "party" democracy—a crucial element for determining how we govern and by who? With an enormous land mass and as the "unwritten" food basket of the country, the North endures and is likely to remain in charge for the foreseeable future. On the other hand, it should also become evident by now that the political survival of the majority and minority in the East, is inextricably linked to each other. The outcome of the 1999 presidential election should finally demonstrate to both that they need each other for their political future. Times have changed, and so instinct and unguarded bravado must yield to a model based on history, reason, and objective self-interest.

The problems of the country did not originate yesterday, and neither will they be solved tomorrow. During Desert Storm (Gulf War 1991), it would have been very easy for the Allied forces to bludgeon Iraq to death in one sudden swoop, but they saw the strategic need to soften the opposition both by buying time and at the same time pulverizing it from the air. When the Allied forces eventually came around to attacking Iraq, the opposition was so weakened from the earlier aerial "war of attrition," that the Iraqi soldiers simply threw away their guns and surrendered en-masse. This is where history could offer a great lesson in patience.

If my reflections lead you to think as I do, then we must allow all our options, no matter how indisposed we may be toward some of them, to confront the issue from different angles at the same time, be they "true" federalism, confederacy, or other alternative choices. We are told that the most dangerous people are those who would hide behind shadows to foment evil, but are too weak to state that which is truly on their mind. And by concealing the true nature of individual conscience, self-deception becomes a permanent threat to every human project. The key problem of Nigeria is not the federal system as a structural model, but it is the lack of political will among entrenched actors and interests to engage the process in such a way that it becomes more adaptable to changing aspirations and to the evolving geodynamics of the political space.

The sooner the debate begins, the sooner the country can avoid the unnecessary consequences of doing without it. If we can confidently assume that there is no easy finality to any of these choices, and in situations where one is less likely to override the credibility of the other without offsetting the dynamics of the negotiation process, why are we so afraid of venturing the possible? That a greater providence may yet await Nigerians is to back-track on a promise so close to realization, an ideal so close that you can almost feel its reverberations, and a voice so precise and noble that you can hear the great words of that fateful Roman orator Cicero, "How great a natal day was thine, O Rome of mine!"

Finally, I will like to point out that to the extent this work reflects a labor accomplished; it is equally a reflection of the unstinting support and encouragement I received from others. I am very grateful for the institutional support of the Council on African Studies at the MacMillan Center for International and Area Studies, Yale University. While much of the actual writing started while I was a research affiliate at the MacMillan Center, my train of thought benefited immensely as a result of insights I drew from the various discussions and exchange of perspectives which I have had over the course of many summers with the foremost research scholar and a leading theorist of democracy Sterling Professor Emeritus Robert A. Dahl of the Department of Political Science, Yale. From our first lunch meeting on September 30, 1998, his interest and support for this work never waned until the date of completion. I thank him very much as a friend and as a mentor. Along the way, my work was made easier by the help I received from very resourceful and kind librarians, in the persons of Dorothy Woodson, curator of the African Collection, Sterling Memorial Library, Yale; and Bassey E. Irele, assistant librarian for Sub-Saharan Africa Collections, Widener Library, Harvard University.

At Auburn University Montgomery, where the manuscript was completed, I have profited in various ways from the supportive environment created by Dr. Bayo Lawal, professor of Mathematics and dean, School of Sciences; and Dr. Tom Vocino, chair, Department of Political Science and Public Administration. I am quite grateful for the financial support that I received through Auburn University Montgomery's Faculty Research Grant. And to all my colleagues in the department including my students who kept up the inquiry as to when this work would be completed, I owe a considerable debt of gratitude. This work is dedicated to my daughter Reneé—in her I see myself as well as draw great inspiration.

1

—m—

Introduction

A Prolegomenon on State and Governance

This work seeks to study the structural and sociological undercurrents of political development and conflict in Nigeria, the role of various actors and processes in facilitating such conflicts, and its implication for federalism and sustained democratic governance. While the study looks at the structural sources of political instability from a historical foundation, it also focuses on the evolutionary transformation of the state system as a critical tool for economic development, political contestation, power and dominance. With the state solely dependent on economic rents from oil production, politics and economics becomes inseparable as central elements in the nature of political discourse and governance. This transformation yields a new political dynamic expressed in the form of *rentier* politics. While the nature of political conflict in Nigeria has been experienced in many different ways including military coups, electoral contestation, ethno-religious strife, political assassinations, and in various other ways; this study reflects an effort to make the case that, contrary to the generally held view, the dynamics of conflict in Nigeria is not necessarily engendered by its multiethnicity, but by specific structural and systemic factors embedded in the very process of national political development. There are three elements that explain the nature of this conflict: religion, the nationality question, and distributive politics tied to issues of relative political and economic inequality.

Nigeria, a country of approximately 144 million people and about 250 ethnic groups is situated in the Western coast of Africa. For much of its political history since it gained independence from Great Britain in 1960, Nigeria has been ruled by its military for approximately twenty-eight years of its forty-seven-year existence as an independent state. Because the various military regimes have oftentimes pursued conflicting political and economic objectives that seem to uphold divergent worldviews; the military has played a central role in reinforcing conditions that engender political instability in the country. In addition to the pathologies of the federal structure, this study also analyzes political development in Nigeria in the context of the interplay between civilian and military governance and demonstrates how the military, buoyed by control of national finance and oil rents, has helped to nurture a culture of perverse competition that, invariably, contributed to escalating the processes of social and political alienation. The civilian regimes that take after the military have also perfected the same method of control and maladministration. While there have been various internal attempts to isolate some of the historical sources of political disagreement in Nigeria, democratic peace will require a dramatic change in the model and institutions of government, from the current limited federalism to perhaps, a more decentralized form of consociational democracy. It is therefore the contention of this study that the factors that breed continuous political instability in Nigeria are not only historical; they are more often than not, structural and systemic.

THE PATH OF THIS PROJECT

Some major works in the literature have provided analytical frameworks for examining the processes of federalism, state formation, and/or democratic consolidation in developing polities such as Nigeria. I refer to the political economy models of Robert Bates (1981, 1988), the state-society relations approach of Naomi Chazan et al. (1992), the neopatrimonialism of Michael Bratton and Nicolas Van de Walle (1997), the Sultanistic regimes model of Chehabi and Linz (1998), and the federalism and ethnic conflict by Rotimi Suberu (2001).[1] Rotimi Suberu's work is of note here, since it deals more particularly with federalism in Nigeria. Among his arguments was that the pre-independence regional and structural arrangement that was imposed on the emergent Nigerian state by the British combined with deeply held primordial inclinations to sustain ethnicity as a key impediment to the workability of the federal system. On the contrary, this project argues that of greater theoretical import should be an exploration of the various ways in which the ethno-religious dynamic in Nigeria undermines the federal system itself, such that the state and its institutions can rarely be relied upon to offer objective remedies to very vexing and perennial problems. The point is that as competing ethno-regional actors conspire against each other for the ultimate price of institutional capture, control of distributive authority, and permanent political subjugation, federalism in the context of division of powers oftentimes becomes the victim rather than an agency for conflict resolution, law and order, and national political integration. First, the answer should go beyond discovering how states are governed, but we should attempt to find out what structural and sociological factors enable them to be governed the way they are governed, and what prospects these present for the attainment of peaceful resolution of political conflicts; or at best how they make the emergence of conflict situations less likely. In fact, by looking at several crisis situations before and after independence, one would expect to find out whether the major sources of conflict in the country were driven more by ethnic differences, or by political (structural), regional, or religious issues that eventually drew on the ethnic factor as a conduit for stoking the fire of mayhem and acrimony. This is the theoretical as well as the analytical void that needs to be addressed.

Second, it seems a rather simplistic notion to suggest that the transition from a nondemocratic authoritarian regime to a liberal democracy begins and end with the replacement of one regime by another. It follows, therefore, that a cultural transformation must also be a central element in the transition process. Hence, where military governments have given up power more or less voluntarily, those militaries have seemed to continue to have substantial influence in their society after their withdrawal from power. Notable examples are Turkey, South Korea, Nicaragua, Brazil, Chile, Nigeria, Zaire, Ecuador, Argentina, Uruguay, Honduras, Guatemala, and many others. While military involvement in Nigerian politics has left its legacy, it remains quite evident that almost all of the regimes lacked, before and after-the-fact, the kind of civil-military relations that Samuel Huntington refers to as "objective civilian control." This development presents enormous problems for the evolution of genuine citizenship and community in transitional states by retaining and reinforcing the paternalistic nature of state-society relations, and by using a de facto military model as a means of civic engagement and democratic discourse. The contradiction generated by this model eventually retards democratic consolidation, engenders widespread conflict, while institutionalizing a "pseudo-military" state by *default*.

METHODOLOGY

Three broad theoretical threads will be utilized in reinforcing the core argument of this project. First, it is argued that the centrality of petroleum and oil as the foremost source of revenue for the economic development of Nigeria creates a condition in which oil rents transcends both power

and authority in the course of the country's political development. Whoever controls political power, invariably controls the oil rents, hence the
nature of distributive politics. Second, as the various regional elements
in Nigeria's power politics struggle for control or for an equitable share
of the nation's oil resources and rents, the ensuing political contestation
essentially manifest itself in overt conflict directed at each other and at
the political center, sometimes both at the same time. Third, in order to
account for the role of the military in state formation and political development, I will argue from the perspective of the praetorian model as developed by Perlmutter (1969).[2] To the extent that it seems very relevant to
the Nigerian case, Alfred Stepan's (1988)[3] work in Brazil and the Southern
Cone provides a crucial model that captures the seeming entrenchment of
military culture in Nigeria's body politic; and how this culture transcend
the way regional issues and conflicts are addressed. In his study of Brazilian politics in the mid-1970s, Alfred Stepan came to the conclusion that a
certain dialectic—which he referred to as "regime concession and societal
conquest"—had begun. It was a retrospective commentary on the military-
controlled party, and a veiled reference to the fact that though the military
may be out of power, it nonetheless remained as a major power broker
within the dominant political party. While the Nigerian military may have
conceded political office in May 1999, it has nonetheless conquered the
political fortunes of the Nigerian state. Hence, an important issue raised
here is whether years of military and dictatorial rule can in its aftermath
generate the conditions necessary for the emergence of political stability,
untrammeled democratic contestation, as well as a deepening of the processes of social capital, civic virtue, and political community.

COMPETING ISSUES OF ETHNICITY AND RELIGION

Previous studies on intrastate conflicts have argued that the multiethnicity of a country makes it impossible or rather difficult to develop a
shared political culture and common interest necessary for political development and peaceful coexistence. Though Nigeria fits into this category,
this work argues that even in light of the current change in political dispensation in Nigeria, the nascent attempt at stable civil governance may
not endure not necessarily because of the multiethnicity of the country,
but essentially due to three main reasons: the cooptation of the state apparatus as an instrument for regional political and economic hegemony,
the role of regional dichotomy as a central factor in the national model of
distributive politics, and the continuing struggle for power between the
entrepreneurial-political class and the retired military oligarchy. In this
volatile mix have also emerged separatist movements, especially in the

oil-rich Niger Delta driven partly by the gross nature of economic and infrastructural deprivation as well as a de facto claim to sovereignty and sole ownership of the mineral resources within the territory. Even though there are more than 250 different ethnic groups in Nigeria, the endemic conflict and violence seem to have been driven more by religious differences than by the ethnic diversity. There has always been a general recognition between Muslims and Christians in Nigeria, that religion is an extremely effective way of mobilizing large numbers of people; and local political and religious leaders have manipulated this with disastrous consequences.

In general, there are two broad perspectives within which conflict and violence occur in Nigeria: conflict between groups or communities within the country; and conflict between groups against the state. The first is driven mostly by issues of religion and political balancing, while the second is driven by issues of distributive politics and political representation in national policy making. By focusing on the deeper sources of these conflicts, we can thus avoid the general tendency to offer generic solutions.[4] This study reflects an effort to make the case that, contrary to generally held opinion, the dynamics of conflict and violence in Nigeria is not engendered by its multiethnicity, but by more recurrent structural and systemic factors. There are three key elements that seem to drive this process: religion, the nationality question, and distributive politics tied to issues of relative political and economic inequality. While the above three elements could be seen as starting points in the development of a broader set of hypotheses; but to fully understand the Nigerian problematic, it is also important to draw from its historical experiences as a nation. In this way, the various efforts at genuine federalism could be contrasted to the structural defects that characterize earlier effort at nation building. These structural anomalies have sought not only to undermine the ideal of genuine federalism, but have also played a central role in the continued sectional agitation and geopolitical crisis in the country. Among the many sources of conflict are issues that deal with constitutional redesign, the issue of distributive justice (reflected in the principle of derivation and resource control), the issue of political leadership (reflected in the six zonal structure for presidential rotation), the issue of an authentic national census, and the diminishing role of the middle class (as the primary anchor for economic growth and job creation). But then, each of these issues manifests themselves severally and in competition with each other.

LAY OF THE LAND

Because the Nigerian federalist model poses both a structural and a governance problem, the theoretical framework of this work draws from contemporary scholarship on federalism, ethno-religious conflict, rentier economy, civil-military relations, and democratic governance. By relying on an array of historical and contemporary literature, I hope to explain how transitional states (Nigeria in this case) can become trapped in a vicious cycle of political, regional and religious acrimony, thereby generating a resurgent crisis of confidence and legitimacy from multiple sources of sociopolitical discontent. By reinforcing the structural and economic basis of these sources of discontent, one is therefore in a better position to understand how they mutate into overt conflict. While I believe that face-to-face across the table (diplomatic) negotiations between two contending parties in a crisis is useful, I see it as a rather superficial way of dealing with the Nigerian situation. The Nigerian case requires more practical approaches and solutions available within Nigeria itself. Some of the things I believe would be crucial are a structural realignment and strengthening of key institutions of national governance (methods of representation, procedural and administrative accountability, and proactively embracing a culture of civism), political empowerment within the context of shared governance, redesigning the inchoate mechanism of distributive politics, development of a macroeconomic regime that encourages private initiative and entrepreneurship, robust quality of life, devolution of programmatic authority to the state and local governments, rule of law grounded in a reformed constitution, stakeholder management principles—finding a governance model that more effectively integrates the divergent sectional interests into an organic framework of national interest.

There are twelve chapters in this work that deal with specific themes tied to the central issues of federalism, regionalism, ethnicity, conflict, militocracy, democracy, economy, governance, and statecraft. Chapter 2 offers an overview of key conceptual and epistemological arguments related to major analytical frameworks of state formation and development. It discusses the relevance of concepts such as state-society relations, political economy, neopatrimonialism, prebendalism, and sultanism as important templates for analyzing the political and economic development of Nigeria as well as the broader developing world. Chapter 3 traces some of the historical schisms in the course of Nigeria's political development as well as the role of the British colonial administration in setting the stage and processes that helped to regionalize Nigeria's politics very early in its formative years as an independent state—with serious consequences for the evolving partisan and ethnic conflicts that seek to undermine the federal system. Chapter 4 delves more in-depth into the structural issues of federalism and how evolving territorial, political, and religious issues eventually become subsumed under ethnic and ethno-religious conflicts. To the extent that it is usually directed at securing a certain political objective, violence is seen as both a response to and as a form of political participation. Chapter 5 discusses the geopolitics of religion and properly situates many of Nigeria's conflicts as driven more by religious differences as opposed to ethnocentric motives. It offers accounts of the causal origins of many of the religious crisis in the North, the Tiv-Jukun crisis, the Hausa-Fulani and the Zango-Kataf, and the deadly Sharia riots in Kaduna, Kano, and elsewhere. In many conflict situations, the role of ethnicity is seen not as a cause but as an inescapable coincidence of nature and irrational human instincts.

In chapter 6, I discuss the genesis of the military's entry into political governance, beginning with the January 15, 1966 coup, the July 1966 countercoup, the civil war, and the aftermath that saw a series of dictatorial military regimes that transformed Nigeria's political culture, more or less, into a praetorian state. Chapter 7 discusses the dynamics of the oil economy and its implications for domestic politics and competition for control of state power, wealth creation and distributive politics, corruption and clientelism. It also discusses the role and influence of international actors (multinational corporations, the world's industrial economies, etc.) as participants in the "rentier economy" and the "rentier space"—and how corruption, public loot, and "squandermania" creates market failures that impede the very process of national development as well as a veritable civic culture. The "rentier space" is developed as a paradigm that seeks to capture the series of domestic and international activities that occur at and are shaped by the confluence of power and economics. Chapter 8 explores the premise that the many years of military rule in Nigeria may have left an indelible mark on the country's evolving political culture to the extent that it could be construed as a "garrison state." In many cases, it has become very difficult to see much difference between the strict military model of governance and the stewardship of civilian politicians under "democratic" rule. Nigerians, in fact, may have become too accustomed to the culture of military rule to the extent that they raise less of an alarm even when it is practiced by the elected civilian political class. In chapter 9, I discuss the politics of party elections, the strategies, and patronage that surrounded the 2007 presidential elections that saw the election of Umaru Yar'Adua as the president of Nigeria's Fourth Republic. I explore the geopolitical implications relative to issues of party candidacy, the tragedy and pitfalls of the electioneering process, and the frames and symbolisms that are highly consequential in terms of how they shape electoral outcomes, dominance and control of state power.

Chapter 10 discusses some of the historical and contemporary issues surrounding the Niger-Delta crisis, the political issues of regional autonomy an self-determination; resource control and the derivation principle, the rise of local insurgency groups such as the Niger Delta People's Volunteer Force (NDPVF) and the Movement for the Emancipation of the Niger Delta

(MEND), the role of multinational oil companies; the central issues of poverty, environmental degradation and the state's responses to the divergent issues of centralized federalism and the quest for sectional autonomy. Chapter 11 focuses on the ideal and efficacy of democracy within a multiethnic federal system, and the competing issues of presidentialism and majority rule. It discusses federalism in the context of other governance options such as confederacy and consociationalism—a kind of "consensual" democracy based on the formation of "grand coalitions." In chapter 12, I broaden the argument by discussing issues of democracy and development within the African context, while highlighting specific implications for Nigeria. As with every other African country or other parts of the developing world, the case is made that the lack of democratic consolidation in many African countries is not due to the absence of the "state"; rather it is due to the weakness or nonexistence of effective institutions. What Nigeria, in particular, and Africa, in general, needs most is the development of *institutional capital* without which democratic consolidation would be difficult to achieve. Taken as a whole, the multidimensional approach of this work and its analyses of the central issues of federalism, conflict, multiethnicity, religion, civil-military relations, political economy and statecraft; offers one more insight into an enduring narrative that continues to shape Nigeria's experience in the course of her political development.

NOTES

1. Robert Bates, *Markets and States in Tropical Africa: The Political Basis of Agricultural Policies* (Berkeley: University of California Press, 1981); Robert Bates, ed., *Toward a Political Economy of Development: A Rational Choice Perspective* (Berkeley: University of California Press, 1988); Michael Bratton and Nicolas Van de Walle, *Democratic Experiments in Africa: Regime Transitions in Comparative Perspective* (New York: Cambridge University Press, 1997); Naomi Chazan, Robert Mortimer, John Ravenhill, and Donald Rothchild, *Politics and Society in Contemporary Africa* (Boulder, Colo.: Lynne Rienner Publishers, 1992); H. E. Chehabi and Juan J. Linz, *Sultanistic Regimes* (Baltimore: Johns Hopkins University Press, 1998); Rotimi T. Suberu, *Federalism and Ethnic Conflict in Nigeria* (Washington, D.C.: United States Institute of Peace, 2001).

2. Amos Perlmutter, "The Praetorian State and the Praetorian Army: Toward a Taxonomy of Civil-Military Relations in Developing Polities," *Comparative Politics* 1, no. 3 (1969): 382–404.

3. Alfred Stepan, *Rethinking Military Politics: Brazil and the Southern Cone* (Princeton, N.J.: Princeton University Press, 1988).

4. See Donald L. Horowitz, *Ethnic Groups in Conflict*, 2nd ed. (Berkeley: University of California Press, 2000); Louis Kriesberg, ed., *Constructive Conflicts: From Escalation to Resolution* (Lanham, Md.: Rowman & Littlefield, 2003).

2

—〜〜—

Analytical Frameworks
of State Formation

In his book *Imagined Communities*,[1] Benedict Anderson vividly narrates the ordeal of new nation-states as many achieved their independence in the post–World War II period.[2] He argues that in the "nation-building" policies of the new states, the blend of popular and official nationalism has been the product of anomalies created by European imperialism: the well-known arbitrariness of frontiers, and bilingual intelligentsia poised precariously over diverse *monoglot* populations. One can thus think of these nations as projects the achievement of which is still in progress, yet projects conceived more in the spirit of Mazzini than that of Uvarov. *Mazzini* stands for the centralizing ambitions of colonial (metropolitan) *absolutism*, while *Uvarov* passes for "Russification"—a subtle but creeping form of bilingual neocolonialism. *Mazzini* and *Uvarov* stand as crucial metaphors that can explain the history and trajectory of state power in Africa. What the colonial regime left, African leaders did not abandoned, but instead, have perfected into the most predatory form of Machiavellian statecraft.

There are contemporary assumptions about what the "state" is, especially in Africa. But when we assume that a universal rule runs through the typical "state" in Africa as in other regions of the world, we run the risk of over-generalization. Different conceptions of the "state" view it "as the organized aggregate of relatively permanent institutions of governance,"[3] or as "a set of associations and agencies claiming control over defined territories and their populations."[4] While these conceptualizations may seem quite basic and self-explanatory, the problem with any analysis of the "state" in Africa is that "its institutions are neither neutral nor aloof; they are organizations with interests of their own."[5] Hence, who controls the state, invariably, controls those interests and would be in a position to determine the critical parameters for social action as well as the authoritative allocation of values.

In *Africa in Chaos*, the Ghanaian economist George Ayittey[6] proclaimed that "the state as usually understood, does not exist in Africa." While Ayittey's seeming frustration might be taken literally, it reflects a genuine revelation of the shattering level of decay and compromise to which the "state" in Africa has been subjected, more or less by its own people. As Claude Ake points out,[7] "when we use phrases such as the 'state in Africa,' we immediately give it the content of our own historical experience. Having named it and given it this content, we feel we have already settled the question of what it is, beforehand. We conflate experience and reality, form and content, because our knowledge is so tied to our language." For Ake, the "'state in Africa' has been a maze of antinomies of form and content: the person who holds office may not exercise its powers, the person who exercises the powers of a given office may not be its holder, informal relations often override formal relations, the formal hierarchies of bureaucratic structure and political structure are not always the cue to decision making power." In essence, control of state power occurs within a tripartite arrangement of indigenous political elites, entrepreneurial capital (the contractor class), and the military aristocracy.

In the Nigerian case as well as in many others, the state has become private property encapsulated and legitimized within the public sphere. "Overwhelmed by societal pressures, its institutional integrity compromised by individual or sectional interest, the state has turned into a 'weak Leviathan,' suspended above society."[8] As the primary source of capital accumulation and social mobility in Africa, the state has become the ultimate price for all political contests. As the state ceases to reflect society in general, and frustrated by the social and economic costs of rudderless governance, the average citizen withdraws and disengages himself from the sphere of public discourse. What is rarely acknowledged is that the contest for democratic rule in Africa is an *intra-elite* struggle for control of state power, rather than a struggle to guarantee fundamental civic rights and liberties for all. In the functional sense of the term, the *state* in Africa exists alone; hence it "cannot be used as a vehicle to take Africans on the 'development' journey."[9]

But others equally hold out some element of optimism. Jeffrey Herbst suggests that by "examining both the environment that leaders had to confront and the institutions they created in light of their own political calculations, the entire trajectory of state creation in Africa can be recovered."[10] Nonetheless, by relying on the role of human agency interacting with powerful geographic and historical forces to bring about a positive reconstruction of the African state, Herbst's argument plays back into one of the main sources of political conflict in Africa: the personalized and patrimonial nature of African political culture. To the extent that systemic and structural forces do constrain the role of human agency, the state in Africa harbors "an intrinsically dual anchorage in class-divided socio-economic structures and an international system of states."[11] The inability to resolve the contradiction generated in the first, makes a true realization of the latter much more difficult.

THE ONTOLOGICAL BASIS OF THE STATE

While theory offers us the opportunity to establish the existence of a logical relationship between two or more phenomena, conceptualization enables us to isolate the attributes of each phenomenon in terms of identity and behavior. "Things conceived or meaningfully perceived (i.e., concepts) are the central elements of propositions and depending—on how they are named—can provide guidelines for interpretation and observation."[12] Concept formation helps us to understand abstract phenomena in terms of their observable or empirical manifestations. For example, there are some common conceptual terms in political science all of which are related in some fundamental and concrete ways. The terms I have in mind are: *nation, state, and government*. While some literature use these terms interchangeably, there has also been an adulteration of the two words in the form of what we call the "nation-state." The irony is that when we use the term "nation-state," we are not speaking about a unique nominal or conceptual term; rather what we are speaking about is the functional "relationship" between a "nation" and a "state" and how this *relationship* is manifested in a legitimate act of governance. A "nation" as a concept is anchored on a specific genealogical and cultural foundation; while a "state" is merely a geographical expression of sovereign authority and power. Hence, concept formation is critical to an understanding of the core distinction between the two.

On the other hand, we conceive "democracy" as being different from "socialism" but when we unify the two concepts into a single term like "democratic socialism," we ought to make it clear that an understanding of "democratic socialism" (as a *political process*) can only be preceded by understanding "democracy" and "socialism" as independent concepts (or constructs) separate from one another. In social scientific inquiry, it is therefore important that we address the initial conditions necessary to understand key operational concepts as well as linkages between key nominal terms, their inherent qualities, and specific functional relationships that serve as building blocks for many of the *grand theories* in the field.

The tendency to limit the argument for the viability of the typical African state has become all too common. The concept of state utilized here embraces not only the central institutions of government, but also the abstract notion of a paternalistic and over-arching agency existing for the purpose of maintaining social order and public good within a geo-political context. The state exists not only in its physical manifestations but also as a concept for which the authority to institute laws as well as sanction social behavior has become internalized by both supporters and opponents. The Hobbesian treatise of the indispensability of a political society presided over by an overbearing state authority stands as one of the fundamental reasons for granting legitimacy to the "state" and its laws. So, when people complain and rail against the "state," they are actually complaining about the "government" or administration that uses the institutions and authority of the state to govern. While the literature on African politics is fraught with several repudiations of the state, such criticisms are rather misplaced because the "state" is nothing but a territorial construct that provides a legitimate basis for the exercise of political power. For those who govern, the "state" therefore offers the legal context for civil and political expression grounded in the law.

Yet the evolutionary path of "state" development in Africa has remained uniformly resilient as a result of the primary conditions that informed its early beginnings. The state was seen as an instrument for grabbing and holding power, but at the same time it became a symbol for ethnocentric group identification as well as the ultimate price of political competition. The primary mission of the state—to provide public goods, domestic and external security—became secondary, at least in the initial phases of sovereign governance following colonial rule. The state-building agenda, which was equally as important as the "state-consolidation" one, was not given early emphasis due partly to the emergent competition for power, and the existence of a fledgling institutional framework that made political accountability quite difficult. The initial problem of state formation in Africa, therefore, "lay in a basic conceptual failure to unpack the different dimensions of 'stateness' and to understand how they relate to economic development"[13] as well as the exigencies of interest aggregation and collective action. As the state-building process came under enormous stress, the ensuing struggle for control of state power and the attempt "to use the public sector to reallocate property rights to the benefit of a particular interest"[14] transcended latter efforts at building a genuine political community.

Nonetheless, the lack of democratic consolidation has been due, partly as a result of the inability to analyze and understand the unique "stateness" problems that each new African state faced. While the easy part has been to enunciate specific national development programmes as a way of providing essential public goods; the problem arises in agreeing to a mutually acceptable framework for the distribution and authoritative allocation of values. While the "current 'regime' may introduce weak reforms that fall short of complete democratization (because it still wants to hold on to power), it oftentimes pushes the opposition to accept a formula that favors incumbent power holders in important ways."[15] One way of doing this would be to permanently embed its own vision and interests within a new constitutional framework that would serve as the basis for the current and future political order.

On the other hand, the state's advantage over other political entities in mobilizing and organizing resources for the application of force as well as for other purposes, raises questions about the survival of other forms of political association or opposition to it.[16] Hence, as it becomes more authoritarian in the attempt to maintain power, the state ends up mobilizing a cross-section of the opposition to the extent that it changes the dynamics of the emerging but nascent political discourse. "As governments that once appeared to operate for the benefit of all the nation's citizens are perceived to have become partisan,"[17] hitherto broad-based national political parties and other organizational frameworks transform into insurgency movements in resistance to the status quo and seeking its replacement. Political mobilization for national development quickly turns into mobilization for control of state power.

Conceptually, a state can be seen as a property that has shared ownership, but that would also need to function on the basis of objective collective interest. But when self-interest replaces the norms of collective interest, the ideal of the state raises issues of property rights and ownership. This is what the typical African state has failed to resolve, especially in the formative years following independence. Who owns the state and to what extent should it be obligated to the welfare of its citizens and vice versa? It is by properly defining and negotiating these normative imperatives that political leaders are able to build the ownership commitment and citizenship needed to advance the course of nationhood. State building and nationhood must be seen as reciprocal as well as mutually reinforcing; the first concerned with constructing effective institutions and procedures critical for a functional system, while the latter focuses on creating a sense of ownership and commitment anchored on untrammeled citizenship. By its actions, the state thus creates awareness within the citizenry of the reciprocal nature of duty, obligation and responsibility. The institutions of the state, therefore, must rest on the authority of the people through their duly elected representatives, and in the methods for making appointments and for passing laws.[18]

Suffice it then to say that for the newly independent postcolonial state, the challenge of state building rests on two crucial assumptions: the ability of political leaders to create an environment of shared ownership, and secondly, the ability to meet the challenge of rising expectations within the polity. To the extent that citizens depend on state institutions, the

values they attach to them, invariably, reflects respect for state authority and legitimacy.[19] As pointed out earlier, states exist to deliver public
goods (including security), enforce law and order, as well as satisfy the
needs of associational ownership to their citizens. "When they function as
they ideally should, they mediate between the constraints and challenges
of the international arena and the dynamic forces of their own internal
economic, political, and social realities."[20] But in societies where strong
associational groupings have emerged, they tend to provide alternative
sources of advocacy for disenfranchised groups to vent their frustrations
against the state. Ironically, instead of serving as an avenue for advancing
a more pluralist form of political engagement, they oftentimes end up creating a situation that undermines the very system they aim to safeguard.
As Macridis and Brown[21] points out, consensus is never universal in complex societies; rather the very openness of communications in democratic
regimes permits dissident elements ample opportunity to clash with each
other, and with the government. For the new state, the urge to democra-
tize must also be seen in light of the domestic capacity to exercise social
control amid the evolving pattern of political engagement. And where
this is not possible (and in order to maintain state control), the postcolonial regime often end up employing much the same set of authoritarian
measures and policies as the colonial authority.[22]

We can also explore the nature and capability of a state in terms of the
extent and scope of its involvement in society's affairs. While some states
allow for a certain level of civil liberties and expression, others inhibit it
as a form of social and political control. "A minimal state seeks to confine
itself to internal order, external defense, basic infrastructure, and the like;
while a maximal state expands state responsibilities to include functions
such as the adjudication of civil liberties, the redistribution of wealth, and
extensive infrastructural development."[23] For the reasons adduced earlier,
and owing to its peculiar condition, the post-independent African state
generally exhibits a minimalist orientation. Hence, as a way of maintaining internal control, the cooptation and exercise of state power becomes a
primary tool for political conquest.

At independence, what the colonial regime left to African countries
were "states" but not governments. While "the state was perceived as an
arena of sovereignty, of territoriality, and perhaps of nation-building; it
was not seen as an interconnected set of institutions with an existence of
its own."[24] It was therefore incumbent on Africans to device their own
forms of government, and to do so meant that they would have to resolve
specific cultural and economic issues of collective governance. Because
of the heterogeneous character of the typical African society, reconciling
disparate cultural assumptions and worldviews became a daunting task
for the postcolonial regime.

The only available alternative, at least in the early years, was to embrace the existing dogma left by the colonial regime. The idea of "state" thus became synonymous with the idea of "government," and this invariably, shaped the problematic existence of the postcolonial African "state." It embraced an idea, but not a "government" to make the "idea" come to fruition. The "state," set apart from every other thing else provides the building blocks for a formative political society, deciding its form, as well as the nature of relationship among its various elements. It conforms to a specific philosophy of ideas about human nature, habit, and logic in both time and space. As an ideal, it offers a pathway as well as a justification regarding how people within a specific geopolitical context can exercise mutual coexistence or what we oftentimes refer to as *nationality*. Mutual and untrammeled coexistence thus becomes a value that needs to be safeguarded for its own sake as well as for social stability. This, therefore, imposes an obligation on the government (the specific holders of public office who have the authority to make policy and enforce the laws) to secure and protect the common value for all citizens within the territory. The government thus becomes the structural and institutional agency for realizing the normative and abstract ideals of the state. While "state" and "government" cannot be the same, they complement each other; the former setting the principles and the latter implementing them. But when we conceive both constructs as the same, we only simplify as well as undermine the distinctions that separate them. The "state, regime, and government may or may not overlap empirically, but in concept, they are quite distinct."[25]

Although out of common and long-term usage, it might seem fruitless to create a dichotomy between a "state" and a "government," but such a distinction is necessary as a way of isolating a crucial element of governance in the typical African state. Hence what is sought here is to clarify an old assumption that explains the ontological basis of the "state" and as a way of redirecting its everyday semantic usage. Because it is desirable for human coexistence and political governance, the idea of a "state" ought not be construed as an anathema and African countries do not necessarily deserve to be characterized as "failed states." Rather what has failed in Africa are not the "states" but the "governments" that emerge, one way or the other, in an attempt to actualize the ideals of the "state." Hence the character of a "state" at any point in time is essentially what the "government" makes of it.

State-Society Relations

The modernizing "state" in Nigeria as well as much of Africa took its shape and sovereignty as a consequence of the end of colonial rule and the declaration of independence. By enforcing obedience, power, and authority over all activities within a defined geographical space combined with recognition by members of the international community, the new "state" also acquired unchallenged legitimacy. Through the use of symbols (flags), anthems, insignias, myths, and other artifacts that invoke the power and nostalgia of a people's history, a "state" stands in parallel relation to the people and culture it represents. In fact, "what has distinguished the modern state from most other large-scale political organizations in history, such as empires, has been its insinuation into the core identities of its subjects. They aim to shape people's entire moral orders—the content of the symbols and codes determining what matters most to them."[26] It is to preserve this moral order, identity, and the cultural history which they embody that governments are created to manage and coordinate the affairs of the "state." Hence, when we discuss the issue of "state-society relations," it ought to be seen as an issue of "government-society relations" since as a matter of fact, states do not govern, but governments do.

Though the term "state" is oftentimes dismissed as a vague abstraction from the past having little empirical meaning or researchable features, the term can refer to concrete structures and observable relationships among them.[27] When particular governments assume power and authority over a state, they utilize standing institutions and laws to advance and consolidate their legitimacy to govern. Such institutions include the executive structures, judiciary, and existing bureaucratic systems—a methodological emphasis generally referred to as the "legal-institutional-descriptive" approach. While the "state" ought to be considered as something more than the "government," its integrative function derives from the continuous administrative, legal, bureaucratic, and coercive systems that attempt not only to structure relations between civil society and public authority (the government) in a polity, but also in structuring many crucial relationships in society.[28] As the primary instrument for law enforcement and the allocation of values, the "state" in Nigeria as well as in many African countries has come to be seen as possessing absolute autonomy and discretion in its relation to society.

This phenomenon is akin to Alfred Stepan's[29] reference to *organic statism,* which in contrast to liberal pluralism and radical Marxism, is seen most importantly as a normative model of the relations and as a mode of articulation between state and society. Organic-statist concepts of the priority of the political community and of the state's responsibility for the common good imply strong constraints on laissez-faire market individualism,[30] but then this is only possible where there is a thriving private market economy and where the source of private capital accumulation does not essentially revolve around state largesse. While elites in many different societies and in many different historical periods, have used variants of the organic-statist model as a legitimizing formula for designing institutions, systems, and administrative structures; such state-structured interactions have played a role in shaping societies in such a way that we are able to assess the comparative weight of the state and/or society in determining various political outcomes.[31]

Nonetheless, many postcolonial states differ in the way they structure civil relationships and the means they employ in enforcing law, order, and continuity. For obvious reasons as will be explored in chapter 3, the Nigerian state fits rather adequately within the organic-statist model. There are fundamental issues that would lead one to this conclusion: the federalizing character of the state, the centralized control of key administrative institutions, sources of revenue, distributive policy, political authority, and the almost absolute control over the authoritative allocation of values. Furthermore, the early creation of regional political fiefdoms was equally instrumental in ensuring that the ensuing pattern of political and civil relations were contained within regional boundaries, but only spilled out unto national politics when narrow regional interests collide with the more general national interest. Hence, considered in light of several coup d'etats, a war, and a continuing political and economic crisis in Nigeria, the search for stability thus makes the role of the state increasingly central in all aspects of state-society relations. In the belief that the state seeks a moral end, and as such should be less disposed to procedural guarantees of civil liberty than the maintenance of social and political stability; the Nigerian government has oftentimes used brute force to quell political unrest and civil society advocacy.

The biological analogy implied in the organic-statist model views the state as a collection of parts; hence the functional role of the state (through its Constitution) and the government (through its policies) becomes one of integrating the various parts to achieve a level of political solidarity and a sense of purpose. But ironically, while popular democratic elections makes it possible for the party that has majority of the votes to win the election, and hence, take control of the government for a specified period of time; it also enables the party to take over state power, thereby opening an avenue to manipulate sovereign institutions and policies of the state for its own political interest. Because the state and government are now assumed to be one, the long-lasting effects of absolute party dominance are rarely obvious until they have reached critical mass.

We can equally note that in states that exhibit the organic-statist inclination, there is a political tendency to move toward greater control over groups through manipulative corporatist politics,[32] as well as tendency to use distributive politics as a means of cooptation and blackmail. It is at this stage that political goals are determined by what could be construed as a party-state vanguard rather than an aggregation of group and popular interests. Nigeria's People's Democratic Party (PDP), while holding majorities in the both the national legislature as well as the Executive branch, and where it can be separated from the government in power, has

acquired enough power that it can engage in arbitrary and de facto constitutional reform, judicial politics and sanctions, vindictive investigations,
unveted contract awards. Disregarding references to the multi-party orientation of the state, the PDP has become exceedingly dominant.

Social Capital and Community Ethos

As a normative aspiration, civil society in Nigeria as well as well as in
many other countries has been considered as the celebrity of democratic
resistance and transition. Civil society refers to that arena of the polity
where self-organizing groups, movements, and individuals, relatively
autonomous from the state, attempt to articulate values, create associations and solidarities, and advance their interests. It includes manifold
social movements (women's groups, neighborhood associations, religious
groupings, professional organizations, trade unions, journalists, business
groups, or lawyers). It has equally been stated that, "without a civil society willing and able to resist authoritarianism, democratic transitions may
only be cosmetic, designed primarily for foreign consumption, or cycli-
cal (as in Latin America), with democratic tendencies reversed by *coups
d'etat*."[33] Hence, at all stages of the democratization process, a "lively" and
independent civil society is invaluable.

But what seems to have been overlooked here is that as long as there
exists in Nigeria and many African countries, a lack of a unifying and
facilitative political culture, deep communal cleavages, lack of mutual
trust, opportunistic tendencies of indigenous elites, the selfish struggle
for control of state power, the authenticity of civil society as an emergent
democratic construct, is seriously undermined. "Deep communal cleavages have a tendency to complicate or even undermine the give-and-take
of democratic competition. Under this condition, electoral politics will
tend to exacerbate divisions, political parties are likely to be formed along
regional and ethnic lines, and victory is interpreted as the victory of one
ethnic or religious group over the others. This perception corrodes the mutual trust on which democratic politics depends, and threatens a decline
into communal violence."[34] As Mahmood Mamdani[35] argues, "the agents
of civil society are intellectuals, who figure predominantly in the establishment of hegemony. Although autonomous of the state, its life cannot be
independent of it, for the guarantor of the autonomy of civil society can
be none other than the state." Hence, "no reform of contemporary civil
society institutions can by itself unravel this decentralized despotism; but
to do so will require nothing less than dismantling that form of power."[36]

Even though civil society may have its virtues, I am of the view that the
development of social capital is a precondition for a credible civil society,
and is perhaps, more relevant in the Nigerian situation. Robert Putnam's
(1993)[37] seminal work on the topic of local governments in Italy con-

cluded that the performance of government and other social institutions is powerfully influenced by citizen engagement in community affairs, or what he calls *social capital*. By social capital is meant features of social life-networks, norms, and trust that enable participants to act together more effectively to pursue shared objectives. "To the extent that the norms, networks, and trust link substantial sectors of the community and 'bridge' underlying social cleavages, then the enhanced cooperation is likely to serve broader interests and to be widely welcomed."[38] In this sense, social capital refers to our relations with one another, and the more we connect with other people, the more we trust them, and vice versa. As Putnam suggests,[39] an amateur choir has economic value because by participating in it people inadvertently learn to trust each other. The consequent reduction in opportunistic behavior reduces transaction costs, because the choir generates an externality—its members learn to trust each other even though this is not the purpose of their interaction.

While Putnam's findings point to the fact that social trust and civic engagement are strongly correlated, with or without controls for education, age, income, race, gender, and other demographic indicators; Ismail Serageldin[40] argues that there is growing evidence that social capital contributes significantly to sustainable development. He views social capital as the internal social and cultural coherence of society, the norms and values that govern interactions among people and the institutions under which they live; hence it is the glue that holds societies together and without which there can be no economic growth or human well-being. It is no wonder that in many African countries, pro-democracy organizations that were once touted as an indication of the resurgence of civil society on the continent, including media houses ended up becoming ethnic and parochial voices of political opportunism.

A key reason could be found in Kate Meagher's (2006) study[41] of the extent to which social networks in the economic organization of two dynamic informal enterprise clusters in the town of Aba (Southeast Nigeria) constitute "social capital" capable of promoting economic development in the context of ongoing liberalization. Her findings, as indicated from the Aba case study, suggest that the weakness of African small-firm networks does not seem to arise from excessive state intervention or from perverse cultural blueprints, but from state neglect and the instability of the wider institutional context in which these networks are embedded. Because formal institutions are weak and are not adequately incorporated into the formal economic framework, it encourages informal firms and occupational associations to turn to cliental forms of economic and political incorporation. As a consequence, informal networks are easily transformed from social into political capital, which invariably, leads to their fragmentation and capture in favor of the machinations of more powerful political forces.[42]

The concept of social capital also dovetails nicely with an earlier argument propounded by Dankwart Rustow.[43] He pointed out that democracy requires a national unity, a sense of affinity between the citizens that surpasses other loyalties. But the problem is that this is frequently lacking, and many states are instead, divided by deep cleavages between different population groups. "These gaps—which are usually ethnic, religious or socio-economic in character—have the result, in the most serious cases, that people feel loyalty and confidence only within their own group and, in recompense, hostility and distrust toward outsiders."[44] Thus, "politicization of ethnic gaps and organizations of parties along such lines instead creates an increasingly intransigent political culture where compromises and coalitions between groups are well-nigh impossible to attain."[45]

To the extent that it undermines public and mutual learning, the seemingly intractable divergence of opinions and interest articulation become the basis for policy and program paralysis. "When policy controversies are enduring and invulnerable to reconciliation, what tends to result is institutionalized political contention, leading either to stalemate or to pendulum swings from one extreme position to another, as one side or another comes to political power."[46] Hence, "where ethnic divisions have not been well handled, as in Nigeria, the result can be a state focused on sharing the spoils, not protecting overall prosperity. Governments are short-lived, and each represents a different ethnic coalition. Military rule alternates with periods of electoral politics, and political life is focused on rent seeking, not productive activity."[47] To sustain an effective civil society, Nigeria would need to find a way to tap into the integrative forces of social capital, without which such claims as "a resurgence of civil society," would in substance reflect only a fleeting phenomenon.

MODELS OF STATE AND GOVERNANCE

Political Economy Models

The premise of political economy is the interaction between the economy and the state in the dynamic process of production. Through micro and macroeconomic policies, the state can shape as well as create the enabling conditions for growth and economic diversification. But the underlying implication of political economy as a model of development arises from a primary belief among economists, especially among methodological individualists, who view economics as a universal science of decision-making under conditions of constraint, scarcity, and choice. Hence to the extent that "political and other forms of social behavior can be reduced to economic motives; government policies, social institutions including the state itself, can be explained through application of formal economic models."[48] While development economists emphasize the role of the state and an activist government in dealing with sectoral market failures in the economy; neoclassical economists argued that developing countries problems were due to government failures (i.e., bad policies) rather than market failures requiring government intervention."[49] But because "the peculiar condition of developing countries goes beyond issues of debt, poverty, and indigenous productivity; successful development would, therefore, depend on the ability to reconcile three competing interests: the liberal and unfettered logic of the market, the domestic capacity to absorb the initial shocks or disruptions of entry into the international market order, and the practical necessity for state intervention."[50] One therefore doubts whether the issue of chronic low economic performance among developing countries can be explained solely by reference to the economic paradigm in use at any particular point in time.

An incentive offered by the liberal economic model is that trade and markets can be made to become the driving force for economic development; hence societies that are economically developed are more likely to have politically stable states. While many African countries have bought into this model, at least in principle, the difference here is that while the "market" drives the economic system in the developed countries, the "state" drives the economy in the less-developed countries. This is due partly to differences in indigenous developmental capacity as well as the asymmetrical trade relations in the international system. But the basic assumption is that as less-developed countries engage in the process of incorporating and transforming their traditional sectors into a modern sector through the modernization of their economic, social, and political structures; they would over time attain higher levels of productive efficiency as well as become more competitively integrated into the global market economy. Political economy thus reflects "the reciprocal and dynamic interaction of the pursuit of wealth and the pursuit of power."[51] "While markets constitute a means to achieve and exercise power, the state can be and is used to obtain wealth; hence state and market interact to influence the distribution of power and wealth in international relations."[52]

But the expectations of the liberal economic doctrine have not yielded many incentives to countries like Nigeria. It is not because such a model could not work if the government developed the political will to engage it; but rather one can point to the peculiar market failures that seem to characterize states with low levels of political and institutional development. Among these would be the inefficient bureaucratic and banking systems, undiversified productive sector, volatility in commodity prices in the international market, high indebtedness, increased regulation, state control and monopoly of critical economic sectors, corruption, and low-skilled labor due to failure of the educational system. The result is that "Nigeria, once considered a country likely to achieve self-sustaining growth, now ranks among the more debt-distressed countries in the developing world."[53]

While the state strives to dictate the pace and direction of economic development; it lacks the geopolitical consensus and the fiscal capacity to deliver on its ever-growing obligations.

But there is a peculiar lesson that seems to be forgotten in this developmental march, and that is, there is nothing that is totally inconsistent with an increased role of the state especially in the early stages of economic transition to a more stable free-market regime. While the international economic system can be described as exhibiting relative capacity in the distributions of economic power, economically weaker states are less able to adjust effectively to dramatic shifts in domestic factor movements because they lack the size and economies of scale necessary to absorb the initial shocks of exposure to the international market. The World Bank and the International Monetary Fund have taken initiatives aimed at assisting economically weak states to take concrete steps to build the capacity necessary to achieve economies of scale so as to become effective participants in the international market regime. Although imposing specific policy conditionalities on beneficiary states, "the standard justification for World Bank structural adjustment lending is that reforms have short-run costs and foreign assistance can help reforms get launched by alleviating these costs."[54] It has therefore held the view that the "objective of policy-conditioned lending is not only to change the policy structure viewed to be at the heart of the problem facing the recipient country, but is also aimed at providing quick-disbursing finance so as to hinder potential defaults on its outstanding loans, as well as loans from influential countries and their commercial banks."

A review of the theoretical literature in political economy points to several factors affecting the likelihood of successful reforms. Among these are general political instability and the identity of the government. Research by Dollar and Svensson[55] argue that political instability has the potential to shorten the time horizon of a reforming government; hence it creates an asymmetry with respect to cost and benefits of reform. For the simple reason that the cost of reform must be born immediately, while the expected benefits occur in the future; the incumbent government is uncertain whether it will be around to reap the benefits of reform. And this may affect the needed incentives to exert adjustment effort in the first place. Reforms also need public support, and this weighs heavily on whether the orientation of the government is "populist" or "ideological" in outlook. A reform proposed by a "populist" government is more likely to be accepted for efficiency-enhancing reasons, than reforms initiated because of ideological tendencies.[56]

In fundamental ways, the type of reforms proposed under the political economy model do not fit the classical market model in its purest form, but rather, they occur at the intersection where the relative interests of the state and the market collide. Despite any existing complementarities, simultaneous economic and political reforms generate at least two clusters of severe conflicts. While the "surge of popular participation and demands that follow from political liberalization often runs counter to the fiscal and monetary restraint needed to cope with severe economic imbalances; the ensuing fiscal cuts and structural reforms are likely to weigh more heavily on the urban industrial and middle class strata"[57]—a group whose continuing support would be needed to make the reform effort successful.

The benevolent view of the state is that of having a limited but specific role in the function of a market economy: "to provide a functioning legal system and a stable macroeconomic environment; to correct market failures; to provide or tax merit goods; and perhaps to subsidize infant industries. All other forms of economic activity are thus, better left to the market which will provide goods as efficiently as possible."[58] Nonetheless, critics see the benevolent view of the state as naïve.[59] They cite the case of the East Asian countries who "rather than focusing on industries in which they had a comparative advantage, they created comparative advantage in specific industries; instead of worrying about allocative efficiency, they concentrated on productive efficiency, and used price to achieve strategic objectives—such as getting firms to invest in key areas, and letting prices be set by the market in the belief that it would lead to optimal outcomes."[60] While it is the responsibility of the state to create an enabling and supportive environment for economic growth, construction of long-term and durable infrastructures, protectionist policies—by providing the opportunity to develop economies of scale and domestic market stability—have been an important and perhaps necessary component of government-led strategies of economic restructuring.

The model of the Association of Southeast Asian Nations (ASEAN) newly industrialized economies (South Korea, Singapore, Taiwan, Malaysia) attest to a simple reality: that the application of protectionist policies, at least in the early stages of entry into the global market can create the enabling conditions (comparative advantage) necessary to acquire the indigenous skills and technology needed to compete in the international market. "By offering subsidies and protection both to offset the disadvantages faced by national firms in international competition and to move the ongoing industrialization toward one with higher value-added, technologically driven and dynamic activities,"[61] the ASEAN NICs were able to reduce the amount of time needed to leap-frog from being low-level agricultural producers to a more advanced technologically driven export-oriented industrialization process. Thus, it follows logically from the assumption that the backwash process dominates the spread effects that nations of low relative productivity will favor protection at home.[62]

This also applies to the liberalization of the financial sector in developing economies. "Given the structure of the financial system in most developing countries; it may be desirable (in the short term) for the financial

sector to support a liberalization of capital movements but take a protectionist stance with reference to the entry of foreign firms."[63] In her work
titled *Financial Politics in Contemporary Japan,*[64] Frances Rosenbluth points
out that decontrol in Japan was propelled by financial institutions, acting
in cooperation with the Ministry of Finance and sometimes politicians,
to construct a new set of rules they needed to compete in a changing
economic environment. The role of the private sector, on the other hand,
is to create wealth through sound investment, building liquidity through
investment in the domestic banking economy so as to create the internal
capacity for domestic lending to small-scale producers, and above all to
create jobs as a way of reducing domestic unemployment.

But the problem for developing economies is that "the adjustable peg
system becomes intolerable when imbalances in the external trade accounts come to be overshadowed (both as a source of problems and as
a response to them) by massive movements of short-term speculative
funds; hence it makes it increasingly difficult for governments to conduct
macroeconomic policy and to support exchange rates under pressure."[65]
Hence, the need for substantial centralized authority to implement
needed stabilization programs runs counter to the fiscal and monetary
reforms needed to fully integrate the productive sector into a liberalized
international market economy.

Neopatrimonialsm

Through their work on democratic experiments in Africa, Michael Bratton
and Nicolas Van de Walle[66] have drawn much attention on the concept of
neopatrimonialism as a useful analytical framework for explaining the nature of state-society relations, especially in developing polities. Compared
to the bureaucratic systems of most western societies, patrimonial political systems explain a situation where an individual rules by dint of personal prestige and power. Authority is entirely personalized, and shaped
by the ruler's preferences rather than any codified system of laws. The
ruler ensures the political stability of the regime and personal political
survival by providing a zone of security in an uncertain environment and
by selectively distributing favors and material benefits to loyal followers
who are not citizens of the polity so much as the ruler's clients.[67]

As with classic patrimonialism, "the right to rule in neopatrimonial
regimes is ascribed to a person rather than to an office, despite the official existence of a constitution. One individual, often a president for life,
dominates the state apparatus and stands above its laws. Relationships
of loyalty and dependence pervade a formal political and administrative
system, and officials occupy bureaucratic positions less to perform public
service, but with the ostensible purpose to acquire personal wealth and

status. Although state functionaries receive an official salary, they also enjoy access to various forms of illicit rents, prebends, and petty corruption, which constitute sometimes an important entitlement of office."[68] A characteristic feature of *neopatrimonialsm*, therefore, is the incorporation of patrimonial tendencies into the workings of bureaucratic institutions, thereby undermining formal rules of governance and the institutions that undergird them. When procedural mechanisms of governmental action are subject to arbitrary interpretation and execution, when the laws they reflect are flaunted, then the institutions that legitimize their public purpose are reduced to irrelevance. If we accept the above notion, then what has been compromised so far is not so much about the nature of governance in most African states, rather it is the *institutions* and the *rules of the game* that are necessary to provide the enabling conditions for good governance. Credible institutions and the rules they enforce should lay the foundation not only for democracy, but also provide an enabling environment for the expression of various rights of citizenship, property, and political participation.

PREBENDALISM

Rather than a nominal construct, prebendalism is an explanatory concept that describes a form of sociopolitical organization, interlocking directorates and structures that unite as well as protect the common interests of political actors. A "prebendal" state is one characterized by a sort of patron-client arrangement in which an office or position is given to a "client" or "agent" as a reward for loyalty or as an avenue for generating specific economic rents for the parties in the network. While "clientelism defines the nature of individual and group relationships within the wider socio-political sphere, prebendalism is primarily a function of the competition for, and appropriation of, the offices of the state—which are then administered for the benefit of individual occupants and their support groups."[69] "As individuals seek out patrons as they move upward socially and materially; they also come to accept ties of solidarity from their own clients which they view as fundamental to the latter's security and continued advancement as well as their own"[70]—hence one sees several chains of patron-client arrangements feeding off a much larger network.

Since independence, Nigeria has never had a stable state-power, and the form of politics which operated at all levels—irrespective of the regime in power (military or civilian)—has always had elements of prebendal politics. "An individual seeks the support and protection of a 'godfather,' while at the same time trying to acquire the basic social and material goods—loans, scholarships, licenses, plots of urban land, employment, promotion—and the main resource of the patron in meeting these requests is quite literally a piece of the state."[71]

The institutionalization of the patron-client relationship in Nigeria's body politic means that most electoral politics are not competitive but are arranged. Electoral contributions and political support are offered in return for guarantees of government contracts or appointments. Ministerial positions and directorships of various public enterprises are, in most cases, "sold" out in advance to the highest bidder in lieu of victory in the election. When these arrangements and negotiated "contracts" fell through after that fact, the ensuing political conflict among the parties presents one among many other obstacles that eventually paralyzes the smooth functioning of public governance. Prebendalism reinforces a culture of corruption in party politics, administrative governance, and continues to present a lasting barrier to the achievement of a veritable and popular constitutional democracy in Nigeria. To the extent that it harbors patrimonial and oligarchic tendencies, prebendal politics tends to bring to the forefront the primordial and ethnic differences that have oftentimes remained the bane of Nigeria's national politics.

Sultanism

The term *sultanism* was introduced into the lexicon of regime types by Max Weber, who considered it an extreme form of patrimonialsim.[72] It is a form of "personal autocracy (personal rulership) in which the ruler enjoys maximum authority and discretionary powers, and is so arbitrary that he becomes a tyrant."[73] Like patrimonialism, sultanism derives as a subtype of Weber's traditional authority, but is more focused on the *discretionary* aspects of personal rule. This definition is not only restrained to military dictatorships or other forms of governments with distinctive characteristics that allow their societies a limited pluralism short of genuine democracy, but also to oligarchic democracies that seeks popular legitimacy as true democracies.

The differences between sultanism and authoritarian or totalitarian regimes are "not merely a matter of degree but lie in their rulers' overall conception of politics, the structure of power, and the relation to the social structure, the economy, and ultimately the subjects of such rule."[74] Because "dictatorships that put on a democratic mask abuse public resources and state power to minimize the competition for elections; elections in these regimes are played with loaded dice—lack of freedom, fairness, and impartiality in their conduct and execution."[75] Invariably, the lack of efficient political institutions and processes results in the supremacy of personal power, which could only be checked by another power and not by the already existing institutions. Government positions, appointments, and authority transcend the will of the personal ruler and his network of cronies, sycophants, and ego-worshippers. Regimes that fit the sultanistic definition include Marcos in the Philippines, Ceausescu in Romania, Stroessner in Paraguay, Saddam in Iraq, Abacha in Nigeria, Somoza in Nicaragua, Hussein in Jordan, Mubarak in Egypt, Franco in Spain, Peron in Argentina, Shah Reza Pahlavi in Iran, Fulgencio Batista in Cuba, Mobutu in Zaire, Jean-Claude Duvalier in Haiti, Francisco Mathias Nguema in Equatorial Guinea, Kim Il-Sung and his son Kim Jong-il in North Korea, Bokassa of Central African Republic, Ghadaffi in Libya, Milosevic in Serbia, and so on.

But what drives sultanism beyond the more traditional patrimonial inclinations is the fact that the laws and the constitution itself (where it exists) become supplanted by the discretionary fiat of the ruler. "The binding norms and relations of bureaucratic administration are constantly subverted by arbitrary personal decisions of the ruler; hence what characterizes such regimes is the weakness of traditional and legal-rational legitimation and lack of ideological justification."[76] There may also be structural issues that work to facilitate the evolution of sultanistic tendencies in both quasi-democratic and nondemocratic regimes. An example of this includes an increasing level of deinstitutionalization (institutional decay) that invariably reduces the level of public accountability but at the same time creates an opening that enables the ruler to arrogate to himself more power over political, social, and economic issues. Because the mechanisms for leadership succession are not broadly nor, in most cases, constitutionally recognized, there is thus the tendency for rulers to seek to perpetuate themselves in office. They seek to find ways to postpone the inevitable, and this is most evident in situations where no natural heir to throne (a son or blood relation) is in the immediate horizon.

One can also point to the fact that in most *rentier* states, by virtue of having a single economic resource (oil, diamond, or uranium) that is greatly in demand and also that earns a greater proportion of the country's foreign currency reserves, the opportunity to control these resources and the economic rents they generate could, in and of itself, lead to oligarchic and *sultanistic* tendencies. This could explain the case in some of the most brutal regimes like Abacha's Nigeria, Mobutu's Zaire, Bokassa's Central African Republic, Charles Taylor's Liberia, and many others. But for Nigeria, the continued domination of the political arena by a civilianized military (retired military officers) and the weakness of its democratic institutions can both be understood as legacies derived from its sultanistic and presultanistic antecedents. In this regard, "the advantages for analysis of situating sultanistic regimes in long-term trajectories of national political development"[77] can point to some of the historical roots of current political instability and lack of democratic consolidation in Nigeria's body politic.

NOTES

1. Benedict Anderson, *Imagined Communities: Reflections on the Origin and Spread of Nationalism* (London: Verso, 1991), 113–14.

2. Excerpted from Kalu N. Kalu, "Embedding African Democracy and Development: The Imperative of Institutional Capital," *International Review of Administrative Sciences* 70, no. 3 (2004): 527–45.

3. Raymond Duvall and John Freeman, "The State and Dependent Capitalism," *International Studies Quarterly* 25, no. 1 (1981): 106.

4. Theda Skocpol, "Bringing the State Back In: Strategies of Analysis in Current Research," pp. 3–37 in *Bringing the State Back In*, ed. Peter B. Evans, Dietrich Rueschemeyer, and Theda Skocpol (Cambridge: Cambridge University Press, 1985), 7–8.

5. Naomi Chazan, Robert Mortimer, John Ravenhill, and Donald Rothchild, *Politics and Society in Contemporary Africa* (Boulder, Colo.: Lynne Rienner Publishers, 1992), 40.

6. George B. N. Ayittey, *Africa in Chaos* (New York: St. Martin's Press, 1998), 227.

7. Claude Ake, *Democracy and Development in Africa* (Washington, D.C.: Brookings Institution Press, 1996), 14.

8. Mahmood Mamdani, *Citizen and Subject: Contemporary Africa and the Legacy of Late Colonialism* (Princeton, N.J.: Princeton University Press, 1996), 11.

9. Ayittey, *Africa in Chaos*, 222.

10. Jeffrey Herbst, *States and Power in Africa: Comparative Lessons in Authority and Control* (Princeton, N.J.: Princeton University Press, 2000), 30–31.

11. Theda Skocpol, *States and Social Revolutions: A Comparative Analysis of France, Russia, and China* (New York: Cambridge University Press, 1979), 32.

12. Giovanni Sartori, "Concept Misformation in Comparative Politics," pp. 24–49 in *Comparative Politics: Notes and Readings*, ed. Roy C. Macridis and Bernard Brown (Homewood, Ill.: The Dorsey Press, 1977).

13. Francis Fukuyama, *State-Building: Governance and World Order in the 21st Century* (Ithaca, N.Y.: Cornell University Press, 2004), 5.

14. Fukuyama, *State-Building*, 16.

15. Yossi Shain and Juan J. Linz, *Between States: Interim Governments and Democratic Transitions* (New York: Cambridge University Press, 1995), 48.

16. Joel S. Migdal, *Strong Societies and Weak States: State-Society Relations and State Capabilities in the Third World* (Princeton, NJ: Princeton University Press, 1988), 21.

17. Robert I. Rotberg, "Failed States in a World of Terror," pp. 131–37 in *Global Politics in a Changing World*, 3rd ed., ed. Richard W. Mansbach and Edward Rhodes (Boston: Houghton Mifflin, 2006), 133.

18. Niccolo Machiavelli, *Discourses on Livy* (New York: Barnes and Noble Publishing, 2005), 57.

19. Robert M. MacIver, "The Myth of Authority," pp. 263–99 in *Comparative Politics: Notes and Readings*, ed. Roy C. Macridis and Bernard Brown (Homewood, Ill.: The Dorsey Press, 1977), 266.

20. Rotberg, "Failed States in a World of Terror," 134.

21. Roy C. Macridis and Bernard E. Brown, "The Political Process," pp. 237–62 in *Comparative Politics: Notes and Readings*, ed. Roy C. Macridis and Bernard Brown (Homewood, Ill.: The Dorsey Press, 1977), 243.

22. See Migdal, *Strong Societies and Weak States*, 56.

23. Fareed Zakaria, *From Wealth to Power: The Unusual Origins of America's World Role* (Princeton, N.J.: Princeton University Press, 1998), 38.

24. Naomi Chazan et al., *Politics and Society in Contemporary Africa* (Boulder, Colo.: Lynne Rienner Publishers, 1992), 38.

25. Naomi Chazan et al., *Politics and Society in Contemporary Africa*, 39.

26. Joel S. Migdal, Atul Kohli, and Vivienne Shue, *State Power and Social Forces: Domination and Transformation in the Third World* (New York: Cambridge University Press, 19994), 13.

27. Alfred Stepan, *The State and Society: Peru in Comparative Perspective* (Princeton, N.J.: Princeton University Press, 1978), xi.

28. Stepan, *The State and Society*, xii.

29. Stepan, *The State and Society*, 9.

30. Stepan, *The State and Society*, 41.

31. Stepan, *The State and Society*, 6.

32. Stepan, *The State and Society*, 45,

33. Sandbrook, *The Politics of Africa's Economic Recovery*, 91.

34. Sandbrook, *The Politics of Africa's Economic Recovery*, 96.

35. Mamdani, *Citizen and Subject: Contemporary Africa and the Legacy of Late Colonialism*, 15.

36. Mamdani, *Citizen and Subject: Contemporary Africa and the Legacy of Late Colonialism*, 16.

37. Robert D. Putnam, *Making Democracy Work: Civic Traditions in Modern Italy* (Princeton, N.J.: Princeton University Press, 1993).

38. Robert D. Putnam, "Turning In, Turning Out: The Strange Disappearance of Social Capital in America," *Political Science & Politics* 28 (1995): 664–83.

39. Robert D. Putnam, *Making Democracy Work: Civic Traditions in Modern Italy*, 1993.

40. Ismail Serageldin, Foreword, to *Social Capital and Poverty*, Paul Collier, Working Paper 4 (Washington, D.C.: The World Bank's Social Capital Initiative), November 1998.

41. Kate Meagher, "Social Capital, Social Liabilities, and Political Capital: Social Networks and Informal Manufacturing in Nigeria," *African Affairs* 105, no. 421 (2006): 553–82.

42. Meagher, "Social Capital, Social Liabilities, and Political Capital," 579.

43. Dankwart A. Rustow, "Transitions to Democracy: Toward a Dynamic Model," *Comparative Politics* 2, no. 3 (April 1970): 337–60.

44. Hadenius, *Democracy and Development*, 112.

45. Alvin Rabushka and Kenneth A. Shepsle, *Politics in Plural Societies: A Theory of Democratic Instability* (Columbus, Ohio: Charles E. Merrill, 1972), 208–17.

46. Donald A. Schon and Martin Rein, *Frame Reflection: Toward the Resolution of Intractable Policy Controversies* (New York: Basic Books, 1994), 8.

47. Susan Rose-Ackerman, *Corruption and Government: Causes, Consequences, and Reform* (New York: Cambridge University Press, 1999), 131.

48. Robert Gilpin, *Global Political Economy: Understanding the International Economic Order* (Princeton, N.J.: Princeton University Press, 2001), 27.

49. Gilpin, *Global Political Economy*, 311.

50. Kalu N. Kalu, "Development and Identity: Framing the South-South Dialogue," in *Vision and Policy in Nigerian Economics: The Legacy of Pius Okigbo*, ed. Jane I. Guyer and LaRay Denzer (Ibadan, Nigeria: Ibadan University Press, 2005), 156.

51. Robert Gilpin, *U.S. Power and the Multinational Corporation: The Political Economy of Foreign Direct Investment* (New York: Basic Books, 1975), 43.

52. Robert Gilpin, *The Political Economy of International Relations* (Princeton, N.J.: Princeton University Press, 1987), 11.

53. Daren Kew and Peter Lewis, "Nigeria," pp. 240–95 in *Introduction to Politics of the Developing World*, ed. William A. Joseph, Mark Kesselman, and Joel Krieger (Boston, Mass.: Houghton-Mifflin, 2007), 258.

54. David Dollar and Jakob Svensson, "What explains the Success or Failure of Structural Adjustment Programs?" Policy Research Working Paper 1938 (Washington, D.C.: The World Bank Macroeconomics and Growth, Development Research Group, 1998): 6–7.

55. Dollar and Svensson, "What Explains the Success or Failure of Structural Adjustment Programs?" 1–36.

56. Dollar and Svensson, "What Explains the Success or Failure of Structural Adjustment Programs?" 9.

57. Joan M. Nelson, "The Politics of Economic Transformation: Is the Third World Experience Relevant in Eastern Europe?" *World Politics* 45, no. 3 (April 1993): 433.

58. Paul Streeten, "Markets and States: Against Minimalism," *World Development Report* 21, no. 8 (1993): 1.

59. See Streeten, "Markets and States"; and Ajit Singh, "Openness and Market-Friendly Approach to Development: Learning the Right Lessons from Development Experience," *World Development Report* 22, no. 12 (1994): 1811–23.

60. Enrique Dussel Peters and Mathew A. Verghis, "The State, Market, and Development: A Rapporteurs Report," Working Paper No. 196. Summary of conference papers and discussion held at the Kellogg Institute, June 1993, 1, at kellogg.nd.edu/publications/workingpapers/WPS/196.pdf.

61. Robert Wade, "East Asia's Economic Success: Conflicting Perspectives, Partial Insights, Shaky Evidence," *World Politics* 44 (January 1992): 270–320.

62. David A. Lake, "Beneath the Commerce of Nations: A Theory of International Economic Structures," *International Studies Quarterly* 28 (1984): 149.

63. Stephan Haggard and Sylvia Maxfield, "The Political Economy of Financial Internationalization in the Developing World," *International Organization* 50, no. 1 (1996): 39.

64. Frances McCall Rosenbluth, *Financial Politics in Contemporary Japan* (Ithaca, N.Y.: Cornell University Press, 1989).

65. John Gerard Ruggie, "International Regimes, Transactions, and Change: Embedded Liberalism in the Post-War Economic Order," *International Organization* 36, no. 2 (1982): 408.

66. Michael Bratton and Nicolas van de Walle, *Democratic Experiments in Africa: Regime Transitions in Comparative Perspective* (New York: Cambridge University Press, 1997).

67. Bratton and van de Walle, *Democratic Experiments in Africa*, 61.

68. Bratton and van de Walle, *Democratic Experiments in Africa*, 62.

69. Richard A. Joseph, *Democracy and Prebendal Politics in Nigeria: The Rise and Fall of the Second Republic* (New York: Cambridge University Press, 1987), 63.

70. Joseph, *Democracy and Prebendal Politics in Nigeria*, 55.

71. Joseph, *Democracy and Prebendal Politics in Nigeria*, 56.

72. See Guenther Roth and Claus Wittich, eds., *Max Weber: Economy and Society: An Outline of Interpretive Sociology* (Berkeley: University of California Press, 1978), 1:231–32.

73. Akbar Ganji, "The Struggle Against Sultanism," *Journal of Democracy* 6, no. 4 (October 2005): 35–51.

74. H. E. Chehabi and Juan J. Linz, eds., *Sultanistic Regimes* (Baltimore: Johns Hopkins University Press, 1998), 3–4.

75. Ganji and Linz, *The Struggle Against Sultanism*, 43.

76. H. E. Chehabi and Juan J. Linz, "A Theory of Sultanism 1," pp. 3–47 in *Sultanistic Regimes*, ed. H. E. Chehabi and Juan J. Linz (Baltimore: Johns Hopkins University Press, 1998), 7.

77. Richard Snyder, "Paths Out of Sultanistic Regimes: Combining Structural and Voluntarist Perspectives," pp. 49–81 in *Sultanistic Regimes*, ed. H. E. Chehabi and Juan J. Linz (Baltimore: Johns Hopkins University Press, 1998), 74.

3

—∽—

History and
Evolutionary Schisms

Nigeria's course of political development could rightly be said to have emerged from very humble beginnings, in the sense that there was an unwritten consensus among key indigenous advocates for her independence from Great Britain; that negotiation rather than violence would be employed in the quest for national sovereignty. Like many African countries, no sooner had the country gotten her independence did the schisms and unresolved issues of cultural integration and elite consensus manifest themselves with uncompromising virulence. Nigeria boasts of a population of about 144 million people—the largest on the African continent. Though three major ethnic groups (Ibo, Hausa, Yoruba) constitute over 40 percent of the population, there are also numerous subethnic tertiary groups that complement the more than 250 ethno-lingual distinctions in the country.

With a modified system of federal government and thirty six states spread across six geopolitical zones (Southeast, South-South, Southwest, Northeast, Northwest, North Central), the central government in the capital city of Abuja establishes much of the decision premises regarding the authoritative allocation of values, national policy, resource distribution, and infrastructural development. With nonexistent or ineffective state constitutions (if they exist), the central government holds sway in matters of program development, national security, and finance. Nigeria's brand of federalism has, in fact, come to reflect an awkward hybrid between popular consent, benevolent dictatorship, and authoritarian regimentation. Much of this had not evolved as an accident of fate, but rather as a

lingering consequence of the disagreements and compromises that befell
the country for much of its forty-seven years existence.

CHARTING STATE AND IDENTITY

Nigeria's independence from Britain was achieved on October 1, 1960, but
from the outset, the new nation was beset by regional and ethnic divisive-
ness that complicated efforts to establish a firm basis for constitutional
rule.[1] The complications arose partly as a result of British colonial policy,
but more fundamentally due to the lack of a regional consensus on the
viability of independence as well as a general unpreparedness by the
indigenous elite to transcend the anti-colonial rhetoric into a wholesome
nationalist culture critical in the formative years of the new sovereignty.
Though British colonial rule in Nigeria lasted for nearly a century, its duration and persistence depended largely on the ability of British colonialists to play one ethnic group against the other. The 1914 amalgamation
of the Northern, Southern, and Lagos Protectorates (which were up until
then a collection of disjointed and virtually independent groups) by the
then British governor general Sir Frederick Lugard into what is today's
Nigeria essentially set the stage for latter events that would occur. The
exit of the British colonial administration exploded the deep-seated tensions that had hitherto been suppressed under colonial tutelage.

In Northern Nigeria, there existed a monolithic class system that distinguished the ruling oligarchy from the ordinary people. The dominant
ethnic groups in the North were the Hausas and Fulanis who invariably
could trace their origins to Northern Africa. An opportune mix of itiner-
ant and nomadic culture created the dynamic for a theocratic conquest of
much of Northern Nigeria by the Hausa-Fulani. The existent class system
provided the British colonialists with judicial and administrative infrastructure that facilitated a sort of "indirect rule" in the North. Because
the emirs and other lower-ranking officials in the Emirate system were
simply designated as colonial officers ruling their subjects on behalf of the
British colonial state,[2] it created an additional privilege and authority for
which they were unwilling to give up easily even at the price of independence. To secure the consent of Northern leaders for independence, much
of the feudal authority system in the region was left literarily intact. This
meant that, in the formative years of Nigeria's independence, two parallel
authorities operated side-by-side, a paternalistic feudal authority in the
North and a federal parliamentary authority for the rest of the country.
More than anything else, the system of indirect rule and the compromise
to allow a quasi-autonomous authority in the North retarded the process
of national political integration as well as sectionalized consequent efforts

at developing a truly Nigerian citizenship. From then on, the evolution of "national" political parties was regionalized, political leadership became personalized, and objective government policy yielded to the allure of primordial inclinations.

In the South, there were relatively egalitarian societies of the Igbos, and the semi-feudal Yoruba principalities claiming common ancestry to a mystical legend called Oduduwa who was said to have migrated from Northeast Africa and eventually settled in Ile-Ife.[3] But in order to replicate the system of indirect rule among Igbos, an area characteristically disposed to a decentralized, communal, and less paternalistic form of traditional governance, it became necessary for the British to impose its own stratification system by inventing a system of warrant chiefs, who in addition to British military force, were used to enforce colonial rule and authority.[4] Among the functions of the warrant chiefs or native officials were the collection of taxes for colonial administration, provision of cheap native labor for colonial public works and the enforcement of colonial regulations and ordinances. In Yorubaland, especially Ile-Ife, Oyo, and Ibadan principalities, the semi-feudal structure of Chiefs and Council of Elders also provided the British the opportunity to utilize the existing traditional authority to implement a de facto system of indirect rule but not to the extent that was in the North.

THE STRUCTURAL BASIS OF DISSENT AND COMPETITION

The literature on multiethnic societies is fraught with the argument that ethnic differences, more often than not, create conditions for political instability. While not discounting the fact that such differences is a potential variable, but it can also be a source of celebration and strength. As with all other matters of state sovereignty, ethnic differences have to be managed through equitable distribution of incentives of citizenship, fair representation in national politics, and in the creation of an enabling environment for the exercise of ethnic identity not as an isolated category, but as the very foundation for collective national interest. For the simple fact that ethnic groups make up the collective national identity, they can hardly be construed as mutually exclusive. Rather it is the structural inequities that different groups experience within states that has the potential to resurface underlying tensions and intraethnic conflict.

The British were never value-neutral before, during, or after colonial rule. First, the geographic size of the North with its arbitrary boundaries extending Southwards beyond the Benue and Niger rivers ensured that it had such a large population and land mass to influence the course of national politics for many years. Second, it also helped to bring under the indirect influence of the feudal authority (the Hausa-Fulani) a large number of smaller ethnic groups that eventually made up the Greater North. There was also a certain level of cynicism on the part of the British. In Nigeria, especially before World War II, the British supported the development of separate institutions and identities for different ethnic and religious communities, a system of "native administration" to reflect communal loyalties; hence it has been argued that Sir Frederick Lugard's most crucial and characteristic decisions as Commissioner for Northern Nigeria (1900–1906) worked against future amalgamation of Nigeria. But his later decision as amalgamator when he became governor general of Nigeria (1912–1918) were said to be aimed at the destruction of his predecessor's achievement in establishing a rational and modern state system.[5]

In a speech entitled "The Amalgamation of Nigeria was a Fraud" which was published in *Guardian Newspaper* of July 2000, the famed jurist Richard Akinjide narrated a poignant account of the background and root causes of Nigeria's problems. As a former federal minister of education in Nigeria's pre-independence cabinet (1959–1966), and latter attorney general and minister of justice in the Shagari Administration (1979–1983), he has remained privy to critical knowledge of many aspects of Nigeria's political development. In his account that follows, Nigeria's problems started at about 1884 and began to take root upon the arrival of Sir Frederick Lugard to the country in 1894. Ironically, Lugard was not originally employed by the British government, but rather arrived in Nigeria first as an employee of British business. After having worked as an employee of different companies including East Indian Company, the Royal East African company, and then by the Royal Niger Company; it was from the Royal Niger Company that he transferred to work for the British government. The Royal Niger Company was chartered in 1886 with the expressed purpose of controlling British trade in Nigeria, but the charter was eventually revoked in 1900 following the creation of the Colony of Lagos and the Protectorates of Northern and Southern Nigeria. In 1912, Lugard was nominated as the governor general of Nigeria with the task of amalgamating the Northern and Southern Protectorates.

In fundamental ways, the period 1906–1912,[6] which preceded the amalgamation, was one of the most crucial in the history of Nigeria, for it marked the beginning of the rejection of standards and customs that had endured for many centuries. It was the beginning of a deepening of Western influence within Nigerian society. Beside new economic opportunities, Christianity as the official doctrine of the colonialists began to spread throughout the pagan areas of both Southern and Northern Nigeria. While new forms of administration and justice were introduced, education as a way of life was made readily available to many Nigerians as a result of the spread of missions. It was in effect the beginning of a silent but creeping revolution in which both religion and education worked in tandem in the process of cultural transformation as well as political socialization. But ironically, the very exception to the principle of *indirect rule* in the North limited further expansion of Christianity and education into the Northern hinterland, a factor that would eventuality work against the sociological and integrative potentials of the new Nigerian state.

For the fact that Nigeria was essentially created as a sphere of British economic and business interests, the consequent administration of the colonial territory by Lugard meant that safeguarding such interests would be foremost in the policies of his administration. As Michael Crowther[7] points out, the immediate reason for the decision to amalgamate the two Nigerias was due to economic expediency. The Northern Protectorate was running at a severed deficit, which was being met by a subsidy from the southern Protectorate, and an Imperial grant-in-aid from Britain of about £300,000 a year. Even though this was at odds with the hitherto colonial policy that each territory should be self-subsisting, resources from the south became a means for sustaining the North until such a time it could become self-supporting. The amalgamation not only made it more conducive to coordinate the colonial railway policy, but it also provided a seaward outlet to the land-locked North for conveyance of produce from the hinterland to the coastal ports. In 1898, Lugard formed the West African Frontier Force initially with 2,000 soldiers. Since 90 percent of the soldiers were from the North and mainly from the Middle Belt region, one can therefore see why Akinjide points this out as the beginning of Nigeria's problems. As of today, the North has maintained a sizeable majority of the military personnel and its leadership cadre, especially in the postwar era. While many of the coup d'etats have been led by Northerners, their control of the military seems to have become the great *equalizer* by nullifying the supposed educational advantage of the South over the North. With control over the use of force, it becomes all the more easier to either take over the reins of political power at whim, or at best, dictate the contours of the emergent political discourse.

Further insights also reveal that between 1898 and 1914, Lugard sent a number of official dispatches to London, which culminated in a rationale for the amalgamation of the Northern and Southern protectorates of Nigeria on January 1, 1914. In those dispatches, Lugard justified the amalgamation by arguing that the British needed the railway from the North to the Coast to facilitate British business interests. The British thus were more concerned about geographical amalgamation as opposed to cultural integration. In fact, a statement attributed to Sir Donald Cameroon, in a terse warning to the British colonial administration offers a window into one of the major reasons why the British sought amalgamation of Northern and Southern

Nigeria: "It should be evident that if we did so frame our policy as to foster the development of the Northern Provinces as a separate political unit we should be merely seeking to revive a state of affairs that the amalgamation of Southern and Northern Nigeria in 1914 was specifically designed to terminate."[8] Because the British government was reluctant to administer the protectorate with taxes paid by her citizens, amalgamation became an expedient means for advancing the financial interests of British business. By arbitrarily carving the boundaries of Northern and Southern Nigeria in such a way that, rather than using the natural and more realistic boundaries offered by the Rivers Niger and Benue, the British overshot through these natural demarcations thereby granting the "North" a permanent majority in any political equation. In fact, if Lugard had accepted earlier recommendations by his Lieutenants for the creation of four provinces in which the Western and Eastern boundaries would simply mirror the geologic contours of the Rivers Niger and Benue; the geographical size of the North would have conformed more to its natural characteristics, thereby tempering its political excesses and eventual claim to legislative supremacy. As in many other details, one also takes note of the dysfunctional effects that were created by the British-sponsored Macpherson Constitution of 1951.[9] While it created a central government and a quasi-federalist structure in an attempt to "nationalize" political institutions; the center remained weak because representation in the unicameral federal legislature was apportioned according to Regional population—which, invariably, produced an automatic preponderance of Northern delegates in that body. Consequent proposals by the East and the West for "unit representation" in which there would be a fixed number of seats from each Region in the national parliament, were rejected by the colonial administration.

It was the colonial high-handedness and brazen bias in favor of the North that partly contributed to the rising electoral tensions that eventually scuttled the partisan coalition in the First Republic (1960–1966) and contributed to the fateful aftermath. Rather than starting the country out as a nation of "equals," it started as a nation of "unequals" with respect to presumed size, population, and legislative hegemony. While reinforcing the principle of "indirect rule" in the North, the British also contributed in fundamental ways to discourage the process of national political integration, especially in the formative years of Nigeria. It was highly consequential, both for education and also for the emergent postcolonial indigenous civil service. While the federal and the Eastern and Western regional governments embarked on a massive replacement of the colonial expatriates by qualified Nigerians, the Northern government on the other hand, adopted the "Northernization" policy in the public service of the Northern region.[10]

The overall effect of this program was that public service employees of Southern origin who were resident in the North, were replaced with persons of Northern origin. The Northern government had feared of Southern domination in the critical institutions of government in an independent Nigeria, but in doing so, laid the foundation for the type of sectoral politics that contributed to the fall of the First Republic as well as a central sore point in the implementation of the "federal character" principle. As A. H. M. Kirk-Greene[11] would reflect later, the concepts of "North" and the "South" evolved into a political terminology that has remained the "trigger-phrases" of Nigerian administrative thought since 1914. From the beginning, Nigeria's transition from a colonial to an independent state was fated and left a lot of unresolved contradictions. The country thus became a perfect breeding ground for internecine wrangling arising out of mutual distrust, suspicions, and misrepresentations due sometimes to purely selfish motives.[12] Because the rationale for amalgamation was ambiguous, or at best self-serving, it would take the forces of inertia culminating in a brutal civil war to resurface the contradictions of nationhood as well as the haphazard manner in which the colonial regime handed over power to Nigerians.

POLITICAL DEVELOPMENT AND THE CRISIS OF GOVERNANCE

Studies in political science have shown that political development[13] is a key element in the determination of the nature of the state, political conflicts, regulation of policies, nature of sanctions, and in the overall exercise of sovereign legitimacy. While most scholars see it as the study of new regimes, the increased role of the state, the expansion of political participation, and the capacity of regimes to maintain order under conditions of rapid change and competition among political groups (classes and ethnic groups) for power, status, and wealth; political development is defined as the effectiveness of political structures in performing major political functions such as interest articulation, interest aggregation, political recruitment, socialization, and communication.[14] But when cast in its contemporary analysis, political development takes on a modernizing and evolutionary characteristics; in the sense that the maturity of new states is expected to be an evolution from primitive, archaic, and authoritarian systems to advanced, industrialized liberal democracies. For many countries, the initial "take-off" is more readily achieved with limited fanfare, but the Achilles heel lay in the inherent and limiting factors of the transition process.

Modern constitutional development began within a few years of the creation of Nigeria as a single colony, with elective office first provided in 1922. An early nationalist leader, Herbert Macaulay, established a political party soon thereafter. As a Nigerian-centered political life grew up among the formally educated (essentially in the South), other organizations arose, and the British colonial administration was pressed with increasing demands for participation.[15] Because of the earlier compromises made to the North, it became very difficult to achieve a flexible consensus among the regional elite regarding the merits of sovereignty and political direction of the nation. As Aborishade and Mundt[16] points out, these differences of opinion were largely a product of the colonial administration's regional approach to governing, which cemented the new country's self-image as a conglomerate of three regions. They resulted in 1954 in the creation of a federal system composed of three regions—Northern (Hausa-Fulani), Eastern (Igbo), and Western (Yoruba)—each dominated by a single ethnic group (in brackets).

Under pressure from their leaders, the Eastern and Western regions were granted self-government in 1957; the North became self-governing in 1959. It is common knowledge that the North had remained quite reticent in the early advocacy for Nigeria's independence either because they had not come to a full understanding of the implications both for the maintenance of the feudal authority or the fear of Southern domination in the new nation. Even after the amalgamation of Northern and Southern protectorate to create Nigeria in 1914, the North did not sit on the Nigerian Legislative Council until 1947. Both sentiments proved quite consequential in the course of the country's political evolution and stability. In the early days of independence, and prior to that, it always proved very difficult to sample Northern public opinion on critical issues of political development in Nigeria. In addition and for the fact that much of the press were in the South, the South was more educated, and the North more sparsely populated, much of early opinions on Nigeria reflected views from the south, and invariably, could not be said to represent that of the North. According to Oluwadare Aguda,[17] this lack of vigorous Northern participation in the national political dialogue, together with the South's over-assertiveness, meant that the North had to press its views with greater bellicosity and violence. Incidentally, the North did not have to worry too much about making its voice heard most of the time, because until January 1966, it controlled the federal government. Aguda hence, concludes that the evident taciturnity of the North together with the assertiveness of the South, due mainly to the South's higher level of education has proven to be one of the most disastrous features of the Nigerian approach to politics.

THE LIMITING STRUCTURE OF POLITICAL REPRESENTATION

The Nigerian independence constitution of 1960 and the republican constitution of 1963 embodied many British parliamentary concepts.

It adopted the British Westminster model[18] at the federal and regional levels, in which the chief executive, the prime minister, was chosen by the majority party. This meant that Northerners came to dominate the federal government by virtue of their "greater" population based on the contentious 1952–1953 census. The ruling coalition for the first two years quickly turned into a Northern-only coalition when the Northern People's Congress (NPC) achieved an outright majority in the legislature. But the adaptations to the Westminster model of government incorporated the regional orientation of Nigerian politics; an unrestrained competition among the regionally based parties thwarted the spirit of compromise indispensable to the effective functioning of parliamentary democracy.[19] In a system where parliamentary opposition was regionally based, this created enormous potential for intimidation,[20] harassment, and violence against opposition supporters, and also against citizens who opt for parties not dominant in their regions. The three main political parties, the National Council of Nigerian Citizens (NCNC), the Northern Peoples Congress (NPC), and the Action Group (AG) had become provincially regionalized in an instinctive attempt to avoid complete crushing by the NPC, which through the Chief Akintola-led Nigerian National Democratic Party (NNDP) was making inroads into the South. While these parties mirrored their respective ethnic-group associations, so were the various minority parties that emerged as representatives of the subethnic groups within the three main regions.

There were other parties such as the Nigerian Elements Progressive Union (NEPU), the United Middle Belt Congress (UMBC), the Middle Zone League (MZL), all formed in the North; while the South produced the Calabar-Ogoja-Rivers State Movement (COR), the Niger Delta Congress (NDC), and the Mid-West State Movement (MSM).[21] Nonetheless, it was a tiered system in which local loyalties remained mostly organized in traditional terms, provincial ones became organized in party-political terms, and national ones were only barely organized at all.[22] From the beginning, the First Republic[23] was thus beset by a threefold structural contradiction: political party formation on the bedrock of ethnic group solidarity and exclusiveness, a constitutional framework which reposted predominant political power with the subnational units, and a federal organization of government at the center. Of these, regional supremacy was decisive and its effects on political life were profound and enduring. No sooner had the NPC assumed full control of the federal government in 1960, the Northern leaders still found themselves incapable of stemming the tide of "Nigerianization" of the new nation. Hence, they adopted a specific method to ensure that the number of Northerners employed in the federal service were dramatically increased. To achieve this meant that entry qualifications for federal civil service were lowered for Northerners; some were transferred to the federal civil service from the Northern public service while foreigners were often hired to replace them in the North, and Northern public servants were often promoted more rapidly than their Southern colleagues.[24]

But the contradiction between political power and socioeconomic development was not the only explosive element in the North's federal predominance. The prominent role of Islamic religion and law in Northern society, the conservative authoritarian social structure and values of the emirates, the historic expansionist tendencies of the Fulani empire—symbolized in Tafawa Balewa's 1948 vow to complete its "conquest to the sea"—and the history of political and ethnic conflict during colonial rule all intensified the refusal of the Action Group and NCNC politicians to accept Northern domination.[25] The absence of a unifying ethos for a truly Nigerian citizenship meant that regional interests took precedent over the collective interest of the nation. Furthermore, the political impenetrability of the upper North was a critical obstacle to the forging of an objective national political challenge along class or ideological lines.[26]

The only time that a sort of alliance emerged between the major political parties was during the preparatory stages of the 1964 federal elections. The NCNC formed an alliance with the Chief Obafemi Awolowo led Action Group (AG) and the NEPU to become the United Progressive Grand Alliance (UPGA)—a progressive, antiregional force; while the NPC formed its own alliance with Chief Akintola's party (NNDP) in the West as well as various minor Southern parties to form the Nigerian National Alliance (NNA). But of more serious consequence was the eventual UPGA boycott of the 1964 elections, and the following showdown between the NPC and the NCNC leadership under Alhaji Tafawa Balewa (prime minister) and Dr. Nnamdi Azikiwe (president), respectively. Wishing to avoid mass bloodshed, and unable to win military and police support, President Azikiwe finally yielded, and the NPC returned to the federal government more powerful than ever, with the NCNC obtaining a reduced role in a new and even more superficial coalition government.[27] It was a compromise that while it strengthened the hand of the ruling NPC government, also inflamed the consequent electoral crisis in the West. Had Azikiwe stood his ground in the face-off with the Prime Minister Balewa and the NPC, a genuine coalition government involving the NCNC could have tempered the political zealotry of the NPC to "control" the government of the Western Region through the election of its main surrogate Chief Akintola as the premier against all indications of electoral fraud.

The consequent destruction and chaos that followed the Western Regional elections of October 1965 could be traced directly to this seemingly innocuous event. Even though some have often pointed to the reason for the January 15, 1966, military takeover of the Nigerian government as having been inspired by the electoral crisis in the Western Region, yet one finds very scant information either from or about the major actors in the coup as to a central relationship to the Western electoral crisis. In the search for the critical mass that led up to the coup, I have been disappointed at the dearth of ideological muster as well as the level of political naivety on the part of the major operators; either from Major Chukwuma Nzeogwu's premier broadcast or Adewale Ademoyega's seemingly Neo-Marxist rhetoric. And this raises a few speculative questions. Was the coup inspired as a result of the fact that the NCNC had lost out to the NPC in the so-called coalition government? Did Dr. Azikiwe's absence from the country during the military putsch in any remote way suggest foreknowledge? Or was the coup imminent as a result of the high-handed, antidemocratic, and extra-constitutional rule of the NPC, especially as it relates to its approach in dealing with the crisis in the West?

If the issue was the Western electoral crisis, then why was the execution of the coup regionalized, rather than being concentrated full-force on the West, especially since the seat of the federal government was in Lagos (in the West)? In retrospect, it seemed that the coup was inspired by a combination of many things, but neither far removed from the above questions. It was a situation where several cleavages, having matured over the years came together and with a vengeance struck decisively at the center of political power. The January 15, 1966 coup was, more than anything else a less than fortuitous event, an unnatural and untimely abbreviation of a dialectic process that was yet to unfold—a process not necessarily inimical to the political evolution and development of a fledgling post-colonial state such as Nigeria. Larry Diamond[28] puts it quite succinctly when he states:

> The continuing political conflict within the West flowed together with the struggle between the ruling parties of the North (NPC) and the East (NCNC) to produce the fraudulent and violent election battle in the West. The resistance of the Western people to the return of a corrupt and patently undemocratic government then exploded in open rebellion. At the same time, a national crisis of confidence was gathering over the political class and its entire regime, swelling in particular among strategically placed young elites in the universities, the press, the civil service and the military, and also among the unions and radical parties that had successfully confronted the regime the previous year. The first three cleavages underlay the crisis in the West. The fourth drew its final burst of momentum from that crisis to bring down the First Republic.

It therefore misses a lot in terms of substance when some ascribe the January 1966 military coup and the consequent abrogation of the First Republic to the Western electoral crisis of 1965. The Western electoral cri-

sis was an *effect* for which the *cause* seemed much larger than the politics
of the region. It was partly the culmination and consequence of other
events that occurred much earlier. The central and most important con-
tributors to that crisis were the failure of the leadership alliance between
the NPC and the NCNC (a responsibility that rests squarely on the
shoulders of two individuals: Tafawa Balewa and Nnamdi Azikiwe), the
controversy over the 1962–1963 national census, and the fateful boycott
of the 1964 federal elections by UPGA. Directly or indirectly, these structural and personality factors generated the critical mass that informed the
general environment for the January 1966 military coup, the death of the
First Republic, and the consequent crisis that eventually metamorphosed
into civil war.

Ironically, while the January coup d'etats seemed to have offered a brief
respite to the tensed situation in the nation, it was the apparent sectional
and political nature of its execution that, more than anything else, gave it
the enduring political footing that would eventually contribute to pushing
the nation beyond the brink of the precipice into civil war. It was a war
fought between the federal side and the former Eastern Region, which
had then seceded from the rest of the country to become the independent
Republic of Biafra. The war lasted for thirty months and formerly ended
on January 15, 1970, when the Biafran regime fell after a brutal onslaught
and was reintegrated into the federal system. Millions of lives were lost
amid a shattered vision of national unity. Though ethnic cleavages have
traditionally tended to provide the undercurrent for much of the political
games played by the Nigerian elite, it seems that early Nigerian political
crisis was neither driven by ideological differences, class, or "overt" ethnicity; although the evolving structure of the federation and the political
environment might make it seem otherwise. Even though the census crisis may have heightened the salience of ethnicity and region in politics, it
marked the beginning of fiercely polarized competition between the NPC
and the NCNC, who were both looking toward the critical federal election
due before the end of 1964.[29] "Region" thus became the common denominator between the two parties. Ethnicity may not have been the spark that
ignited the fire, rather it was a political crisis engendered by the regional
struggle for control of state power and the resources at its disposal.

There are great lessons to be drawn from Nigeria's experience. Since
the average person during the pre-independence days lacked the educational background to conceptualize the merits or demerits of various
political ideas, he or she relied on the personality of the regional party
leader as a surrogate for judging what was in the public interest. The
January 1966 military coup may have ended the First Republic, but it
also made the emergence of an ideologically driven national political
party more difficult. In fact, the use of coercive powers on issues that

require a purely political-diplomatic approach points to the ideological barrenness of the governing class.[30] While the supposed objectives of military coups are assumed to be "corrective" in outlook, but once civilian rule is restored, the citizens simply revert back to their old ways of doing things—and once again, justified or not—giving flimsy cause to the military for another round of intervention. Perennial military interventions into the political affairs of the state have made it quite difficult to develop appropriate democratic coalitions or alignments, but nonetheless have aided in shaping particular orientations toward narrow and conflicting political objectives. Amid an increasing level of social ambivalence, the party system has equally not been spared. As was the case in the "Great Debate" over the structure of the Second Republic (1979–1983), many Nigerians have begun to question the viability of political parties for democracy in the country.

After forty-seven years of independence from Great Britain, Nigeria is yet to devise a stable mechanism that could mitigate the ethno-regional trajectory of national politics. In fact, the endemic political tensions reflects widespread cynicism with party politics, and some have even called for a zero or one party system—as the solution to the increasing level of political corruption, fraud, violence, and boss politics—that have become the bane of party politics in Nigeria. The noble ideal of elected political representation has been replaced with a paternalistic form of political godfatherism. As with many other developing countries, Nigeria has too many problems to solve at the same time. Overlapping crisis of national identity, ethnocentrism, secularism, illiteracy, poverty, and distributive politics must be resolved in the same parallel process of state consolidation and nation-building.

GUARDIANSHIP WITHOUT DISCOURSE

As indicate earlier, Nigeria started on a hurried platform of political sovereignty without adequate corporate foundation. Such could be seen in the rigid and abject indifference to the art of political compromise by the political leadership of the Northern Peoples Congress, even as Dr. Azikiwe made overt proposal for constitutional checks and balances of executive power. Even though rebuffed, why Azikiwe remained so willingly to acquiesce or unilaterally abdicate his strong points for a constitutional government built on division of powers was quite befuddling. The fallout was that the individual compromises that he made at various stages in the formation of the postcolonial Nigerian government emboldened the Northern leadership, which also controlled a functional majority in the parliament. In fact, Azikiwe continued to push for alterations in the federal constitution up until the last days of the First Republic. In a 1965 *West Africa* magazine titled *Visioner in a Gilded Age*,[31] Dr. Azikiwe ushered in a debate on the federal constitution with a series of proposals that, though highly imaginative, attracted very little interest on the part of the dominant Northern Peoples Congress.

Dr. Azikiwe's first proposal was, in line with popular opinion then, that the Head of State should also be the "chief executive." He argued that Nigeria then was not ready to have a constitutional head of state (president) with hollow responsibilities but working parallel with a power-loaded "head of government" (prime minister). But without pushing this argument to its logical conclusion, Azikiwe also left room both for his own political future and for the sake of mutual coexistence. He accepted the fact that majority of adult Nigerians then, were still illiterate and would most likely supplant personality to the realities of power when both positions (president and prime minister) are put forth for analysis. Though he knew that the position of president in a coalition government was symbolic, he was willing to play the role of a "prisoner in a Gilded cage," since he (surprisingly) had "no personal ambitions." He felt that as a safeguard for the federation, the presidency should be given some powers, even if the office of the prime minister was retained.

Among the minimum responsibilities that Azikiwe urged for the presidency were control of the Federal Public Service Commission, the Federal Audit, the Federal Electoral Commission, and the Federal Census Board. In this way and by placing these under the presidency, they could be insulated from being subverted for parochial ends. In order to make it impossible for political parties to use the armed forces for partisan purposes, he suggested that a privy council consisting of past and current presidents, governors, premiers, speakers, and others be enabled to advise the president on the use of armed forces for internal security; and on matters of civil crisis and war, the prime minister can use the police and, inside Nigeria, the armed forces. However, it was not lost on him as to the changing character of the emerging Nigerian society in which tribalism seemed to have displaced patriotism as the new center of political gravity. For him, the problem of federalism in Nigeria was how to coexist in harmony within a common citizenship. While urging for the unification of the federal judicial system, he also argued for the creation of more regions along geographical boundaries so that no one region would be in a position to dominate others. But it was clear that from the ideas Azikiwe put forward, many of them were unlikely to appeal to the Northern Regional Government or the Northern Peoples Congress, which was in power at the center, and which with its ally, the NNDP, also controlled two regions. Furthermore, the timing of Azikiwe's proposals were suspect because they should either have been presented during the early constitutional talks for independence or during the NPC-NCNC negotiations for a coalitions government—a process that saw Azikiwe cede the role of prime minister to the NPC, but settled for the ceremonial role of head of state.

Because the NPC already controlled a majority in the legislature, Azikiwe lacked the political leverage to make his proposals stand on their own merit. Furthermore, the key cabinet ranks in the first executive were already taken by the NPC which held such critical ministerial portfolios as defense, internal affairs, transportation, works, economic development, mines and power, Lagos affairs, establishments. The prime minister Alhaji Tafawa Balewa also held the portfolio of External Affairs. With all the critical portfolios controlled by the Northern People Congress, one can reasonably argue that the First Republic was not really a coalition government as many took it be, rather it was an imperial government set apart in its tradition of regional and political hegemony. Under these circumstances, it was also surprising that the famed jurist Rotimi Williams also rejected Azikiwe's constitutional proposals and argued that by giving the president power as a check on the prime minister one would merely be providing for two captains in one boat, which would be a dangerous experiment. While he indicated that the proper check on the prime minister would be the Parliament, the Judiciary, and educated public opinion, he also forgot that in such a situation where the prime minister's party controls the parliament (which was the situation then), the institutional role of the parliament as a check on presidential excesses would be severely compromised.

In sum, the paralyzing crisis of democratic political discourse in Nigeria's formative years could be traced to a combination of factors including the incompetent manner in which early electoral machinery were operated, the undemocratic nature of electioneering campaigns which were marred by violence, lawlessness, and boycotts. Other remote political causes that accentuated the problems of federalism in the country relates to the arbitrary exercise of executive, legislative, and judicial powers. All these can be traced to the fact that the most basic flaw in the federal structure was that one region was, by design or default, more populous and hence more politically powerful than all the others combined.[32] The ensuing combination of region, religion and ethnicity transcended a "witches brew" of primordial politics, subterfuge, and sustained acrimony that has, in various mutations, remained the bane of Nigerian political discourse. Although Clifford Geertz[33] points out the impossibility of replacing primordial ties and identifications by civil ones, he agrees that by modernizing ethnocentrism, it can thus be more easily reconciled to the presence of developed national political institutions. What is required is an adjustment mechanism that allows the processes of government to proceed freely without seriously threatening the cultural framework of personal identity, such that whatever discontinuities in "consciousness of kind" happen to exist in the general society does not radically distort political functioning.

EXCURSUS ON EARLY BRINKMANSHIP

An important account of what we observe today in the evolution of Nigeria's political development also reflects aspects of earlier thinking and disposition of the British colonial regime. The British were not sure of what kind of government they would want for Nigeria, but instead preferred, in the interim, a process of slow growth and gradual development in such a way that development can proceed on natural lines without slowing down the pace below that which internal pressures renders desirable. In his memorandum on the future political development of Nigeria, then colonial governor B. H. Bourdillon noted that the extent to which steady progress was maintained in Nigeria's political development was mainly due to the adoption and vigorous prosecution of the policy of "indirect rule."

In consideration of the history and theory surrounding the adoption of the policy as then practiced in Northern Nigeria, he points to three historical reasons that Lord Lugard noted in his *Political Memorandum* no. 9 of 1918 as follows: the large staff needed for direct administration was not available; a similar policy had been successful in the Indian Native States; and that it would have been obvious folly, with our (colonial administration) limited knowledge of local conditions, to attempt drastic reforms which would dislocate that traditional administration. Although the policy of "indirect rule" allowed for the feudal authority of the emirates and other indigenous institutions, it was never meant to be an end in itself, but merely a means to the government of the people. For the simple fact that the feudal emirates already had a fairly simple and straightforward machinery of administration, which could be maintained or restored with little alteration; the policy was seen as the best means for securing the peace, prosperity and contentment of the people at a price that they could afford to pay. Furthermore, it was felt that no other policy could have secured whole-hearted loyalty to the British Empire.

There were also reasons adduced for not applying the same policy of "indirect rule" in the South and parts of Yorubaland. The administrative units in these areas (where they existed) were smaller and the existing organizations more complex, obscure, and loosely connected, with no simple indigenous administrative machines that could be handled and adapted on. Hence the idea of "indirect rule" in the North was seen as consistent with the prevailing social and political order of the region, as well as the colonial policy of "slow and natural development." According to Sir Donald Cameroon in his *Principles of Native Administration*, the idea was to seek a form of authority which according to tribal tradition and usage has in the past regulated the affairs of each unit of native society and which the people were willing to recognize and obey. Nonetheless, the emphasis on the criterion of "tradition" was simply a way of tapping into one of the social instruments through which acceptability and obedience can be secured in the typical African cultural context.

It is equally possible to speculate on the fact that the British colonial regime had a healthy appreciation of what was then possible or not in Nigeria, at least, on matters pertaining to the challenge of transforming a political system with so much inconsistencies. In the deliberations concerning the political and constitutional future of Nigeria, the colonial governor in Lagos sent a formal dispatch to London, dated December 6, 1944, and addressed to the Right Honorable Oliver Stanley, the secretary of state for the colonies. It was a brusque recognition of a central problem that would, invariably, remain a perennial issue in the course of Nigeria's political evolution even after independence. He stated that the problem of Nigeria was how to create a political system which contains the living possibility of an orderly advance—a system within which the diverse elements may progress at "varying" speeds, amicably and smoothly, toward a more closely integrated, economic, social, and political unity—without sacrificing the principles and ideals inherent in their divergent ways of life. While we generally interpret this to mean an emphasis on achieving "unity in diversity," but the difficulty in Nigeria remains how to satisfy the independent demands of each, without making both mutually exclusive.

NOTES

1. Harold D. Nelson, eds., *Nigeria: A Country Study* (Washington, D.C.: Foreign Area Studies, American University, 1982).

2. Padre Badru, *Imperialism and Ethnic Politics in Nigeria, 1960–1966* (Trenton, N.J.: Africa World Press, 1998), 69–71.

3. Badru, *Imperialism and Ethnic Politics in Nigeria*, 69–71.

4. Badru, *Imperialism and Ethnic Politics in Nigeria*, 69–71.

5. E. Wayne Nafziger, *The Economics of Political Instability: The Nigerian-Biafran War* (Boulder, Colo.: Westview Press, 1983), 32.

6. Michael Crowther, *The Story of Nigeria* (London: Faber and Faber, 1962), 206.

7. Crowther, *The Story of Nigeria*, 213.

8. Sir Donald Cameroon, *Memorandum on Native Administration*, July 13, 1934, para. 5. Also see A. H. M. Kirk-Greene, *Lugard and the Amalgamation of Nigeria: A Documentary Record* (London: Frank Cass, 1968), 17.

9. William D. Graf, *The Nigerian State* (Portsmouth, N.H.: Heinemann, 1988), 27.

10. Benjamin Nkemdirim, *Social Change and Political Violence in Colonial Nigeria* (Devon, Eng.: Arthur H. Stockwell Ltd, 1975), 105.

11. Kirk-Greene, *Lugard and the Amalgamation of Nigeria*, 35.

12. Oyeleye Oyediran, eds., *Survey of Nigerian Affairs, 1978–1979* (Lagos, Nigeria: Nigerian Institute of International Affairs, 1988), 263.

13. Edward K. Hwang, "Simulation of Political Development, Political Conflict, and Regulation Policies," *Journal of Political and Military Sociology* 25 (Winter 1997): 249–78.

14. Hwang, "Simulation of Political Development," 251.

15. Oladimeji Aborishade and Robert J. Mundt, *Politics in Nigeria*, 2nd ed. (New York: Longman Publishers, 2002), 9.

16. Aborishade and Mundt, *Politics in Nigeria*, 9–10.

17. Oluwadare Aguda, "The Nigerian Approach to Politics," African Studies Seminar Papers 2, Sudan Research Unit, Faculty of Arts, University of Khartoum, Sudan, 1969, 4.

18. Darren Kew and Peter Lewis, "The Making of the Modern Nigerian State," pp. 240–95 in *Introduction to Politics of the Developing World*, ed. William A. Joseph, Mark Kesselman, and Joel Krieger (Boston: Houghton-Mifflin, 2004), 247.

19. Nelson, *Nigeria: A Country Study*, 190.

20. Larry Diamond, "Nigeria: Pluralism, Statism, and the Struggle for Democracy," pp. 351–409 in *Politics in Developing Countries: Comparing Experiences with Democracy*, ed. Larry Diamond, Juan J. Linz, and Seymour Martin Lipset (Boulder, Colo.: Lynne Rienner Publishers, 1990), 358.

21. Graf, *The Nigerian State*, 31.

22. Clifford Geertz, *The Interpretation of Cultures [Selected Essays]* (New York: Basic Books, 1973), 304.

23. Graf, *The Nigerian State*, 32.

24. Okechukwu Okeke, *Hausa-Fulani Hegemony: The Dominance of the Muslim North in Contemporary Nigerian Politics* (Enugu, Nigeria: Arena Press, 1992), 58–59.

25. Larry Diamond, *Class, Ethnicity, and Democrcay in Nigeria* (Syracuse, N.Y.: Syracuse University Press, 1988), 293.

26. Diamond, *Class, Ethnicity, and Democracy in Nigeria*, 299.

27. Diamond et al., *Politics in Developing Countries*, 360.

28. Diamond et al., *Politics in Developing Countries*, 277.

29. Diamond et al., *Politics in Developing Countries*, 359.

30. Arthur Nwankwo, *The Military Option to Democracy: Class, Power, and Violence in Nigerian Politics* (Enugu, Nigeria: Fourth Dimension Publishers, 1984), 141.

31. *West Africa* (No. 2495), "Zik Starts a Debate," March 27, 1965, 333.

32. Diamond, *Class, Ethnicity, and Democracy in Nigeria*, 292.

33. Clifford Geertz, *The Interpretation of Cultures [Selected Essays]*, 308.

4

—⚋—

Restless Federalism

Critical Arguments on Conflict and Governance

The perennial debate and confusion on the efficacy of Nigeria's federal system of governance stem from two interrelated sources. The first is a conceptual misunderstanding of the ideal of federalism as a "process" of governance that ought to be held accountable when competing issues of national interest are not satisfactorily addressed. The second stems from the centralizing tendencies of national governments in most developing polities—a tendency that, more often than not, generates the kind of administrative overreach that often blurs the boundaries between the constitutional prerogatives of the center and the political imperatives of the constituent units. While federalism offers a structural model for guiding the relationship between the central and state governments; it is the responsibility of the various political actors to ensure that administrative actions follow the established constitutional order.

But where the constitutional order is weak or its key provisions are arbitrarily circumvented, it generally undermines the smooth functioning of the federal system. One of those abrogations of the constitutional order is the many years of military rule that Nigeria has suffered since its independence in 1960. As the sovereign authority of the constituent units in specific policy areas thus gave way to the monologic autocracy of dictatorial military fiat, it generated an unnatural imbalance in the functional relationship between the national and state governments. For federalism to work, the structure (division of powers) and the process (functional constitutional procedures) must complement each other in such a way that they reinforce a credible level of political legitimacy. Because military rule in Nigeria essentially made a nuisance of the idea of federalism, it was not surprising to read the former military head of state Yakubu Gowon argue that under his government (as well as consequent military regimes), "the spirit of federalism was preserved in the organ of the Supreme Military Council where all states of the federation were represented by their (military) governors."[1] Firstly, the Supreme Military Council reflects a forum for collective decision-making within the military hierarchy. It does not reflect the concept of "division of powers" or distribution of policy responsibilities between the center and the peripheral units as called for in a robust federal system. Secondly, the Supreme Military Council, more often than not, operates outside the existing Constitution and holds supremacy over the "sovereign" authority of the states in specific policy domains. Ironically, rather than helping to preserve the integrity of Nigeria's federalism, the Supreme Military Council balkanized it. "The appropriation of all fiscal authority by the central government under military rule severely injured the utilization of the principle of derivation in the allocation of federally collected revenue to various tiers of government."[2] This also had the negative effect of strengthening the power of the central executive over the constituent states as the dominant institution of the Nigerian political system—a situation that allowed the presidency to control important and critical elements of national distributive politics.

Thirdly, the nascent call for "true federalism" from many groups and political persuasions is a flawed and misplaced advocacy. The problem of federalism in Nigeria is not in the ideal itself, but in the very processes and instruments of government that give it direction and legitimacy. The most prominent of these instruments is the federal Constitution. While the most critical issues of federal governance were, perhaps deliberately, excluded from the Constitution, important provisions are either circumvented or not adhered to in the intergovernmental processes needed to run an effective and accountable system. Such has generally been the case that "in the history of constitution making in the country there has never been on the agenda a discussion of the various contentious issues that have so far plagued the federation, including those relating to identity, nationality, the rule of law, citizenship, and language."[3]

The continued clamor "for autonomy is a consequence of the over-concentration of power at the center relative to other tiers of government (state and local governments), and in the executive relative to other institutions of the national government (legislature and the judiciary)."[4] While the later is less an issue of contention, especially in a situation where the same party controls the executive and the legislature; the most serious default is that the executive can (and often does) use its appointive powers to sway the nominations and membership of the judiciary, and the legislature can use its power of ratification to approve nominees who, at best, owe "political" allegiance to the executive as well as to the ruling party doctrine. It would therefore not be an overstatement to point out that as the country professes federalism, it becomes more and more a de facto "unitary" state. I do not put the onus of this type of perverse federalism completely on the arbitrary whims of political actors or partisan politics, but rather on the coincidences of fate that befell the Nigerian state in its formative years.

OF INCOMMENSURABILITY: AUTHORITY WITHOUT POWER

The concept of authority and power are ubiquitous names in political science, organization theory and behavior, human resources management, and in many other disciplines. They are also central concepts in the crafting of constitutions and in the establishment of a federal system of government. While authority pertains to the office or a specific position in government, power reflects the ability to make others do what they would not ordinarily have chosen to do without any external compulsion. Because both concepts imply two different meanings, they also offer a pathway for understanding some of the reasons for the chronic tensions and the desirability of building a functional civic culture within the umbrella of a shared political identity in Nigeria.

The Nigerian independence constitution of 1960 and the republican constitution of 1963 embodied many British parliamentary concepts, that none the less complicated later efforts to consolidate federal rule. "The adaptation to the Westminster model of government incorporated the regional orientation of Nigerian politics—an unrestrained competition among the regionally based parties thwarted the compromise indispensable to the effective functioning of parliamentary democracy."[5] The difficulty in subsuming the different regional identifications within the structure of federalism meant that the country lacked a collective political virtue necessary to come to an early agreement concerning the central issues of nationhood. It remains the case that "when a people disagree over comprehensive moral and political doctrines, they will also have difficulty agreeing on a conception of justice to regulate the basic institutions of society."[6] Today, there are two legal systems in Nigeria seeking essentially two different approaches to law, order, and jurisprudence. One is the constitutional law that serves as the traditional basis for federal law as well as the law in approximately half of the states in Nigeria. But there is also the Sharia law that serves, in most cases, as the legal (civil) code for some of the predominantly Muslim states in the Northern part of the country. While it is "a religious obligation for Muslims to adhere to the body of laws that make up the Sharia and that includes the 'personal law' relating to marriage, divorce, and inheritance;

the interpretation and application of the law is often a complex matter as well as one of the principal mechanisms by which the *ulema* (clerical authority) maintain their control over Islamic society."[7] Hence in societies with a sizeable Muslim population, "the Sharia invariably emerges as a symbol of conflict between the *ulema* and the secular political elites (Muslims and non-Muslims) who wish to establish a centralized state for which they consider a modern legal system essential."[8]

What makes it even more complicated is that the role of Sharia in the politics of Northern Nigeria has a long history that dates back to the colonial period of indirect rule. The British[9] recognized very early in the administration of the North that religion (Islam) was a crucial element in the political system and social order of the Northern feudalities; but since this did not seem to be an obstacle to the attainment of essential British economic and political objectives, it was therefore expedient to preserve and respect aspects of the Islamic laws as principles of local government administration. But it subordinated this law to the superior British legal systems integrated into the colonial legal system. A major premise, therefore, of the policy of indirect rule in the North was the granting of legitimacy to the traditional emirate authorities. This legitimacy necessitated the administration of Sharia law by emirates and the recognition by the colonial power of the religious basis of legal authority in the North. Consequently, the Sharia became a crucial incentive in the political compromise that buoyed the confidence of the Northern feudal authorities in the unfolding process of independence. For the simple fact that "religion as a factor in the political arrangement of the country suited the North and instead of regarding religion as separate from the affairs of the civil society, the British emphasized religion as an instrument of political order. Religion instead of being the affairs of the individual became the concern of the corporate state, thus sowing the seed of dissension which religion has been noted to do in world history."[10] Consequently, Nigeria has not been an exception.

Because both legal systems originate from two different philosophical premises, it is difficult to see how the federal Constitution can exert supremacy over the Sharia law in the Northern states; and also how it can be used to reconcile conflicts in the law when both deal with similar issues in different ways. Moreover, the fear that the *ulema* would be able to mobilize the mass of Muslims in Northern Nigeria in opposition to any efforts to reform their personal law has, by default, "enabled them to hold hostage both the secular Muslim political elites and all Muslim political leaders who seek to represent Muslim interests."[11] Ironically, Muslim political elites on the other hand, have found the Sharia useful as a symbol in their conflicts with non-Muslim political elites for political influence in the Muslim community and as such have remained quite unwelcoming of any reform. The point is that while the dual approach to law undermines federalism as an effective model for governing a multiethnic society such as Nigeria; the creation of more states, on the other hand, has deepened the imbalance of political power, thus intensifying regional agitation and increased quest for devolution of the federal system.

BEYOND IDEALISM AND PRACTICE

One of the most contemporary works on Nigerian federalism is Rotimi T. Suberu's *Federalism and Ethnic Conflict in Nigeria*.[12] By combining historical and sociological analyses of the Nigerian political space, Suberu argues that the evolution of federalism in Nigeria seems to have been set up for failure even before it began. He points to the arbitrary 1914 Lord Lugard's Amalgamation of Northern and Southern Nigeria and the consequent structure of "British administrative regionalism or the colonial divide and rule syndrome,"[13] which seemed to favor the less-developed North at the expense of the more cosmopolitan South. This assumption also has ominous implications for the ongoing democratization exercise in Nigeria, especially when considered in light of the inherent primordial inclinations, the monoeconomic characteristics of its productive sector (oil), and the *rentier* nature of state power and political control. It also points to the fact that there is a practical difference between federalism in the context of decentralized authority and federalism as a form of division of powers.

Among the key issues that seem to have confounded Nigeria's gamble with federalism are: the intergovernmental sharing of powers, the reorganization of constituents states and local units, the manipulation of census data for regional political ends (a process that was initiated by the 1962–1963 national census), and the loss of ideal and efficacy in the various applications of the *federal character* principle. But Suberu argues that such putative attempts at political decentralization without the requisite powers to the constituent units breeds a situation where competition for political influence at the center generates its own destabilizing effect. As the clamor for the creation of more states and local governments increase at the periphery, and as ethnic and religious differences are exploited, the ideal of federalism as practiced in Nigeria becomes more of a destabilizing rather than a unifying force. The *federal character* principle seems to have become a victim of Nigeria's restless attempts at federalism. Although it was meant to "involve the equal devolution of federal development patronage to the states, its primary purpose was not to disperse resources away from the center but to establish an ethnically representative and inclusive center."[14] But unfortunately, the ideal became an avenue for guaranteeing ethnic and religious group domination in the critical institutions of the national government. While much of the political conflict is rooted in maldistributive federalism, it has also recently seen itself manifested in a religious transformation of power politics. The agitation for the Islamic Sharia law in many of the Northern states and the consistent call for *ethno-religious* representation in national institutions highlight a much more serious problem in the integrative potentials of the Nigerian polity. These latent issues as much as they embody ramifications yet unknown, were not part of the original bargain for Nigerian statehood, but none the less, portend a dangerous cleavage in the growing pains of national political integration.

While the country's federalism developed as an "institutional response both to the federal character of society and to the explosive demographic configuration of the ethnic structure which pitted three major ethnic nationalities (Yoruba, Igbo, Hausa-Fulani) in fierce competition with one another, such redistributive inclinations led to the political manipulation of the ideal of state creation, first to sooth the unceasing agitation from the periphery, and second, to accord greater legitimacy to the controlling elite at the center."[15] By tracing the evolution of revenue sharing under Nigerian federalism from the Richard's Constitution of 1946 through a series of other distributional structures, Suberu concludes that the centralized budgetary control effectively enshrined the supremacy of vertical over horizontal revenue sharing formulae. By linking the various local governments to the central government through a hierarchical system of local government finance, would mean that the political party at the center could use its partisan control of local governments to oppress political opponents. In addition, Suberu argues that the centralizing culture of military doctrinaire, its governance by dictatorial fiat, and its dominance by Northern military personnel, more than anything else, helped to scuttle any possibility for an emergent progressive federalism in Nigeria. While he discussed various reform options like rotational presidency (zoning), a Swiss-type federalism, a unity government, territorial/regional restructuring, and confederacy, one is left in doubt as to whether the problem of Nigerian federalism is solely that of institutional redesign, as opposed to a broad-based ideological and sociological transformation without which any institutional reengineering will falter.

Suffice it then to state that "although there may be no better alternative to federalism in Nigeria, the challenges involved in overcoming the pathologies of the country's federal system are truly enormous."[16] It is therefore debatable to what extent these reform measures would offer the menu of choices needed to address the triple issues of religious intolerance, the nationality question, and the skewed nature of distributive politics. While these may provide partial explanations of the processes of state formation, regime transitions, and intra-state conflict in the Third world in general, and Africa in particular; they are inadequate and cannot be used to capture or explicate the multidimensionality of the political and social forces that affect the emergence of conflict situations, peaceful coexistence, and why conflict situations generally result into overt violence in Nigeria.

But of greater theoretical import is the general idea that ethnic conflict, the nature of which has been seen among many developing polities, is not always manifested in overt violence, but more often than not, embodies a structural dialectic that is essentially more insidious. As competing ethno-regional actors conspire against each other for the ultimate price of institutional capture, control of distributive authority, and permanent political subjugation, federalism in the context of division of powers oftentimes becomes the victim. This development can partly be traced back to the Lyttleton Constitution of 1954[17] which, while it made the immediate federal future of Nigeria possible, also created an adverse situation where the former administrative regions (North, West, East), rather than the capital of Lagos, became the foci of political activity. Each of the main political parties then had a base from which to defy, and if possible erode, the power of their rivals in the other regions and in the central government.

Furthermore, because of the Lyttleton Constitution's insistence upon the employment of locally born people wherever possible, it became difficult for qualified personnel from other regions to gain employment or to make occupational progress outside their own native regions—the eventual Northernization policy of the Northern region was thus regarded as a fait accompli. The consequent grant of internal autonomy to the Eastern and Western regions in 1957 further reinforced the ethnic basis of political power; and although regional loyalties were temporarily forgotten in the emerging prospect of national independence when the North also became self-governing in 1959, the federal elections of 1957 set the tone for an eventual Northern dominance and control of the federal government. The consequent attempt by the North to use the fraudulent 1962–1963 census figures to consolidate its power at the center and the resulting opposition from the other regional actors exposed very early the structural defects in Nigeria's attempt at federalism.

CRITICAL MASS: FROM PERIPHERY TO THE CENTER

Beyond the 1967–1970 civil war, a series of low-intensity conflicts have also continued to present stark reminders of a process yet unsettled. Prominent among these have been the "Maitatsine religious riots that occurred (1980–1984) in Dan Awaki ward, Kano (1980), Bulunkutu near Maiduguri (1982), and Jimeta near Yola (1984); the Kafanchan riots (1987), the Bauchi riots (1991), the religious crisis in Funtua (1993), the Kaduna crisis (2000), the Jos crisis (2001), and the crisis in Wase, Plateau state in June–July 2002."[18] The Jos crisis of September 2001 which happened in the predominantly Christian Plateau state is particularly noteworthy as to its cause. On September 7, a Christian woman supposedly crossed a street that Muslims had blocked off for their prayers. That event provided the pretext for an orgy of violence in which Muslims attacked unsuspecting Christians; and by the time it was over, more than 5,000 people were dead and property worth millions of naira destroyed.

But it was gathered later that the remote cause of the crisis was the fact that one Alhaji Mohammed Muktar Usman was appointed (in August 2001) by the federal government as the Jos North Coordinator of the National Poverty Eradication Programme—an appointment which the "indigenes" refused to accept claiming that the land belonged to them (the Berom) and not the Jasawa (Hausa "settlers") where Usman belongs. It should also be noted that the brief political life of Alhaji Usman has not been without controversy, even before his latest appointment as coordinator of NPEP. Earlier in December 1998, he was forced to step down as Chairman of the newly created Jos North local government after he was alleged to have falsified his credentials. Hence his subsequent appointment to the coveted post of poverty eradication coordinator was seen by some as a provocation and was strongly opposed by Christian groups. Because of alleged threat to his life, Usman abdicated his office, but the bad blood was already sown between the two ethnic groups over political control of Jos North local government. As if unfolding events were following a script, the simmering internecine conflict between the Tiv and Jukun ethnic groups shot into national prominence after some 19 federal soldiers were abducted by ethnic Tiv militiamen and hacked to death on October 12, 2001. In a hurriedly organized scorched-earth reaction, Nigerian soldiers were dispatched to Plateau state to "stabilize" the area and to apprehend the perpetrators of the crime. In a ruthless crackdown, soldiers opened fire on villages and razed four communities to the ground. The ensuing massacre began in the village of Gbeji and spread to the neighboring areas of Vaase, Anyiin, and Zaki-Biam, and when it was over, two hundred people were dead.

On February 24, 2004, Christians in an early morning prayer meeting were surrounded and massacred by local Muslims in the town of Yelwa, Plateau state. Between February and April 2004, fighting between Hausa-Fulani Muslims and the mainly Christian Tarok people and the surrounding areas of Rwang Doka and Jenkur in the southern part of Plateau state had claimed more than 233 lives and displaced more than 6,000 people across three neighboring states. On May 2, 2004, a heavily armed militia and tribesmen from the Christian Tarok ethnic group retaliated and slaughtered Muslims in Yelwa, triggering a massive refugee exodus. The following week, dozens of Christian villagers were killed in a sudden outbreak of violence near the town of Yelwa, Plateau state. The raids were perpetrated by armed Muslim groups who attacked the nearby Christian villages of Karese, Sabon Gida, Jirim, Gidan Sabo, and Bakin Ciyawa, as reprisal for the earlier tit-for-tat attack against Muslims in the town of Yelwa on May 2. Christians in the Muslim-dominated city of Kano were also killed in reprisal. While some reports put the death toll in Kano at two hundred, local Christian leaders claimed that about six hundred Christians were killed there and thousands more remained missing.

The May attacks and the scope of atrocities which it generated forced President Olusegun Obasanjo to declare a state of emergency in Plateau state on May 18, 2004, sacked its elected governor Joshua Dariye, dismissed the state legislature and appointed former army major general Chris Alli to run the state for the next six months. In his national broadcast imposing the state of emergency in Plateau state, President Obasanjo proclaimed the following as one of his reasons:

> Considering my constitutional responsibility as President of the Federal Republic of Nigeria and having exhausted all possible avenues to have and help the Governor of Plateau state to ensure security of life and property generally in that State, and cognizant of the proven inability and incompetence of the Governor to maintain security of life and property generally in the state and particularly in Langtang, Wase, and Yelwa-Shendham in the past few months, I have painfully come to the point that I have to resort to the last constitutional option available to ensure security of life and property of all citizens of Nigeria and non-Nigerians alike residing in any part of Plateau state.

The presidential action was overwhelmingly endorsed by the national legislature, with more than two-thirds of the 369 members of the House as well as 90 members of the Senate voting in favor of the measure. Constitutionally, the measure was endorsed based on the provisions in Section 305 (2) and 305 (6)(b) of the 1999 Constitution (and order 134 and 135 of Senate rules) which would empower and authorize the president and commander-in-chief of the Federal Republic of Nigeria to declare a state of emergency in any part of the country where there is a breakdown of law and order. But the emergency decree represents a rather superficial and belated attempt to tighten the lid on a simmering pot instead of finding ways to reduce the heat. The undercurrents of these conflicts are historical as well as political. "This is especially true of the North where various minorities still confront the threat of Hausa/Fulani domination by way of religion, Hausa/Fulani settlers migration, the imposition of village and district heads by the powerful Emirs, and the attempt to reconstruct Northern political unity based on Hausa/Fulani hegemony."[19] Hence, "Violent ethno-religious conflicts, demands for autonomous chiefdoms and local government councils, and new forms of Middle-Belt nationalism, which reject Hausa/Fulani hegemony, are some of the ways in which the minorities have responded to continued domination."[20]

It is therefore easy to see how a localized dispute between ethnic groups competing for political control, land and economic resources could quickly turn into a full-fledged religious conflict, extending well beyond the boundaries of the originating state. President Obasanjo was quite aware that to impose an equivalent state of emergency on any of the other equally violent Muslim-dominated states could elicit a more explosive situation that could threaten the very political stability that he seeks to attain, and of course, his own support among key Northern political elites within his own party hierarchy. Hence making an example of Christian-dominated Plateau state and its governor became the safer bait. There are also other structural sources of conflict that many agree would continue to generate perennial sources of acrimony between groups and within states for the foreseeable future. Among these would include the competition "over the creation of new local government councils, the location of headquarters of the state government or local council, access to and ownership of land and water resources, order ranking of traditional rulers, and in the Niger Delta, disputes over territories with oil."[21] Because some of these crises were inspired by multiple factors, both subjective and objective, it is quite difficult to pinpoint exactly a single causal origin. The confluence of ethnicity, religion, region, economics, and property in many conflict situations undermines a proper understanding of the causal sequence in which they occur as well as the explanatory power of each factor.

In Nigeria, "ethnic and communal conflicts often emerge as simultaneously religious and cultural, especially where the religious cleavage between Muslims, Christians, and traditional religion practitioners coincide with ethnic and communal cleavages; and because of this interconnectedness, most conflicts—no matter how localized—have the potential of getting out of hand and threatening the peace and stability of the Nigerian state."[22] While perceived "inequalities at the federal level seem to have shaped the national template of inter-ethnic animosity, most of the conflicts have arisen out of perceptions of inequalities at the local and state levels."[23] But as the mutual mayhem unfold, they are viewed more as transitory and episodic shocks as opposed to a systematic "peeling-off" of the fabric that must bind together to sustain a virile federal system.

VIOLENCE AS POLITICAL PARTICIPATION:
CATEGORIES WITH A DIFFERENCE

In many developed and developing polities, one cannot help but to see a resort to violence as a form of political participation even when it is normally abhorrent as well as contrary to rule of law. While violence may be relative in terms of degree and type, suffice it to say that they are generally meant to achieve a political objective or to attract attention to an issue of importance to the party or parties engaged in the act. But what drives most violent acts in politics is not necessary the issue in contention, but more often than not, it is the lack of political opportunity or formal access to bring forth a case to the prevailing authorities. When such opportunity does not exist or their possibility seems remote, collective anger and frustration transforms into a violent form of political advocacy.

In his seminal work on the social psychological model of "civil strife," Ted Robert Gurr[24] carried out quantitative analyses of a variety of forms of conflict through national measures of protest and rebellion. His work was driven by an interest in the individual-level variable of "relative deprivation," but he mainly drew on aggregate national demographic data to operationalize his major variables. A few years later, his work in *Why Men Rebel*[25] drew attention to some of the political determinants of conflict. While he pointed to such factors as "the relative balance of institutional support and coercive control," he was mainly interested in the determinants of collective contention that could be cross-nationally correlated with various measures of conflict.[26] Contemporary scholars have drawn inspiration from Gurr's earlier work and have sought to analyze different conflict situations including civil wars. For example, Collier and Hoeffler[27] found significant correlations between civil wars and high levels of primary commodity exports, large populations, low levels of secondary education, low economic growth, low per capita income and the presence of previous civil wars. They also found out that the lack of democracy was significant, that inequality was insignificant, and that ethnic and religious fractionalization was surprisingly unimportant. While Nigeria meets the above characteristics, the later finding is also very pertinent for the simple fact most civil strife in Nigeria are almost always attributed to ethnic or religious foundations, even when other structural but remotely placed factors may be at work.

This observation becomes more important when we look at later works by Fearon and Laitin.[28] Proceeding from a similar numerical violence definition of civil war and from similar microeconomic premises as Collier and Hoeffler, they too found that primary exports—and especially oil—were highly correlated with civil war outbreaks. Their other major conclusion was that civil wars are most likely to occur in countries governed by weak but nondemocratic governments, and where there is political instability. Of equal relevance was that they found civil wars as not statistically correlated with ethnicity. There are some crucial lessons to be learned in matters of conflict and violence within political communities. "Violence is by nature instrumental; and like all means, it always stands in need of guidance and justification through the end it pursues."[29] And like the various forms of political participation, "power and violence, though they are distinct phenomena, usually appear together; but wherever they are combined, power has been found to be the primary and predominant factor."[30]

However, the context in which this proposition is cast pertains to situations where distinct groups seek political, economic, religious, or cultural supremacy over other competing elements in society. In federal systems with very weak institutions and corrupt governance practices, competing groups are more likely to use extra-constitutional means as a way of dealing with conflict situations. It is therefore not inconceivable to view the endemic conflicts in Nigeria as a result of the inevitable quest for power and control between the elite layers of the political and social strata. As Hannah Arendt[31] would argue, power needs no justification, being inherent in the very existence of political communities; rather what it does need is legitimacy. But many Nigerians, having become so enamored by the level of violence and communal acrimony befalling the country, have become more pronounced in their call for increased devolution of power to the regions and to the many ethnic groups seeking effective representation at the center. But it still begs the question, what type of devolution and how? Since May 1999, various ethnic and pressure groups have emerged spearheading one advocacy or the other in the country. We have the Odua Peoples Congress (fighting for the Southwest Yoruba states), the Arewa Consultative Forum (seeking the interest of the Northern states), the Middle Belt Forum (seeking to reaffirm a geopolitical identity distinct from the Greater North), the Ohanaeze (seeking a new political affirmation for the southeastern states), and the South-South Forum (seeking increased representation in the political leadership of the country). There are also the Egbesu Boys and the Ijaw Youth Council (seeking a redistribution of Nigeria's oil and petroleum rents in favor of the impoverished oil-producing region of the Niger Delta), Movement for the Actualization of the Sovereign State of Biafra (fighting for the renaissance of a new Biafran state), and many other vigilante and criminal groups with "ideologies" that shift much faster than the desert sand. Nonetheless, these portray a classic case of hitting the head in order to spite the bottom.

NOTES

1. Yakubu Gowon, "Federalism and Nigerian Unity: Problems and Prospects," in *Federalism and Nation-Building in Nigeria: The Challenges of the 21st Century*, ed. J. Isawa Elaigwu, P. C. Logams, and H. S. Galadima (1994), 23–28.

2. Sola Akinrinade, "Constitutionalism and the Resolution of Conflicts in Nigeria," *Round Table* 368, no. 1 (2003): 47.

3. Akinrinade, "Constitutionalism and the Resolution of Conflicts in Nigeria," 41–52.

4. Akinrinade, "Constitutionalism and the Resolution of Conflicts in Nigeria," 41–52.

5. Harold D. Nelson , ed., *Nigeria: A Country Study* (Washington, D.C.: American University Press, 1982).

6. Duncan Ivison, "Modus Vivendi Citizenship," in *The Demands of Citizenship*, ed. Catriona McKinnon and Ian Hampsher-Monk (London: Continuum, 2003), 127.

7. Paul R. Brass, *Ethnicity and Nationalism: Theory and Comparison* (Newbury Park, Calif.: Sage Publications, 1991), 80–81.

8. Brass, *Ethnicity and Nationalism: Theory and Comparison*, 81.

9. The following account is partly based on the perspective of Professor Ikenna Nzimiro as one of the members involved in the proceedings "Nigeria Marches On: Story of Nigeria From the Origin and Articulate Opinions on Matters of the Moment to Mark Nigeria's Silver Jubilee of Independence 1960–1985," (1985), 9–14. This proceeding was a kind of stocktaking and reflection on the history and development of Nigeria after twenty-five years of independence.

10. Ikenna Nzimiro, "British-Fulani Conquests Weakened National Unity," in "Nigeria Marches On" (1985): 12.

11. Paul R. Brass, *Ethnicity and Nationalism: Theory and Comparison*, 81–82.

12. Rotimi T. Suberu, *Federalism and Ethnic Conflict in Nigeria* (Washington, D.C.: United States Institute of Peace, 2001).

13. Suberu, *Federalism and Ethnic Conflict in Nigeria*, 20.

14. Suberu, *Federalism and Ethnic Conflict in Nigeria*, 16.

15. Suberu, *Federalism and Ethnic Conflict*.

16. Suberu, *Federalism and Ethnic Conflict*, 206.

17. Kenneth Ingham, *Politics in Modern Africa: The Uneven Tribal Dimension* (London: Routledge, 1990), 70.

18. O. Oche, "Low Intensity Conflicts, National Security and Democratic Sustenance," in *Nigeria Under Democratic Rule, 199–-2003*, ed. Hassan A. Saliu (Ibadan, Nigeria: University Press PLC, 2005), 2:113.

19. Eghosa E. Osaghae, "Explaining the Changing Patterns of Ethnic Politics in Nigeria," *Nationalism and Ethnic Politics* 9, no. 3 (Autumn 2003): 63.

20. Osaghae, "Explaining the Changing Patterns of Ethnic Politics in Nigeria," 63.

21. Osaghae, "Explaining the Changing Patterns of Ethnic Politics in Nigeria," 63.

22. Eghosa E. Osaghae, "Regulating Conflicts in Nigeria," *Peace Review* 14, no. 2 (June 2002): 218.

23. Ukoha Ukiwo, "The Study of Ethnicity in Nigeria," *Oxford Development Studies* 33, no. 1 (March 2005): 17.

24. Ted Robert Gurr, "A Causal Model of Civil Strife: A Comparative Analysis Using New Indices," *American Political Science Review* 62 (1968): 1104–24. Summarized in Sidney Tarrow, "Inside Insurgencies: Politics and Violence in an Age of Civil War," *American Political Science Review* 5, no. 3 (2007): 588.

25. Ted Robert Gurr, *Why Men Rebel* (Princeton, N.J.: Princeton University Press, 1970).

26. Sidney Tarrow, "Inside Insurgencies: Politics and Violence in an Age of Civil War," *American Political Science Review* 5, no. 3 (2007): 588.

27. Paul Collier and Anke Hoeffler, "Greed and Grievance in Civil War," Policy Research Paper 2355, World Bank, 2000. Summarized in Sidney Tarrow, "Inside Insurgencies: Politics and Violence in an Age of Civil War," *American Political Science Review* 5, no. 3 (2007): 587–600.

28. James D. Fearon and David Laitin, "Ethnicity, Insurgency and Civil War," *American Political Science Review* 97 (February 2003): 75–90. Summarized in Sidney Tarrow, "Inside Insurgencies: Politics and Violence in an Age of Civil War," *American Political Science Review* 5, no. 3 (2007): 588.

29. Hannah Arendt, *On Violence* (New York: Harcourt, Brace & World, 1970), 51.

30. Arendt, *On Violence*, 52.

31. Arendt, *On Violence*, 52.

5

—m—

The Geopolitics of Religion
Conflated Origins of Ethnic Crisis

The idea of explaining ethnic crisis in Nigeria as due to differences in ethnicity is a rather simplistic notion that misses the point. It offers an escape mechanism that minimizes the cultural and historical roots of interethnic rivalry in the country. Such rivalries have, if nothing else, been exacerbated by the increasing level of political and economic competition in both the public and private domains. And to get a larger share of the pie, political elites on both sides evoke hitherto subdued memories of ethnic chivalry, superiority, conquest and oppression as an affirmation of strength as well as injustice perpetrated against them. As ethnic groups seek to redefine their stakes in the ensuing contest with others, they draw enormous inspiration by invoking the greater glories of their past and using that as a basis for threading the thorny pathways of today's political journey.

As the parallel processes of ethnic identification and historical nostalgia assert themselves in tandem, the unfolding dynamic tends to mask the implicit and final objective for political supremacy. Hence to the extent that "a satisfactory understanding of the reasons for the chronic tension in new states could be based on the need to maintain a socially ratified personal identity and the desire to construct a powerful national community,"[1] it behooves us to move beyond the specific "micro-level mechanisms to the larger empirical context so that we can make better initial assumptions about what sorts of mechanisms are most common and important empirically."[2]

THE CULTURAL FOUNDATIONS OF AUTONOMY

Take for instance the ongoing series of conflicts between the Itshekiri and the Urhobo of the Niger Delta region. For as long as time could remember, these two geographically adjoining communities have traded, married across ethnic lines, and essentially lived peacefully with each other—at a period when Nigeria was a relatively poor country without the economic resources from oil revenues. Contrary to most conclusions, the contemporary crisis between the Itshekiri and Urhobo, part of the Itshekiri-Urhobo-Ijaw triangle is not due particularly to differences in ethnicity, since they have all acquired enough integration over time to make such differences minimally visible. Rather, the political import of such differences come to the surface as past history and cultural experiences are used as place-holders to address contemporary issues of political development and redistribution—whether such issues concern land boundaries, oil drilling rights, the location of local government headquarters, or mechanisms for the distribution of incentives from both government largesse and the local oil drilling conglomerates. In fact, from the following accounts, it would thus be more defensible to make the argument that much of these crises are driven by a combination of political and economic factors. As the most obvious feature, ethnicity thus becomes an intervening but unavoidable variable in the conflict equation.

It is neither the cause of these conflicts nor is it the effect, but rather it is a natural coincidence that could, on the one hand, be used to lend more fire to a crisis situation; and on the other hand, is seen as the most salient variable that stands out in any consequent attempt at conflict resolution. The issue of inter-ethnic rivalry in Itshekiri-Urhobo relations, as well as many other Nigerian ethnic groups, is not new. But the sources of these rivalries have historically been driven by exogenous factors such as trade disagreements, slavery, royalty, and ethno-nationalistic feelings of superiority no matter how self-proclaimed. Obaro Ikime's[3] account of Itshekiri-Urhobo relations during the period of early European activities in the Niger Delta (1485–1883) is noteworthy. He argues that even though the Itshekiri and Urhobo had historically traded and married with each other, the evolving "blood relationship" did not metamorphose into a wholesome political unit with a common objective and worldview. For the Itshekiri, consciousness of belonging to a greater Urhobo community was absent until the late 1930s, but even then, both sides began to demand a larger share of the political action. The interethnic slave trade that existed between the Itshekiri and the Urhobo culminated in a disproportionate number of Urhobo slaves in Itshekiri hands, which invariably was used by the Itshekiri as evidence of lordship over the Urhobo. Due to the absence of a centralized rulership among the Urhobos, the British administrators detested dealing with the various village communities, each of which was virtually independent of each other. On the other hand, the British felt more comfortable with the more centralized form of administration practiced by the Itshekiri to the effect that it afforded them a means of exerting firmer control on the subjects. "Consequently, the centralizing and federalizing tendencies of the British Government were to be more easily acceptable to the Itshekiri than to the Urhobo. Stress and strains began to develop between the Itshekiri and Urhobo when these tendencies, more acceptable to one group, were forced on the other in a manner which, intentionally or incidentally, gave the impression of subjecting the Urhobo to institutions (British institutions) dominated by the Itshekiri."[4]

There were also issues of geography in the matter of Itshekiri-Urhobo relations. For the simple fact that Itshekiris inhabited the more proximate coastal areas of the Niger Delta, they were first to come into contact with Portuguese missionaries and their culture. This was not the case for the Urhobos that lived much farther in the agricultural hinterland. Because the Itshekiri culture had been much affected by their early contact with the Europeans, "the Urhobos were more or less dependent on the Itshekiris not only for such knowledge of the Europeans as they had, but for European manufactures as well."[5] This nonetheless became a primary source for the feeling of superiority that the Itshekiri has historically had over the Urhobo. However, the end of slave trade in the nineteenth century in the riverine areas of the Nigeria Delta and its consequent abolition in Britain made the trade itself less profitable, hence British investment shifted to the hinterland away from the riverine areas which was mostly inhabited by the Itshekiri. "The trade in palm oil, which was only a fraction of the trade at the earlier period, now replaced the trade in slaves, calling for new methods of organization in the process. The European merchants now finding their hulks inadequate began to build 'factories' on land."[6] These developments meant that over time, the Itshekiris as their British protégés moved inland to Urhoboland to establish businesses—which eventually earned them economic dominance or control of the commerce in Urhoboland. This again became a source of friction and seething acrimony between the two communities, and all the more reinforced by the historical feeling of superiority of one side over the other. This disposition continues to manifest itself in the contemporary political arena where the contestation for power is grounded on historical antecedents laced with ancient myths, victories, and past glories of conquest and subordination.

The recent upsurge of crisis between the Itshekiris, Urhobo, and Ijaws in the Warri area of Delta state is a phenomenon that began in the 1990s. As T. A. Imobighe[7] points out, the basic root of the crisis stems from the claims and counter-claims by the three main ethnic groups in Warri over the ownership of Warri land. These conflicting claims have, by extension, led to the questioning by the Ijaws and the Urhobos of the title of the Olu of Warri as the paramount ruler of Warri. And besides the issue of land ownership, there is also the issue of political authority and territorial supremacy or jurisdiction of the Olu of Warri. There is also a question of economics, since Warri has now become a cosmopolitan center of commerce and industry, driven partly by the growth in the oil economy and an increasing level of urbanization. "As the petroleum business accelerated the growth of Warri and as more and more people moved into the city, the heightened clamor for the city's limited resources and land helped to aggravate the already tensed rivalry between the three major ethnic groups. These inter-ethnic rivalries have degenerated into recurring violence, thereby turning Warri into a city in a state of persistent crisis."[8]

In similar vein, the Ife-Modakeke communal crisis in (Osun state) the Western part of the country is rooted in the ancient history of both communities and their interrelationships over the years. It has always been a question of who owns the land and who settled on it first. While the Ifes felt that the "alien" Modakekes should be sent away from Ile-Ife, old history and the mythology of inter-communal migration were reinforced to make "legitimate" claims for political authority and territorial jurisdiction. Dramatic changes were set in motion by the collapse of the Old Oyo Empire in the early part of the nineteenth century following the revolt against the Alafin by Afonja, the Are-Ona Kakanfo, the head of the Oyo Calvary force and consequent invasion of Oyo by Fulani Jihadists from Ilorin.[9] In the attempt to fill the political leadership vacuum created by the fall of the Old Oyo Empire, there were a series of wars in different parts of Yorubaland between 1840 and 1894.[10] As noted by Isaac Olawale Albert,[11] "these two historical events, the collapse of the Old Oyo Empire and the subsequent wars that occurred up till 1893, led to mass movement of Oyo refugees to different parts of Yorubaland." He further points out that as the Fulani invasion continued, most of the Oyo refugees fled to Ile-Ife and the surrounding communities. The Ifes welcomed the new refugees, land was granted to them for their farms, and a history of intercommunal marriages began to plant deep roots.

In 1835, the Oyo citizens in Ibadan challenged the political authority of the Ife war chief, Okunade. He was consequently killed in the battle of Gbanamu, thereby making it possible for the Oyo citizens (Modakekes) to take over the political leadership of Ibadan (now capital of Oyo state). The Ifes responded by seeking the ouster of the Oyos from "their" territory and sending most of them to Ipetumodu, Gbongan, and Ikire in 1847—a process expedited following the defeat of the Fulani invaders at the battle of Osogbo in 1840. The first attempt to mediate the Ife-Modakeke crisis was made by Ooni Abeweila who decided to create a separate settlement for the Oyo (Modakeke) refugees who had no homes to return to, hence the area now known as Modakeke. And "shortly after the establishment of Modakeke, the Ife people started regretting the 'mistake' of Ooni Abeweila; but for the Oyo refuges (Modakekes), as they began to see themselves as having a separate identity from the Ifes, they also saw themselves as an independent political sovereign."[12] As the Ifes saw their political influence over the Oyo refugees (Modakekes) wane, they reacted. This thus set the stage for the many years of crisis, violence and acrimony that persists today between the two communities.

As issues connected with the overt subethnic conflict became increasingly politicized, "the conflict itself was detached from its original causes to become its own self-energizing cause."[13] The whole crisis came to a head in 1997 over the location of the headquarters of the Ife East Local Government from Oke-Ogbo (Ife area) rather than Modakeke. The destruction and violence that followed, invariably, became an outlet for a crisis that supposedly had its genesis in the years between 1840 and 1894. And since this type of historical account (depending of which account is more tenable) cannot be easily changed or pacified, it makes the search for permanent solutions less likely to be successful. Unfortunately, the "notion that an *entire* ethnic group is devotedly out to destroy another ethnic group, can in such cases, shatter any ability to perceive nuance and variety; and it can also be taken to suggest that efforts to foster elite accommodation are essentially irrelevant and therefore bound to prove futile."[14]

REGIONALISM AND POLITICAL CONTROL

Although deriving from different historical origins, this is the same kind of situation that the Igbos face in many other parts of Nigeria, especially the North—where many of them have established dominant economic interest in their host communities. The rise of a progressive "alien" economic culture in some parts of Nigeria breeds a tenuous condition where local political and economic disadvantages are sooner or later traced to the economic prominence of non-natives over natives as the more proximate cause. In many cases, the blinding rage resulting from such misplaced feelings have been enormously consequential when these businesses and economic interests become the primary source of hate, anger, and destruction. These tendencies which sooner or later are passed off as interethnic acrimony are actually driven by political and regional factors that have minimal causal implication for ethnicity. In many ways, "the higher levels of ethnic violence associated with cases of this nature are probably due as much to the nominal and historical connection between a group and a piece of territory as to more material and strategic implications of geographic concentration. In fact, given the norms and practices under-pinning the modern states system, the coincidence of a named region and ethnic group creates a basis, and even an incentive, for claims to political autonomy and sovereignty; hence such claims also have the potential to generate violent conflict with the state that officially controls the territory in question";[15] or in most cases, against a competing ethnic group as a scapegoat. One can thus reject the theory that intermixing of the ethnic groups within the same geographical space is enough, in and of itself, to dispose them to violent conflicts.

Even in the pre-independence days, the notorious Kano (Northern Nigeria) riots of May 1953, though it may seem otherwise, were at best superficially connected to ethnicity. "It was the first collective outburst between the Southern and Northern Communities, or more importantly, between the principal political parties contending for influence or control over the operations of the Government of Nigeria."[16] The most obvious causes of that riot which lasted for about three days from May 16–18, 1953, can be traced to differences in political party affiliation, the rise of a seem-ingly alien economic hegemony in Kano, and the increasing population of "foreigners" (non-indigenes) among the local population that made their presence and political affiliation much more noticeable than before. Hence to appreciate the circumstances which gave rise to the Kano riots of 1953 and many more in later years, it is important to draw from the socioeconomic and cultural cross-currents at work. The city of Kano was the main center of the groundnut industry of the then Northern Nigeria as well as its major commercial center; hence the centrifugal forces of wealth creation attracted a vibrant cosmopolitan population from all parts of Ni-geria and beyond. "In terms of population, Kano city itself had a popula-tion of 93,000 while a further 34,000 lived in the suburbs. The Emirate had a population of 3,000,000 approximately, 1,000,000 of which reside within a long day's march of Kano city. Of the 3,000,000 in the Emirate, all were of Northern origin with the exception of approximately 16,000 Ibos and Ibibios, 7,500 Yorubas, and 3,500 from other Southern races."[17]

One can equally note that "in the 1921 Census, Kano township (popula-tion 4,670) which then included the Sabon Gari (stranger's quarters) had a total Southern population of less than 2,000, and 1,478 of whom were Yorubas. The Ibos were insufficient in numbers then to merit special men-tion. There were, in fact, less than 3,000 of them in the entire Northern Region."[18] While much of the interethnic conflicts were less evident during much of the pre-independence years, one sees a trend that may suggest that as the population of other ethnic groups built up in Kano and the sur-rounding environs, it began to change the socioeconomic and possibly, the political landscape in very fundamental ways. On a psychological level, it created a feeling of self-alienation and imposition on the part of the native population. It was this feeling of insecurity and uncertainty that some Northern political elites played on to foment the imaginary scenario of an impending "political domination."

"Even by 1931, the total population of Kano township had only risen from 4,670 to 7,643, but the racial percentages were: Northern races 60.2, Yorubas 17.7, Ibos 14.6, and others 7.5. The number of Ibos had risen to nearly 12,000 (in 1932). But in 1952, there were over 100,000 Ibos, less than half the number of Southern Yorubas."[19] While this increase in population from the South was an essential corollary to the economic development of the North, it was the fear of imminent political domination,[20] which more than anything else caused the Kano riots of 1953. The crisis therefore was a consequence of a struggle for power among the mobilized power blocs over the instrumentalities of political, social and economic control within the political community. Although the population of Northern Nigeria was approximately two-thirds Muslim, the population of Kano then was 99 percent Muslim. Ethnic differences were more or less an inescapable factor in the whole scheme of violence that ensued. In fact, during the killings and plunder that followed the rioting, many Northerners were known to have sheltered Southerners in Fagge and Southerners sheltered Northerners in Sabon Gari, most obviously at risk to injury to themselves and their families. To the extent that "ethnicity proved essentially to be simply the characteristic around which the perpetrators and the politicians who recruited and encouraged them happened to array themselves; it was important as an ordering device or principle, but not as a crucial motivating force."[21]

Nonetheless, there were two main undercurrents to the crisis, "the relationship existing between the average Northerner and the Southern petty officialdom, as well as the southern staff of the big commercial firms."[22] Because Southerners found themselves in charge of key federal government ministries and commercial firms in the North, the underlying feeling of resentment began to shape a more aggressive Northern attitude that invariably filtered into the political development of the day. "The immediate spark which caused the Kano riots was the proposed Action Group tour headed by Chief Akintola. Even since the return of the Northern representatives from the earlier Budget Session at Lagos early in April 1953, resentment had been growing, firstly as a result of the Lagos demonstrations (where Northern delegates were booed and satired for voting contrary to popular expectation regarding the tenets of national independence and self-government), and secondly as a result of the alleged hostile press campaign which had taken place immediately afterwards."[23]

It should, nonetheless, be noted that the Northern region had been more reserved, or rather reluctant to accede to an outright and immediate self-government from Britain. This was due partly to the fact that having been granted partial autonomy by the British colonialists as a result of the system of indirect rule which thus preserved, almost intact, the fiefdoms of the Northern Emirs; most Northerners and certainly the Emirs, were reluctant to abdicate such preferential treatment (privileges) for the yet uncharted waters of Nigerian nationhood. Their resolve was even more strengthened by what they felt was a sheer demonstration of "intolerance" among some Southern elements for reproaching them for voting in accordance with their conscience and for what made "sense" to them at that particular point in time. In fact, Northern leaders strongly held "the claim that unless there was a fundamental reorganization in the structure of government and in the division of powers between regions and the federal government, creating a truly federal system, the proposed self-government in 1956 would mean unquestioned continuation of Southern predominance in the higher levels of the central and regional civil services and police."[24] Equally, it could also mean eventual Southern dominance in the national legislature, especially in the ongoing campaign of Southern-based parties to create a political alliance with the Middle Belt parties opposed to the more conservative and status quo–based Northern Peoples Congress.

As the rioting evolved, it slowly began to manifest as a struggle between the supporters of the Northern Peoples Party (NPC) dominated by Northerners, and the Action Group (AG) dominated by Southern Yorubas. With the rising population of Ibos in Kano, many of whom were naturally members of the National Council of Nigeria and the Cameroons (NCNC), it became obvious that it too would be drawn into the ensuing political conflict. Coincidentally, it just happened that most of the members of the AG were Southern Yorubas, and most of the members of the NCNC were Southern Ibos. On the other hand, most of the members of the NPC were Hausa/Fulanis of the North and mainly Muslims.

The crisis set out as a political issue between the major political parties, which by implication drew also on their region of dominance and ethnic origins. Had the political issues been tamed, or had the party formations, by either design or default, not been drawn essentially along ethnic lines, the ethnic factor would have been minimally consequential if at all. In a dynamic federalism where specific powers are devolved to the constituent units, it would not be considered totally inappropriate for any region of the country to seek a commensurate degree of political autonomy from the center or from other units of the whole, but the argument remained moot at that time since Nigeria was yet to become a federation. Rather what it did was to superimpose a regional mindset on the national question, albeit very early in the series of political discussions for national sovereignty. One can therefore see how purely partisan and regional issues of autonomy and control can very quickly become immersed in the generally emotive atmosphere of religious ethnocentricism.

IS ETHNICITY A SUFFICIENT CONDITION?

While this is not to argue that individuals could not hate each other simply because of differences in ethnicity, but what is most important is to argue whether such differences could become the sole catalyst for conflict and violence between them. On balance, it could be argued that Nigerians, perhaps, may not dislike each other solely due to ethnic differences; but if and when they do, it is more about how these differences manifest themselves as the basis for power, autonomy, competition, and in the distribution of relative political and economic opportunities. It is the relative disadvantage that accrues from the political calculus that spurs one group to see the other as its main obstacle, hence deserving of any negative attitude directed at them.

In this regard, it is useful to draw from some of the issues surrounding the military coup of January 15, 1966. While there is less evidence of ethnic motivation, the more proximate causes were generally rooted, firstly, in the political situation in the country at that time and, secondly, in the various adjustments at addressing emerging anomalies in the federal system. The timing of the coup in itself, barely six years after the country's independence, may have been its greatest source of failure. This was still a time of growing and teething pains in the political evolution of the country, when it was yet bent on recreating its own indigenous political space distinctly apart from the colonial orthodoxy. Judging from its antecedents as well as the eventual outcome, the July 29, 1966 countercoup by Northern soldiers had a political objective of capturing power at the center; but the killings and the ethnic undercurrent that drove it became overpowering than the objective it was supposed to achieve. While General Ironsi had sought the promulgation of the Unification Decree No. 34 on May 24, 1996, "the dissolution of the hitherto regional structure and the establishment of a provincial system forced the emirs, as new regional intermediaries, into the center-stage of national politics; but the dominant political class in the upper North 'feared' that the 'abolition' of Nigeria's federal structure would expose their region to 'takeover' by the more advanced South."[25] In a matter of days, the decree sparked waves of murderous violence in several Northern cities, notably Kano, Kaduna, Zaria, Jos, and Bukuru.[26] And in the crosscurrent of events, ethnicity became the reluctant victim.

In fact "tribal factors are by no means absent from African politics, the more so as local political leaders generally tend to exploit the pattern of

tribal allegiance in other to achieve their ends. While tribalism (or ethnicity) is essentially an instrument in African politics, it is not a moving force
or an independent factor by itself; tribalism only becomes explosive within
an already explosive political situation, such as existed in Nigeria in the
mid 1960s."[27] As Ola Balogun[28] argues, "the explanation of the events of
May–July 1996 should not be sought in tribal feelings or in alleged tribal
antagonisms, but rather in the general political evolution of Nigeria since
independence, and more specifically, in the political crisis that led to the
January 1966 coup and its aftermath. This crisis could most accurately be
described as a gradual breakdown of the machinery of government in the
country over the years since independence, and partly as a result of an in-
tensification of the struggle for power among the various ruling groups."

RELIGION AND PARTISANSHIP:
SHAPING THE POLITICAL MINDSET

The end of World War II generated increased fervor for constitutional reform preparatory to the discussions on Nigeria's independence. While the
"Nigerian nationalists wanted a greater representation of Nigerians in the
governing bodies of the country; they also agreed that the two main issues
to be dealt with within the framework of a reformed constitution were the
question of national independence and the problem of regionalism—that
is the relations between the various regions and the national federation."[29]
The first pre-independence Constitution, the Richards Constitution became effective on January 1, 1947. While it divided Nigeria into three
regions (North, East, and West) perhaps as a matter of deliberate design,
it also by default divided Nigeria into two religious groupings consistent
with a North-South distinction—the North being mainly Muslim and the
South and Middle Belt being mostly Christian.

Because the regional powers wanted more autonomy than was granted
under the Richards Constitution, the resulting series of constitutional
conferences produced a new constitution, the Macpherson Constitution, which was put into effect in 1951. The seeming inadequacy of the
Macpherson Constitution very early in its inception led to further constitutional conferences in London in 1953 and 1954, which eventually
produced another new constitution. "The main difference between the
Macpherson Constitution and the new (1954 Constitution) was a distinction between the powers of the federal government and the regional as-
semblies."[30] In addition to the fact that federal and regional elections were
separated, any residual powers not granted to the federal government
was implicitly ceded to the regional governments. "The federation as a
whole became an independent state within the British Commonwealth

in October 1960, and under yet another new constitution, the Northern People's congress (Northern-based party) gained a parliamentary majority with Sir Abubakar Tafawa Balewa as the first Prime Minister of an independent Nigeria."[31] Although this resembled the beginnings of an institutionalized federal system in the country, the geopolitical layout would certainly become consequential for the eventual evolution of early party politics in Nigeria.

The development of political parties in post-independent Nigeria emerged out of local and regional ethnic associations in the three dominant regions of the country. While "the two dominant parties in the central Islamic part of Northern Nigeria were the Northern People's Congress (NPC) and the Northern Elements Progressive Union (NEPU); the NPC became the main opponent of the Christians because it was generally seen as the party which more than anything else embodies the Hausa-Fulani dominance in Northern Nigeria."[32] From its inception in 1951, the NPC was dominated by the Islamic power elite in Northern Nigeria, its elected representatives were drawn from the Native Authority system or from the local Northern aristocracy"[33] and cronies of the Emirate system. The NEPU, on the other hand, could be considered a renegade partisan offshoot of dissatisfied elements within the Northern political establishment, but with a more radicalized ideological bent and bias for social equity and the upliftment of the more disadvantaged lower ranks of the social order—like the *talakawas*.

The other party of interest was the United Middle Belt Congress (UMBC) covering the mid-section of the country and extending throughout the areas bordering the Rivers Niger and Benue. "As was the case with the NPC and the NEPU, the origin of the UMBC can be traced to a tribal union called Birom Progressive Union from the Jos Area of today's Plateau state. It was the party which all Christians in Adamawa supported and which had one of its strongholds in the Bachama-Numan area."[34] Though favored by the early Christian missionaries, its religious inclinations drew from a common fear of being dominated by the Muslim Fulani elite, unless there was an attempt at organized resistance that drew on key cultural identifications. "To both Nigerian and Danish Protestants in Adamawa, religious and ethnic competitions were intimately linked";[35] hence to the extent the missionaries accused the Muslim Fulani elite of mixing religion and politics, they also saw Muslim conversion campaigns as a program of political domination.

As early as 1953, "the major political parties in the country, the NCNC, AG, and the NPC had become associated with the three major ethnic groups, Igbo, Yoruba and Hausa, in line with the three regions of the country, East, West, and North, respectively."[36] The dominant party in the West was the Action Group (AG) which drew its political support mainly from the Yoruba ethnic group who are mostly Christians but with a recognizable Muslim population; the NPC became dominant in the North which is mostly Muslim; and the National Convention of Nigerian Citizens and the Cameroons (NCNC) became the dominant party in the East inhabited mostly by Ibos and other Christian ethnic groups. The NCNC was later to become the National Council of Nigerian Citizens after Southern Cameroonians opted to become part of Cameroon as opposed to remaining part of Nigeria.

As Okwudiba Nnoli points out,[37] while the 1954 Constitution institutionalized regionalism in the country, it provided a geographical basis for the emergent regional political class to carve out spheres of economic and political influence. As the regionalized party system was used as a way of mass political mobilization, the ethnic factor became effective instruments for political brinkmanship. Nonetheless, the political class "succeeded in creating the false impression that the various political parties were the champions of the interest of various ethnic groups, and that the struggles of these parties for political dominance represented the struggles of the various ethnic groups for political ascendancy in the society." The acquisition of political power became a means, not for addressing the many problems affecting the society but for actualizing the 'self-interest' of the ethnic group. In Northern Nigeria, in particular, this more than anything else "contributed to hostilities among ethnic groups in major towns and communities."[38] And "the inevitable consequence, thus, was the politicization of ethnicity."[39]

For the simple fact that it is easier to switch partisan alliances based on one's political calculations, it is rather difficult to change ones religious affiliation since this, in and of itself, draws from a deeper level of human sensitivity, belief, conscience and emotion. It therefore became very difficult to isolate the religious foundations of political strife from the more practical issues of party affiliation, ethnicity, and ideology. "Religion and politics have always been intimately fused in the North as a result of the establishment of the Sokoto Caliphate over the greater part of that region. To that extent, Islam was able to blunt the sharp edge of ethnic identity and substituted it with a broad distinction between those who accepted emirate control and spoke Hausa, and those who either had resisted Islam or lived in areas where little attempt had been made to propagate the religion."[40] In fact, it has been pointed out that "the history of the establishment of the Sokoto Caliphate and the subsequent directive by Lord Lugard (the Colonial Administrator) that Christian missionaries should confine their activities to only part of the North where Islam was least thoroughly established made the Middle Belt region a fertile ground for the Christian missionary enterprise. This invariably, set the stage for some of the future religious crises in the North"[41] as Christian and Muslim communities clash over political and economic empowerment. The primacy of religion in political statecraft is even more meaningful for the average Muslim, especially when considered in light of the fact that Muslims believe in the inseparability of "church" and state, and see religious dogma as the centerpiece for a well-ordered society and a fulfilling life. It is the emotional and psychological attachments drawn from these beliefs that makes people kill in the name of religion even when such actions contributes to social disorder and political disunity. Hence, the ambiguity created at the intersection where religious doctrinaire clashes with state authority offers a breeding ground that is easily exploited by false prophets and religious zealots.

A classic case that conjures up this type of apostasy is the Maitatsine sectarian violence that erupted in the Northern city of Kano in late December 1980. Led by Alhaji Muhammadu Marwa, members of this heretical Muslim sect numbering about 3,000 stood in opposition to the secular state authority. The ensuing orgy of violence only took the army and the air force to restore order after an eleven-day mayhem. By the time it was over, more than 4,000 people were dead, property worth millions of naira were destroyed, and many were arrested. Nonetheless, more riots by Maitatsine followers broke out again in late December 1982 in Maiduguri and spread to other parts of the North including Kaduna. By the time it was over, more than 188 civilians and 18 policemen were killed. In February 1984, and against all odds, members of the now proscribed Maitatsine sect struck again, this time in northeast Nigeria and in Yola, the capital of Gongola state. Although the army was called in to restore order, the sectarian violence left more than 700 persons dead, 30,000 made homeless, and about 2,000 homes destroyed or damaged. In the following April 1985, adherents of the same Maitatsine sect inspired a series of riots in Gombe that claimed more than one hundred lives. The trail of violence extended to and pitted Christian and Muslim students in the various secondary schools and universities in Kano, Zaria, and Bauchi against each other.

ZANGO KATAF: TERRITORIALISM OR ETHNICITY?

On May 14, 1992, one of the most brutal carnages in the history of Nigeria's communal conflict occurred in the area of Kaduna state known as Zango Kataf. It was a clash of wills and mayhem between the "alien" Hausas who are mostly Muslims, and the native Katafs who are mostly Christians of Southern Kaduna state. At the end of that conflict, no fewer than three hundred persons were killed and many more injured, and scores of churches, mosques, and property worth millions of naira destroyed. But what most people including political leaders see as an ethnic conflict was certainly an economic and historical issue that has festered for more than 150 years. The real irony in a case of this nature is that once it is pronounced and taken as an ethnic conflict, it limits the search for more lasting solutions to the underlying historical and other proximate causes of the crisis. The mere feeling that there is little one can do to change people's ethnic origins tempers the zeal for a more aggressive approach to get to the root of the problem. As reported in the *African Guardian* of June 1, 1992, "the causes of the current conflict, though seemingly inter-ethnic, are deeply rooted in history and economics." One explanation was that the settler Hausa community of Zango Kataf provoked the indigenous Kataf people (also known as the Atyap), by marching onto their farmlands in the areas of Ungwar Tabo, Rahogo, and Wakili on that Thursday night (May 14, 1992), destroying months of labor and any hope of useful harvest from the remaining crops and yams.

As the Hausas and the Katafs became locked in battle with each other over the destruction of the farmlands, the Katafs repeated a constant refrain about the underlying issues between the two communities: the emirate institutions imposed on them by the Hausas, and the domination of the government by the Zango elites. While there was also a counter-charge that it was the Katafs and not the Hausas who first engaged in the act of farm destruction; but what was surprising was how such a land issue was quickly drawn into the religious realm, which in the case of Nigeria, can be a potent rallying cry more than anything else. In addition to the historic nature of the Hausa-Kataf rivalry, the *African Guardian* of June 1, 1992, made reference to the contents of an earlier letter written on May 9, 1992, to the Sultan of Sokoto, Alhaji Ibrahim Dasuki, by one Aliyu Jibril on behalf of the local branch of the New Aid Group of the Izalatul Bidia (religious) sect—claiming that the Katafs had made life difficult for the Hausas through murder and the night-time destruction of their farms. According to Jibril, "since all the Hausas are Muslims, an attack on Hausas was in fact a veiled assault on Islam for which the Sultan, being the spiritual leader of Nigerian Moslems, ought to be alerted."[42] Jibril threatened "holy war" or Jihad against the Katafs.

But the Hausa-Kataf crisis has a long history. The fundamental and perhaps, more central issue has remained the Kataf's rejection of the seeming autocracy of the Emir of Zaria—as embodied in a memorandum submitted to the judicial commission of inquiry into a similar riot at Zango Kataf market on February 6, 1992, where about ninety people were killed. The complaint of the Kataf Youth Development Association (KYDA) was that the Hausa-controlled Emirate system had unacceptable control over the Katafs; and that the exclusive pattern of Hausa-dominated settlements in Zango was apartheid-like. These circumstances have led to the deployment of Hausa district heads to Zango since 1915 until 1967 when the first indigenous district head, Mallam Bala Dauke was appointed. Other grievances were the employment of Islamic cultures to hinder the economic development of the Katafs like restrictions on the sale of pigs, pork, and locally brewed beer; the alleged humiliation of Kataf women, as well as the location of the local Zango market which the Hausas, because of their relative economic success, insisted would not be moved. "Fearing an attempt to reverse their economic fortunes, the Hausas have consistently opposed the relocation of the market, but the Kataf people, canvassing a case for modernization, thought it was time to have a befitting market built and controlled by the local government. Nonetheless, the relocation effort seemed to be an aspect of the plan to redress what the Kataf considered to be a historic injustice."[43]

THE ECONOMICS OF POWER: PAST AS PROLOGUE

With the rising wave of "democracy" in Nigeria, the Hausas of Zango were concerned of seeing their traditional political power wrestled from them by a resurgent Kataf political activism. The *African Guardian*[44] reports that the Hausa-Kataf acrimony that led to the immediate crisis dates back to 1650. As part of the informal satellite markets on the Trans-Sahara trade route, the Hausas saw in the Kataf basin a market to purchase elephant tusk, camwood, iron ore, honey, in exchange for which they sold red caps, horses, swords, and bangles. The success of this commercial relationship eventually led to the founding of a transit camp (Zango) in Kataf on the political accord that the Hausas will pay annual tribute for protection and peace. But by 1750, the Hausas planned a "coup" of sorts; they stopped paying tributes but instead sought to capture the trade routes, having linked up in the plot with their kins in the areas of Zaria and Kaura. The Kataf quickly foiled the plot and in the process declared the Hausas unwelcome in the area for the ensuing two decades. By 1800, some understanding was reached between both parties but the tensed relationship remained for many years amid a series of scorched battles. The battles were long and costly for both sides until victory came for the Kataf only in the 1920s. But it was Pyrrhic victory complicated more or less by the advent of colonialism.

The British were less interested in creating enabling conditions for decentralized governance, especially when such was anchored on historical sentiments and fiefdoms. They were more interested in the principle of "indirect rule" through the existing traditional institutions, which nonetheless had favored the alien Hausas to the native Katafs. Hence when Nigeria secured her independence in 1960 and the exit of the British, the prevailing colonial institutions still held sway as the dominant orthodoxy. Since then, the Hausas and the Katafs have viewed each other with misgivings, resulting sporadically in ethnic and communal clashes between them. Of relevance are the Kasuwan Maganis riot (1984), Zango Kataf (1984), Kahugu-Gure (1985), Kafanchan (1987), Zonkwa (1991), and Zango Kataf (1992). While "the struggles in the Middle Belt at the end of the twentieth century seem generally to be argued on the basis of events that occurred hundred of years before,"[45] it is noteworthy to indicate that above all, the common denominator in these crises was the struggle for political power on the one hand, or differences in religion, on the other. What the Zango Kataf/Hausas-Fulani, the Shayawas and the Fulanis, the Tivs and the Jukun conflicts[46] indicate is a festering political question anchored on religious differences.

"In recent times, religious crises have assumed a frightening dimension, threatening the very foundation of the nation."[47] Okey Ekeocha provides a narrative of the causal origins of an ethno-religious crisis that erupted in 1985 in Gombe, Bauchi State. The cause was that the Shayawa indigenes were accused by the Hausa-Fulani settlers of slaughtering pig in the Gombe central abattoir contrary to Islamic injunctions. But beneath the surface of the Shayawa-Hausa-Fulani crisis was the demand by the Shayawa for the control of their own destiny that had come under the emirate system. It took a turn for the worse in April 1991 when the Shayawa demanded for a separate local government outside of the emirate system. By the time it was over, about 764 people were killed and property worth millions of naira was destroyed. "Religion was again the catalyst in the 1987 Kafanchan riots, so were the ones in Zaria and Kaduna. Katsina and Kano have also witnessed ethno-religious crisis in which many lives and property were lost; the strife in Kano being caused by an overt invitation to a German Preacher."[48]

The series of intercommunal conflicts that were witnessed in the country in the later part of 1980s and early 1990s over the introduction of the Islamic Sharia law in many states of Northern Nigeria were also religious as they were political. While Christians and non-Muslims saw it as a surreptitious attempt at islamization "one piece at a time" and as a religious preference that contradicts the secular status of the country; Muslims argued that it was a central element in their religion the denial of which would demonstrate non-inclusiveness. While the "opposition to sharia law stems from two major sources, the fear that it would be applied to non-Muslims in spite of the assurance of the state governments involved, and the fear that it would be imposed on the predominantly Christian populations of Bugoro, Tafawa Balewa, and Das local government areas of Bauchi state; the ensuing debate precipitated a costly crisis between the Sayawa and the Hausa-Fulani ethnic groups, as well as increased tensions in southern Zaria."[49] "Since this form of Islamic law was first introduced in Nigeria in 2000, more than 5,000 people have been killed as a result of sectarian crisis."[50]

The underlying issue concerning the introduction of Sharia in the North lies in its political significance, the relative population of Christians and Muslims in the North and its consequent implication for the distribution of political and economic incentives based on the principle of majority rule. But contrary to the widely held belief of the absolute and numeric majority of Muslims in the North, the statistics paints a rather different picture. "In states such as Nassarawa, Taraba, Gombe, Plateau, Benue, Kaduna, Adamawa, Christians hold sway; while in Bauchi, Borno, Yobe, Kebbi, Niger there is a substantial number of Christians. In states such as Kano, Zamfara, Jigawa, Sokoto, they are overwhelmingly Muslim."[51] But the reality is a bit more complex than simple numbers. The point is that prior to the creation of an additional nine states in 1991, "Muslims were dominant in only six of the eleven northern states; Christians constitute the majority in the remaining five states. In the South, Muslims constitute the majority in two states, with Christians dominant in the remaining eight states; but the presence of 'animists' (adherents to traditional religions) in most of the southern states and in parts of the Middle Belt is most often ignored."[52] While Christians constitute a sizeable proportion of the population, the general belief among them is that in spite of the impact of Christianity in the north, many Muslims still believe that Christians do not belong to the northern society as of right.[53] But as a matter of political realism and without pandering to the idea of Sharia, no candidate, governor or legislator in predominantly Muslim parts of the northern states could hope to be elected or reelected. In fundamental ways, the Sharia idea serves as a social filter through which politics and religion come to shape government officials' disposition toward critical issues of public policy.

INTERNATIONAL DYNAMICS AND EMERGENT FAULT LINES

There is a new and much more insidious paradox emerging in the context of many of the religious and sectional crisis in Nigeria—that is, the quickness by which international events can provide the match that turns the tinder into a violent inferno. While it has been alleged that financial support from some Middle Eastern countries was partly responsible for the rise of religious fundamentalism in Northern Nigeria, it is one of those situations where human action seems to defy ordinary common sense or any sense of proportionality in light of the issue in question. Many people were quite shocked after it became evident that the match that set off the

Muslim-Christian riots that broke out in mainly Muslim Kano (in Northern Nigeria) on October 12, 2001, was the U.S. bombing of Afghanistan following the terrorist events of September 11, 2001. As Muslim mobs attacked Christians and burned churches, Christian mobs responded by attacking Muslims and burning mosques, and after two days of clashes more than eighteen people were dead. The saddest thing in this episode was that the central issue that sparked the riots had very little to do with Nigeria or with those who consequently paid with their lives.

Another classic example is the "Miss World riots" which occurred in Kaduna (Northern Nigeria) in November 2002, when protests relating to the Miss World beauty pageant scheduled to be held in the Federal capital of Abuja spiraled out of control. By the time it was all over, 250 people have been killed as Muslim and Christian groups fought each other for three days. As in many earlier situations, religious intolerance, political disputes, and ethnic and partisan rivalries came together in one violent outburst of death and destruction. In consideration of many varying accounts, the Human Rights Watch[54] offered a rather comprehensive account of the events leading up to and during the November riots, and it is from that source that the following account is presented. The decision to hold the 2002 Miss World contest in Nigeria was an option that arose because the winner of the previous contest was a Nigerian; but the political import, particularly among conservative sectors of the Muslim community in the North who had opposed the beauty contest on moral grounds became an obstacle that loomed behind the scene. Initially scheduled to take place at the end of November, it was eventually postponed to December 7, to avoid coinciding with the Muslim holy month of Ramadan. The "spark" came on November 16, 2002, when an article that was published in one of the national newspapers *This Day*, suggested to the effect that "Prophet Mohammed would have been less disapproving of the Miss World Contest, and would probably have chosen a wife from among them." The article provoked a series of protests from Muslims, which started on November 20, especially in Kaduna. On November 21, Muslim groups in different parts of Kaduna town attacked Christians, churches, homes, schools, and businesses owned by Christians.

On November 22, Christian groups began to retaliate by attacking Muslims, burning mosques, homes in Muslim areas, setting up roadblocks and interrogating those who passed by to ascertain their religion, then singling out Muslims for attack. On the afternoon of November 22, the violence spread to the federal capital of Abuja (about 185 kilometers south of Kaduna), where Muslim groups began smashing vehicles and lighting fires in the city center. On Friday, November 22, the newspaper *News Day* published an extensive apology by its editor for any offense caused by the original article; retractions and apologies had already been published in two earlier editions, on November 18 and 19. However, the apologies, barely noticed by the rioters, made no impact as the violence continued to spin out of control. The mayhem in Kaduna continued into Saturday, November 23, and by this time the violence had taken on a life of its own. Ironically, some of the rioters did not even know what had sparked off the fighting but were nevertheless systematically hunting down members of the other faith and destroying their property; others seemed more interested in looting than in killing. In addition to those killed in the fighting, scores of people were shot dead by security forces, either wittingly or unwittingly. By the time the carnage ran itself out, approximately 250 people were killed in Kaduna and about 30,000 people displaced

While it is relevant to examine the "Miss World Riots," we also need to look at some of the factors that provided the political and religious undercurrent for the ensuing violence. The Human Rights Watch[55] points specifically to the earlier event of February and May 2000, in which at least 2,000 people were killed in intercommunal violence between Christians and Muslims in Kaduna. The fighting began following debate around the proposed introduction of Sharia in Kaduna State. To demonstrate their opposition to Sharia, between eight to ten thousand Christians took to the streets of Kaduna on May 21, 2000. On their way back, the conflagration which eventually consumed the city erupted with reckless abandon.

Although Sharia had existed in northern Nigeria for many years, it had only been applied to personal and domestic law. But in a bold move which was popular among many conservative Muslims but highly controversial and destabilizing in the context of Nigerian federalism, the year 1999 saw a number of northern state governors extending its application to criminal law and other areas that had not been previously regulated. Zamfara was the first state to do so; others soon followed, and by the end of 2001, most of Nigeria's northern states had adopted some form of Sharia in criminal law. Today, there are twelve geographically contiguous states (Sokoto, Zamfara, Katsina, Kano, Jigawa, Yobe, Borno, Kebbi, Niger, Kaduna, Bauchi, and Gombe) that have adopted some form of the Sharia legal code. Although designed to apply *only* to Muslims living in these states, its application has been strongly opposed by Christians, who find themselves directly or indirectly affected by it in different ways. For example in some of the states, the sale and consumption of alcohol is prohibited, and women are prohibited from traveling with men in public transport vehicles.

Aside from these practical effects, many Christians oppose the application of Sharia for reasons of constitutionality, politics, and principle, arguing that its spread is a way of perpetuating the political influence of the Muslim North. It was never lost on officials that in light of Kaduna's

large Christian population, the possibility of introducing Sharia in Kaduna State would likely attract controversy and rejection more than in
other northern states. Although it was estimated that the 2000 Kaduna
killings resulted in the death of between 2,000 to 5,000 people, it left long-
lasting scars on the people and the state. The memories were still fresh
when violence struck again two years later in 2002, as many communities
felt that their grievances had not been addressed and old scores needed to
be settled. Furthermore, the 2000 violence caused large-scale population
displacements, leading to a sharp segregation of communities in some
areas. As "Christians and Muslims increasingly moved to areas which
were dominated by people of their own faith in the hope of finding safety
there; the later violence of November 2002 helped to exacerbate the deepening polarization in what was once a genuinely mixed population."[56]
But above all, Kaduna state stood a unique position—"as an environment
where both the demand for and the opposition against the Sharia was
equally resolute and unyielding."[57]

Then there was also the Danish cartoon episode[58] in which many lives
were lost in Northern and Southeastern Nigeria following several days
of killing and destruction. In early February 2006, rioting began when
Muslim mobs, mostly Hausas, destroyed thirty Christian churches and
killed eighteen people in the northeastern city of Maiduguri, Bornu state.
A few days later, those attacks were followed by rioting in Bauchi, where
another twenty-five people died over a two-day period. On February 22,
after a bus carrying bodies of victims from the Maiduguri riots arrived at
the bus terminal in Onitsha in the southeastern part of the country, the
people reacted and went into an orgy of reprisal attacks against Muslims
living in the area. More than thirty people were left dead. Soon, the rioting spread to other nearby towns of Enugu, Owerri, Aba, and Umuahia,
and when it was all over, more than eighty people were killed nationwide
and property worth millions of naira were destroyed. The attacks in Nigeria began almost six months after a Danish newspaper first published a
cartoon satire of Prophet Mohammed, and weeks after it ignited a wave
of unrest in Muslim countries from Egypt to Indonesia that left about
twenty-eight people dead.

What made the Nigerian case most revolting was the sheer incompre-
hensibility of it all, and why innocent, and mostly illiterate and ordinary
people will have to die for events that occurred thousands of miles away
in "winter-cold" Denmark—a place where very few of those involved in
the mayhem would have been able to pick out on a political map of the
world. While security forces were essentially responsible for the deaths
in essentially all of the other countries where riots occurred, but in Nigeria, neighbors and communities set upon each other simply for the sake
of "differences" in faith. What can be gleaned from these events is that

ethno-religious crises in Nigeria could be drawn from multiple sources of discontent such as issues over land or property, but also represents a constantly evolving pattern of political struggle and competition subsumed under the rubric of group and religious identity. Hence, any issue, no matter how remotely placed, could very well provide the catalyst for conflict with potentially disastrous consequences.

NOTES

1. Clifford Geertz, *The Interpretation of Cultures: Selected Essays* (New York: Basic Books, 1973), 309.

2. James D. Fearon and David D. Laitin, "A Cross-Sectional Study of Large-Scale Ethnic Violence in the Postwar Period," Unpublished Draft Paper, University of Chicago (September 30, 1997), 1–39. Paper based on a longer version "Explaining Ethnic Violence" which was issued as a Working Paper of the Juan March Institute, Madrid, Spain.

3. Obaro Ikime, *Niger Delta Rivalry: Itshekiri-Urhobo Relations and the European Presence, 1884–1936* (Harlow, UK: Longmans, 1969), 41–68.

4. Ikime, *Niger Delta Rivalry*, 43.

5. Ikime, *Niger Delta Rivalry*, 57.

6. Ikime, *Niger Delta Rivalry*, 57.

7. T. A. Imobighe, "Warri Crisis in Historical and Contemporary Perspectives," in *Conflict and Instability in the Niger Delta: The Warri Case*, ed. T. A. Imobighe, Celestine O. Bassey, and Judith Burdin Asuni (Abuja, Nigeria: Spectrum Books, 2002), 36–52.

8. Imobighe, "Warri Crisis in Historical and Contemporary Perspectives," 36.

9. I. A. Akinjogbin, "The Oyo Empire in the 18th Century: A Reassessment," *Journal of the Historical Society of Nigeria* 3, no. 3 (December 1966): 449–60.

10. J. F. A. Ajayi and R. Smith, *Yoruba Warfare in the Nineteenth Century* (Cambridge: Cambridge University Press, 1964). Also see S. A. Akintoye, *Revolution and Power Politics in Yorubaland, 1840–1893* (London: Longman, 1971).

11. Isaac Olawale Albert, "Ife-Modakeke Crisis," pp. 142–83 in *Community Conflicts in Nigeria: Management, Resolution and Transformation*, ed. Onigu Otite and Isaac Olawale Albert (Ibadan, Nigeria: Spectrum Books, 1999), 143–44.

12. Albert, "Ife-Modakeke Crisis," 145.

13. Albert, "Ife-Modakeke Crisis."

14. John Mueller, "The Banality of 'Ethnic War,'" *International Security* 25, no. 1 (Summer 2000): 42–70.

15. Fearon and Laitin, "A Cross-Sectional Study of Large-Scale Ethnic Violence in the Postwar Period," 1–39.

16. Bernard Nkemdirim, *Social Change and Political Violence in Colonial Nigeria* (Devon, UK: Arthur H. Stockwell Limited, 1975), 60.

17. Northern Regional Government, *Report on the Kano Disturbances* (Nigeria: Government Printer, 1953), 1.

18. Northern Regional Government, *Report on the Kano Disturbances*, 1.
19. Northern Regional Government, *Report on the Kano Disturbances*, 2.
20. Nkemdirim, *Social Change and Political Violence in Colonial Nigeria*, 107.
21. Mueller, "The Banality of 'Ethnic War,'" 63.
22. Northern Regional Government, *Report on the Kano Disturbances*, 2.
23. Northern Regional Government, *Report on the Kano Disturbances*, 4.
24. Nkemdirim, *Social Change and Political Violence in Colonial Nigeria*, 67.
25. Olufemi Vaughan, *Nigerian Chiefs: Traditional Power in Modern Politics, 1890s–1990s* (Rochester, N.Y.: University of Rochester Press, 2000), 123.
26. Ola Balogun, *The Tragic Years: Nigeria in Crisis* (Benin, Nigeria: Ethiope Publishing Corporation, 1973), 27.
27. Balogun, *The Tragic Years: Nigeria in Crisis*, 73–74.
28. Balogun, *The Tragic Years: Nigeria in Crisis*, 74.
29. Niels Kastfelt, *Religion and Politics in Nigeria: A Study in Middle Belt Christianity* (London: British Academic Press, 1994), 69.
30. Kastfelt, *Religion and Politics in Nigeria*, 70.
31. Kastfelt, *Religion and Politics in Nigeria*, 71.
32. Kastfelt, *Religion and Politics in Nigeria*, 71.
33. Kastfelt, *Religion and Politics in Nigeria*, 72.
34. Kastfelt, *Religion and Politics in Nigeria*, 73.
35. Kastfelt, *Religion and Politics in Nigeria*, 76.
36. Okwudiba Nnoli, *Ethnic Politics in Nigeria* (Enugu, Nigeria: Fourth Dimension Publishers, 1978), 158.
37. Nnoli, *Ethnic Politics in Nigeria*, 158.
38. Nankin Bagudu, *Identity, Political Religiosity and Communal Violence in Nigeria: Implications* (Jos, Nigeria: League for Human Rights, 2003), 9.
39. Nnoli, *Ethnic Politics in Nigeria*, 159.
40. R. T. Akinyele, "Ethnicity, Religion and Politics in Nigeria," in *The Amalgamation and Its Enemies: An Interpretive History of Modern Nigeria*, ed. Richard A. Olaniyan (Ile-Ife, Nigeria: Obafemi Awolowo University Press, 2003), 123–47.
41. R. T. Akinyele, "Ethnicity, Religion and Politics in Nigeria," 129.
42. African Guardian, *A Savage Carnage*, June 1, 1992, 22.
43. African Guardian, *A Savage Carnage*, June 1, 1992, 23.
44. African Guardian, *A Savage Carnage*, June 1, 1992, 22.
45. Karl Maier, *This House Has Fallen: Midnight in Nigeria* (New York: Public Affairs, 2000), 194.
46. See Shedrack Gaya Best, Alamveabee Efhiraim Idyorough, and Zainab Bayero Shehu, "Communal Conflicts and the Possibilities of Conflict Resolution in Nigeria: A Case Study of the Tiv-Jukun Conflicts in Wukari Local Government Area of Taraba State," in *Community Conflicts in Nigeria: Management, Resolution and Transformation*, ed. Onigu Otite and Isaac Olawale Albert (Ibadan, Nigeria: Spectrum Books Limited, 1999), 82–117.
47. Okey Ekeocha, "A Hardy Perennial," *African Guardian*, June 1, 1992, 27.
48. Okey Ekeocha, "A Hardy Perennial," 27.
49. R. T. Akinyele, "Ethnicity, Religion and Politics in Nigeria," 141. Also see Mathew Hassan Kukah and Toyin Falola, *Religious Militancy and Self-Assertion: Islam and Politics in Nigeria* (Aldershot, UK: Avebury, 1996).

50. Nankin Bagudu, *Identity, Political Religiosity and Communal Violence in Nigeria*, 156.

51. Nankin Bagudu, *Identity, Political Religiosity and Communal Violence in Nigeria*, 155.

52. Ladipo Adamolekun, "Introduction: Federalism in Nigeria," *Publius: The Journal of Federalism* 21, no. 4 (Autumn 1991, 9): 1–11.

53. *Guardian* 16, no. 7667, November 10, 1999.

54. Human Rights Watch, "The 'Miss World Riots': Continued Impunity for Killings in Kaduna," 15, no. 13 (July 2003): 1–32, at www.hrw.org.

55. Human Rights Watch, "The 'Miss World Riots,'" 4.

56. Human Rights Watch, "The 'Miss World Riots,'" 5.

57. The Comet, "The Making of Kaduna Sharia War," June 30, 2000.

58. Craig Timberg, "Christians Turn on Muslims in Nigeria, More than 30 Die," *Washington Post Foreign Service*, February 23, 2006.

6

—〰—

The Praetorian Orthodoxy[1]
Pathways to Civic Soldiering

The Praetorian Guards of the Roman Empire were established as a special military unit for the protection of the emperor. They ended up using their military power to overthrow emperors and to control the Roman Senate's "election" of successive emperors.

—Eric Nordlinger[2]

The irony of civil-military relations and the tendency to arbitrarily circumvent legally constituted means of acquiring political authority is very much underscored by Nordlinger's commentary above. Equally, and for most developing polities, the trade-off between the primary role of the military as a security apparatus, and as a governing institution, has been quite costly in the course of their political development. "Two events in Nigeria's political development in the 1960s had profound consequences for the evolution of the federal system: the advent of military rule, and the consequent civil war."[3] The emergence of military rule, at least in its first few days, rarely generates mass political protests. This may be as a result of understandable frustration with the previous regime, or simply due to a basic human inclination for self-preservation. Nonetheless, when sporadic anti-military protests do occur, there has always been the tendency to construe them as a resurgence of mass political "consciousness" or the awakening of "civil society";[4] when, in fact, these are external manifestations of internal conflicts due to disagreements within the dominant ruling orthodoxy.

ASSAULT ON THE POLITICAL SPACE

Many reasons have been put forth as the driving force behind military incursions into the political sphere. Among the most predominant reasons are to maintain the security and stability of the state, to arrest declining social and economic conditions, to prevent social and political anarchy, to combat rampant corruption, or any combination of the above. One can also include individual ambition for power, conflict and factionalization within the military class, or conspiracy with certain elite groups within the civilian population. But whatever the justification, it should be obvious that military participation in politics is the antithesis of objective civilian control. Hence, civilian control decreases as the military become progressively involved in institutional, class, and constitutional politics.[5] The consequence being that the satisfaction of professional performance and adherence to the professional code, are replaced by the satisfaction of power, office, wealth, popularity, and the approbation of various non-military groups.[6] It is this loss of professionalism that may have prompted Morris Janowitz[7] to argue that a professional soldier is incompatible with holding any other significant social or political role.

Cracks in the Military Monolith

The ability of the Nigerian military to adhere strictly to its professional role and to stay away from political governance was shattered on January 15, 1966, following a military coup, partly as a result of the political crisis and social decay created within the civilian sector, especially in the Western region of the country. The general reason provided for this revolt was to preserve national unity and the integrity of the state, and to root out corruption and nepotism. It therefore seems plausible to argue that this bold step at national rescue nonetheless opened a Pandora's Box that exploded the deep tensions between a cross-section of the military elite and the political class. It may have also exposed the early stages of an alliance between a faction of the military leadership and their civilian surrogates in the First Republic, who were bent on capturing a monopoly of political power throughout the country. A. R. Luckham[8] argues that institutional instability within the Nigerian armed forces was engendered by the progressive and rapid indigenization of the officer corps in the immediate aftermath of independence. This was a direct result of political as opposed to military imperatives, and so this kind of localization led to erosion of skill and in many cases to a breakdown in discipline and military *esprit de corps*. What happened later, in essence seem to vindicate the views expressed by Alfred Stepan.[9] He argued that in terms of the military's contribution to national unity, much evidence exists that in many developing countries, not only is the military not isolated from the tensions experienced by the general population and therefore not able to act as an integrating force; but the military is itself an element in the polity that may transform latent tensions into overt crisis.

When the final account is written, history will show that the Nigerian military, for one reason or the other, has been its own worst enemy. In all its ramifications, military coups in Nigeria have contributed more than anything else to rob the country of its most cherished military talents.[10] The January 15, 1966 military coup spearheaded by Major Chukwuma Kaduna Nzeogwu, and which incidentally brought Major General J. T. U. Aguiyi Ironsi to power was perhaps the first attempt in which the indigenous military set upon itself in the quest to rescue the same country it has vouched to protect. The coup and its aftermath led to the deaths of the prime minister of the Federation, and some top military and political leaders from the North, West, Midwest, and one from the East.[11]

While he was not part of the original putsch, Ironsi nonetheless became a reluctant head of state if for nothing but in the interest of preserving the integrity of the state apparatus. In the following July 1966, another faction of the military elite from the North initiated a countercoup that led to so much carnage and blood-letting that one could appropriately think that they were two armies from different countries fighting against each other in a duel to the finish.[12] The countercoup was spearheaded by a group of Northern soldiers, the most prominent of whom were Lieutenant Colonel Murtala Mohammed (inspector of signals, Army), Major Theophilus Y. Danjuma (4th Battalion, Ibadan), Majors Martin Adamu (Brigade Headquarters, Apapa), Shittu Alao (staff officer, Air Force Headquarters), Baba Usman (staff officer II, Intelligence), and Abba Kyari. But generally speaking, "many other officers and men, ex-politicians, and civil servants of Northern origin were eventually involved or complicit at one stage or the other in the planning, supervision, or execution of the operations."[13] When it was all over, the commander-in-chief of the armed forces General Ironsi, and the military governor of the Western Region Lieutenant Colonel Francis Adekunle Fajuyi were dead along with more than two hundred elite soldiers, mostly Igbos from the East, at the hands of their fellow brethrens-in-arm. The demolition job was total. While then Lieutenant Colonel Yakubu Gowon became the new commander-in-chief of the armed forces, the inability of the military to resolve the widening cracks within its institution as well as other serious issues of state, eventually led to the secession of Eastern Nigeria, which became the Republic of Biafra. The ensuing carnage culminated in a fratricidal war that lasted from July 1967 to January 1970, amid the loss of millions of lives and a shattered sense of national unity.[14]

It is therefore noteworthy to touch on a few milestones relative to the January 15, 1966 coup, the July 29, 1966 countercoup, and the eventual civil war that followed. Although a lot of reasons have been given as to why the January coup occurred, it remains to be seen to what extent it was inspired by some form of revolutionary ferment. Neither the initial broadcast by Major Nzeogwu nor Adewale Ademoyega's book *Why We Struck*[15] has been able to shed a more credible insight into the genesis of the coup or the ideological underpinnings that drove it. While the 1962–1963 census controversies and the outcome of the 1964 federal elections may have contributed to the political unrest in the Western Region; one gets the sense that Nzeogwu's initial broadcast was aimed, more or less, at relieving the nation of the existing scourge of corruption, bribery, political profiteering, and brigandage. These were no new issues and everyone already knew that they pervade almost every aspect of the country's political culture. Or perhaps, they struck because of the fear that some sections of the military elite had forsaken their professional ethic, and thus, allowed themselves to be recruited into the ongoing power play between various elements of the political class. Either way, had some of the major actors not died very early in the crisis, the world would have had a deeper understanding about the true motivations for the putsch and its aftermath. Ademoyega's book, though highly instructive, does not seem to offer a convincing portrait of a full-fledged revolutionary or ideological movement, and how Nigeria of that time would have offered a most receptive political and cultural environment for its implementation. And because the coup did not succeed, we may never know how the revolutionary ideal would have unfolded in practice.

But in all its ramifications, and despite the suggestive manner in which the January coup turned out, as well as the ethnic orientation of the primary actors who were mostly Igbos, there is no indication or evidence to suggest that it was ethnically motivated. On a political level, not only did it add a new complexity to the regional political calculus; it also amplified an already increasing sense of anxiety that may have hitherto been kept under control within the military hierarchy. Because the major weakness of the coup and, invariably, its failure was in the pattern of its execution, the ensuing passion and the vengeful intent that it generated so much beclouded further debate on the issue that it would have been very difficult to grant credence to any form of ideological justification. Nonetheless, it would still be acceptable to state that a successful coup d'etat always requires good political advisers. There are few politicians, not even among the Igbos, who would have sanctioned the coup in the way it eventually unfolded. In fact, the consequent events of July 29th notwithstanding, the Igbos lost a lot as a result of the January 15 coup. Prior to the coup,

Nigeria was only five years and three months old as an independent state, but that was how long it took for the Igbos to lose their strategic footing so suddenly in the formative years of the new republic. Like other Nigerian groups, they were ejected overnight from the political and administrative hierarchy that they had occupied in the federal system during the First Republic. While the political elite quietly ruminated over the unfolding events in the country and its broader implications, many others were less discerning until a new awakening set in with a deafening virulence. The intensity of the July 29th countercoup by Northern soldiers (mostly Hausa-Fulani) was further magnified by the widespread massacre and pogrom that saw Northerners kill more than 30,000 individuals of Igbo and Eastern Nigeria origin. It was the viciousness and scope of these two events that set Nigeria on an "irreversible" collision course which, despite all efforts at resolution, it never recovered from.

One of the most widespread reasons given for the July 29 coup was the North's fear that General Ironsi's proclamation of Decree No. 34 of 1966 (otherwise known as the Unification Decree 34 of 1966) on May 24, 1966, would centralize the federal civil service, thereby making it more convenient for the more educationally disposed Igbos to dominate it. While this interpretation took on a life of its own, it eventually became a rallying cry not only against the Ironsi regime as a government, but also against his ethnic group as a form of collective guilt. But if one should look more closely at the decree itself, it offers indication of executive centralization only in name (section 3.1); but operationally, it actually decentralized authority to the new provinces that were created (as in sections 4.1, 4.2, and 4.3). And whatever could not be accommodated was allowed to remain as they were before (section 8.3). It actually granted more authority to the regional military administrators (section 2.3 and 2.4). The decree, in fact, decentralized some of the responsibilities from the national public service commission to the provincial public service commissions. Also section 8.3 of the decree stated that "Nothing in this Decree shall affect the validity of anything done before the appointed day," which meant that it was not retroactive and was not meant to change anything that was already in existence.

Instead it was more of a document for the future, but one that enhanced both the authority of the military administrators as well as the provincial public service commissions. And because the regional public service commissions had reverted into provincial commissions, each of the regions now had more public service commissions than it had during the First Republic. One weakness though in the document was its wordiness and its rather confusing redundancy. In fact, section 4.1 (which conferred appointment and promotion powers on the National Public Service Commission) duplicates the same power and authority by assigning it to the

Supreme Military Council (section 5.1). Even though section 5.1 refers primarily to the Permanent Secretaries of Government agencies, the additional provision of "or any other office of equivalent rank in the National Public Service," created further ambiguity that opened up the decree to different kinds of motives and interpretations.

There is another important factor that seems to be overlooked in most analyses of the decree. The whole concept of the document itself reflects a natural feature of military culture and practice: a natural tendency toward structure and organizational control. In the same way that "the military's orientation towards combat and special socialization processes leads to a greater concern for corporate autonomy, fear of factionalism, and an emphasis on hierarchy and chain of command; these functional requirements, in fundamental ways, do set the military apart from other institutions in society."[16] In an ironic way, General Ironsi—the man called "Ironside," may have been a victim of his own professional training and military culture; more than the propaganda surrounding the "Decree No. 34" issue that his killers used as a ruse to fell him along that desolate stream on the outskirts of Ibadan. When Lieutenant Gowon took over power following the death of Ironsi, and as the pogrom against the Igbos and Easterners continued in the North, he initiated a series of *Ad Hoc Constitutional Conferences* aimed at "stabilizing" the political situation.

The first one began in Lagos on August 12, 1966, the second on September 12, 1966, and the third on September 20, 1966—all in Lagos. Following another orgy of massacre of innocent Igbo civilians in the North on September 20, 1966, Gowon abruptly suspended the ad hoc conference and began to exercise dictatorial powers. A meeting of the Supreme Military Council and the Government of Eastern Region under then Lieutenant Colonel Odumegwu Ojukwu took place at Aburi, Ghana. The latter repudiation of the tenets of the Aburi meeting by Gowon on advice from his permanent secretaries exacerbated the tension. The conflict between the central government and the Eastern Region further escalated when Gowon on May 27, 1967, created twelve new states out of the existing four regions. Ojukwu responded by declaring the Eastern Region as the *Republic of Biafra* as it seceded from the federation. The ensuing war began on July 6, 1967, and formerly ended on January 15, 1970, following Biafra's defeat. In the end, more than 2 million lives were lost and the fortune of a whole generation squandered. Despite all odds, Gowon and Ojukwu had ample opportunity to resolve the crisis without further bloodshed, but their personal dispositions toward each other would not let them put their egos behind them in the pursuit of a course nobler than the feelings of two individuals. As the chief protagonists, both men, therefore, must accept a greater responsibility as to why resort to war was the only available option despite earlier efforts and other opportunities at resolving the crisis.

THE AFTERMATH AND GROWING PAINS

At the end of the war, the factionalization within the military class remained even more obdurate. For this reason alone, the rather unrestrained incursions of the Nigerian military into political leadership cannot be dismissed solely on such simplistic assumptions as selfish whims or individual lust for power. It represents the external vestiges of an internal power struggle between two major elite groups that emerged in the military at the end of the civil war (Nigeria-Biafra war). While the Igbos who had occupied a majority of the officer cadre and engineer corps of the army were effectively neutralized as a result of the July 1966 countercoup and also the civil war, the vacuum created led to a power contest between the traditional military wing from the core North (controlled by the Kaduna Mafia),[17] and a progressive military wing from the Middle Belt region (controlled by the Langtang gang).

While the countercoup of July 1966 was meant to reassert Northern control of the country, the subsequent Murtala Muhammed coup of July 1975 that overthrew the regime of Yakubu Gowon (a Middle Belter) was said to have been meant to reestablish the political authority of the "Kaduna Mafia." It should equally be noted that Gowon, who hails from the Middle Belt Plateau state which is the domain of the "Langtang gang," was never really considered the "great white knight" of the North, simply because he is a Christian and also did not belong to the dominant Hausa-Fulani oligarchy. Nonetheless, the abortive Dimka/Bisalla coup of February 1976 in which General Murtala Muhammed was also killed seemed to be a desperate attempt by the "Langtang gang" to retake control of the military institution and the power of the state that goes with it. Consequently, scores of Middle Belt officers who were implicated in the coup were executed.

When the Buhari-Idiagbon clique came to power in December 1983 after overthrowing the democratically elected government of Shehu Shagari, some of the draconian steps that it took to address the endemic corruption and waste in the country ran head on to the traditional interest of the "Kaduna Mafia," and it reacted. On August 17, 1985, the Buhari-Idiagbon regime came to a crashing end, and the Ibrahim Babangida regime took over the reins of government. However, over the course of the Babangida regime, the "Langtang gang" struck twice, first by the General Vatsa "attempted" coup which was supposed to take effect on December 17, 1985, barely four months after Babangida came to power. General Mamman Vatsa was the minister for the Federal Capital Territory of Abuja and a member of the Armed Forces Ruling Council. A second coup against the Babangida regime took place on April 22, 1990, this time led by the dashing Major Gideon Orkar. Both coup attempts failed and the "Langtang" faction of the military, including several military officers from the then Bendel State (now split into Edo and Delta states) paid very dearly due to the consequent executions.

General Babangida's reign ended in June 1993 when he handed over power to an Interim National Government headed by Ernest Shonekan, but the ensuing political crisis paved the way for General Sani Abacha (then minister of defense in the Interim Government) to initiate a coup de grace and smoothly eased himself into the mantle of Nigeria's political leadership. His regime was further strengthened as a result of wholesale purges within the military hierarchy. However, the selective nature of these purges indicated that a greater proportion of those removed or prematurely retired from the military were from the Middle Belt (domain of the Langtang gang), and some from the Southwest, but were mostly Christians. Abacha's rule was characterized by a high-handedness that has remained unparalleled in the annals of Nigeria's military history. Through arbitrary arrests, murder, and police brutality, he was able to muscle and brutalize the opposition into silence.

Even members of his own military were not spared on the slightest suspicion. On March 1, 1995, a group of army officers led by Colonel Lawan Gwadabe were arrested on alleged charges of plotting a violent overthrow of the Abacha regime. Some were sentenced to life, and others for various jail terms. On December 27, another group of army officers including Abacha's second-in-command Lt. General Oladipo Diya who was the army's chief of general staff, were arrested for allegedly plotting to overthrow the government. In all, the special military tribunal tried thirty accused persons. Six were found guilty of treason and conspiracy and were sentenced to death, four received life imprisonment, while six were sentenced to various jail terms. Fourteen were acquitted. However, while all denied the charges against them as a calculated ploy to eliminate "imaginary" enemies, the executions never took place because they were pardoned and released by General Abdulsalam Abubakar, who had become the new head of state after the death of General Abacha on June 8, 1998. Nonetheless, it can appropriately be stated that each military regime in Nigeria has followed essentially three processes: legitimacy crisis, grand idealism, and decay or revolt (table 6.1):

Legitimacy Crisis: As Fatton[18] points out, legitimacy crisis activates infra-politics, a realm where the people create a political world of their own and where they ridicule the wisdom of the rulers. "The temper of legitimacy crisis which Nigerians call, *political impasse*, is beyond the political realm. It is as if the rulers declared war on those they ruled; but they blew harsh flutes instead of the mellifluous music of good company."[19] As the particular regime tries to proffer some basic reasons to justify its taking

Table 6.1. Trajectory of Praetorian Rule in Nigeria, 1966–1999: From Inception to Decline

Leader (s)	Legitimacy (Entry)	Grand Idealism	Decay or Revolt
Aguiyi Ironsi (January–July 1966)	Coup de grace	National stability and unity, Centralization of Public service	Overthrown and killed barely six months in office.
Yakubu Gowon (July 1966–July 1975)	Coup d'etat	Reconstruction, Rehabilitation, and Reconciliation, (NYSC)	Overthrown in a bloodless coup.
Murtala Muhammed/ Olusegun Obasanjo (July 1975–Oct 1979)	Coup d'etat	Probity in government, Accountability	Muhammed killed in an abortive coup in February 1976. Obasanjo takes over, rules for about three years and hands over to a civilian government in October 1979.
Buhari/Idiagbon (Dec 1983–Aug 1985)	Coup d'etat	War Against Indiscipline (Social Engineering)	Overthrown in a palace coup.
Ibrahim Babangida (August 1985–June 1993)	Palace coup	Economic reconstruction, Social justice, Self-reliance; War Against Indiscipline and corruption, SAP	Survived two aborted coups, scores of plotters executed. Hands over to a civilian-led Interim National Government following much public protest.
Sani Abacha (November 1993–June 1998)	Coup de grace	Sultanistic inclinations, Vision 2010	Survived two "alleged" coup plots. Massive corruption and graft. Economy and national reputation in shambles. Died in office on June 8, 1998, of natural causes.
Abdulsalam Abubakar (June 1998–May 1999)	Selected by the Provisional Ruling Council after death of Abacha	Pledged to return nation to democracy and elected government	Buoyed by international pressure and public agitation, handed over to a civilian elected government of Olusegun Obasanjo on May 29, 1999. (General Obasanjo was a former military Head of State who ruled Nigeria from February 1976 to October 1, 1979.)

over political authority, it also launches a massive public relations program to coopt various domestic and international interests for support.

As Hannah Arendt points out,[20] "power needs no justification, being inherent in the very existence of political communities; what it does need is legitimacy." The Aguiyi Ironsi regime came to power in order to *restore national stability and unity*, the Murtala Muhammed regime took over the government to stamp out *corruption* and to lay the groundwork for a return to *civilian rule*, while the Sani Abacha regime came to power under the guise of seeking to stem the ensuing tide of *political anarchy*. The above are some of the common justifications that have oftentimes been put forth as the basis for the military intrusion into the political domain. In a 1979 address entitled *The Military Regime and the Nigerian Society*,[21] then Brigadier Joseph Garba (former commander of the Federal Guards who led the overthrow of the Yakubu Gowon regime), stated that much of the military's popular acceptance or legitimacy was attributable to its self-proclaimed transitional tenure in power, deriving its vitality from a self-image of a "hard-headed and practical approach" which was at the same time "symbolic of the revolutionary tradition."

Grand Idealism: The utility of an idealistic approach to praetorian governance is that it enables the regime to create a public perception that it has indeed isolated a key national problematic and is actually leading the way in taking concrete steps to remedy it. It also provides the regime a rallying cry for shaping popular support as well as a basis for evoking nationalistic or patriotic sympathies. A concerted advocacy for a grand idealism warrants the regime a basis for public acceptability and the concomitant legitimacy that goes with it. The Gowon regime presented a plan for national reconstruction after the war; the Murtala Muhammed regime presented its framework for an African-oriented foreign policy, the creation of more states as a politically balancing act, and the quest for probity and accountability in public service; the Buhari/Idiagbon regime opted for a new code for public morality (the War Against Indiscipline); while the Babangida regime presented its MAMSER (Mass Mobilization for Social Justice, Self-Reliance, and Economic Recovery). The Abacha regime while still battling with its program for a return to civilian rule in 1998, inaugurated its Vision 2010—a grand design aimed at ensuring a progressive economic growth and stable democratic governance that would propel Nigeria into the dawn of the twenty-first century and beyond.

Decay or Revolt: The only military regimes in Nigeria that have peacefully handed over political power to an elected civilian government are the Obasanjo and Abubakar regimes. Others have essentially been removed by forceful means, except for the Abacha regime. As the socioeconomic condition of the state continues to decline, the consequent decay is used as another excuse by a segment of the military to strike once again at the political center, as one regime replaces another. The military life cycle in Nigeria typically seems to follow a bell-shaped curve. First, is its entrance into political governance and coveting of civic loyalty; second, as it solidifies its hold on executive authority, its political and economic power rises until it reaches critical mass; and finally, either by internal dissension or public outcry, it abdicates or is overthrown by another military clique. Under the same token, the absence of effective political institutions in Nigeria generates a condition in which power is fragmented, and in which authority and office are easily acquired and lost.

THE PRAETORIAN MODEL

Although literature on praetorianism delineates distinct types or models,[22] there is a general agreement that a praetorian society is one in which the military has established itself not only as a power broker in terms of current political discourse, but also as the primary institution responsible for the authoritative allocation of values in society. As Amos Perlmutter points out, a praetorian society is one in which the military plays a disproportionately large political role, such that it has a greater tendency than is found in the Western democracies to intervene in politics, and to dominate the executive.[23] Such a role for the military in Third world societies is a function of the weak level of development of civilian political institutions that normally would subordinate the military to civilian purposes.[24] Perlmutter further delineates the general social and political conditions that contribute to praetorianism.[25]

At the social level, he indicates: low degree of social cohesion—due to ethnicity and primordial attachments; the existence of fratricidal classes—the bottom, middle, and top classes that are always in conflict; social polarity and unconsolidated middle class, ineffective, and politically impotent; recruitment and mobilization of resources—the lack of commonly valued patterns of action and symbols toward mobilization for social and political action. From the early days of the Nigerian state, primordial inclinations presented the main obstacle to a broad-based sociopolitical consensus. The ethnification of national politics and the inordinate desire to interpret every aspect of national issues from ethnocentric prisms has remained the bane of the state. Crozier et al.[26] contend that the viability of democracy in a country is related to the social structure and social trends in that country; and as such a society deeply divided between two or more polarized ethnic or regional groups would not be conducive to democracy. The ethnic cleavages between the three major groups in Nigeria (the Hausa-Fulani, Igbo, and Yoruba) has tended to diminish an objective and impersonal evaluation of internal political structures and objectives, thus shifting the focus of public interest, not on the condition of the state per se, but on what it can provide to each of the contending groups.

It would not be an overstatement to state that "in Nigeria, a mix of tribal loyalties and intertribal animosities permeates the whole society."[27] In the early years following independence, there were three major political parties, the National Council of Nigerian Citizens (NCNC), the Action Group (AG), and the Northern Peoples Congress. There was fierce competition between them for control of the central government. "As in most new nations, the initial stages of modernization tended to exacerbate traditional conflicts and intensify primordial sentiments, which more often than not, express themselves in violence. But they were felt in the army even more strongly because the requirements of cooperation, obedience, and command were more intense within the military than in society at large, hence antagonisms were amplified."[28] It was under this atmosphere that some portions of the military elite became coopted into the political activities of regional politicians, and remained ever more willing to do their bidding. The power to "socialize to national identity" of the army, thus became very weak.

At the political level, Perlmutter cites above all, the inter-class conflict between center-periphery; low level of political institutionalization and lack of sustained support for political structures; weak and ineffective political parties; and frequent civilian intervention in the military. "In most cases, civilians turn to the military for political support when civilian political structures and institutions fail, when factionalism develops, and when constitutional means for the conduct of political action are lacking."[29] Perhaps, it was the suspected military-politicians partnership that formed part of the undercurrent for the January 1966 coup. The aborted Major Orkar coup of April 1990 was also alleged to have been funded by a civilian fisheries magnate known as Great Ovedje Ogboru, an Urhobo who hails from Abraka, in Ethiope Local Government Area of then Bendel State (now split into Edo and Delta states). When General Babangida ended his reign in June 1993 and handed power over to an Interim National Government headed by a civilian Ernest Shonekan, he created a constitutional as well as a political crisis. It was under this atmosphere that key members of the political elite, especially those not favored by the emerging dispensation called for the military to step in.

According to Ebenezer Babatope[30] who claims to be a "progressive revolutionary," but later became a minister of transportation in the General Abacha regime, "the Abacha coup of November 17, 1993, was not an ordinary coup, but was a coup that had a lot of direct input by civilians. Many politicians were involved in inviting the military in." He states that "the June 12 crisis was becoming so serious that many people started nursing the genuine fear of a possible disintegration of the country. Some felt that the military should be made to come and effect solutions to the problem a section of it had created with the June 12 palaver. Newspapers in Nigeria had their pages flooded with open invitations to the military to reenter the stage by removing the Interim National Government."[31] Bolaji Akinyemi, a former External Affairs minister in the General Babangida regime, and even M. K. O. Abiola himself, were also mentioned as people who had made overt calls for the military to take over the government. This was one of those rare situations when the military never fails to answer what it considers a "legitimate" call. It matters very little how far corporate hypocrisy may have eaten away at the sole of genuine patriotism, especially when the military is considered as a "savior" and as guardian of the state. On July 19, 1993, General Sani Abacha gave an address to senior military officers at the National War College in Lagos, in which he made the following statement:

> The success of the military profession depends on the disciplined subordination of the officers and men of the armed forces to the Constitution of the Federal Republic of Nigeria that we have all sworn to uphold. Thus you must resist all attempts to be used by unpatriotic people to subvert the Constitution. It is your cardinal duty to defend the Constitution. The nation, and indeed the whole world expect no less of you.[32]

Ironically, on November 17, 1993, General Sani Abacha, having suddenly become oblivious to the above oath, overthrew the Interim National Government and took over the reins of political power. "Military rhetoric in the twentieth century has kept alive the image of the army as the guardian of all the values and historical constants of the people to which it belongs."[33]

In fact, looking at Nordlinger's[34] typology of praetorian military intervention in which he distinguished between praetorian moderators, guardians, and rulers, the Nigerian brand of praetorianism seems to approximate his "praetorian guardians." This is also informed by the fact that none of the military regimes in Nigeria has been revolutionary in nature, but have essentially opted to make incremental modifications within the dominant institutional framework. Nordlinger points out that praetorian guardians take governmental control in order to preserve the status quo, but also aim to correct socioeconomic malpractice and deficiencies. Praetorian guardians generally have a bias against mass political activity, and find it unnecessary to create a mobilization regime capable of penetrating the population.

It is well understood that by allowing the creation of political institutions and other infrastructures of political mobilization such as secondary associations, interest groups, or professional organizations, the praetorian regime would have implicitly laid the foundation for popular political dissent against it. Thus by defining the scope and parameters of civil expression, the praetorian regime not only exercises maximum control, but also remains in a powerful position to scuttle any semblance of organized resistance to its supremacy.

One can only point to the General Abacha regime that lasted from November 1993 to June 1998, as one of the most brutal in the history of Nigeria's experience with military rule. The U.S. Department of State's release on "Nigeria: Country Report on Human Rights Practices for 1996," provide a catalogue of endemic human rights abuses during the Abacha regime. Under him, the supposed winner of the annulled June 1993 presidential election was charged with treason, after having arbitrarily declared himself the president of the country. He was put in detention where he eventually died on July 7, 1998. On October 6, 1995, hired assassins suspected of being security agents of the regime gunned down Alfred Rewane, a key prodemocracy activist, in his house. On November 10, 1995, an Ogoni activist Ken Saro Wiwa and eight other members of the Ogoni tribe were hanged for alleged anti-government and subversive activities. They were charged with being responsible for the deaths of four Ogoni chiefs whose charred and broken bodies were found in a burnt out automobile. On June 4, 1996, Kudirat Abiola, the feisty wife of M. K. O Abiola, the business tycoon believed by some to have won the June 1993 presidential election, was murdered by assassins thought to be agents of the Abacha regime. The government conducted a perfunctory investigation of the murder that included the detention of leading National Democratic Coalition (NADECO) activists and Abiola family members. All were later released. Even Alex Ibru, publisher of the Guardian, one of the country's leading newspapers, who also became a civilian Minister of Internal Affairs in the Abacha regime, was also shot and permanently injured by gunmen.

Amid many political and extra-judicial killings, the government continued to enforce its arbitrary authority through the federal security apparatus (the military, the state security service, and the national police force) and through decrees blocking action by the opposition in the courts. The right of habeas corpus was suspended; political prisoners were given long jail terms or death sentences, and the courts could no more be relied upon to deliver an impartial justice. Though academic freedom was generally respected, security forces routinely monitor and on occasion break up conferences they perceived as forums for pro-democracy groups. A few days before the sudden death of General Sani Abacha, the Joint Action Committee of Nigeria, a group of thirty-five human rights and prodemocracy organizations had planned a March on June 4 and 12, 1998, to commemorate the assassination of Kudirat Abiola, and the annulment of the

June 19993 elections, respectively. The Nigerian police immediately instituted a ban on a series of mass protest actions planned by the opposition
coalition against military rule. In fact, the Lagos state police commissioner
Abubakar Tsav announced that his forces would not allow any marches
to be held, and warned parents not to allow their children to associate
themselves with such protests.

Constitutional provisions providing for freedom of speech and the
press were not enforced because of continued suspension of constitutional
rights. Journalists were constantly harassed, jailed, or murdered, as in the
case of the famed journalist Ray Ekpu who had died a couple of years
earlier during the Babangida regime, when a letter bomb exploded in his
face. Security forces used permit requirements as one of the justifications
for their regular practice of disrupting pro-democracy conferences, book
introductions, and seminars. While permits are not normally required
for public meetings indoors, and permit requirements for outdoor public
functions are often ignored by both government authorities and those as-
sembling, the Abacha government retained legal provisions adopted by
the General Babangida government, banning gatherings whose political,
ethnic, or religious content it believed might lead to unrest. The political
witch-hunt also extended to organized labor. The government employed
a variety of tactics to divide and intimidate labor. "Although basic labor
legislation dating to 1974 remained in place, decrees enacted in 1994
that dissolved elected national executive councils of the Nigerian Labor
Congress (NLC) and two key oil sector unions (The National Union of
Petroleum and Natural Gas Workers, and the Petroleum and Natural Gas
Senior Staff Association) and placed them under the authority of govern-
ment-appointed sole administrators."[35]

The unfolding dynamic very much captured the essence of Samuel
Huntington's account, pointing out that because "there are no political institutions, no corps of professional political leaders are broadly recognized
or accepted as the legitimate intermediaries to moderate group conflict,
or to decide the procedures to be used for the allocation of office and the
determination of policy, social forces are more apt to confront each other
with increasing rapidity and virulence."[36] It ensures that any agreement
on national priorities would be severely contested as a zero-sum game, issues and choices polarized along ethnic and religious lines, and economic
interests hijacked to reflect the welfare of those in positions of authority as
well as those in the upper echelons of the social strata. Amid this state of
affairs, each group undoubtedly employs means which reflect its peculiar
nature and capabilities: the wealthy bribe, students riot, workers strike,
mobs demonstrate, and the military coup.[37] Thus, the praetorian regime
instead of maintaining order and stability has the potential to exacerbate
the crisis into a state of *anomie*. As Thomas Pickering, then U.S. under

secretary of state for political affairs, remarked in his speech delivered at the *Council on Foreign Relations' Conference on Nigeria*, on January 30, 1998, "It seems evident that after 30-plus years of being in charge the military has failed to bring enduring stability to Nigeria. It has fostered division over diversity and patronage over patriotism."

Ogbu Kalu[38] argues that, "the praetorian culture is characterized by patrimonialism, politics of the belly, clientelism, and corruption. Instead of a legal rational authority, the patrimonial system borrows its idiom from primal society: the personal self and the official are not distinguished; loyalty is a core value and is encapsulated within the distribution of patronage, as a hegemonic alliance of reciprocal elites welds the dominant class." In Nigeria under the Abacha regime, "corruption turned into looting the public treasury. It is estimated that he left an estate worth $10 billion, and a vast business empire controlled by his son and Lebanese brother-in-laws under the corporate name of *Chougry and Chougry*."[39] To explore only the outer edges of praetorian patrimony in Nigeria, one only has to read a report by *Tell Magazine*.[40] It concerns the construction of a steel mill in Nigeria known as the Ajaokuta steel. The Russians were the main contractors, and the government of Nigeria owed them $2.5 billion dollars. Abacha's son negotiated to buy the loan and paid half-billion dollars to the Russians. But he gave the federal government a bill for the full sum and kept 2 billion dollars, all in one contract deal. He forced Ministers to pay him money in order to gain access to his father. The mother also controlled importation of petroleum products into the country, and in order to support her business, the government simply refused to pay for the turnaround maintenance of the country's four refineries. While cars queued for miles to buy petroleum in an oil-producing nation, the scarcity enabled Mrs. Abacha to sustain a monopoly on this trade and to amass untold profits. General Abacha died suddenly on June 8, 1998.

On May 26, 1999, his immediate successor General Abdulsalam Abubakar confiscated unto the government what many believe was a fraction of the embezzled and misappropriated wealth of the Abacha regime. The government recovered US$625,000,000, £25,000,000, N100,000,000 in local currency (Naira), a host of other choice and prime property and real estate scattered all over the country. Millions of dollars were also recovered from Minister of Finance Anthony Ani, Security Chief Ismaila Gwarzo, and one of Abacha's own sons. National largesse was also extended far beyond Abacha's family circle. As Arthur Nwankwo argues,[41] "we have a situation where new military dictators court, persuade, wine, dine, and place in strategic national positions old dictators they accused of various sins, crimes and misdemeanors, some of which are unarguably treasonable." He cites the case of General Yakubu Gowon who was overthrown in August 1975 on the basis of his government being "corrupt, aimless, and drifting," but was consequently and fully rehabilitated and given strategic chairmanship positions in key national economic and health institutions.

There is also that of General Muhammadu Buhari whose overthrow as head of state was announced by General Sani Abacha, but was later appointed the chairman of the Petroleum Trust Fund (PTF), a virtual alternate government with over N800 billion (local currency worth billions of dollars) to disburse and contract out as it so desires. Over the years, "an increasing number of retired senior military officers have found themselves appointed to the governing councils or boards of important government agencies, investment companies and industrial concerns, including banks where the government had controlling shares."[42] "With the trend towards privatization and commercialization initiated under the structural adjustment program (SAP), many state-owned economic concerns have been sold-off to the rich and influential including retired military officers or to currently serving officers through their surrogates."[43] As a consequence, many retired military officers have emerged as dominant figures in certain sectors of private business, industry, and agriculture. In Nigeria, military officers have become economic entrepreneurs—a factor that has sustained them as a potent force in the ongoing struggle for control of the political space.

MILITARY LORDS AND CIVIC SUBORDINATION

The Nigerian military has over the years become politically savvy. They have mastered one basic principle of control, and that is, to cut off all three heads of the Hydra at the same time and let the body to die a slow but painful death. For example, over a three-month period between July 1994 and September 1994, the oil union workers and the Nigerian Labor Congress went on strike in protest to the military regime of Sani Abacha over its arrest of M. K. O. Abiola and other leaders of the pro-democracy movement. The strike essentially paralyzed the economic sector including the export of oil (which is the main revenue earner for the country), and if it had continued a little longer, many believed it would have effectively brought down the military regime.

However, in order to forestall further damage from the strike as well as continued erosion of its authority, the military simply arrested or immobilized the elite leadership of the oil workers union, the Nigerian Labor Congress, the pro-democracy movements; it issued retroactive decrees,[44] arrested hundreds of demonstrators, and as many as three hundred persons were believed to have been shot dead by security forces. As the masses looked up to the elite leadership of their organizations to set the action premises, none was forthcoming. The protest movement either evaporated, went underground, as many of the leaders were coopted by the military into the mainstream of political power. A particularly interesting example was the case of Bana Kingibe who was the vice presidential candidate under the presidential ticket of M. K. O. Abiola when they ran in the June 1993 elections. The election was immediately annulled, thus paving the way for General Sani Abacha to become head of state. As soon as Abacha took over the reins of government, he coopted Baba Kingibe to become his Foreign minister, the latter exhibiting little quiver to the brutality meted out to Abiola. Furthermore, because Abiola had flown out of the country on a self-imposed exile, only to return to the country many months later, "his long absence from Nigeria afforded opponents of the pro-June 12, 1993 election the opportunity not only to consolidate their power, but also to bribe into submission some of the key leaders of the June 12 (pro-democracy) movement."[45]

In fact, the shameless ease with which so-called pro-democracy and "June 12" activists in Nigeria abandoned the struggle for democracy to join the conservative military junta of General Sani Abacha in November 1993 shows the opportunistic character of the power elite in Africa in general.[46] While the elite may have provided the vast majority of the leaders of the pro-democracy movements, their involvement in these movements was mainly a tactical maneuver;[47] hence, to the extent the masses looked up to them for leadership, therein lay their vulnerability. The political, economic, and military elites make up the political class in Nigeria. It makes very little difference whether they are in or out of office, or whether they profess for the masses today or remain indifferent tomorrow. The corporate interest that unites the elite system, and the intimacy of power between the praetorian state and the political elite, makes the emergence of civil society impossible. When the Nigerian elite preach democracy, they mean "economic democracy," even as the unsuspecting masses campaign and stampede for civil democracy. The gap in elite-mass linkage has grown wider ever since. Robert Putnam[48] makes a good case when he argues that the degree of concordance between mass preferences and elite actions in doubtless, as long as such preferences are dictated by elite values. Accepting the fact that effective mobilization is always interactive, and in many post-independence societies, a consequence of this elite-mass gap is the progressive parochialization of national elites.[49]

In the absence of any obvious external threat to the security of the state, the Nigerian military has continued to redefine its role as the sole instrument for maintaining internal security and unity. The "old professionalism" of safeguarding the state from external aggression, has now been replaced by the "new professionalism" of maintaining internal order and unity (table 6.2). Under the guise of saving the state from inevitable

Table 6.2. Contrasting Paradigms: The Old Professionalism of External Defense, the New Professionalism of Internal Security and National Development

	Old Professionalism	*New Professionalism*
Function of the military	External Security	Internal Security
Civilian attitudes toward government	Civilians accept legitimacy of government	Segments of society challenge government legitimacy
Military skills required	Highly specialized skills, incompatible with political skills	Highly interrelated political and military skills
Scope of military professional action	Restricted	Unrestricted
Impact of professional socialization	Renders the military politically neutral	Politicizes the military
Impact on civil-military relations	Contributes to an apolitical military and civilian control	Contributes to military-political managerialism and role expansion

Source: Alfred Stepan, "The New Professionalism of Internal Warfare and Military Role-Expansion," in Alfred Stepan, ed., *Authoritarian Brazil* (New Haven, Conn.: Yale University Press, 1973), 53.

anarchy, military insubordination is nonetheless excused as a moral calling. A close analysis of the emergence of these regimes underscores the fact that this "new professionalism" figured prominently in the military's self-justification for their vastly expanded role in politics.[50] On October 1, 1974, the then military head of state General Yakubu Gowon made an Independence Day broadcast to the nation. He had ruled the country for almost eight years, and this was at the peak of the oil boom when the country was awash in wealth and prosperity. Instead of announcing to the nation his plans for the resurrection of political activities in preparation for a return to civilian democratic rule, read his explanation for hanging on to power even as his government was bedeviled by corruption and other excesses:

> Our own assessment of the situation as of now is that it will be utterly irresponsible to leave the nation in the lurch by a precipitate withdrawal which will certainly throw the nation back into confusion. Therefore the Supreme Military Council, after careful deliberation and full consultation with the hierarchy of the armed forces and police, have decided that the target date of 1976 is in the circumstances unrealistic and that it would indeed amount to a betrayal of trust to adhere rigidly to that target date.[51]

Amid rising inflation, high cost of living, and a general public frustration at the indefinite postponement of the end of military rule, a series of labor strikes in vital areas of the economy created hardship both for the

public and private sectors. On July 29, 1975, Yakubu Gowon was overthrown while he was attending an Organization of African Unity summit
conference in Kampala, Uganda. He was replaced by one of his lieutenants, thirty-eight-year-old Brigadier Murtala Muhammed who was formerly the inspector of signals and the commissioner of communications.
Muhammed's first statement to the nation was not far removed from the
usual pretexts, and it read thus:

> The armed forces came to the conclusion that certain changes were inevitable.
> After the civil war the affairs of the state, hitherto a collective responsibility,
> became characterized by lack of consultations, indecision, indiscipline and
> even neglect. Indeed, the public became disillusioned and disappointed—the
> trend was clearly incompatible with the philosophy and image of our cor-
> rective regime. The nation was thus being plunged inexorably into chaos. It
> was obvious that matters could not, and should not, be allowed to continue
> in this way.[52]

It had become obvious to Nigerians that while the military has its "reasons" for taking over political power, it nonetheless invokes the "chaos
theory" argument simply to acknowledge its role as the primary arbiter of
internal security and national unity. It often plays on this fear to justify a
hard-nosed, centralized and undemocratic regime. "Yet these factors only
constitute an incomplete explanation of why the military chose to strike;
they do not reveal the logic of the timing and substance of the coup."[53]
Nonetheless, and in its limited history, the Murtala regime attained
remarkable successes in many areas. He reorganized the national bureaucracy, introduced more stringent fiscal responsibility in governance,
attacked corruption and incompetence, and pursued a more vigorous
African-focused foreign policy. Barely six months in office, Lieutenant
Colonel Burkar Dimka assassinated him in an aborted coup. General
Olusegun Obasanjo, who was the chief of staff, Supreme Headquarters,
assumed the mantle of leadership, and ruled from February 1976 to October 1979, before handing over power to the civilian elected government
of Alhaji Shehu Shagari.

In many of the military coups, it would later become obvious that personality conflicts, uncontrollable egos, and internal policy disagreements,
have been the major inspiration. A good case would be the Babangida
coup of August 1985, which overthrew the Buhari-Idiagbon regime, the
abortive Mamman Vatsa coup of December 1985, and the failed Gideon
Orkar coup of April 22, 1990, both directed against the Babangida regime.
General Babangida was a member of the Armed Forces Ruling Council in
the Buhari-Idiagbon regime, and Vatsa was a friend and the Minister of
Federal Capital Territory in the Babangida regime. The personality conflict and policy disagreements within the Armed Forces Ruling Council

culminated in a tragic ending, when Vatsa was executed for plotting to overthrow the regime.

PATHWAYS TO CIVIC SOLDIERING

The Nigerian military has become very comfortable with political governance, and when officers and commanders are seen carrying fashionable "walking sticks" to inspect military commands and on various public occasions, they essentially exhibit the same "grandeur" and vanity that has become typical of the equally maligned civilian political class. One is always baffled at the ease in which the distinction between traditional military ethos and political governance is discarded with very little credence given to the institutional boundaries that separate them. In Nigeria, military officers rarely retire from the domain of the state; they simply change occupations. When soldiers operate in the political arena, they are in a different territory. A military regime, whether popular or scorned, cherishes very minimal or no opposition to its rule. To achieve this outcome, the Nigerian military is aided by its coercive power (control over the means of destruction), the nature of political participation, the unitary state system, budgetary monopoly, and political education

Coercive Power and Monologic Autocracy

The Nigerian military has on many occasions demonstrated its willingness to use force to quell political protests, and to govern by means of arbitrary and retroactive decrees. The military's concern about maintaining the national integrity of "the postwar state led it to establish rigid, dogmatic distinctions between progressive versus atavistic administration. Progressive administration is civil and democratic, while atavistic nonprogressive administration is command-oriented, hierarchical, and militarized."[54] By abolishing the constitution, the military takes the first step in the nullification of the primary institutions of civil government, and along with it, the concomitant liberties that undergird civil political expression. By means of arrests, elite cooptation, bribery, manipulating the contours of the national political agenda, murder and intimidation, the military is able to scuttle, or at least delay the emergence of a stable democratic framework. Some have argued that the three-month worker's strike in Nigeria, which extended from July to the end of September 1994, represented a new awakening of "civil society."[55] To the extent that the military reacted quickly, by arresting the most vocal leaders of the pro-democracy movement, shutting down universities and media houses, tightened security around the country, and expanded its cooptation network,[56] the basis for the emergence of civil society and its various expressions[57] came to an abrupt end.

Although lacking in the political art of governance, the Nigerian military has been able to legitimize its political footing by engaging in a strategy of sharing administrative functions with civilian employees while retaining executive and policy making control,[58] either through the Supreme Military Council, or the Armed Forces Ruling Council. By controlling the executive and policy making functions, the military is able to neutralize various social forces such as labor movements, the press, professional organizations, and scores of other secondary organizations that could provide the catalyst for mass political mobilization. The monologic autocracy of military reasoning negates the ingredients necessary for a broad-based consensus on critical national issues. It is therefore difficult to see how basically undemocratic military regimes can school civil politicians in the ways and manner of democratic rule.[59]

The Nature of Political Participation

It can be argued that love of country and service to mankind may not be the over-riding force that inspires the average Nigerian political aspirant. Here is a situation in which state office is sought for its instrumental role as a means to an end, but not necessarily as an end in itself. To the extent that motivation for public office is premised on self-interest, greed, and patronage, the moral basis for seeking public office becomes irredeemably flawed, and so is everything that comes thereafter. Even those who maim, kill, and plunder in the name of political participation or campaign, are on average driven more by hysteria and primitive ecstasy than by a serious rationalization of the political stakes.

Furthermore, due to the current adverse economic condition in the country, the uncelebrated entry of much of the "middle class" into the rural caste has no doubt contributed considerably to the near absence of a consistently powerful grass-roots mass-driven political consciousness. The importance of economic welfare seems to have taken precedent over pressing political imperatives. This new development, however, is not without cause. According to A. A. Ujo, the civil war period (1967–1970) coincided with the "oil boom," when the basic necessities of life were available in sufficient quantities, while the sudden increase in wealth in the early 1970s caught the people by surprise.[60] There was a sudden rise in the number of people who were brought into the modern sector, who in turn needed goods and services. But while development in public services like public transportation, banks, post offices, and social services lagged behind, a situation of bottlenecks developed around these services, which in turn led to jungle laws where only the fittest survived. This was the beginning of moral decay as each sought his own way of getting what he wants. More often than not, political participation has become a means to an instrumental end rather a sincere and substantive national quest. Generally, most members of the elite class as well as a cross section of the mass public opt for politics as a means of economic salvation to the extent that it would lead to lucrative contracts, official appointments, access to powerful personalities, or as a means to secure a position that gives one access to public plunder and corrupt practices.

This situation is also confounded by the low average growth in literacy rate, thereby making it possible for the cosmopolitan elite to hijack mass political expression and personify it in terms of "politics of personality." Joseph Lapalombara[61] has argued that it is difficult enough for citizens to sort out issues, evaluate candidates, and otherwise prepare themselves for meaningful electoral participation in countries of wide literacy; but where illiteracy is the rule, the probability is sharply raised that an entrenched elite will be able to manipulate voters pretty much as they please. In Nigeria today, there are formal and informal factors that inhibit as well as dictate the structure of mass political opportunity. Military doctrinaire seem to have seriously affected attempts to create secondary associations at the mass level, as distinguished from primary associations such as family, neighborhood organizations, schools, or churches. But before citizens can vote, or even run for public office, the act of participation must first pass military scrutiny and approval. These notwithstanding, a variety of informal factors also determine whether people will actually exercise this right when given. For example, rural residents may in many cases be disadvantaged regarding easy access to information that might spur participation. This is partly due to the absence of effective mass political parties as agents of mass political indoctrination (that could convert parochial objectives into public goals); widespread illiteracy in the rural sector; fewer mobility channels and the lack of bureaucratized patterns of political recruitment.[62]

The "Unitary" State System

The centralizing nature of the Nigerian state makes it more amenable to dictatorial military rule than to a democratic government. While this observation may be challenged in terms of the moral imperative that it evokes, suffice it to say that it is driven more by practical realism than by any other relevant value criteria. The centralized nature of federal executive authority concentrates overwhelming power at the political center. And so, as soon as the military wrestles the center from civilian authorities, they can easily exercise absolute control. The nature of the executive branch and the various obligations that accrue to it, in fact, makes it possible and even tempting for military takeover. The preponderance of authority and functions at the executive level has indeed become legendary.

Today, there are three branches of the Nigerian government: federal, state, and local governments. However, real authority resides at the federal level either through the Federal Executive Council as the premier policy making body of the country, or through the Council of States, which is also an appendage of the Federal Executive Council. We can examine the scope of authority reposed in the executive branch of the Nigerian government. Among these are the Executive Office of the President, Ministries and Departments, Public Enterprises and Parastatals, Council of States, Code of Conduct Bureau, Federal Civil Service Commission, Federal Judicial Service Commission, National Boundaries Commission, National Defense Council, National Economic Council, National Population Control, National Primary Education Policy, Revenue Mobilization Allocation and Fiscal Commission, the National Security Council, the Nigerian Police Command, Public Complaint Commission.[63] In addition, the headquarters of the major national ministries or agencies are housed in a single administrative complex (the Secretariat). Hence, as soon as the military takes over political authority, it becomes quite expedient and possible for it to quickly establish a chokehold on the critical nerves of government.

Budgetary Monopoly

Generally, the idea of Nigeria as a *rentier state*,[64] means that the greater majority of state revenues accrue from taxes or "rents" on production, rather than from productive activity. Taxes and "rents" collected from oil exploration in Nigeria account for about 90 percent of total government revenue. The primary national agency responsible for the oil economy is the Nigerian National Petroleum Corporation (NNPC), which is essentially under the control of the Executive Branch. As William Graf points out,[65] oil revenues enter the political economy virtually intact, via the central government of Nigeria. The central government, military or civilian itself spends well over half of these revenues and distributes the rest to state and local governments (for whom centrally distributed funds make up over 90 percent of all income). "Unfortunately, successive military regimes have displayed massive corruption and obscene exploitation of society drawing on the large revenues that the federal government controls from oil exports, and on the patronage available through overseeing major construction contracts and foreign exchange allocations."[66] Hence, by taking over the central agency responsible for the oil economy (NNPC), the military is able to take command of the only major source of revenue that makes possible the authoritative allocation of values in the country. Budgetary allocations to the "inflated military bureaucracy creates career opportunities for thousands of middle-class officers whose loyalty to the state ultimately rests on its reliability as an employer."[67]

Political Education

The habit of establishing separate and independent "political centers" for the military seem to have convinced the military elite that political governance may in fact be part of their manifest destiny. The number of military training and indoctrination centers has become redundant to the extent that many of their functions duplicate each other. For example, the Nigerian Defense Academy, Kaduna, was established in 1964 for professional military training. In 1976, the Command and Staff College was established in Jaji for the specialized training of the officer corps in both military logistics and general administration, a function partly duplicated by the Nigerian Defense Academy. The National Institute for Policy and Strategic Studies, Kuru, (Jos) was built as a school for the education military personnel (though not exclusively) on various elements of policy making and strategic planning related both to military and civilian purposes. In 1981, the Training and Doctrine Command (TRADOC) was built in Minna, Niger State as the primary "think tank" of the Nigerian army. In 1991, the National War College was also established. To the extent that subsequent civilian administrations opt to leave these institutions to operate independently as de facto centers of "political" training, it will continue to inspire a persistent contest of will in which the military can equally feel that it has the necessary political wherewithal to govern. Hence, they strike at the political center with impunity.

This is not to suggest that the military as an institution should not have the benefit of developing a professional "political" dimension. In fact, "military systems can retain essential parts of their traditional configuration (i.e., discipline and order), more or less, and still develop an intellectual dimension of the profession with a value system closely linked to society";[68] but there should be a mutual recognition that "political knowledge, political interests, and awareness are not the same as political action and bipartisan politics."[69] Hence, in order to develop the political dimension of military professionalism compatible with liberal democracy, the process would need to be anchored on a concept of professionalism that recognizes the complexities of the real world—particularly the political-social components of political systems.[70] By "pursuing a professional education based on enlightened advocacy—with emphasis on horizons and perspectives that consider political and social implications of military decisions beyond battlefield necessities—it would offer a means of socializing military personnel into reinforcing their commitment to the political system and in their understanding of the political-social dimensions of their role as soldiers."[71] It stands as a great mystery as well as a contradiction when the military (even if justified) take over political power on the premise of seeking to restore and protect democratic rights when, in fact, they themselves entered into political office by undemocratic means.

SOCIAL ETHICS AND "MORAL" REVIVAL

There was a time when it became obvious, even to the ordinary Nigerian, that the level of etiquette and individual disposition toward one another was intolerable. Life in a Hobbesian state of nature could have been more understandable since there were no man-made laws. But in the unfolding Nigerian society where laws are deliberately flaunted, and where strangers on first contact can easily become mortal enemies, and where impatience breeds vulgarity and violence, very few complained when the military unfolded its latest attempt at social engineering. One of the most concerted efforts to create some form of a normative idealism within the Nigerian polity occurred in March 1984, when the Buhari/Idiagbon regime instituted what was known as the War Against Indiscipline (WAI). Against the backdrop of incredible social decay and growing indifference to ordinary humane behavior and civility in interpersonal relations and public etiquette among Nigerians, this served as a welcome promise to save a nation tittering on the brink of a lost civilization.

Though lacking in ideological content, it was nonetheless the first major attempt to provide a systematic program to deal with the loss of civic culture and moral values among the Nigerian citizenry.[72] But unfortunately, the program had inherent pitfalls, for the attempt to transfer military culture and discipline onto the civic populace generated a contradiction that eventually toppled both the Buhari/Idiagbon regime and its program of social moral sanctification.[73] The top-down and draconian way in which the WAI program was implemented became overly regimented for the hitherto unmindful Nigerian populace to accommodate, even as obedience to the new moral dispensation was extracted more out of fear than by a sincere dedication on the part of the average individual to accept change. The program negated the role of the family, and early education as critical elements in the socialization process. Very little was done to find out why Nigerians, of all people, behave the way they do. As soon as the Buhari/Idiagbon regime fell, the people simply returned to their usual way of doing things, so much that the social irresponsibilities that have become part of the Nigerian drama took on a more institutionalized form.

Following the footsteps of the *War Against Indiscipline*, the later Babangida regime on July 25, 1987, instituted a program known as MAMSER (Mass Mobilization for Social Justice, Self-Reliance, and Economic Recovery). The aim was to mobilize the Nigerian masses for self-reliance, social justice, and economic recovery; promote political education—by promoting a framework for creating the basic institutions and norms of democracy at all levels of society; generate a consciousness about power and the proper role of government in serving the collective interest of Nigerians. However, the failure of MAMSER laid both in its emphasis and in the channels selected for its dissemination. First, the primary objective of MAMSER was essentially what any duly elected government ought to have pursued as part of its administrative obligations, but not as an arbitrary dogma created for sheer political profiteering. Second, ideas about power, authority, and the proper role of government in its relationship to the citizenry become more effective as an integral part a dynamic political culture; than as a tool for mass political indoctrination and consequently regime legitimization.

NOTES

1. This chapter and the account that follows is an updated version of my article that was first published as, "The Praetorian Orthodoxy: Crisis of the Nigerian Military State," *Journal of Political and Military Sociology* 28 (Winter 2000): 271–92.

2. Eric A. Nordlinger, *Soldiers in Politics: Military Coups and Governments* (Englewood Cliffs, N.J.: Prentice Hall, 1977), 3.

3. Ladipo Adamolekun, "Introduction: Federalism in Nigeria," *Publius: The Journal of Federalism* 21, no. 4 (1991): 5.

4. See Julius O. Ihonvbere, "Are Things Falling Apart? The Military and The Crisis of Democratization in Nigeria," *Journal of Modern African Studies* 34, no. 2 (1996): 202. He holds the view that the five-day protest (July 5–9, 1993) that occurred predominantly in the Western part of Nigeria represented an awakening of "civil society."

5. Samuel P. Huntington, *The Soldier and the State: The Theory and Politics of Civil-Military Relations* (New York: Vintage Books, 1957), 83.

6. Samuel P. Huntington, *Political Order in Changing Societies* (New Haven, Conn.: Yale University Press, 1968), 95.

7. Morris Janowitz, *The Military in the Political Development of New States* (Chicago: University of Chicago Press, 1964).

8. A. R. Luckham, *The Nigerian Military: A Sociological Analysis of Authority & Revolt, 1967–1970* (London: Cambridge University Press, 1971).

9. Alfred Stepan, *The Military in Politics: Changing Patterns in Brazil* (Princeton, N.J.: Princeton University Press, 1971).

10. Lawrence Mayer, John Burnett, and Susan Ogden, *Comparative Politics: Nations and Theories in a Changing World* (Upper Saddle River, N.J.: Prentice Hall, 1996), 370.

11. Those who were killed during the January 15, 1966 military coup included Sir Abubakar Tafawa Balewa, prime minister of the Federation of Nigeria; Sir Ahmadu Bello, Sarduana of Sokoto and premier of the Northern Region; Chief Samuel L. Akintola, premier of the Western Region; Chief Festus Okotie-Eboh, federal minister of finance; Brigadier Zakariya Maimalari, Brigade Commander, 2nd Brigade, Apapa, Lagos; Lieutenant Colonel Yakubu Pam, adjutant general, Army Headquarters, Lagos; Colonel Kur Mohammed, general staff officer, Army Headquarters, Lagos; Lieutenant Colonel Aborgo Largema, officer commanding 4th Battalion, Ibadan; Lieutenant Colonel Arthur Unegbe, quartermaster general, Army Headquarters, Lagos; Brigadier Samuel Ademulegun, brigade commander, 1st Battalion, Kaduna; Colonel Ralph Shodeinde, commandant, Nigeria Military Training Center, Kaduna.

12. Among those who were killed during the July 1996 countercoup by Northern soldiers were Major General J. T. U. Aguiyi-Ironsi, head of state and commander-in-chief of the Armed Forces; Lieutenant Colonel Francis Adekunle Fajuyi, military governor of the Western Region; Lieutenant Colonel Gabriel Okonweze, garrison commander, Abeokuta Garrison; Major John Obienu, inspector, 2nd Reconnaissance Squadron, Abeokuta Garrison; Lieutenant Orok, Abeokuta Reconnaissance Squadron; Major Christopher Emelifonwu; Lieutenant Colonel Israel Okoro, infantry unit commander, Kaduna; Major Ebanga Ekanem (provost marshal); Major J. O. Ihedigbo; Captain J. Chukwueke; and Major T. E. Nzegwu of the air force, to name but a few. Major Donatus Okafor, of the Brigade of Guards was buried alive. In addition, more than two hundred elite soldiers and officers of Eastern Nigeria origin, particularly Igbos, were murdered in the ensuing melee as Northern soldiers went on an uncontrollable rampage of blood and death. Beginning on May 29, 1967, Northern soldiers and civilians embarked on a massive pogrom in which they killed about 30,000 Easterners, mostly Igbos, who were living in the North.

13. Luckham, *The Nigerian Military*, 63.

14. For more detailed account of issues leading up to and during the civil war, consult some of the following sources: John De St. Jorre, *The Nigerian Civil War* (London: Hodder and Stoughton, 1972); A. H. M. Kirk-Green, *Crisis and Conflict in Nigeria: 1967–1970*, vol. 2 (London: Oxford University Press, 1971); Alexander A. Madiebo, *The Nigerian Revolution and the Biafran War* (Enugu, Nigeria: Fourth Dimension Press, 1980); Olusegun Obasanjo, *My Command: An Account of the Nigerian Civil War, 1967–1970* (Ibadan, Nigeria: Heinemann, 1980); Ikenna Nzimiro, *The Nigerian Civil War: A Study in Class Conflict* (Enugu, Nigeria: Fourth Dimension Press, 1979); Adewale Ademoga, *Why We Struck: The Story of the First Nigerian Coup* (Ibadan, Nigeria: Evans Brothers Publishers, 1981); Zdenek Cervenka, *The Nigerian War, 1967–1970* (Frankfurt am Main, Ger.: Benard & Graefe Verlagfur Wehrwessen, 1971); John J. Stremlau, *The International Politics of the Nigerian Civil War, 1967–1970* (Princeton, N.J.: Princeton University Press, 1971); Ola Balogun, *The Tragic Years: Nigeria in Crisis, 1966–1970* (Benin, Nigeria: Ethiope Publishing Corporation, 1973); Jimi Peters, *The Nigerian Military*

and the State (London: Tauris Academic Studies/Tauris Publishers, 1997); Joe O. G. Achuzia, *Requiem Biafra* (Enugu, Nigeria: Fourth Dimension Publishers, 1986); David Akpode Ejoor, *Reminiscences* (Lagos, Nigeria: Malthouse Press, 1989); Robin Luckham, *The Nigerian Military: A Sociological Analysis of Authority & Revolt, 1960–1967* (Cambridge: Cambridge University Press, 1971); Bernard Odogwu, *No Place to Hide: Crisis and Conflict Inside Biafra* (Enugu, Nigeria: Fourth Dimension Publishers, 1985).

15. Adewale Ademoga, *Why We Struck: The Story of the First Nigerian Coup* (Ibadan, Nigeria: Evans Brothers Publishers, 1981).

16. Henry Bienen, "Military Rule and Political Process: Nigerian Examples," *Comparative Politics* 10, no. 2 (1978): 207.

17. According to William Graf in his book, *The Nigerian State: Political Economy, State Class and Political System in the Post-Colonial Era, 1988,* 172, the term "Kaduna Mafia" was first coined in 1978 by Mvendaga Jibo, a Nigerian journalist at the Constituent Assembly, and since then the term has gained popular currency. It is a powerful, relatively cohesive group of Northern-based but nationally operative interests; and is said to comprise a technocratically and "modernization"-oriented coalition of Northern Nigeria intelligentsia, top economic and political managers of local power.

18. R. Fatton, *Predatory Rule: The State and Civil Society in Africa* (Boulder, Colo.: Lynne Rienner Publishers, 1992).

19. Ogbu Kalu, "Harsh Flutes: The Religious Dimension of the Legitimacy Crisis in Nigeria, 1993–1998," lecture delivered at the Center for the Study of World Religions, Harvard University, February 24, 1999, 4.

20. Hannah Arendt, *Crises of the Republic* (New York: Harcourt Brace Jovanovich, 1972), 151.

21. Joseph Garba, "The Military Regime and the Nigerian Society," Address to a Seminar on 'Nigeria in Transition," September 11, 1979. Also reprinted in the "New Nigeria" Supplement on "Nigeria in Transition," September 28, 1979.

22. See Amos Perlmutter, "The Praetorian State and the Praetorian Army: Toward a Taxonomy of Civil-Military Relations in Developing Polities," *Comparative Politics* 1, no. 3 (1969): 382–404; and Amos Perlmutter, "Civil-Military Relations in Socialist Authoritarian and Praetorian States: Prospects and Retrospects," pp. 310–31 in *Soldiers, Peasants and Bureaucrats,* ed. Roman Kolkowicz and Andrzej Korbonski (London: George Allen & Urwin, 1982). Also see Eric A. Nordlinger, *Soldiers in Politics: Military Coups and Governments.*

23. Amos Perlmutter, "The Praetorian State and the Praetorian Army: Toward a Taxonomy of Civil-Military Relations in Developing Polities," *Comparative Politics* 1, no. 3 (1969): 382–404.

24. Janowitz, *The Military in the Political Development of New States.*

25. Perlmutter, "The Praetorian State and the Praetorian Army," 385–90.

26. Michael Crozier, Samuel P. Huntington, and Joji Watanuki, *The Crisis of Democracy: Report on the Governability of Democracies to The Trilateral Commission* (New York: New York University Press, 1975), 5.

27. Stepan, *The Military in Politics,* 10.

28. Stepan, *The Military in Politics,* 11.

29. Perlmutter, "The Praetorian State and the Praetorian Army," 390.

30. Ebenezer Babatope, *The Abacha Regime and the June 12 Crisis: A Struggle for Democracy* (Lagos, Nigeria: Ebino Topsy, 1995), 7.

31. Babatope, *The Abacha Regime and the June 12 Crisis*, 8.

32. Babatope, *The Abacha Regime and the June 12 Crisis*, 16.

33. Carolyn P. Boyd, *Praetorian Politics in Liberal Spain* (Chapel Hill: University of North Carolina Press), x.

34. Nordlinger, *Soldiers in Politics*, 1977.

35. U.S. State Department, "Nigeria: Country Report on Human Rights Practices for 1996," Bureau of Democracy, Human Rights, and Labor, January 30, 1997.

36. Huntington, *Political Order in Changing Societies*, 196.

37. Huntington, *Political Order in Changing Societies*, 196.

38. Kalu, "Harsh Flutes: The Religious Dimension of the Legitimacy Crisis in Nigeria, 1993–1998," 2.

39. Kalu, "Harsh Flutes: The Religious Dimension of the Legitimacy Crisis in Nigeria, 1993–1998," 2.

40. "Plundering and Looting Unlimited," *Tell Magazine*, August 24, 1998, 12–32.

41. Agwuncha Arthur Nwankwo, *Nigerians As Outsiders: Military Dictatorship and Nigeria's Destiny* (Enugu, Nigeria: Fourth Dimension Press, 1996), 73.

42. J. Bayo Adekanye, "Military Occupation and Social Stratification," *An Inaugural Lecture delivered at the University of Ibadan*, November 25, 1993 (Ibadan, Nigeria: University of Ibadan), 29–30.

43. J. Bayo Adekanye, "Military Occupation and Social Stratification," 29.

44. Under the State Security (Detention of Persons) Decree No. 2 of 1984, as amended in September 1994 by Decree No. 11 of 1994, the chief of general staff—and in addition—the inspector general of police may order the detention without charge or trial of any person considered a threat to the security of the state for an initial period of three months—doubled from a previous maximum of six weeks. However, the Nigerian military government routinely treated the initial period of arrests as indefinitely renewable, detaining people for months or years without charge or trial. Some of the arrests included M. K. O. Abiola, Frank Ovie Kokori, secretary general of the National Union of Petroleum and Natural Gas Workers (NUPENG); Olu Aderibigbe (Nigerian Labor Congress); Francis A. Ado, of the Petroleum and Natural Gas Senior Staff Association of Nigeria (PENGASSAN), Wariebi Kojo Agamene (NUPENG); Chief Amadi, G. A. B. Paschal, Akpabi Okoronwata (NUPENG), and a host of others.

45. Babatope, *The Abacha Regime and the June 12 Crisis*, 40.

46. Julius O. Ihonvbere, "Beyond Governance: The State and Democratization in Sub-Saharan Africa," *Journal of Asian and African Studies* 5 (1995): 154.

47. Claude Ake, "Is Africa Democratizing?" Guardian Lecture, Nigerian Institute of International Affairs, Lagos, Nigeria, December 11, 1993.

48. Robert Putnam, *The Comparative Study of Political Elites* (Englewood Cliffs, N.J.: Prentice Hall, 1976), 161.

49. Robert Putnam, *The Comparative Study of Political Elites*, 164.

50. Alfred Stepan, *Rethinking Military Politics: Brazil and the Southern Cone* (Princeton, N.J.: Princeton University Press, 1988), 13.

51. Anthony Kirk-Green and Douglas Rimmer, *Nigeria Since 1970: A Political and Economic Outline* (London: Hodder and Stoughton, 1981), 7.

52. Kirk-Green and Rimmer, *Nigeria Since 1970*, 11.

53. William D. Graf, *The Nigerian State: Political Economy, State Class and Political System in the Post-Colonial Era* (Portsmouth, N.H.: Heinemann, 1988), 154.

54. James A. Stever, "The Glass Firewall Between Military and Civil Administration," *Administration and Society* 31, no. 1 (1999): 43.

55. Julius O. Ihonvbere, "Are Things Falling Apart? The Military and the Crisis of Democratization in Nigeria," *Journal of Modern African Studies* 34, no. 2 (1996): 202. Also see Julius O. Ihonvbere and Olufemi Vaughan, "Nigeria: Democracy and Civil Society. The Nigerian Transition Programme, 1985–1993," pp. 71–91 in *Democracy and Political Change in Sub-Saharan Africa*, ed. John Wiseman (London: Routledge, 1995).

56. Ihonvbere, "Are Things Falling Apart?" 202.

57. In light of the fact that the emergence of "civil society" involves a "deepening" of those common values that would make it possible to achieve socio-political consensus across a broad spectrum of the society including the military which still maintains "absolute" power, and to the extent this was not the case, it may therefore have seemed premature to invoke the concept of "civil society" to explain the three-month protest, which for all practical purposes was mostly constrained to the Western part of the country, and more or less in some of the oil-producing areas of the South with wide differences in efficacy.

58. Lawrence Mayer, John Burnett, and Susan Ogden, *Comparative Politics: Nations and Theories in a Changing World* (Upper Saddle River, N.J.: Prentice Hall, 1996), 371.

59. Kunle Amuwo and Bayo Okunade, "Political Democracy and Economic Dictatorship: Notes of Paradoxes and Illogicalities of a Transiting Neo-Colonial State," in *Toward the Survival of the Third Republic*, ed. A. T. Gana and S. G. Tyoden (Jos, Nigeria: Department of Political Science, University of Jos, 1990).

60. A. A. Ujo, *Citizenship in Nigeria* (Kaduna, Nigeria: Passmark International, 1994), 101.

61. Joseph Lapalombara, *Politics Within Nations* (Englewood Cliffs, N.J.: Prentice Hall, 1974), 484.

62. Joseph Lapalombara, *Politics Within Nations*, 482.

63. A. A. Ujo, *Citizenship in Nigeria*, 36.

64. See William D. Graf, *The Nigerian State: Political Economy, State Class and Political System in the Post Colonial Era, 1988*, 219. Graf argues that the Nigerian economy has come to conform to the classic profile of a mono-mineral, dependent enclave economy, and as such has come to be viewed by many scholars as a rentier state. The essential feature of the rentier state in the world market is that it serves the link between production and distribution. State revenues accrue from taxes or "rents" on production, rather than from productive activity. This production depends, however, on techniques, expertise, investments—and markets—generated outside the territory controlled by the state. For this reason, practically all aspects of exploration, production, and marketing are dominated by international capital, typically in the form of transnational corporation. For a detailed account of the *rentier state* and *rentier politics*, see chapter 7 in this volume.

65. Graf, *The Nigerian State.*

66. Stephen Wright, *Nigeria: Struggle for Stability and Status* (Boulder, Colo.: Westview Press, 1998), 431.

67. Boyd, *Praetorian Politics in Liberal Spain*, 8.

68. Sam C. Sarkesian, "Military Professionalism and Civil-Military Relations in the West," *International Political Science Review* 2, no. 3 (1981): 295.

69. Sarkesian, "Military Professionalism and Civil-Military Relations in the West," 293

70. Sarkesian, "Military Professionalism and Civil-Military Relations in the West," 293

71. Sarkesian, "Military Professionalism and Civil-Military Relations in the West," 294.

72. Ujo, *Citizenship in Nigeria*, 108.

73. Ujo, *Citizenship in Nigeria*, 108.

7

———〰〰———

Rentier Politics

The Confluence of Power and Economics

The American Heritage Dictionary defines the word "rentier" as "one who derives a fixed income from property rentals or returns on investments";[1] but its use as a defining characteristic of most states offers a theoretical as well as a methodological pathway for explicating the ways and means by which some states acquire economic power. The concept of the "rentier state" is a complex of associated ideas concerning the patterns of development and the nature of states in economies dominated by external rent, particularly oil rent.[2] While much of the literature has been focused on the later, the problem arises in the attempt to construct an all-embracing theory that could explain the mechanisms of governance in majority of the oil-endowed states. A key principle for theory building is to draw from basic elements or universal principles and to use that as a basis for the analysis of specific empirical observations. Hence what matters, in most cases, is the approach or methodology used in the process of establishing a degree of congruence between theory and an observable event or phenomenon. Social science deals with knowledge of society and the social world, hence is focused on the study of socially constructed phenomena and how they relate to each other, the structure of society and the activity of its members.

While "methodology" helps us in the development of a logical structure and procedure for social scientific inquiry; the challenge, therefore, of theory building is to provide a pathway for understanding how specific social relations can become predictable. A theory building that draws from the past is often fueled by an interest in what it might tell us about the present and the future. The task of social scientific inquiry is to convert lessons of history into a comprehensive theory that encompasses the complexity of the phenomena or activity in question and to establish its truth or falsity. "Although textbooks often state that theory is meant to describe, explain, or predict; theory almost always is meant to explain in order to predict."[3] Predictability simplifies the future for us, and reduces the burden of gathering information and resources necessary for making public policy in a timely manner.

Theory building is hardly an exaggeration. It requires an ability to see things or patterns that others have not been able to see, to identify the many conditions and variables that affect historical outcomes, to sort out the causal patterns associated with different historical outcomes, and to synthesize disaggregated parts into a new whole. By doing so, "theory accounts for the variance in historical outcomes; it clarifies apparent inconsistencies and contradictions among the 'lessons' of different historical cases by identifying the critical conditions and variables that differed from one case to the other."[4] While theory offers us the opportunity to establish the existence of a logical relationship between two or more phenomena, conceptualization enables us to identify the characteristics of each phenomenon in terms of identity and behavior. "Things conceived or meaningfully perceived (i.e., concepts) are the central elements of propositions and depending—on how they are named—can provide guidelines for interpretation and observation."[5]

DEFINITIONAL PROSE AND CONCEPTUALIZATION

To accurately define a term means that we must know the concepts and the functional relationships that make it up. Concept formation helps us to understand abstract phenomena in terms of their observable or empirical manifestations. For example, there are some common conceptual terms in political science all of which are related in some fundamental and practical ways. The terms I have in mind are: *nation, state, and government*. While some literature use these terms interchangeably, there has also been an adulteration of the two words in the form of what we call the "nation-state." The irony is that when we use the term "nation-state," we are not speaking about a unique nominal or conceptual term; rather what we are speaking about is the functional "relationship" between a nation and a state and how this *relationship* is manifested in a legitimate act of governance. A "nation" as a concept is anchored on a specific genealogical and cultural foundation; while a "state" is merely a geographical expression of sovereign authority and power. Hence, concept formation would be critical to a proper understanding of the core distinctions between the two.

Alternatively, we see "democracy" as being different from "social-ism" but when we bridge the two concepts into "democratic socialism," we ought to make it clear that an understanding of democratic social-ism (as a *political process*) can only be preceded by an understanding of "democracy" and "socialism" as independent concepts separate from one another. On a practical level, what this means is that the foundation of social scientific inquiry must at the same time seek to reinforce the conditions necessary to understand as well as internalize its operational concepts, the linkages between key nominal terms, and how they facili-tate the reciprocal processes of theory-building and knowledge creation. Theory makes it easier to understand policy making or the ideal behind specific state behaviors in international and domestic affairs. Policy mak-ing (as we know it) is not just a legislative exercise; it is also a negotiation between agencies, political elites, and interest groups that operate from different ideological paradigms and worldviews; even if the primary ac-tors involved are not always aware of the theories they propound. While most textbooks often emphasize world events from a particular theoreti-cal perspective, it has become crucial in today's international system for students to develop a working knowledge of central theories of interna-tional relations and foreign policy. A good starting point would require the ability to understand and articulate the interrelationships between theories and models and the kinds of explanations they bring to bear on practical real world situations.

The concept of "rentier state" was postulated by Hossein Mahdavy[6] in his studies of Iran during the reign of Shah Reza Pahlavi; but saw its advancement in the latter works of Beblawi and Luciani[7] in their studies of the Middle East and Arab oil producing economies. For a country like Nigeria, oil has dominated practically every sphere of its economic, social, and political activity since the civil war (1967–1970), so much so that it has been characterized as a "rentier" state. "The essential feature of the rentier state in the world market is that it severs the link between production and distribution; state revenues accrue from taxes or rents on the production of a single commodity (oil), rather than from productive activity."[8] To the extent that the external component of this production process depends on "techniques, expertise, investments and markets generated outside the territory controlled by the state, the role of international capital in the form of transnational corporations becomes dominant."[9] Because the *rentier* state is typically a mono-resource producer, it is also a dependent economy both with respect to international capital, technology, and mar-kets. This is what makes it a much more complex phenomenon as well as a potentially precarious system.

William Graf articulates four primary reasons that could make the rentier state extraordinarily crisis-ridden.[10] He points to fluctuations in global demand, the collateral effects of worldwide recession, technical breakdowns, and labor disputes may reduce the flow of "rents" and thus undercut national budgets and development plans. There is also the fiscal crisis that could result as a result of continued outflows of revenues due to expenditures on vital and luxury imports, ongoing net outflow of transnational corporation profits, and interest payments on foreign loans. Furthermore, the over-reliance created by the dependence on oil revenue generates an economic dislocation that eclipses other hitherto productive sectors of the dependent economy—as experienced in the underdevelopment of agriculture and parallel distortions in the industrial and manufacturing sectors. It is in this regard that Beblawi and Luciani characterize the rentier state as a subset of a broader rentier economy—in which the state is examined primarily through its size relative to the sources and structures of its economy. It is also important to note that "states that use the control of a specific domestic source of rent to extract surplus from society are not rentier states, because they are supported by society rather than vice versa."[11] A key feature of rentier economies is that the rents acquired by the state derives from external sources, they accrue directly to the state, and because of the size of the rents at the state's disposal, it thus makes domestic taxation unnecessary.

From the above considerations, one comes out with the view that in descriptive terms, the idea of a "rentier state" is perhaps a misnomer. It does not explain the nature of the state per se, but the *activities* undertaken by it; hence it is a *process*-driven phenomenon as opposed to a nominal term that accurately defines what a particular state is. Beyond the critical neo-Marxist undertones of many of the literature on the rentier state, the point is that states are not the ones that decide whether or not to engage in rentier activities; it is the combination of a specific natural resource endowment and the external demand for it that creates the international market from which the state extracts rents. The practice of rent seeking is relative as well as prevalent among all states whether the economy is diversified or not; hence the general inclination to tag oil-producing states as "exclusively" *rentier* tends to diminish the role of states whose economy depends exclusively on other kinds of commodities, such as cocoa, diamonds, gold, or coffee. The principle behind the idea of comparative advantage is that a state should concentrate on producing those goods and services for which it can bring to the market, at a lower cost and maximum benefit more than other competing states. Hence if a state can produce oil because its natural factor endowments dictates so more than other products, it should focus on that not as a defining characteristic but as a means of participation in the international market and exchange system.

THE POLITICAL ECOLOGY OF RENT SEEKING

When viewed in purely competitive free-market terms, rent seeking among oil-dependent economies leads to a persistent market failure both in terms of allocation of resources, and in the distribution of the incentives for participation. The role of the state in mediating between public owner-ship (property rights) and private capital in the free-market creates a situ-ation where politics, not markets determines the incentives of ownership. Because "the state receives revenues which are channeled to the economy through public expenditure, the allocation of these public funds between alternative uses has great significance for the future development pat-tern of the economy."[12] Because most public infrastructures are not profit making, they must be supported by continuous appropriation of public funding generated through external rents, despite the performance of other sectors of the domestic macroeconomy.

Even though state expenditures on public sector infrastructures can help to create jobs thereby reducing unemployment; it can also provide additional sources for extracting legal and illegal rents (corruption) from the public treasury. "Oil-related rents (royalties, taxes, oil export earnings, interests on joint-venture investments, etc.) are the lifeblood of Nigeria's economy; but in spite of Nigeria's vast oil resources, the World Bank es-timates that as a result of corruption 80 percent of the oil that accrues to the domestic front benefit only 1 percent of the population."[13] "Factions of the country's elite, with strong interests in the allocation, appropria-tion, and use of oil revenues, dominate all levels of government; hence their interests combine conveniently with those of the state to support a regime of predatory accumulation and lawlessness."[14] And this points to an important factor in the development process, that is, rentier economies rarely spread the wealth, but rather concentrates it in the hands of those who control the apparatus of the state.

There is "considerable evidence that point to the fact that a strong natu-ral resource base does not necessarily promote economic development";[15] but instead, can create the false illusion of an economic cushion that could enable the state to overcome future periods of economic crises. Ironically, it may simply allow the state to "postpone painful decisions by masking underlying problems that would have produced an immediate crisis in less fortunate countries."[16] To the extent that "talented people and those who seek to get rich concentrate their effort on rent-seeking rather than on productive entrepreneurship,"[17] the "private profitability of rent-seeking ac-tivities rises above their social value and may crowd out productive invest-ment."[18] Hence "instead of promoting growth, a valuable natural resource may simply make control of the state more worthwhile."[19]

Because rentier states inherit a political order from history, they do not create their own political order.[20] Rentier politics and the rent seeking that goes with it has always been a historical part of the evolution of modern political culture in Nigeria. Even though it predates the period of independence, it still resonates today but in varying dimensions. It began with the "constitution of 1954 which not only created a genuinely federal system, but granted enormous autonomy and control over resources to each of the three regions. As the regions became the primary centers of power and wealth in Nigeria, the ensuing struggling between the three regional parties for socioeconomic resources came to dominate the country's politics—on such issues as the timing of self-government, revenue allocation, and the consequent NPC's effort to purge southerners from the Northern bureaucracy and economy."[21] Hence much of the early inter-party conflicts, the struggle for state power at the federal level, the malpractices that followed the 1962–1963 election, the labor union strikes of June 1964, the UPGA boycott of the 1964 elections, the 1965 Western regional elections, and in fundamental ways, the military putsch that ended the First republic, could all be categorized as extensions of rentier politics.

In other to deny the then Eastern Region (became the "Republic of Biafra" on May 30, 1967) control of the oil resources of the Niger Delta, *rentier politics* was, by design or default, introduced into Nigeria as a result of the creation of the twelve state structure by General Yakubu Gowon on May 27, 1967. "Of the four political regions that existed in the mid-1960s, only the Eastern and Midwest regions were oil producers."[22] Contrary to the widely held view that it was the 1967–1970 civil war that introduced a dispute over oil ownership into Nigerian politics;[23] rather it was the creation of the twelve states structure which used the territorial location of oil resources as its primary criteria in the political and economic dismemberment of the Eastern Region. By this very act alone, and for the first time in the country's history, a war fought for the preservation of rights, suddenly became in the minds of many a war over oil and territorial control. In the ensuing dispute over revenue allocation and the authority of the federal government over the natural resources of the federating units, the government of the then Eastern Region demanded oil companies operating in the region to pay rents, royalties and taxes to the newly created Republic of Biafra. "The Nigerian government, on the other hand, countered by insisting that royalties be paid to it, and it moved to impose a naval blockade on Bonny and Port Harcourt—the two main external terminals for oil export."[24]

In November 1969, a month to the end of the war, "the Nigerian government initiated the Petroleum Decree that nullified all concessions held by oil companies and granted itself the power to issue new oil exploration licenses and production leases." "The decree vested in the state the control and ownership of all petroleum in, under or upon any lands in the country; all petroleum under the territorial waters of Nigeria; and all land forming part of the continental shelf of the country."[25] But the country's transition into a dominant "rentier state" did not take root until the end of the civil war in 1970 when oil became the centerfold of the national economy. In 1971, the federal government created the Nigerian National Oil Corporation (NNOC), later to be renamed the Nigerian National Petroleum Corporation (NNPC) to prospect, produce and market oil, and also began to acquire equity stake in the oil companies.[26] "From a modest 5% of total national revenue in 1965, the share of oil revenue rose to 26.6% in 1970, 43.6% in 1971, and 80% by 1980."[27] Prior to that, the contribution of agricultural exports to national development exceeded that of the petroleum industry by more than 3 to 1. "Although palm produce exports declined dramatically as a result of the war (since a high proportion came from the former Eastern Region); cocoa (of which Nigeria was the world's second largest producer) earned £54.7m (pounds sterling) in 1967; groundnuts (of which Nigeria was the world's largest exporter) earned £35.4m; rubber £6.3m; cotton £6.4m; and timber £3.5m."[28] "This array of crops made Nigeria one of Africa's most diversified economies agriculturally and their earnings, although progressively forming a smaller share of total export earnings (67% in 1962 and 47% in 1967), continued to pay for most of Nigeria's existing industries and infrastructure at that time."[29]

But the end of the civil war changed all that. Because the propaganda on both sides of the war and the security and financial interests of British, French and American oil companies made oil a salient factor in their respective country's disposition toward the war, it meant that oil would also feature prominently in Nigeria's postwar reconstruction. In addition, Nigeria needed the funds to pay for the enormous amount of military arsenal it acquired from both the Soviet Union and Britain. Furthermore, the 1973–1974 Arab-Israeli war and the attendant "oil embargo" (even if superficially)[30] not only raised the price of oil, it also made it a central part of international politics and the international market economy—a powerful combination that not only changed the structure of international trade but also exposed the vulnerability of the West to the oil brinkmanship of hitherto weak oil-producing states. In addition to having acquired membership in the oil-producing cartel—the Organization of Petroleum Exporting Countries (OPEC)—in 1971, Nigeria was able to benefit from the incentives of collective action in terms of influence over the supply and price of oil in the international market.

As the economic rents from oil continued to increase beyond anyone's imagination, the country became more and more entrapped by its own "natural" blessings; and slowly, by design or default, its commitment to promoting and supporting the agricultural and other sectors of the economy dissipated. Oil thus, became the centerpiece of economic development and, invariably, political contestation and government largesse. Out of this development has evolved a cabal of political-tycoons and their "freelance celebrities"—oftentimes a synthetic product of warped electoral machinery—as major donors to the political parties that seeks control of the central government.[31] "Locked into a mainly self-created process of unmitigated accumulation, immune from countervailing pressures from above or below and unconstrained by ideological or moral scruples, the tycoon class initiated a whole series of self-enriching projects and designs that allowed it to appropriate and export huge quantities of the national wealth."[32]

Elections in Nigeria (at the federal, state and local government levels) have become victims of the worst aspects of rentier politics. As a means of maintaining control over state power as well as ensuring the continuous flow of "informal" rents, new-age "political-tycoons" and robber-barons (many with unsavory backgrounds) use their financial contributions (or electoral support) as prebends or "down payments" for the "purchase" of choice ministerial portfolios which they will, in turn, designate their own representatives or cronies for formal appointment. Traditional rulers, emirs, chiefs, sultans, and other inexplicable temporal lordships have also abandoned their "sacred" duties and gotten into the fray as political contractors and arbiters of choice political opportunity. Because it enables extra-governmental actors access to and control over agency budgets and contract awards, the political "capture" of public offices has unfortunately become a much-desired instrument of rent seeking. Besides making a caricature and mockery of the electoral system, it also undermines the credibility of the public vote by using it as a conduit for "legitimizing" fraud.

Corruption as Political Mining

The term *political mining* is a descriptive construct that captures the relentless quest and use of politics as means for securing instrumental rewards. Political engagements are not sought for their objective utility and as a means of serving the public interest; rather they are sought solely for reasons of self-interest. The distinction between private economic interest and the public purpose are, at best, ambiguous. The most concrete example of *political mining* is corruption—a form of illegal "rent"—especially when it occurs at the highest levels of government and in other aspects of public-private relationships and transactions. Because "governments frequently transfer large financial benefits to private firms through procurement contracts and the award of concessions,"[33] "the public official's behavior depends not only on the total economic rents that accrues to the government but also on the share that he or she can extract in dealing with corrupt beneficiaries."[34] If several officials have authority over the allocation and transfer of such financial benefits, the problem often multiplies as each tries to extract a share of the "informal" rent. "In a corrupt regime, economic actors who engage in illegal businesses may be able to achieve comparative advantage";[35] but the cost to society is that it is caught in a corruption trap where "toleration of corruption in some areas of public life can facilitate a downward spiral in which the malfeasance of some encourages more and more people to engage in corruption over time."[36]

Even when corruption and economic growth coexist, financial payoffs (bribery) introduce costs and distortions. Because bribery is a form of "informal" rent, "the price mechanism, so often a source of economic efficiency and a contributor to growth, can become distorted to the extent that it undermines the legitimacy and effectiveness of government."[37] But to view bribery, solely in financial terms, is to arbitrarily limit the scope of its damaging effects. Bribery, especially in the public sector, extends to appointments based on nepotism and cronyism, award of contracts to cronies, using one's public office to seek for or as a compensation for personal favors, changing the rules of the game to create a favorable advantage for one's clients, and using unauthorized public assets and resources for electoral campaigns and vote-baiting. Corruption in Nigeria, therefore, incorporates both "formal" and "informal" aspects of rentier politics. It is, in fact, a form of "illegal" rent.

According to one of the mildly circulated publications[38] in Nigeria, the most enduring legacy since the country's independence in 1960 has been the uncanny ability to produce millionaire military generals. It has been noted that corruption was the main reason given as to why the five majors struck and brought down the First Republic on January 15, 1966; and why General Murtala Muhammed overthrew General Yakubu Gowon. When Murtala Muhammed was assassinated in 1976, his successor General Olusegun Obasanjo handed over power to the civilian government of Alhaji Shehu Shagari in 1979. However, it took the civilians only four years to surpass the military in profligacy and corruption. When General Muhammadu Buhari took over the reins of power in December 1983, he accused the civilians of corrupt practices and launched a war against indiscipline. The Babangida and Abacha years (1985–1998) saw a level of unbridled corruption in which the nation's wealth was siphoned away into private coffers. As confirmed by the Okigbo Panel report, a $12 billion oil profit windfall that accrued to the country (during the Babangida administration) due to a sharp rise in oil prices following the Iraq-Kuwait conflict (Gulf War 1991) disappeared into thin air and remain unaccounted for; military officers accused of corruption and public theft were also shielded from legal prosecution. Before his death in office in June 1998, General Abacha was believed to have siphoned-off more than $5 billion of public funds into his private accounts in various foreign bank accounts. In a most-brazen act of economic patronage, General Abacha appointed the former head of state Yakubu Gowon to serve in his economic and health ministries. General Muhammadu Buhari, another former military ruler, who ironically, was overthrown by the duo of Babangida and Abacha, was appointed to head the Petroleum Trust fund—a vital program that manages revenues from the sale of Nigeria's oil.

In 2006, a controversial $90 million oil bloc scandal between Addax Petroleum of Canada and little known "Starcrest Energy" of Nigeria threatened to expose collusive activities between top presidential officials, their cronies, and the foreign oil conglomerate. It was also discovered in 2006 that some foreign contractors in the oil and gas sector connived with officials of the Nigerian National Petroleum Corporation (NNPC) to siphon-off revenue totaling $20 billion through the award of construction contracts for work that were either not done or remained uncompleted. In November 2006, the director of the Department of Petroleum Resources was fired over what was alleged to be official impropriety in the award of oil bloc bids. Top officials of the NNPC have been alleged to have milked the nation of oil revenues to the tune of billions of dollars through various frauds including contract awards to bogus companies, and producing crude oil far in excess of assigned OPEC quotas and converting the proceeds to political electioneering and personal interests. Between 2006 and 2007, about thirty-one of Nigeria's thirty-six state governors, scores of federal officials and private individuals charged with corrupt practices, money laundering, theft and embezzlement of public funds, were dragged before the Code of Conduct Tribunals by the Economic and Financial Crimes Commission (EFCC) under the chairmanship of Nuhu Ribadu.

While is noteworthy that in the course of Obasanjos's eight-year administration, "the country earned $233 billion, two and a half times the amount earned over the previous eight years; the EFCC estimates that the country has lost about $400 billion since independence in 1960."[39] Also in 2007, the *Sun Newspaper* reported that the U.S. Department of Justice claimed that a U.S. oil company Wilbros had bribed the Nigerian government and top leaders of the ruling People's Democratic party millions of dollars in order to secure award of a $387 million Eastern Gas Gathering System project. While the Wilbros case does not stand out from others, it remains an essential feature of Nigerian power politics that oil has had a profound impact in undermining any sense of political morality and responsible governance. It has become a galvanizing force as well as the epicenter that attracts all sorts of characters, hawkers, and charlatans into a politico-economic chess game that could only be characterized as *orga-*

nized amateurism. The objective is not necessarily to achieve any definitive public purpose, but to maintain political control of the oil economy in such a way that the rents would continue to circulate within the cabal of political power brokers and their clients or surrogates. By pooling their resources together and "electing" one of their own into public offices and strategic positions, they are able to work the system to their advantage.

The *News Magazine* of December 18, 2000, published a long list of well-connected personalities, both in and out of office, who control and "manage" the political and economic affairs of the Nigerian state. Among those mentioned were the Chougry Brothers, who are Lebanese-Nigerians said to have extensive business partnerships with prominent military leaders such as the late General Abacha and retired General Theophilus Danjuma; Alhaji Aliko Dangote, a Nigerian business mogul with business interests in virtually every sector of the economy; Bode George, a retired navy commander and former governor of Ondo State; Remi Oluwode, chairman of one of the nation's leading insurance firms; General Ibrahim Babangida, former head of state; Adamu Ciroma, former minister of finance and a key member of the Arewa Consultative Forum; Sambo Dasuki, son of the former sultan of Sokoto and former military aide-de-camp to Ibrahim Babangida; Olusegun Obasanjo, head of state 1999–2007; Chief Tony Anenih, former minister of works and housing; Atiku Abubakar, former vice president; Chief Barnabas Gemade, former chairman of the Peoples Democratic Party; and Major General Mohammed Aliyu Gusau, former national security adviser to President Obasanjo. And the list is endless.

Nonetheless, it is from this epicenter that elite interests originate and is circulated outwards to those at the periphery (including the foot soldiers). In fundamental ways, the arrangement of power and influence within the political machine is arranged in an onion ring formation with those closest to the inner core being the most powerful. But either collectively or individually, they are able to cast their net over "a wide range of interests and issues in governance, including who gets what, who should occupy which post, who should lead the Senate or the House of Representatives and who should not lead."[40] While this is not to suggest that the political machine always functions as a unitary actor; they oftentimes conspire and engage in subterfuges against each other, but the political objective of state control remains essentially the same.

OIL RENTS AND MARKET FAILURES

Nigeria is the largest oil producer in Africa and the seventh largest exporter of crude oil in the world. "The country's daily output of 2.2 million barrels accounts for 80 percent of state revenues and 90 percent of foreign exchange earnings. The state owns all oil rights and has a majority interest in every oil company operating in the country."[41] According to the Oil and Gas Journal (OGJ), Nigeria has 35.9 billion barrels of proven oil reserves as of January 2006.[42] When it created the Nigerian National Petroleum Corporation (NNPC) in 1977, its primary function was to oversee the regulation of the Nigerian oil industry, with secondary responsibilities for upstream and downstream developments. In 1988, the Nigerian government divided the NNPC into twelve subsidiary companies in order to better manage the country's oil industry. The majority of Nigeria's major oil and gas projects (95 percent) are funded through joint ventures (JVs), with the NNPC as the major shareholder. The largest joint venture is operated by Shell Petroleum Development Company (SPDC), producing nearly half of Nigeria's crude oil. Additional foreign companies operating in joint ventures with the NNPC include ExxonMobil, Chevron, ConocoPhillips, Total, and Agip. The remaining funding arrangements are comprised of production sharing contracts (PSCs), which are mostly confined to Nigeria's deep offshore development program. Oil accounts for about 90 percent of the country's total export revenue. Because Nigeria's oil-dependent economy is more or less determined by its international component, it makes it difficult to initiate a national development plan without taking into account its potential effects on the economic interests of the major oil companies that help to generate the nation's revenues. Tough measures needed to protect indigenous industries and to regulate economic behavior in the oil industry are circumvented and sacrificed in the process of acquiescing to the patronage politics of oil interests and their clientele.

For the simple fact that key members of the political and economic elite are connected to the rentier economy through various forms of patronage, they are less receptive to making the tough decisions needed to address major market failures as a result of over-reliance on oil rents. Due to the increased dependency on oil rents, other sectors of the economy have also been neglected. Because the productive sector is less diversified, goods that could have been produced or manufactured locally are imported thereby making their prices exorbitantly high. And for the fact that the choice of alternative consumer products are limited, the consequent rise in the price of imported commodities sparks a series of inflationary spirals that snow-balls throughout the whole economy. Excessive reliance on imported commodities to serve the needs of a growing and modernizing economy such as Nigeria creates a disincentive for producing the same kind of goods locally. The benefits to the national economy in terms of employment, taxes, and economic synergies are lost and the process of indigenous development further undermined. The unrestrained expectation of making a "fast killing" (quick and easy money) from oil rents stifles personal innovation, initiative, and kills the entrepreneurial spirit even before it is born.

There is also an illegal dimension to the oil trade and economy. The "illegal marketing of oil in Nigeria reached its peak in the 1980s, when oil syndicates (with ties to senior government, military, and police officials) not only sold an overwhelming bulk of all the oil traded, but produced and refined oil themselves. Because these illegal cartels have secret refining stations, terminals, tank farms and ships that stock-pile and redirect oil in the high seas to exclusive locations; billions of petrol dollars accruing to the concessionary states were siphoned through the activities of syndicates (through a process known as bunkering)."[43] It is estimated that with an average oil pilferage of about 200,000 barrels a day, and at $65 a barrel, Nigeria would be losing approximately $13 million dollars daily. Due to the fact that much of this subterranean economy operates outside of the formal channels of fiscal accountability (in complicity with official and government stakeholders), the loss to the nation's treasury in the form of taxes and royalties have been enormous. And because a disproportionate amount of the illegal rents are scooted away to foreign banks and investment outfits, they represent negative outflows of cash that, if spent locally, could have helped to generate new investments as well as create increased demand for domestic goods and services.

The ease with which oil rents accumulate into the coffers of the Nigerian state creates a situation of rising expectations that depends on expected future oil revenues for their actualization. But because oil revenues, for the most part, are dependent on fluctuations in the international supply and demand, it is difficult to guarantee when or if these expectations would be met. The consequent distortion in national development planning and budgets discourages further investment in other productive and related sector markets. There is also the issue of excessive liquidity or too much cash in circulation. The enormous and sudden inflow of oil revenues often creates excess liquidity relative to demand (or absorptive capacity) in the productive sectors of the economy, which, invariably, leads to high inflationary spirals.

Though inflation remains high in the country, the government has managed (to a limited extent) to mitigate its most devastating effects by using some of the surplus oil rents to pay off and service some of its foreign debts, and to embark on capital-intensive projects that require massive outflows of cash payments from the country's economy. Inclusive of the billions of dollars siphoned-away and/or stolen through official corruption, embezzlement, over-invoicing, and other "innovative" mechanisms, the country has managed, in a rather perverse way (contrary to the expected effect), to sustain a marginally stabilizing effect on what would otherwise have been the "mother" of all run-away inflations. Nonetheless, an unconventional approach to "monetary policy"—the Nigerian way.

THE RENTIER SPACE: A PARADIGMATIC APPROACH

The concept of the *rentier space* comprises the series of formal and informal activities centered at the confluence of state power and the oil-driven rentier economy (figure 7.1). While the state serves as the epicenter (the fulcrum) that holds together the internal and external components of the rentier space; its sovereign authority enables it to preside over the distribution of oil dividends (rents) as well as arbitrate emerging conflicts between major actors and stakeholders operating within the boundaries of the rentier space. As domestic and international actors enter or exit the permeable boundaries of the rentier space, the centrifugal and centripetal (push-pull) forces of inertia act to create an organic (changeable) system sustained under a dynamic equilibrium.

It is noteworthy to point out here that the activities that occur within the rentier space are not only driven by individual or group interests;

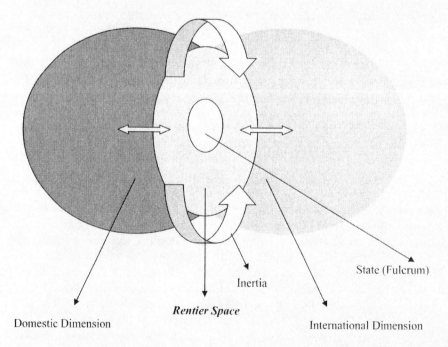

Figure 7.1. The Rentier Space: A Phenomenon at the Intersection of Power and Economics

but are for the most part, driven by various domestic and international events, crises, economic growth or decline, monetary exchange rates, changes in political regimes, elections, petroviolence, ecoterrorism, ethnic revolts and insurgencies, and other exogenous factors. The state thus, is one among many other actors engaged within the rentier space. Over time, as the rentier space takes on a life of its own, it is thus able to select those actors and players who will remain as well as those who will be removed or denied access for continued participation. It can expand or contract according to relative shifts in the balance of interests. *Rentier politics* takes place and is centrally located within the porous borders of the *rentier space*.

There are crucial lessons to be gleaned from the above analysis. To the extent that only a portion of the state is engaged in the rentier economy, the greater majority of society is not centrally connected to it. It is also a fallacious argument to state that rentier states are not necessarily "productive" economies, simply because their economy is dependent on oil rents. But the point is that while oil resources can serve as raw material for other productive enterprises, it can also provide the source of revenue for industrialization as well as synergies in other sectors of the economy. And because of its overall contribution to GDP per capita as well as to a country's credit worthiness; the impact of oil revenues permeates the whole fabric of the economy (into other productive sectors) in such a way that it would be misleading to see it as having only a one-sided effect on the revenue side of the national budget. There is nothing fundamentally wrong in being characterized a "rentier state," rather the issue should be on how the country manages the evolving politics of the rentier space to deal with various critical issues of national development.

The Domestic Dimension

In fundamental ways, it would not be an overstatement to view the evolution of Nigeria's federal system as a continuing struggle between state and class, rather than in the traditional sense of division of powers between the center and peripheral units. "With oil as the mainstay of the national economy, oil interests and control of the accruable revenues, have become a major defining influence upon the Nigerian state and its politics."[44] "Mindful of its equity interest and joint venture partnerships with the major oil corporations, the Nigerian state usually intervenes on behalf of the oil industry using legislation, public policy, and sometimes, military reprisals to resolve conflicts between the oil industry and host communities, especially in the Niger Delta."[45] As Larry Diamond[46] points out, state power has remained obdurate as the primary source of national wealth and as the primary route and access to the resources and opportunities of class formation; hence it oftentimes becomes "tempting for a democratically-elected ruler of a rentier state to become authoritarian, as soon as he acquires control of the oil rent and the great power this gives to him over society."[47]

While the productive economic activity fades in appeal, access to and manipulation of the government-spending process becomes the golden gateway to fortune. In the ensuing shift from "nurture capitalism" to "pirate capitalism," the quest for political power replaces effort as the basis of social reward. As "politics translates into open warfare and a matter of life and death, the enormous premium on political power degenerates into political chaos, intolerance, and instability—exemplified by impeachments, decampments, expulsions, thuggery, rioting, arson, electoral fraud—that denies the government any sense of legitimacy."[48] The domestic actors engaged in rentier politics include the state, interest groups, ethnic groups and militia movements, media, domestic corporations, banks and financial institutions, government agencies and parastatals, elected public officers and political appointees, oil workers unions (NUPENG and PENGASSAN),[49] individuals, criminal gangs and oil syndicates. The formal or informal actions taken by each of these actors are, in most cases, directly or indirectly tied to the petropolitics of the state—hence should be construed as an aspect of rentier politics. To the extent that they involve theft of public funds and official malfeasance tied to oil scandals, the gale of legislative and gubernatorial impeachments that occurred in the country from 1999–2007 could, directly or indirectly, be tied to rentier politics.

When key ministerial portfolios such as Defense, Finance, Energy and Petroleum resources are skewed in favor of people from a particular geopolitical zone of the country (a practice that has historically favored the North), it offers a mirror through which rentier politics can be used to entrench oligarchic interests at the apex of state power. Other examples of these activities abound with respect to their relative impacts on the supply and price of oil in both the domestic and international markets. In June 2007, the Nigerian oil unions called a general nationwide strike in protest of a government price hike on automobile fuel. This caused an immediate rise in oil and gasoline futures pushing the international market price above $68. Stocks of major airlines fell on the news of higher oil prices, thus ending the Dow Jones transportation average down 38.35 (0.74 percent) to 5,138.63. It is common knowledge that most of the time, Nigerian labor unions threaten to go on strike only to settle at the last minute; but by the time negotiations are over, the financial damage would have been done. Strikes, or even the threat of strikes, can become powerful tools in the practice of rentier politics.

The environmental protests against the state and the oil companies, especially in Ogoniland (the Niger Delta) during the 1990s, and which saw its climax in the consequent execution of Kenule Saro Wiwa in 1995, was on both sides, an integral part of rentier politics. So is the emergence of the ethnic militia movements such as the Niger Delta Volunteer Force, Movement for the Emancipation of the Niger Delta (MEND), the Ijaw Youth Movement, the Egbesu boys, and many others. The regional advocacy for resource control and disagreements over the derivation formula have become central issues linked to oil politics, fairness, equity, and often times self-determination. Various aspects of the inter-minority conflicts such as the series of Ijaw-Itshekiri-Urhobo disputes reflect a struggle for control of informal rents derived from oil resources.

Nigeria has also experienced increased pipeline vandalism over the years. The U.S. Energy Information Administration,[50] reports that in October 2005, a pipeline fire in the southwestern Delta State of Nigeria resulted in the deaths of about sixty people. This was followed by a December attack, in which armed men in speedboats dynamited Shell's pipeline in the Opobo Channel. In January 2006, a pipeline attack from the Brass Creek fields to the Forcados terminal forced Shell to announce a suspension of operations. Additional attacks made on the pipeline and the Forcados terminal in February made it necessary for Shell to extend an earlier force majeure beyond the end of the February date. Shell estimated that 455,000 bbl/d (barels per day) of its oil production was shut-in because of the attacks. Also another February 2006 attack on the Escravos pipeline, that supplies oil to the Warri refinery, caused the refinery to shutdown, this in spite of the fact that the Nigerian government had recommissioned the Escravos-Warri pipeline in January 2005 after eighteen months of repairing the damage caused by sabotage during the 2003 Niger Delta Crisis.

The Energy Information Administration further reports that, in addition to pipeline vandalism, there has been a marked increase in kidnappings of expatriate oil workers in the Niger Delta region. In January 2006, four foreign employees of Royal Dutch Shell were kidnapped and then held for nineteen days before being released on "humanitarian grounds." In February 2006, nine additional oil workers were kidnapped in the Niger Delta region. The Movement for the Emancipation of the Niger Delta took responsibility for the kidnappings and for blowing up a crude oil pipeline owned and operated by Royal Dutch Shell. While six of the nine hostages were released as of March 3, 2006; MEND presented a series of conditions that must be met before the remaining three hostages would be released. Among the conditions were the release of Ijaw prisoners and the establishment of a United Nations inquiry that would investigate the environmental and economic problems of the Niger Delta (see figure 7.2).

Figure 7.2. Lacking fuel for cooking. Many people in the Niger Delta use the heat generated by natural gas flares for drying foodstuffs (oblivious of the gaseous fumes and toxic emissions).
Source: Jacob Silberberg/New York Times/Redux, 2006.

By drawing attention to some of the key problems of the region (most of which are tied to the oil economy) and making political demands for their resolution, groups such as MEND and others are also engaged in rentier politics.

The International Dimension

As Africa's leading oil exporter and the fifth biggest supplier of U.S. oil imports, Nigeria's participation in the international market and finance is inextricably tied to its production and supply of oil. With approximately 40 billion barrels of proven petroleum reserves, its economy is webbed into the specific economic and security interests of key international stakeholders, notably, multinational oil corporations, global financial and lending institutions, the Organization of Petroleum Exporting Countries, international investors and speculators, other non-OPEC oil producers; as well as specific policy shifts in the decision-making of major world industrial powers like the United States and Great Britain. As indicated in the Energy Information Administration's 2007 Country Analysis Briefs,[51] the majority of Nigerian crude exports go to markets in the United States and Western Europe, with Asia and Latin America becoming increasingly important destinations. In 2005, Nigerian petroleum export to the United States averaged 1.15 million bbl/d, and is expected to grow in the coming years. This thus makes uninterrupted access to Nigerian oil an integral part of U.S. energy and economic security. The security concern over the continuing crisis in Nigeria's oil-rich Niger Delta featured prominently in the decision that led to the creation of a separate military command for Africa—the Africa Command (AFRICOM) by the United States in February 2007.

Multinational oil conglomerates such as Total, Chevron, Agip, and ConocoPhillips are centrally involved in the upstream and downstream sectors of the Nigerian oil economy. There is also the presence of oil service companies like Schlumberger, Halliburton, Transocean, and Brazil's Petrobas. The country relies on their technological know-how and financial resources for the exploration and development of new oil fields at both onshore and offshore deepwater locations. Chinese firms are also becoming increasingly involved in the Nigerian oil sector. In December 2004, Sinopec and NNPC signed an agreement to develop the Niger Delta's OML 64 and 66; and in July 2005, a trade agreement was reached in which Nigeria will supply China with 30,000 bbl/d of crude oil over the next five years.[52] Along with the increased foreign investment in the oil sector, the Nigerian government has also embarked on a Joint Development Zone (JDZ) initiative shared with the neighboring country of Sao Tome and Principe (STP)—a project that contains 23 exploration blocks and could potentially hold up to 14 billion barrels of oil reserves. In past years, the amount of oil that Nigeria produced has led to disputes with the Organization of Petroleum Exporting Countries (OPEC), as Nigeria frequently exceeded its production quotas which had been set at 2.3 million bbl/d. While the multinationals see Nigeria's OPEC production quota as a major hindrance to increased production at several deepwater fields; the economic pressure to over-produce reproduces itself as a source of conflict between state sovereignty, corporate rent, and the collective interest of OPEC membership.

In his recent article titled, *The First Law of Petropolitics*, the New York Times columnist Thomas Freidman attempts to build on the argument that there is an evident correlation between rises and falls in the price of oil with rises and falls in the pace of freedom in petrolist countries. As figure 7.3 indicates, the price of oil is inversely related to the degree of economic and political freedom granted by the Nigerian state. As the pace of freedom starts to decline, the price of oil invariably starts to rise. Hence if the argument holds true, then the higher oil price levels would certainly have long-term effects on the nature of politics in many weak or authoritarian states; and this, in turn, could have a negative global impact on the post–Cold War world as we have come to know it.

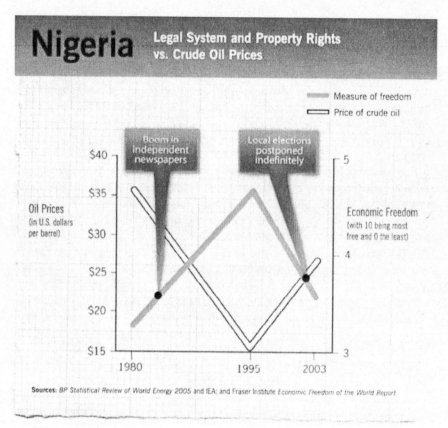

Figure 7.3.   Correlation Between Changes in Oil Price and Economic Freedom.
Source: BP Statistical Review of World Energy 2005 and IEA; and Fraser Institute *Economic Freedom of the World Report.* Reprinted from: Thomas J. Friedman, "The First Law of Petropolitics," May/June 2006, p. 5. www.foreignpolicy.com

Part of the reason for the rise in oil prices is due to the growth in the number of new entrants into the global market economy and the surge of rising expectations among their populations. With an increasing energy appetite coming from countries such as Brazil, China, India, Japan, and Latin America, we should expect a concomitant pressure on the price of oil in the foreseeable future. "Politically, that will mean that a whole group of petrolist states with weak institutions or outright authoritarian governments will likely experience an erosion of freedoms and an increase in corruption and autocratic, antidemocratic behaviors. Leaders in these countries can expect to have a significant increase in their disposable income to build up security forces, bribe opponents, buy votes or public support, and resist international norms and conventions."[53]

Citing the corresponding rise in authoritarian rule in Putin's Russia and much of the oil-producing Arab states as prices rose in the late 2000s, Friedman argues that as more and more oil wealth pile up in petrolist countries, it could really begin to distort the whole international system and the very character of the post–Cold War world. Pointing to the fact that when the Berlin Wall fell in 1989, there was a widespread belief that an unstoppable tide of free markets and democratization had been unleashed. While the proliferation of free elections around the world for the next decade made that tide very real; it is now running into an unanticipated counterwave of petro-authoritarianism, made possible by more than $60-a-barrel of oil. Suddenly, "regimes such as those in Iran, Nigeria, Russia, and Venezuela are retreating from what once seemed like an unstoppable process of democratization, with elected autocrats in each country using their sudden oil windfalls to ensconce themselves in power (as Obasanjo tried in 2006 to persuade the Nigerian legislature to amend the constitution to allow him to serve a third term), buy up opponents and supporters, and extend their state's chokehold into the private sector, after many thought it had permanently receded."[54]

Overall, the concept of rentier politics and the boundaries of the rentier space offer meaningful approaches for dealing with the complex of issues that influence oil politics within developing polities as well as in the international system. While it would be insufficient to look only at the patterns of rent accumulation; it would equally be useful to explore the structural and sociological forces that drive the accumulation process as well as the web of collateral interests that draw inspiration from it. While we cannot be able to determine in every single case, what the independent behavior of political actors would be; but it can be argued that the rentier space is robust enough to capture both formal and informal activities that occur within it, as well as the more deleterious effects on the practice of governance and public accountability. Nonetheless, I remain less inclined to the view that it is a "curse" to have oil in one's territory; but what could really be a "curse" is when dubious men and women are entrusted with managing the proceeds from oil rents and when such are diverted for unscrupulous gains. As could be said, it is not nature that should bear the "guilt," rather it is the "people."

NOTES

1. *The American Heritage Dictionary of the English Language*, ed. William Morris (Boston: Houghton Mifflin, 1976), 1102.

2. Douglas Yates, *The Rentier State in Africa: Oil Rent Dependency and Neocolonialism in the Republic of Gabon* (Trenton, N.J.: Africa World Press, 1996), 11.

3. Pamela Shoemaker, James W. Tankard, and Dominic L. Lasorsa, *How to Build Social Science Theories* (Thousand Oaks, Calif.: Sage Publications, 2004), 6.

4. Alexander George, "Case Studies and Theory Development: The Method of Structured, Focused Comparison," in *Diplomacy: New Approaches in History, Theory, and Policy*, ed. Paul Lauren (New York: Free Press, 1979), 44.

5. Giovanni Sartori, "Concept Misformation in Comparative Politics," pp. 24–49 in *Comparative Politics: Notes and Readings*, ed. Roy C. Macridis and Bernard Brown (Homewood, Ill.: The Dorsey Press, 1977).

6. Hossein Mahdavy, "The Pattern and Problems of Economic Development in Rentier States: The Case of Iran," in *Studies in the Economic History of the Middle East*, ed. M. A. Cook (Oxford: Oxford University Press, 1970), 428.

7. Hazem Beblawi and Giacomo Luciani, *The Rentier State, Volume II* (London: Croom Helm, 1987).

8. William Graf, *The Nigerian State: Political Economy, State Class and Political System in the Post-Colonial Era* (Portsmouth, N.H.: Heinemann, 1988), 219.

9. Graf, *The Nigerian State*, 219.

10. Graf, *The Nigerian State*, 220–22.

11. Giacomo Luciani, "Oil and Political Economy in the International Relations of the Middle East," pp. 79–104 in *International Relations of the Middle East*, ed. Louise Fawcett (New York: Oxford University Press, 2005), 91.

12. Beblawi and Luciani, *The Rentier State, Volume II*, 12.

13. Kenneth Omeje, "Oil Conflict and Accumulation Politics in Nigeria," Report from Africa: Population, Health, Environment, and Conflict, *ECSP Report* 12 (2007): 45. Also summarized in Energy Information Association (EIA), *OPEC Revenues: Country Details*, at www.eia.doe.gov/emeu/cabs/orevcoun.html.

14. Kenneth Omeje, "Oil Conflict and Accumulation Politics in Nigeria," Report from Africa: Population, Health, Environment, and Conflict, *ECSP Report* 12 (2007): 46.

15. Alan Gelb et al., *Oil Windfalls: Blessing or Curse?* (New York: Oxford University Press, 1988). Also see Jeffrey Sachs and Andrew M. Warner, "Natural Resource Abundance and Economic Growth," Development Discussion Paper 517a, Cambridge, Mass.: Harvard Institute for International Development, October 1995.

16. Susan Rose-Ackerman, *Corruption and Government: Causes, Consequences, and Reform* (New York: Cambridge University Press, 1999), 214.

17. Anne O. Krueger, "The Political Economy of a Rent-Seeking Society," *American Economic Review* 64: 291–303.

18. Arne Bigsten and Karl Ove Moene, "Growth and Rent Dispensation: The Case of Kenya," *Journal of African Economics* 5 (1996): 192–93.

19. Rose-Ackerman, *Corruption and Government: Causes, Consequences, and Reform*, 213.

20. Luciani, "Oil and Political Economy in the International Relations of the Middle East," *International Relations of the Middle East*, 92.

21. Larry Diamond, "Nigeria: Pluralism, Statism, and the Struggle for Democracy," pp. 351–409 in *Politics in Developing Countries: Comparing Experiences with Democracy*, ed. Larry Diamond, Juan J. Linz, and Seymour Martin Lipset (Boulder. Colo.: Lynne Rienner Publishers, 1990), 356.

22. John Boye Ejobowah, "Who Owns the Oil? The Politics of Ethnicity in the Niger Delta of Nigeria," *African Today* (1999): 35.

23. See Ejobowah, "Who Owns the Oil?" 35.

24. Ejobowah, "Who Owns the Oil?" 35.

25. Kayode Somerekun, *Perspectives on the Nigerian Oil Industry* (Lagos, Nigeria: Amkra Books, 1995). Also summarized in Ejobowah, "Who Owns the Oil?" 35.

26. Ejobowah, "Who Owns the Oil? 35.

27. Augustine Ikem and Comfort Briggs-Anigboh, *Oil and Fiscal Federalism in Nigeria* (Aldershot, Eng.: Ashgate, 1998), 140. Also summarized in Ejobowah, "Who Owns the Oil?" 35.

28. *West Africa*, No. 2747, "Nigeria After the War: Lubricating the Economy with Oil," Saturday, January 24, 1970, 99.

29. *West Africa*, No. 2747, "Nigeria After the War," 99.

30. See Luciani, "Oil and Political Economy in the International Relations of the Middle East," 89. At the outbreak of the Arab-Israeli conflict in October 1973, the Organization of Arab Oil Exporting Countries (OAPEC) declared an embargo on the United States and the Netherlands. Even though oil prices rose sharply as the international market experienced its first "energy crisis," Luciani argues that the so-called oil embargo never occurred and remains fictional at best. In fact, oil was never used as a weapon. By referencing a British Petroleum Statistical Review of World Energy and Oil production by region (1970–1980), it showed that Middle East Oil Production increased steadily and rapidly until 1974; but only declined the following year due to recession and decrease in oil demand that was triggered by the increase in oil prices. He states that, although the episode was a success from the point of view of provoking an increase in prices, it was a politically disastrous failure, which the Gulf oil producers still regret to this day.

31. Graf, *The Nigerian State*, 110.

32. Graf, *The Nigerian State*, 110–11.

33. Rose-Ackerman, *Corruption and Government*, 27.

34. Rose-Ackerman, *Corruption and Government*, 14.

35. Rose-Ackerman, *Corruption and Government*, 3.

36. Rose-Ackerman, *Corruption and Government*, 26.

37. Rose-Ackerman, *Corruption and Government*, 9.

38. Scrutiny, "The Missing Billions," 1, no. 9 (July 1998): 1.

39. Jean Herskovitz, "Nigeria's Rigged Democracy," *Foreign Affairs* (July/August, 2007): 119.

40. "The Leader of the Leader," *The News*, December 18, 2000, 17.

41. Ike Okonto, "Nigeria: Chronicle of a Dying State," pp. 213–17 in *World Politics*, Annual Editions, 27th ed., ed. Helen E. Purkit (Dubuque, Ia.: McGraw-Hill, 2007), 214.

42. This information and what follows in the rest of the paragraph were gleaned from the Country Analysis Briefs of the EIA, U.S. Department of Energy (International Energy Annual), 2007.

43. Okey Ekeocha, "The Scramble for Oil," *The African Guardian*, March 5, 1990, 18.

44. Kenneth Omeje, "The Rentier State: Oil-Related Legislation and Conflict in the Niger Delta, Nigeria," *Conflict, Security and Development* 6, no. 2 (June 2006): 212.

45. Omeje, "Oil Conflict and Accumulation Politics in Nigeria," 45.

46. Diamond, "Nigeria: Pluralism, Statism, and the Struggle for Democracy," in *Politics in Developing Countries: Comparing Experiences with Democracy*, 384.

47. Luciani, "Oil and Political Economy in the International Relations of the Middle East," 92.

48. Diamond, "Nigeria: Pluralism, Statism, and the Struggle for Democracy," 384.

49. The National Union of Petroleum and Natural Gas Workers (NUPENG) and the Petroleum and Natural Gas Senior Staff Association of Nigeria (PENGASSAN) are the leading labor unions in Nigeria's oil sector.

50. U.S. Energy Information Administration, *Nigeria: Country Analysis Briefs*, Department of Energy, April 2007, at www.eia.doe.gov.

51. U.S. Energy Information Administration, *Nigeria: Country Analysis Briefs*, Department of Energy, April 2007, at www.eia.doe.gov.

52. Information in the rest of the paragraph were gleaned from the U.S. Energy Information Administration, *Nigeria: Country Analysis Briefs*, Department of Energy, April 2007, at www.eia.doe.gov.

53. Thomas L. Friedman, "The First Law of Petropolitics," May/June 2006, 5, at www.foreignpolicy.com/story/cms.php?story_id=3426&print=1.

54. Friedman, "The First Law of Petropolitics," 7.

8

—ɱ—

The Garrison State
Bridging Civil-Military Transitions

It is a rather simplistic notion to suggest that the transition from a non-democratic authoritarian regime to a liberal democracy begins and ends with the replacement of one regime by another. If follows therefore, that a cultural transformation must also be a central element in the transition process. "Where military governments have given up power more or less voluntarily, those militaries will continue to have substantial influence in their society after their withdrawal from power. Notable examples are Turkey, South Korea, Nicaragua, Brazil, Chile,"[1] including Nigeria, Zaire, Ecuador, Argentina, Uruguay, Honduras, Guatemala, and many others. The Nigerian military coup of January 1966 ended civilian rule; but in order to widen its base of support before and during the civil war (1967–1970), it became expedient to put civilian politicians in cabinet-level positions. As Henry Bienen points out, "this civilian-military diarchy existed from mid 1967 until towards the end of 1974 (a practice that also continued into 1999 with successive military regimes) because the military government thought civilian help was necessary to mobilize civilian energies, to handle representative functions at both central and grassroots levels, and to unify disunified states in the federation."[2] But while the "military created institutions, in which civilian politicians could participate, be used, and also controlled; these institutions were, in turn, used by the civilian leaders to build a power base independent of the military."[3]

Suffice it then to state that "military involvement in Nigerian politics has left positive and negative legacies. The negative legacy that came mainly in the second part of military rule (1984–1999) was the legacy of tyranny, divisive leadership and corruption."[4] But almost all of these authoritarian military regimes lacked, before and after-the-fact, the kind of civil-military relations that Samuel Huntington refers to as "objective civilian control." On this note, Harold Lasswell's[5] seminal thesis comes to mind—when he argued that a military administration working in concert with civil administration could turn the modern state into a "garrison state." This development poses enormous problem for the evolution of citizenship and democracy in transitional states, by retaining and reinforcing the patrimonial nature of state-society relations, and by using a de facto military model as a means of civic engagement and democratic discourse. The contradiction generated by this model eventually retards democratic consolidation while institutionalizing the military state by *default*. Hence, the praetorian military state becomes embedded in the political structure by transforming itself and coopting the domain of political discourse in the public space. In this chapter, I will explore the political consequences of the many years of mingling civil and military culture in Nigeria's body politic.

THE DIALECTICS OF POWER AND POLITICAL RELEVANCE

In Nigeria, there seem to be an evolving public perception that the leadership of previous military regimes and that of subsequent civilian democratic governments essentially complement or mirror each other. When authoritarian regimes take over political power, their first attempt is to impose a regimented dictatorial order. But in its aftermath, the legacy of such order endures in the mindset and expectations of the civilian population as a behavioral fait accompli. Civilian political leaders more often than not embrace the same governing style and worldview as their military predecessors. They become reluctant agents in the facilitation of a nondemocratic political culture. Aside from witnessing the same autocratic tendencies in dealing with crucial domestic policy issues, there is also an evident breakdown in law and order to the extent that the only practical way to deal with the rising problem of social dissension (with the attendant ethno-religious undertones) is to crack down.

Nigeria's experience points to the fact that the current "economic reform has been stymied, has become unpopular with a restive public, and has been manipulated to benefit members of the old authoritarian elite. Crime and corruption have increased to the extent that they have been elevated to an acceptable work of art. Human rights guarantees in the new (military directed) constitution have been routinely violated; the press has been controlled or subverted; and political party systems have been fragmented and personalized, incapable of producing either effective governments or responsible oppositions. While the removal of overt authoritarian controls has permitted and even helped to stimulate heightened communal (ethnic and religious) consciousness and violence, the democratic deficiency has generated, in most cases, an authoritarian nostalgia, as people (in desperation) look back with longing at dictators who provided for basic needs and made things work (no matter how painful)."[6] There are two trajectories to this seemingly diametrically opposed political norm: the individualized claim to political citizenship whether military or civilian, and the more general impact on the macro-political culture of society at large. The moral dilemma created here is that when the military abdicates power in most transitional states, they are equally entitled as every other citizen to the benefits and privileges of the new democratic order.

In almost all transitional states, regime legitimacy is not necessarily assured no matter how efficient and committed a new government seeks to operate and consolidate its power. Rather, *time* is the most critical element that enables the transition process to solidify and generate enough capacity to bridge the different orientations of the military and civilian cultures. But unfortunately, most transitional regimes do not have much *time*. They are, more often than not, overthrown as a result of tensions generated within the same regime they seek to secure. Though having been in power before, the soldier-turned-civilian is able to use his knowledge of the nuances of governmental control to seek a new civilian electoral mandate that brings him back into the saddle of power, but this time with a greater sense of legitimacy anchored on the popular will. "As a rule, military establishments are uncomfortable with the enforced inactivity of peacetime,"[7] hence by seeking electoral office, they invent new ways to secure and retain their institutional and personal relevance. But when old habits die hard, one is therefore forced to ask the question: Can military culture be genuinely subsumed under a participatory democratic governance? Can they abandon the military emphasis on hierarchy and chain of command for the more gradualist and consensual politics of civilian life?

REGIME CONCESSION AND SOCIETAL CONQUEST

In his study of Brazilian politics in the early 1970s, Alfred Stepan[8] came to the conclusion that a certain dialectic—which he referred to as *regime concession* and *societal conquest* had begun. It was a retrospective commentary on the military-controlled party, and a veiled reference to the fact that though the military may be out of power, it nonetheless remained as a major power broker within the dominant political party. While the military may have conceded political office, they have conquered the political fortunes of the society. As Nigeria engages in a process of transition from years of authoritarian regimes to that of a democratic political order, it remains to be seen how far it would avoid a crisis of democratic consolidation typical of most developing polities. The military may have for once shade its colors but the marching order and sentiments remain buried in the political struggles for perpetual power and control. With its immense population and multiethnic orientation, as well as its historical antecedents, Nigeria serves as a very useful case study that explains the essential problematic indicated here.

The history of military rule in Nigeria and the periodic spurts in civilian governance presents a crucial basis from which to address the above questions (table 8.1). In an ironic way, the institutional role of the Nigerian army (defense and national security) is combined with its instrumental role as citizens (participants in the governance and maintenance of the functional integrity of the state).

It is in the later that the military role is confused when considered in light of the democratic potentials of the country and in the choice and methods of political engagement and participation. So much is therefore evident that "the institutional role of the Armed forces in the new democratic regime remains, as in all cases, a matter of conflict between political and military elites."[9] Though the military directly or indirectly, tries to preserve a tutelary role over the civilian government, it is nonetheless the very process of political engagement that eventually would determine the ways in which the Armed forces are integrated into the democratic system. Hence, "different patterns of democracy would, in turn, have diverse

Table 8.1. Dimensions of Political and Military Leadership in Nigeria, 1966–2007

Date	Head of State	Type of Regime
1960–1966	Abubakar Tafawa Balewa	Civilian
Jan. 1966–July 1966	Maj. Gen. Aguiyi Ironsi	Military
July 1966–1975	Lt. Colonel Yakubu Gowon	Military
1975–1976	Brig. Gen. M. Muhammed	Military
1976–1979	Lt. Gen. Olu Obasanjo	Military
1979–1983	Alhaji Shehu Shagari	Civilian
1983–1985	Maj. Gen. M. Buhari	Military
1958–1993	Maj. Gen. I. Babangida	Military
June 1993–Nov. 1993	Ernest Shonekan	Civilian (Interim)
1993–1998	Gen. Sani Abacha	Military
1998–1999	Maj. Gen. A. Abubakar	Military
1999–2007	Olusegun Obasanjo	Civilian (former military head of state, 1976–1979)
2007–present	Alhaji Umar Yar'Adua	Civilian

consequences for the resulting types of democracy."[10] Although democracy developed under military tutelage in Nigeria, the struggle over the form and scope of that tutelage still finds general expression in the chaotic and pseudo-dictatorial tendencies of the civilian regime.

On May 29, 1999, Nigeria elected a new civilian president in the person of retired army general Olusegun Obasanjo. Obasanjo had ruled Nigeria from February 1976 to October 1979, when he handed over the reins of government to the elected civilian administration of Shehu Shagari, and retired from the military. In the Obasanjo civilian government, many retired military generals found their way back into political governance. No fewer than five former generals were elected into the legislature. Some became state commissioners or ministers, while others, though out of the military, remained politically active behind the scenes. In fact, it has become an undisputed fact that the 1999 election was greatly funded by a clique of wealthy retired military officers. Among them was the former military head of state General Ibrahim Babangida who also has become enormously wealthy due to the limitless opportunities provided by control of the state apparatus.

However, upon taking office, Obasanjo surprised many of his former military colleagues by retiring more than 150 military officers, removing any soldier who held political office between 1985 and 1999. The first list of retirements in the army included nine major generals, sixteen brigadier generals, and twenty colonels. There were also other top-rank retirements in the navy and the air force. Many of the officers were known to be close to the late military dictator General Sani Abacha. On June 5, 1999, he inaugurated a panel headed by Christopher Kolade to review all contracts, licenses, and awards made by the last military regime between January and May 1999. He established a new set of civil service rules to curb official corruption, established a committee headed by a former Supreme Court judge to examine the cruelties and human rights abuses that took place since 1983.

In the effort to professionalize the military and prepare it for its traditional role of defending the territorial integrity of the country, Obasanjo stated that "the military is not only morally disadvantaged on account of the abysmal failure of past political adventures, but that public opinion is decidedly against the soldiers."[11] But there was increasing public anxiety that despite the purges, the military would still be in control of the Nigerian government, but only this time in civilian clothes. Of greatest concern was former Lt. General Theophilus Danjuma, a one-time member of the Supreme Military Council under the Obasanjo military regime of 1976 to 1979. Apart from working with other retired generals to persuade Obasanjo to contest for the presidential elections, he also participated in raising funds for his campaign. After Obasanjo won the February 1999 election, Danjuma was selected to chair the Presidential Policy Advisory Committee (PPAC) that recommended ministerial and parastatal positions. He was consequently appointed as minister of defense in the Obasanjo administration.

After many years of presiding over the "looting and plundering" of the Nigerian treasury, military personnel (both serving and retired) have become the largest repository of private capital accumulation, unrivaled in many countries of the world. They are able to fund their own individual political campaigns, or that of their surrogates in any part or region of the country. Many civilian state governors and other candidates were funded through the financial benevolence of retired military generals. From this vantage point, the military, directly or indirectly, is able to shape the nature of policy making as well as the allocation of values within the administrative state. As Amos Perlmutter points out, some tutelary political structures established under military rule have weaknesses similar to those of the political structures they replace, and others are no more than a shadow of the military-dominated state.[12]

CITIZENSHIP AND CIVIC CULTURE: DICTATING THE CONDITIONS FOR INTEGRATION

The conceptualization of citizenship in this particular case goes beyond the idea of individual identity but embraces the notion of "identity in relation to others" within the same political community. What is sought in this interpretation is a more constructive worldview of citizenship that allows an individual to view cultural as well as political events through various analytical lenses. In other words, is what makes one a citizen the same as that which is understood to be so by others similarly situated? Can different cultural dispositions (military or civic) offer different interpretations of citizenship and the requisite individual obligations? When the military sheds its dictatorial tendencies for the imperatives of civilian governance, does it retain its military culture or does it replace it with a more tolerant civic culture?

If we consider the dichotomy in cultural dispositions, we can therefore see that the inherent problem of the military turned civilian political leaders is a problem of *cultural transformation*. When this fails, it obfuscates and interrupts what would normally be construed as a smooth path toward democratic consolidation. This is not to say that the military cannot change its original cultural disposition, but this is a phenomenon that requires time as well as the will to do so. Citizenship, therefore, "is a final good only for citizens who are citizens in the full cultural sense."[13] As Thomas Bridges points out,

> Citizenship is in many ways a difficult and peculiar way of life. Even the minimalist citizenship called for by *modus vivendi* liberalism—the citizenship that requires no more than the cultivation of an attitude of "live and let live," a posture of benign mutual indifference in the name of civil peace—can be difficult for many who have strong commitments to totalizing life ideals. If such minimalist citizenship can be burdensome to many, then even more difficult is the practice of full cultural citizenship that alone insures the success of liberal political institutions.[14]

Because it lacks full cultural citizenship in the civic and integrative sense of the term, the military mindset remains a serious challenge to liberal democratic ideals. Such is the case that when cultural identities and commitment (civic or military) create a sense of belonging simultaneously to the state and to another institutional community (the military) "that is distinct from the state but at the same time contained within it,"[15] the authenticity of individual loyalty becomes more ambiguous. Where then does military loyalty lie? Is it in the simultaneous cultivation of the military ethic while seeking its replacement under the guise of the emergent democratic order?

Beyond Frameworks and Heuristics

The modus operandi of a professional military is anchored on sets of behavioral scripts or standard operating procedures that have overtime become regularized and encoded in the very character of that institution. While the expectation of loyalty and conformity is an ingrained part of the disciplinary framework, transitional states find it hard to unfreeze much of the behavioral habits retained by the military as it attempts to embrace a new democratic doctrine. It should therefore be understood that "retention systems are not simply repositories for interpretations that have been selected and discarded over time. They affect subsequent actions; they are frequently edited; they are protected in elaborate ways that may conflict with variation and selection (other opinions); they are coercive only to the degree that members are informed of their contents; and they contain items that frequently are opposed to the self-interest of persons who must implement these items (rules)."[16]

The psychology of military rule is based on the concept of power and control. When they abdicate military rule for the more tolerant culture of civilian political governance, it does not reflect a change in their interpretation of the imperatives of public service, rather it is a continuation of the institutional quest for power and control. Rather than seeing power as intercursive or pluralistic, the military sees "power as something which benefits one group at the expense of another, rather than something that benefits everyone."[17] This is the prism through which former military leaders in Nigeria embrace the civic culture as they attempt to transform themselves into civilian political leaders. They are not always successful, driven partly by the difficulties they confront in the process of cultural transformation, and on the other hand, by the nostalgia of a regimented life devoid of the uncertainty and the characteristic horse-trading of political life.

The issue therefore is whether a means of persuasion can be found sufficient enough to motivate all individuals and groups to seek political governance as a civic ideal, rather than as an instrumental objective. While it may be true that "the practice of political virtue is parasitic on our holding our beliefs and interests—and, importantly, those of others—in the right way, but failing the emergence of such a disposition, the goods of political interaction and cooperation can remain elusive."[18] While some seek political governance as an extension of power and control, others see it as a means of long and short-term economic security. But considered in light of the general population, very few see it as a sacrifice or as a public good. It is the dearth of citizens who fall in the middle category that sways the consequent abuse of democratic opportunities in favor of those who see it as a means of achieving both instrumental and self-aggrandizing objectives. And herein lays the difficulty for all citizens (military and civilians) to acquire a common political virtue conducive to long-term democratic consolidation, without resulting in the ambiguity of national purpose.

The uncertainty created by this also makes it possible for the military turned civilian political leaders to secretly shed their overt democratic credentials for the more expedient and covert military regimen. Some authors on Nigerian politics[19] have written about what they see as a "transition without end," but in fact, what they have really tried to expose is the continuous attempt of the Nigerian military and its old-guard mentality to fill the political vacuum resulting from the ambiguity and multiple interpretations of the nation's civic culture. The military engages in the institutional process of drawn-out transitions, the manipulation of elections, or the deliberate construction of civil strife to ensure that its agents in the civilian political class remain in control. As Juan Linz and Alfred Stepan point out,[20] "if the costs of rule by the *military as government* are considered too great for the *military as institution*, a free election may become part of the extrication formula for the hierarchical military in charge of an authoritarian regime." Hence, support for popular democratic elections is not necessarily a sine qua non to support for political democracy as an ideal. Rather it presents a strategic opportunity for the military to rethink and retool its next step in the cultural quest for power and control. The military, in fact, never leave government; they just change the playing field.

Such can be explained by the fact that when General Babangida (August 1995–June 1993) ended his reign in June 1993 and handed power over to an Interim National Government headed by a civilian Ernest Shonekan (June 1993–November 1993), he (either by design or default) created a constitutional as well as a political crisis. It was under this atmosphere that key members of the political elite, especially those not favored by the emerging dispensation, were said to have favored a military takeover of government. Then on November 17, 1993, General Sani Abacha initiated what most people would qualify as a coup de grace and overthrew the civilian-led Interim National Government, thereby abbreviating the transitional path toward democratic consolidation. In consideration, it is therefore relevant to note that "the characteristics of the previous nondemocratic regime have profound implications for the transition paths available and the tasks different countries face when they begin their struggles to develop consolidated democracies."[21] Hence, the above scenario exemplifies in a dramatic way the residual problems stemming from a transition initiated by nondemocratic regimes. The death of General Abacha led to rule by another interim government headed by General Abdulsalam Abubakar (1998–1999) and "a constitution-making process (the 1999 Constitution) heavily conditioned by nondemocratic pressures. The process consequently resulted in the creation of 'reserve domains' of power that precluded, as long as they were in place, the completion of the democratic transition and consolidation."[22]

MACROPOLITICAL AND ECONOMIC
DIMENSIONS OF THE TRANSITION PROCESS

The major problems affecting civil-military relations in transitional or new democracies are: the potential for military intervention in politics (the *latency effect*), the disruption in preexisting military privileges, the possibility of prosecution by the new regime, and the enduring desire for power and legitimacy—to preserve the fleeting institutional integrity of the army and the recognition of its past and present heroes. While the frequency of coup attempts against aspiring democratic governments have been numerous, Huntington points out that many such coup attempts with the exception of—Nigeria, Sudan, and Haiti—have failed. He asked an apt question: "If well-established military forces are challenging new regimes, which have a somewhat fragile existence and are potentially unstable, why have they gone down in defeat?"[23] He states that the answer to that question lies primarily with each country's level of economic development and modernization. The economic development thesis posits thus that:

> The process of economic development from the 1950s through the early 1970s laid the basis for the movement toward democracy beginning in the mid-1970s. Economic development has also ensured the failure of almost all of the subsequent coup attempts. Without embracing absolute economic determinism, one can thus cite a useful economic guideline. There is a coup attempt ceiling and there is a coup success ceiling, both of which can be defined more or less in terms of per capita GNP. Countries with per-capita GNPs of $1,000 or more do not have successful coups; countries with per-capita GNPs of $3,000 or more do not have coup attempts. The area between $1,000 and $3,000 per-capita GNP is where unsuccessful coups occur, while successful coups in Nigeria, Sudan, and Haiti were in countries with per-capita GNPs under $500.[24]

However, beyond the bold conclusion relative to the above thesis, there are assumptions that underestimate the role of other generally non-economic factors in the preponderance of coup attempts among transitional states. In the case of Nigeria, we can thus highlight specific cultural issues that impede the process of stable transitions as well as democratic consolidation. These indicators attest to the generally low level of human development, democracy, rule of law, civil society, and governmental effectiveness in Nigeria (tables 8.2–8.6). These indicators are very important because their effects are cumulative and extend to previous years. On a scale, Nigeria ranks very low (at 148) out of approximately 173 countries.

What is indicated by the cumulative effect of the above indicators is that they are probably not unique to different regime changes, but

Table 8.2.   Nigeria: Democracy, Subjective Indicators of Governance, 2000–2001

Indicators	Democracy	
	Country Score*	Parameter
Polity Score	4	(–10 to 10)
Civil Liberties	4	(7 to 1)
Political Rights	4	(7 to 1)
Press Freedom	55	(100 to 0)
Voice and Accountability	–0.44	(–2.50 to 2.50)

Note: *Higher is better.
    Human Development Indicators Rank (148).

Source: United Nations Development Programme, *Human Development Report 2002: Deepening Democracy in a Fragmented World* (New York: Oxford University Press, 2002), 40–41.

Table 8.3. Nigeria: Rule of Law and Government Effectiveness, Subjective Indicators of Governance, 2000–2001

	Rule of Law/Government Effectiveness	
Indicators	Country Score*	Parameter
Political Stability	–1.36	(–2.50 to 2.50)
Law and Order	2.0	(0 to 6)
Rule of Law	–1.3	(–2.50 to 2.50)
Govt. Effectiveness	–1.0	(–2.50 to 2.50)
Corruption (Graft)	–1.05	(–2.50 to 2.50)

Note: *Higher is better.
Human Development Indicators Rank (148).

Source: United Nations Development Programme, *Human Development Report 2002: Deepening Democracy in a Fragmented World* (New York: Oxford University Press, 2002), 40–41.

Table 8.4. Nigeria: Political Participation, Objective Indicators of Governance, 2000–2001

	Political Participation	
Indicators	Country Score*	Parameter
Voter turnout**	41%	(0–100%)
Seats in Legislature (Women)	3.3%	(0–100%)
Women in govt. (at ministerial level)	22.6%	n/a
Civil Society (Union membership)	17%	(0–100%)***
Non-governmental organizations	894	n/a

Notes: *Higher is better.
**Latest election for lower or single house (1999)
***As a percentage of nonagricultural labor force.
Human Development Indicators Rank (148).

Source: United Nations Development Programme, *Human Development Report 2002: Deepening Democracy in a Fragmented World* (New York: Oxford University Press, 2002), 44.

Table 8.5. Nigeria: Human Development Index, Objective Indicators of Governance, 2000–2001

	Human Development Index	
Indicators	Country Score*	Parameter
Life expectancy at birth	51.7	n/a
Adult literacy rate	63.9%	(0–100%)
Primary/Sec. Enrollment**	45%	(0–100%)
GDP per capita	$896	n/a
Gini Index***	50.6	(0–100)
Life expectancy index	0.44	n/a
Education index	0.58	n/a
Human Dev. Index****	0.462	n/a

Notes: *Higher is better
**Percentage 15 and above
***The *Gini index* measures *inequality* over the entire distribution of income or consumption. A value of zero represents *perfect equality*, and value of 100 *perfect inequality*.
****Nigeria has been ranked consistently *low* on *Human Development Index* trends 1975–2000.
Human Development Indicators Rank (148).

Source: United Nations Development Programme, *Human Development Report 2002: Deepening Democracy in a Fragmented World* (New York: Oxford University Press, 2002), 44.

Table 8.6.   Nigeria: Flows of Aid, Private Capital and Debt, Human Development Indicators Rank (148).

Flows of Aid, Private Capital and Debt			
Indicators	*Country Score**		*Parameter*
Official Dev. Assistance (ODA)	$184.8m		n/a
ODA per capita	$1.6		n/a
Net FDI as a % of GDP**	2.1 (1990)	2.6 (2000)	n/a
Private Capital flows (% of GDP)	0.4 (1990)	−0.4 (2000)	n/a
Debt Service (% of GDP)	11.7 (1990)	2.5 (2000)	n/a
Debt Service (% of exports)	22.6 (1990)	4.3 (2000)	n/a

Notes: *Higher is better.
          **Net foreign direct investment inflows as a percent of Gross Domestic Product (GDP).

Source: United Nations Development Programme, *Human Development Report 2002: Deepening Democracy in a Fragmented World* (New York: Oxford University Press, 2002), 205.

in a way, serve as explanatory factors that suggest more endemic and fundamental problems in the political and developmental character of Nigeria. Though the various regimes might be different both in name and disposition, the fundamental logic that drives the character of political stewardship remain the same. As Arthur Nwankwo argues,[25] "the tragedy of political transitions in Nigeria thus far is that no credible attempt has been made to address the fundamental issues in the national question." The clientelist nature of the relationship between the military and the elite political class ensures that the established principles of governmental action and institutional reciprocity remain unchanged. In fact, "if the underlying relationships based on corruption, family connections, and patronage are not changed, standard macroeconomic prescriptions are less-likely to succeed."[26] In the long run, democracy yields minimal or no dividends in terms of improvements in civil liberties and quality of life issues.

So the principal problem facing most transitional states is not the endemic oscillations between democratic and nondemocratic (autocratic) regimes; rather it is an inherent problem of the inability to differentiate between the boundaries of the military and civilian political cultures because both have severely permeated each other. Simultaneous economic and political crises challenge state legitimacy and thus drive sane political discourse into what might seem as a perpetual state of *anxiety*. "Though economic and political crises are costly and risky preconditions for reform, they are often preceded by long periods of slow decline in the effectiveness of the state,"[27] hence when they occur, the violence and chaos which they generate are often too difficult for transitional states to contain as the instability continue to multiply.

DEMOCRACY AS IDEAL: RECONCILING CITIZENSHIP

Drawn from historical experience, one can argue that democracy and citizenship are not mutually exclusive. While this is not to argue as to which one precedes the other, but where they exist, each individually serves as a necessary safeguard for the other. "In democratic theory, the notion of citizenship is anchored in the legal definition of rights and obligations."[28] But "clearly crucial to real citizenship is the civil (liberal) component whereby the members of the collectivity (society) affirm themselves autonomously, in a way that not only dispenses with the state but may even involve acting effectively against it."[29] But in many transitional states, such demonstration of democratic liberalism is considered a threat to national security and might even provide a ruse for the military to reconquer government. The political dilemma therefore is how to contain the potent forces unleashed by political liberalization without uprooting the very foundation upon which that process is based. As Nigeria wrestles with this situation, it has always seemed to take the easiest route out by applying the same brutal machinery of control used by previous military regimes to subdue political protests. It is yet to reconcile the fact that though "the articulation between the need for governability and representation on the one hand, and participation and citizens' control of government administration on the other, are often portrayed as incompatible, the construction of democracy requires both processes."[30] While "the expansion of the social base of citizenship (i.e., granting of voting rights to all, fair representation, protection of minority rights), inclusion of minorities or of dispossessed social groups as members of the citizenry (in national policy making), and the claim of equality before the law are ever present issues in contemporary history," but unless they endeavor from the outset to institutionalize the means of citizen participation and control, new and weak democracies cease to be democratic.[31]

In this chapter, I have tried to advance the general thesis that the long years of military rule in Nigeria has made it rather difficult to assimilate a civic culture that efficaciously accommodates both military and civilian norms. In fact, it may have destroyed Nigeria's democratic potentials for the foreseeable future. Since January 15, 1966, the Nigerian army has cultivated a long-standing disposition to intervene in political governance. Beyond the rhetoric, its inclination toward political activism sprang from three sources: First was the political ambitions of senior generals who had exploited civilian weaknesses to further their own careers. The second was the professional dissatisfaction of junior officers (especially majors) who saw political governance as a quick avenue for fulfilling career aspirations and wealth. The third was the personality conflict among key members of the senior officer cadre. As the army became increasingly identified with unpopular or repressive policies; and as the possibility for effective military reform diminished, the gap between it and the rest of society widened. "Since the abuses, the privileges, and the inefficiency were daily visible, the army became the institution most frequently blamed by critics of the regime."[32] In fact, the civil-military crisis of the Babangida and Abacha years was the most significant example of a general crisis of democratic consolidation affecting Nigeria, as her politicians struggled unsuccessfully, to repair a shattered sense of national credibility.

As the Nigerian military abdicates direct political power, there has to be a concern about the "crisis of mission" it is bound to face. This is even made more relevant due to the fact that a lack of "professional mission should be seen as a dangerous destabilizing force that could motivate the military to reconquer government."[33] In the presidential elections of 2003 and 2007, no less than three former military generals and two military heads of state declared interest to contest for the civilian presidency. While they may have the funds and the machinery to do so, but the question remains as to their true motivations. If people must embrace beliefs and practices that are suitable to, or consistent with the notion of democracy, they also must learn how to act within the renewed constitutional order. "The challenge of democratization lies in the capacity to combine formal institutional changes with the expansion of democratic practices and the strengthening of a culture of citizenship."[34] The military, whether in their professional role as *praetorian* guards of the state, or as political administrators, are nonetheless public servants. The problem for transitional states (developing polities) in general, and Nigeria in particular, is how to make the military permanently subordinate to civilian purposes.

NOTES

1. Samuel P. Huntington, "Reforming Civil-Military Relations," pp. 3–11 in *Civil-Military Relations and Democracy*, ed. Larry Diamond and Marc F. Plattner (Baltimore: Johns Hopkins University Press, 1996): 9.

2. Henry Bienen, "Military Rule and Political Processes: Nigerian Examples," *Comparative Politics* 10, no. 2 (January 1978): 209–10.

3. Bienen, "Military Rule and Political Processes," 210.

4. Anthony Akinola, "Phases of Nigerian Democracy," *West Africa* (No. 4283), July 9–15, 2001, 11–12.

5. Harold D. Lasswell, "Sino-Japanese Crisis: The Garrison State Versus the Civilian State," *China Quarterly* 2 (1937): 643–49. Also see Harold D. Lasswell, "The Garrison State," *American Journal of Sociology* 46, no. 4 (1941): 455–68.

6. Huntington, "Reforming Civil-Military Relations," 4.

7. Juan Rial, "Armies and Civil Society in Latin America," in *Civil-Military Relations and Democracy,* ed. Larry Diamond and Marc F. Plattner (Baltimore: Johns Hopkins University Press, 1996): 47.

8. Alfred Stepan, *The Military in Politics: Changing Patterns in Brazil* (Princeton, N.J.: Princeton University Press, 1971).

9. Carlos A. Acuna and Catalina Smulovitz, "Adjusting the Armed Forces to Democracy: Success, Failures, and Ambiguities in the Southern Cone," pp. 13–38 in *Constructing Democracy: Human Rights, Citizenship, and Society in Latin America,* ed. Elizabeth Jelin and Eric Hershberg (Boulder, Colo.: Westview Press, 1996), 33.

10. Acuna and Smulovitz, "Adjusting the Armed Forces to Democracy," 33.

11. Ndulue Mbachu, "Nigeria's Military Purge Seen as Timely," *Reuters Ltd,* June 11, 1999.

12. Amos Perlmutter, "The Praetorian State and the Praetorian Army: Toward a Taxonomy of Civil-Military Relations in Developing Polities," *Comparative Politics* 1, no. 3: 382–404.

13. Thomas Bridges, *The Culture of Citizenship: Inventing Postmodern Civic Culture* (Albany: State University of New York Press, 1994), 167.

14. Bridges, *The Culture of Citizenship: Inventing Postmodern Civic Culture,* 168.

15. Joseph H. Carens, *Culture, Citizenship, and Community: A Contextual Exploration of Justice as Evenhandedness* (New York: Oxford University Press, 2000), 65–66.

16. Karl Weick, *The Social Psychology of Organizing,* 2nd ed. (New York: McGraw-Hill, 1979), 126.

17. Gibson Burrell and Gareth Morgan, *Sociological Paradigms and Organizational Analysis* (Burlington, Vt.: Ashgate, 2000), 215.

18. Duncan Ivison, "Modus Vivendi Citizenship," in *The Demands of Citizenship,* ed. Catrioni Mckinnon and Iain Hampsher-Monk (London: Continuum, 2000), 123–43.

19. Larry Diamond, Anthony Kirk-Green, and Oyeleye Oyediran, eds., *Transition Without End: Nigerian Politics and Civil Society Under Babangida* (Boulder, Colo.: Lynne Rienner Publishers, 1997).

20. Juan Linz and Alfred Stepan, *Problems of Democratic Transition and Consolidation: Southern Europe, South America, and Post-Communist Europe* (Baltimore: Johns Hopkins University Press, 1996), 65.

21. Linz and Stepan, *Problems of Democratic Transition and Consolidation,* 55.

22. Linz and Stepan, *Problems of Democratic Transition and Consolidation,* 116.

23. Huntington, "Reforming Civil-Military Relations," 8–9.

24. Huntington, "Reforming Civil-Military Relations," 9.

25. Agwuncha Arthur Nwankwo, *Nigerians as Outsiders: Military Dictatorship and Nigeria's Destiny* (Enugu, Nigeria: Fourth Dimension Press, 1996), 146.

26. Susan Rose-Ackerman, *Corruption and Government: Causes, Consequences, and Reform* (New York: Cambridge University Press, 1999), 212.

27. Rose-Ackerman, *Corruption and Government,* 212.

28. Elizabeth Jelin, "Citizenship Revisited: Solidarity, Responsibility, and Rights," pp. 101–19 in *Constructing Democracy: Human Rights, Citizenship, and Society in Latin America,* ed. Elizabeth Jelin and Eric Hershberg (Boulder, Colo.: Westview Press, 1996), 102.

29. Fabio Wanderley Reis, "The State, the Market, and Democratic Citizenship," in *Constructing Democracy: Human Rights, Citizenship, and Society in Latin America*, ed. Elizabeth Jelin and Eric Hershberg (Boulder, Colo.: Westview Press, 1996), 127–28.

30. Jelin, "Citizenship Revisited," 107.

31. Jelin, "Citizenship Revisited," 106–7.

32. Carolyn P. Boyd, *Praetorian Politics in Liberal Spain* (Chapel Hill: University of North Carolina Press, 1979), 42.

33. Alfred Stepan, *Rethinking Military Politics: Brazil and the Southern Cone* (Princeton, N.J.: Princeton University Press, 1988), 86.

34. Jelin, "Citizenship Revisited," 102.

9

—⟋⟍—

Elections and Electioneering
On the Democratic Deficit

While issues drive elections in most developed polities, there exist a peculiar characteristic that seem to drive presidential elections in a developing country such as Nigeria. These are personality and party affiliation. A vote for a particular political party is also seen as synonymous with a vote for the party's choice candidate. While there are major domestic issues facing the country such as inflation, unemployment, health system and infrastructural decay, crime and corruption, as well as a multitude of other social ailments, it is difficult to get from most average Nigerians a more convincing reason as to why they voted one way or other. Nonetheless, Nigerians seem to be generally animated and engaged in the electioneering process, more or less, than in the outcome of the election itself. It is therefore easy to observe that electoral violence, vandalism, and killings, attain epic proportions during the campaign process; but once the result is announced, a calming effect descends on the nation as a deep sense of resigned indignation sets in among both winners and losers, at least until the next round of elections.

Unlike many other African countries (including but not limited to Cote D'Ivoire, Senegal, Sierra Leone, Liberia, Togo, Equatorial Guinea, Kenya), Nigeria has managed to avoid the kind of post-election crisis of the type that befell Kenya between the period of January 2 to 4, 2008. As people protested against the presidential election results that declared incumbent President Mwai Kibaki as winner over his opposition challenger Mr. Raila Odinga; the protest quickly degenerated into an anti-government and interethnic confrontation between Kibaki's Kikuyu and Odinga's Luo tribes. By the time it was over, more than 500 persons had been slaughtered and some 255,000 displaced from their homes. No matter where the guilt lay, it was a most macabre display of "primitive" Africa at its worst; and possibly one of the costliest political violence in Kenya since independence from Britain in 1963. But in Nigeria, most challengers to unfavorable election results have generally sought redress through petitions to election tribunals or actual suits and litigation in the courts. Hence taken alone on its own merit, this development ought to be seen as a "success" story and as an encouragement in the slowly but evolving democratic culture in Nigeria. Individual responses to undesired electoral outcomes could also take the form of political realignments as partisan opportunists switch political affiliations and issue positions in a strategic bid to reposition themselves for the expected political and economic rents they could draw from the victorious camp.

THE 2007 PRESIDENTIAL ELECTION:
PARTY PATRONAGE AND SUPREMACY

From inception, the 2007 presidential election was a classic case of a party-controlled program, where the outcome was already decided even before the process began. It began the previous year with President Obasanjo's failed attempt to change the federal constitution so that he could stay in power for a third successive term. As "king maker," the president ended up casting his support to his hand-picked successor Alhaji Umaru Yar'Adua, the ascetic former governor of Katsina State, who eventually became the nominee of the ruling People's Democratic Party (PDP). The choice certainly added more fuel to the long-running tension between Obasanjo and Alhaji Atiku Abubakar, his feisty vice president who had to decamp the PDP to become the presidential candidate for the rival Action Congress party (AC). As part of his strategy, "Obasanjo seemed to have done everything within his power to try and knock Abubakar out of the race, using the government-sanctioned Economic and Financial Crimes Commission (EFCC) as the weapon."[1] Nonetheless, the election was held on April 21, 2007, and the Independent National Electoral Commission (INEC) declared the presidential candidate of the PDP as the winner, garnering 70 percent of the votes cast (figure 9.1).

According to electoral rules, a presidential candidate must have 25 percent of the votes from two-thirds of Nigeria's states to win the first round of elections; which means that the candidate must have one-fourth of the votes cast from twenty-five out of the thirty-seven states including the Federal Capital Territory. Yar'Adua's candidature won the support of five of the six geopolitical zones with 24.6 million votes against 6.6 million votes of his closest rival, former military ruler Muhammadu Buhari who

PRESIDENTIAL RESULT

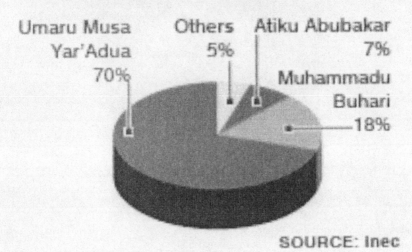

Umaru Musa Yar'Adua 70%

Others 5%

Atiku Abubakar 7%

Muhammadu Buhari 18%

SOURCE: Inec

Figure 9.1.   INEC Electoral Results, 2007

ran on the ticket of the All Nigeria Peoples Party (ANPP). Alhaji Atiku Abubakar, the vice president who ran on the presidential ticket of the Action Congress (AC) came in third with a total vote count of 2.6 million. With a population of about 144 million people, the number of eligible voters has been estimated to be between 60 and 70 million people; but how many of these actually vote, or are able to vote their choice on election day remains anybody's guess.

DESCENT INTO A HORNET'S NEST

What made this election not so unique were the general environment in which it was undertaken and the usually predictable outlook that has always informed national elections in Nigeria. About twenty-five parties fielded presidential candidates, a factor that may have over-weighed the administrative and monitoring capacity of the INEC, thereby enabling the whole process to run out of control (see appendix A). Beside the ensuing violence and electoral banditry which cost more than two hundred lives, the process experienced various logistic and voter registration problems, intimidation, and security loopholes that made it possible for fraud to occur at many voting stations. In most cases, polling hours were deferred into the late hours of the day, closed early or failed to open at all, transportation carrying ballot papers were either delayed, or deliberately sent

Figure 9.2.   Stolen Ballot Papers Scattered along a Bush Path (Ilongwuro), in Egbu Umuenem Community, Otolo Nnewi, Anambra State
Source: Sun News, Nigeria, 2007.

to different locations where they were not needed. Ballot papers meant for some polling stations were callously discarded away (see figure 9.2).

No sooner had the election results been announced that protests and widespread calls for its nullification ensued amid complaints of ballot rigging, manipulation, and wholesale electoral fraud. The presidential candidate of the Action Congress, Alhaji Atiku Abubakar filed a petition with the Presidential Election Petition Tribunal to strike out the election results. He argued that the April 21 election was inconsistent with the 1999 Constitution and the Electoral Act of 2006. His petition was denied. The European Union which had about 150 observers described the polls as a "fraud and a charade," while the Commonwealth group of 17 observers remained ambivalent about whether the election was "free and fair." While the U.S.-based International Republican Institute that had fifty-nine observers questioned whether the entire electoral process met international standards; the civil rights lawyer and activist Gani Fawehinmi decried the election results as a gross violation of the stipulations in the 1999 Constitution. The Washington, D.C.-based National Democratic Institute (NDI), which sent an international observer team headed by former U.S. secretary of state Madeleine Albright passed a vote of no confidence indicating that the electoral process had failed the Nigerian people. The governments of the United States, Britain, Germany, and Canada also expressed reservations over the conduct of the elections. "Nigeria's largest domestic election monitoring group, the Transition Monitoring Group, a coalition of some sixty civil society organizations which fielded 50,000 poll watchers across the country, called for a cancellation of the election results."[2]

Similar calls for cancellation came from Nobel Laureate Wole Soyinka, the Afenifere, and the Ohanaeze leadership. Two of the opposition parties, The Action Congress Party (AC) and the All Nigeria Peoples Party (ANPP) challenged the results citing that the Chairman of the INEC, Maurice Iwu had erred when he declared the election results for the entire thirty-six states when only the results from eleven states had so far been collated. In his response, Iwu unapologetically noted that "the challenge of conducting the elections were enormous, but the fact that the elections took place at all was a thing of joy to all Nigerians and their friends; and the very fact that the election was successful, even with its imperfections, shows the tremendous love God has for the country."[3] He went further to note that the election was the first time in the history of Nigeria that one democratically elected government has served its two terms in office and would be succeeded by another democratically elected government. While many saw a direct complicity between the police, army and INEC officials to micromanage and rig the election result in favor of the ruling People's Democratic Party; there was a general recognition of the rise of a more vibrant media that has created channels for the dissemination of information and the expression of divergent views and public opinion on important national issues. Ironically, while the immediate post-election disillusionment seemed to have subsided rather quickly; it nonetheless gave way to the rise of new expectations regarding improvements in the quality of life and new ways for dealing with the many vexing problems of the nation.

OF IMPERATIVES, PATRONAGE, AND INSTITUTIONAL CAPTURE

The path to the nomination and eventual ascent of Umaru Yar'Adua to the presidency did not come about without its own geopolitical calculations and horse-trading that threatened, once again, to divide the nation along ethno-regional lines. Besides having produced a majority of the leaders that have ruled Nigeria since independence, the North has had a disproportionately greater number of representations than the other regions at the federal level. Even though the country has been split into six geopolitical zones for presidential electoral purposes (three in the North, and three in the South), there is also the popular lexicon of "North-South" dichotomy that essentially sees national politics in terms of competition between the north and south of the country.

Since the outgoing president Obasanjo is a Southerner (Yoruba from the Southwest), the Arewa Consultative Forum and a forum of Northern governors argued that the next president should come from their zone. The southeast geopolitical zone through its sociocultural organization Ohanaeze Ndigbo in addition to some of the seating governors insisted that it was the turn of the zone, and specifically an Igbo person to become the president of the nation. "The Igbos premised their demand on power rotation among the six geopolitical zones rather than on an unwritten North-South power shift formula which formed the basis of the claim from the North."[4] To buttress its case, the Ohanaeze pointed out that since power had shifted from Abdulsalim Abubakar (Hausa-Fulani from the North) in 1999, to Obasanjo (Yoruba from the Southwest), it should therefore, naturally be the turn of the Igbos (Southeast) as one of the three major ethnic groups in the country, to produce the next president of the country.

But the issue became more complicate for three main reasons. Firstly, many of the key leaders in both the North and the Southeast belonged to the ruling Peoples Democratic Party (PDP), "hence their campaigns and counter-campaigns for the party's presidential ticket gradually became another 'backbone' breaker"[5] for the unity and integrity of the party—and its consequent electoral victory at the polls. Secondly, while president Obasanjo was generally ambiguous about what zone the party candidate should come from, the PDP National Chairman Audu Ogbe broached a statement to the effect that the North would likely produce the party's presidential candidate. It is also equally important to note that "the presidential adviser on Political Matters, Professor Jerry Gana, who also doubles as the Secretary of the PDP Board of Trustees (a most unusual conflict of interest that can rarely be ignored in most other countries), was among key northern political figures who were covertly pushing for the North to produce the next president."[6] Thirdly, it was indicated that there was a deal between PDP stakeholders in 1999 (at the beginning of Obasanjo's first term as president), that the North would fill the vacancy at the expiration of Obasanjo's second tenure—a likely "payback" for garnering northern support for his reelection in 2003.

What could be learned thus far, is that in Nigeria, the party machinery is central (not necessarily the voters) to a candidate's nomination and eventual victory in presidential elections. The leadership of the party is also quite instrumental, hence whatever clique or coalition of interests that controls the party and its leadership organ, would be in a powerful position to dictate the conditions for the party's national electoral choices. This development is generally consistent with the politics of structural choice, a situation where the ideal points of partisan choice making will not simply be a reflection of what members and constituents want, but will generally reflect what the party leadership or the governing coalition wants. In other words, party leaders have a greater measure of autonomy in decision making and, in most cases, micro-managing legislative and executive actions in conformity with party orthodoxy. In "the analytical world of social choice, we see citizens as voting on candidates and parties while legislators vote on public policies. But in the typical state of nature, where voters are taken as equals, the social choice is determined by a preexisting rule, usually majority rule."[7] But where this process is truncated, the party reigns supreme in its arbitrary exercise of public authority. It engages in a "politics of structural choice in which the winners use their temporary hold on public authority to design new structures and impose them on the polity as a whole."[8] In the same way that "these structures become vehicles by which they pursue their own interests, often at the expense of the losers; they also, invariably impose new constraints on the way the political game will be played in the future, constraints that give today's winners advantages over their opponents in tomorrow's jockeying to exercise public authority."[9] Progressively, as the electoral system undergoes a process of institutional capture, the state itself slowly transforms into an instrument of a de facto "one-party" state that seeks total use of power for the restructuring of society's social and economic system. At the apex of the party system resides a revolving oligarchic leadership system that could qualify under the term *mafiocracy*—a presumed "democratic system" that actually operates more like a "Mafioso" state; a development that, invariably, undermines a genuinely competitive party system.

The efficacy of political parties goes beyond elections and electioneering; it is about power, domination and control. In democracies, as well as in totalitarian one-party systems, "they represent the principal instrument through which segments of the population compete to secure control of elective institutions, and through them to exercise predominant influence over public policies."[10] In recognition of the basic power role of political parties, V. O. Key once remarked that they "provide a good deal of the propulsion of the formal constitutional system."[11] "It is not simply that parties are central to elections and to policy making, or that they make and break governments, administer patronage, and take decisions that deeply affect a nation's welfare";[12] they also have the instrumental effect of shaping political and social behavior. "Under their aegis, mass publics are mobilized for good and evil, revolutions are fomented, dissidents are arrested, tortured and killed, and ideologies are turned into moral imperatives."[13] In the case of Nigeria, "mass publics" are quickly transformed into "party publics" as different groups form allegiances to advance the course of one party or the other. Mass publics and the "elite" leadership, therefore, are easily manipulated or "bought over" by party patronage and financial largesse; and thus, can hardly serve as the inspiration for a collective populist movement.

THE ART OF LANGUAGE, FRAMES, AND SYMBOLISMS

I will also like to point out specific nuances and symbols that characterized the event of the 1999 presidential elections in the hope that it can
shed more light on the dynamics of presidential elections in Nigeria. The
election pitted Olusegun Obasanjo (PDP) and other candidates, including
his closest challenger former military head of state Muhammadu Buhari
of the All Nigeria People's Party (ANPP). In the same way that political opposition has a "cost," its rewards are also innumerable. A simple
cost-benefit analysis may suggest that the reward oftentimes could be so
profound as to diminish within days, the sacrifices that may have been
made years before. In the early years of Nigerian electoral politics, and
notwithstanding its crudeness, the Yorubas with specific reference to the
Action Group embraced the opposition front to the ruling political orthodoxy. Their combined experiences in both the First and Second Republics,
and specifically during the Babangida and Abacha regimes, undoubtedly
made the Yorubas (accepting a certain level of generalization) masters of
the "opposition" doctrine as far as Nigerian politics was concerned. They
have mastered how to drive the "opposition" without cutting important
"bridges" to emerging political opportunities.

But what made it very unique was that they did it without at the same
time alienating themselves from the status quo against whom they have
been fighting. They were able to keep key elements of their political elite
within the nucleus of both the "establishment" and "opposition" camps,
in such a way that whichever side wins, their loss would be minimal.
From the annulment of the June 12, 1993 election, the "surgical" demobi-
lization of Yoruba personnel from key elements of the armed forces (during the Abacha era), to the consequent death of MKO, powerful Yoruba
forums continued to advocate on critical issues such as a sovereign national conference, restructuring of the military, political autonomy, ethnic
marginalization, and many others. These were issues that the Northern
establishment did not want to hear, and to make them disappear from the
mainstream of national political discourse, the North decided to "compromise." It was a compromise framed and constantly wrapped around
the catchword "concede." To "concede" means to grudgingly and hesi-
tantly acknowledge a person to have something, to allow, permit, or to
grant a certain right or permission. The connotation here is that somebody
is giving up something for the sake of peace and so the burden of guilt
and reciprocity must rest on the person to whom that concession was
being given. The psychology behind the consistent reference to the word
"concede" was meant to sooth and placate Southern emotions which was
already boiling toward an inevitable but decisive outcome. This seemingly innocuous word became as disarming as it was effective. In a bold

masterstroke, the troubled legacy of almost thirty-nine years of Northern political dominance was forgotten, because the North has finally "conceded." As soon as it began, vocal outbursts from the South, particularly the Southwest region of the Yorubas subsided.

The idea of "conceding" the presidency to the South was a major test of the political maturity of the North. It offered them a great opportunity from which they could both maintain power as well as wreck havoc on the political disunity of the South. First, by creating a situation where the dominant Igbos of the Southeast will have to compete with the dominant Yorubas of the Southwest, the North ensured that even after the election is over, recrimination and finger pointing between the Igbos and the Yorubas would continue. By throwing the presidential aspiration of Southern minorities into the same political melee as a "wild card," the North also ensured that there would always be a perennial voice of political discontent within the South. In the midst of all this, the fundamental principles that were previously agreed during the constitutional convention were sidelined or forgotten. There was no more discussion about restructuring the military, or reassessing the inequality in federal ministerial appointments. The glaring inequity and crude partiality of Nigerian distributive politics was all but forgotten. And as was expected, in their usual but studied disposition, the North waited silently, plotted strategically, and was ready to up the ante should unfolding events move in an unexpected direction.

By conceding the presidency to the South, the North not only saved Nigeria to live another day, they also institutionalized their role as the premier "power broker" of Nigerian politics. In order words, no individual (Southwestern, Southeastern, or South-South) could hope to become the president of Nigeria without Northern support (that is, if we relied exclusively on the "North-South" dichotomy). It also points to a very destructive flaw in the temperament of Northern politics, and that is, self-interest comes first before partisan loyalty and ideological conformity. Accepting the fact that the 1999 election was a referendum on preserving either the "status quo" or "progressive change," but when Northern members of the Alex Ekwueme wing of the PDP absconded and voted for the Obasanjo camp, what then does that mean for ideological conformity?

It is said that each man acts only for his own self-interest, but how can one qualify this act except by inventing base intentions and strategic motives to account for them. The issue of political and economic marginalization was a credible issue, which the Igbos championed a long time before the start of the 1999 presidential elections. But the case for "marginalization" as a rallying cry for a renewed political "opposition" was ironically dealt a savage blow when it became trivialized from all corners of Nigeria's political spectrum. Accepting the fact that the issue of regional and ethnic marginalization existed in other parts of Nigeria ante-bellum, it remained undisputed that the Igbos who have been its foremost victims, gave it its contemporary political appeal. As soon as the southern minorities, the Yorubas, and Middle Belt political leaders developed their own versions of "marginalization," the Northern "establishment" quickly discovered the political incentive of creating its own advocacy for marginalization. It soon became evident that there were too many different shades of "marginalization" that was being peddled by the various groups and sections of the country. All that was needed was to add one more to make it total and complete, and to argue that "everybody has always been marginalized." The Hausa-Fulani simply came out and decried that it too has been "marginalized" for years. Even the natives on whose land the federal capital of Abuja was built came out and cried "marginalization." And it worked. The Southerners suddenly lost the stomach for championing the cause of "marginalization."

The Igbos lost as well as the Southern minorities partly because the minorities having single-handedly charted the course for their own political salvation were all too eager to go it alone. Because the Igbos and the southern minorities had divergent views on the issue of "marginalization" and what it represented, this not only opened it up for political caricature by others, but also may have been the single most important factor that laid it to rest for good. The outcome and intrigue that spearheaded the 1999 election should have indicated to the Igbos and the Eastern minorities that they need each other for their mutual political future. The strength of Ndigbo in numbers and otherwise must be seen as an asset to the minorities, while the quest of the minorities for distributive justice and equity in representation must not be seen as inimical to the larger political interest of Ndigbo. It is now evident that in those circumstances where both sides refused to cooperate, both sides have lost. In an era where sane and strategic thinking must prevail, it is very important that the simmering and historic ambivalence that characterized the past few decades should not have stood in the way of a genuine partnership premised on mutual self-interest.

In another strategic ploy to build party consensus, the PDP hierarchy brokered an agreement to "concede" the Senate presidency to the southeast (Igbo), invariably, as compensation to the Alex Ekwueme "wing" of the party. But no sooner had the decision been made, that it started to tear apart at the political fabric of the southeastern (Igbo) states. Abia and Imo states want the position to be given to them; Enugu wanted it and so did Ebonyi. But Anambra must have it, especially since Ekwueme is from that state. It was therefore this "politics-against-thy-brethren" that occupied and sapped the political resources of the Igbos, and kept them at bay for the remainder of the election period from seeking or challenging the party's decision to grant the candidacy to Obasanjo. But beyond the tokenism, the more disarming effect and danger was that it created the impression that the Igbos have been accommodated within the ruling government, and as such may be less disposed to pursue a more focused and aggressive reconstruction of their bruised political strategy.

It is also important to address two specific words that are often used in reference to the Igbos, and to suggest their political and electoral significance. The two words are "South-East" and "Igbo-Speaking." There was a time when Cross-River and Akwa-Ibom states were collectively known as the South-Eastern state, but now the name has reverted to the five mainland Igbo states. Understandably, the geopolitical influence of the Igbos during the First Republic was much greater when there was the "East"; the same applies to the North and the West. But for the North, even though it has been divided into many smaller states, the ideal of a "Greater North" still resonates as a potent political force. To an extent, the same goes for the West, who having emerged so far as they did, have now understood that they can get anything they want from Nigeria without firing a single shot, even in the midst of delayed providence.

Because the word "Southeast" with its connotation of a limited and smaller geopolitical space is an arbitrary boundary drawn under a punitive postwar mind-set of ethnic separation; the idea of "Igbo-speaking," on the other hand, is a misnomer and must be viewed in the same way as a postwar phenomenon with a dangerous underbelly. The point is that you are either Igbo or you are not. "Igbo-speaking" could not possibly serve as a mediating factor, and must be seen only as a cultural derivative of being Igbo. But the political significance and consequence of this coinage is that it may have enabled some sectors of the borderline Igbo communities to attempt for a new identity, contrasting assimilative coincidences in language with more genuine and indisputable issues of genealogy. The territorial and psychological balkanization of a once veritable majority into an artificial minority status remains a powerful political weapon—in the evolving drama of Nigerian elections and electioneering.

NOTES

1. "A Blacklist to Bolster Democracy," *The Economist* 382, no. 8516 (February 17, 2007): 50.
2. J. Peter Pham, "Nigeria: Crisis of Legitimacy," *The National Interest Online* April 24, 2007, at www.nationalinterest.org.
3. "AC, ANPP Protest Yar' Adua's Victory," *Guardian Newspaper*, April 24, 2007, 1–2, at www.guardiannewsngr.com.
4. Kunle Oderemi, "2007 Presidency: Arewa vs. Ohanaeze No Retreat, No Surrender," *Sunday Punch*, May 16, 2004.

5. Oderemi, "2007 Presidency: Arewa vs. Ohanaeze No Retreat, No Surrender."

6. Oderemi, "2007 Presidency: Arewa vs. Ohanaeze No Retreat, No Surrender."

7. Terry M. Moe, "Political Institutions: The Neglected Side of the Story," special issue, *Journal of Law, Economics, and Organization* 6 (1990): 215.

8. Moe, "Political Institutions," 222.

9. Moe, "Political Institutions," 222.

10. Joseph Lapalombara and Jeffrey Anderson, "Political Parties," in *Encyclopedia of Government and Politics,* ed. Mary Hawkesworth and Maurice Kogan (New York: Routledge, 1992), 1:393.

11. V. O. Key, *Politics, Parties, and Pressure Groups* (New York: Thomas Y. Cromwell, 1964), 154. Also summarized in Lapalombara and Anderson, "Political Parties," 1:393.

12. Lapalombara and Anderson, "Political Parties," 1:393.

13. Lapalombara and Anderson, "Political Parties," 1:393.

10

—⚭—

The Niger Delta

A Platform Under Duress

The Niger Delta issue has existed in Nigeria even before oil became a central element in the country's economy. Because the crisis has, at one time or the other, revolved around competing issues of territorial autonomy, economic opportunity, environmental control and compensation, infrastructural development, political representation, and/or self-determination; it is rather difficult to accurately pinpoint which single issue has been at the forefront of the conflict. But beyond the transitory shocks of overt violence, which continues to be witnessed in the area, there is a general feeling that the region will continue to experience one stress after another for the foreseeable future. For the simple fact that the bulk of Nigeria's oil exports and petroleum reserves are linked to this region more than any other place, the increasing level of infrastructural underdevelopment and poverty in the area exposes a glaring inequity in the distributional incentives of Nigeria's federalist system.

Located in the southern part of the country and comprising a sizeable proportion of the country's Atlantic coastline, the Niger Delta region (about 40,000 square miles of swamps, creeks, and mangrove forests) has seen a growing increase in the population accounting more than 30 million people (in 2005) and representing 23 percent of Nigeria's total population. "The population density is among the highest in the world with 265 people per square kilometer, and a growth rate of about 3% per year."[1] As poverty and urbanization rates increase, the lack of accompanying economic growth and employment opportunities works against the emergent spirit of rising expectations and quest for improvements in the quality of life.

Nonetheless, a proper appraisal of the Niger Delta issue should reflect back on some of the historical events that informed it. As an area mostly inhabited by several minority ethnic groups, the largest of whom are the Ijaws, Urhobos, Itshekiri, Ogonis, Andonis, Annang, Isoko, and many others, the issue of autonomy from the influence of the majority ethnic groups in the country was always a major factor in the demand for state creation even before independence. To deal with this issue, the Willink Commission on state creation was inaugurated at the constitutional conference held in London in September 1957. While state creation has generally served as a unit of reference in the allocation of offices and amenities at the federal level; it is also a crucial variable in the distributive politics of the revenue allocation formula. As pointed out by R. T. Akinyele, "the British government decided to set up the commission after delegates to the constitutional conference disagreed on the number of states to be created in order to eliminate the fears of ethnic domination in Nigeria."[2]

"While the Northern Peoples Congress (NPC) strongly resisted the creation of new regions, the National Council of Nigeria and the Cameroons (NCNC) called for the division of the country into 17 states";[3] and "the Action Group (AG) expressed support for the immediate creation of Calabar-Ogoja-Rivers (COR) state, the Midwest and Middle Belt states and the insertion of a clause in the constitution to make state creation an ongoing exercise."[4] In the end and after much deliberation, "the commission rejected the request for the creation of Rivers, Mid-West, Middle Belt and COR states in the belief that their creation would initiate fresh minority problems."[5] But then, this was actually what eventually happened. The later creation of the Mid-West region in 1963, fueled an increased passion and discontent among the Eastern minorities who had been asking for a COR state. In a way, while the creation of the Mid-West helped, by default, to make Awolowo's Action Group Party the "enlightened" champion of minority political rights; he masterfully used it as political fodder to endear his party to much of the electoral support it received from a cross-section of the Eastern minority population during the First Republic.

However, parts of the Niger Delta remained in the Eastern and the Mid West Regions, but it was after the first military coup of January 15, 1966, that the issue emerged once again onto the national political scene with a more militaristic punch. On February 23, 1966, Isaac Adaka Boro, an Ijaw and a former student of the University of Nigeria Nsukka who also hails from the Niger Delta Region, took up arms against the federal military government in a fervent attempt to "secede" from Nigeria. "The objective of his military action was to seize power and to declare a separate 'Niger Delta Republic' in the Delta area of the Eastern Region."[6] Boro's short-lived insurrection met its Waterloo on March 7, 1966, when he was captured by federal forces; but he died a year and a few months later in the civil war fighting on the federal side. In retrospect, it would seem that his last charge to his troops, some fifty men named the Niger Delta Volunteer Service (NDVS), remains an enduring testimony of the contemporary state of the Niger Delta. He had exhorted them to "remember your 70-year old grandmother who still farms to eat, remember also your poverty-stricken people and then remember, too, your petroleum which is being pumped daily out of your veins and then, fight for your freedom."[7]

While Boro's statement resonates some of the perennial issues of contention (poverty, resource control, and ethnic self-determination for the Ijaws), the political landscape as well as the dynamics of the oil economy has changed dramatically from what they were during his time. If he was as committed to the ideal of "self-determination," many wondered how he could have achieved that when he "sidelined" the cause, and instead opted to fight on the federal side against Biafra so early in the war. By that singular act, the initial zeal and commitment for pursuing a sovereign identity for the region was severely weakened. Nigeria today has a thirty-six-state structure and his own Ijaw hometown of Kiama is now part of Bayelsa state. Nigeria has earned enormous wealth from oil resources generated from the region, Abuja has become Nigeria's federal capital made possible by oil revenues, many of the youth remain uneducated and unemployed, local communities and renegade militias are still up in arms, interethnic rivalries abound, and the environmental consequences of the oil wealth has become more manifest and devastating. And poverty and economic deprivation remain equally as vicious, as state authorities look the other way.

THE RISE OF ECOPOLITICS:
"SELF DETERMINATION" INTERRUPTED?

The end of the civil war saw the new states of the Niger Delta discovering themselves and seeking to live up to the independent aspirations of statehood. Among the most contentious issues on the political horizon was the issue of "abandoned" property in which property belonging to their mostly Igbo owners were arbitrarily taken over under de jure authority of the state, in this case the Rivers state. But as the economic incentives derived from oil rents started to trickle down, the ideal and argument for self-determination (at least to the extent that Boro had envisioned it) became more mooted. But then a new dynamic began to unfold in the "struggle." The conflict took on a more ferocious bent "in the early 1990s due to rising tensions between foreign oil corporations and a number of Niger Delta's minority ethnic groups who felt that they were being exploited, particularly the Ogoni as well as the Ijaw."[8] As the environmental consequences of unregulated oil exploration and drilling resulted in the pollution of rivers and creeks, destruction of farmlands and agriculture, and a rise in toxic-related diseases, the crisis took on a more global dimension (figure 10.1).

Prodded by international non-governmental organizations, human rights and environmental groups, and some local civil society associations, Kenule Saro Wiwa, then leader of the Movement for the Survival of Ogoni People (MOSOP, which emerged in 1990) saw the oil politics of the country and its consequent environmental degradation as a serious issue that impinged on the survival (livelihood) of his ethnic Ogoni people (numbering about 500,000 people). As he decried the economic exclusion of the Ogonis from the oil rents drilled from their land, he also railed against the multinational oil companies and the Nigerian state then under the military dictatorships of Generals Babangida and Abacha, for its complicity in the environmental damage that has been visited on his people. Ironically, his justified focus on the environmental problems of the area (especially Ogoniland), while they won him international acclaim and drew global attention to other pressing issues of the region; the

Figure 10.1.   A Deadly Mix of Toxic Smoke and Gas Flares Darkens the Sky in the Niger Delta. (There are few safe places left for oil companies in the Niger Delta, the epicenter of Nigeria's petroleum industry.)
Source: Jacob Silberberg/*New York Times*/Redux, 2006.

ensuing loss of multiethnic consensus undermined the political quest for "self-determination" and economic autonomy for the Niger Delta region as a whole. Saro Wiwa was eventually hanged in 1995 by the Abacha regime for his alleged involvement in the death of four Ogoni Chiefs who had challenged his leadership of MOSOP.

Since then, "competition for oil wealth has continued to fuel violence between innumerable ethnic groups, causing the militarization of nearly the entire region by ethnic militia groups as well as Nigerian military and police forces."[9] What thus has become more salient to the country and the international community is the rising spate of violence, kidnappings, and murder that pervades the region; and in the midst of all this, the more central and authentic issues such as the endemic poverty, environmental pollution, and the wholesale pilferage of the oil resources have almost been lost, or rather overshadowed by the more immediate physical manifestations of anarchy and disorder.

IDEOLOGICAL TENSIONS

Among the many challenges facing the Niger Delta region is how to channel the collective anger to the political center in such a way that it transcends a living ideology. But to do that, the multiple issues would need to be more tightly connected to each other (or at least made to seem so), and then projected through a more formal platform for collective action, such as a political party. That is, an ideologically based political party anchored on the unique and specific realities of the Niger-Delta experience. For example, a recognized political party such as a "Niger Delta Republican Party" or "Niger Delta Democratic Party" could offer a platform through which the people of the region would be able to pull their issues and collective votes together as they engage the political and electoral process for influence and control at the national level. It would be of little consequence whether such is a "minority" or "majority party," but what it does is that it centralizes the various expressions of popular discontent and projects a unified vision and leverage at the political center.

But what has obtained so far is that core issues have become disaggregated as different ethnic-based organizations from the region provide multiple platforms for advocating bits and pieces of the central issues. The lack of coherence in what was supposed to be a collective advocacy remains the foremost obstacle to the development of a unified political thrust. This has, therefore, opened up the various groups to the "divide and rule" strategy that has been employed against them by both the federal government and the multinational companies. Such ethnic-based organizations like the Movement for the Survival of Ogoni People (MOSOP), the Movement for the Survival of Ijaw Ethnic Nationality (MOSIEN), and the Ijaw Youth Council have played central roles in the cross-sectional mobilization of protest movements in the region. While the execution of Saro Wiwa seemed to have weakened the political influence of MOSOP, various Ijaw and other ethnic groups have emerged more forcefully on the scene but under different types of persuasion that range from the right to share in the oil wealth from their land, compensation for environmental degradation, political oppression, economic disenfranchisement, and many others.

The various Ijaw youth groups have splintered into organs such as the Egbesu Boys, the Chicoco Movement, the Ijaw Youth Council, the Federated Niger Delta Ijaw Communities, and the Niger Delta Volunteer Force—furthermore sapping their organizational and collective strength. Many of these splinter groups have also turned to extortion, hijackings, sabotage and kidnappings for ulterior motives. Furthermore, pronouncements and demands from the various groups tend to run counter to each other and sometimes focus on bread and butter issues, more or less, than on other central issues of sovereignty and economic autonomy. For instance, in August 1992, an event occurred involving another ethnic group in the region. A group of "Isoko youths in Igibide closed off the road to Shell's Orion flowstation for 5 days demanding employment, water, and electricity."[10] On December 11, 1998, the Egbesu Boys and other members of the Ijaw Youth Council issued an ultimatum under their *Kiama Declaration* setting the deadline of December 30 for all the multinational corporations operating in Ijawland and territorial waters to withdraw from the region; as well as all military forces of "occupation" by the Nigerian state. In response to the threat, the government deployed additional forces and declared a state of emergency in Bayelsa state. By the time the tension subsided on January 4, 1999, at least twenty people had died in the various clashes between government troops and Ijaw youths. Immediately thereafter, the Niger Delta Volunteer Force, regarded by most to be the armed wing of the Ijaw youths, made a list of demands on the government and oil companies. The demands, however, are insightful both in their diversity and in the obvious de-linking from the traditional issues of territorial sovereignty, self-determination, and economic autonomy. They included:

- The construction of twenty major link roads in the oil-producing states of the country
- Creation of additional three states and 120 local council areas for the Ijaw ethnic group
- Construction of gas turbines to generate and supply electricity to all towns and villages in oil-producing communities

- Participation of oil-producing communities in the operation of oil companies, with equity holding of 20 percent
- Employment of Ijaw youths, both on quota basis and on merit, by oil companies.[11]

While the oil companies ignore much of these demands because they do not wish to set a precedent for other oil-producing communities; they also hold fort that it is the responsibility of the government to provide these amenities. They see their role not as pre-empting state responsibility but as working in "partnership" with it to the extent that their contractual interests are protected. While the government does not wish to be seen as caving in to such a demand, its reluctance to negotiate is driven more by the belief that the state has proprietary claim to all land and minerals in the country, as well as by its overwhelming command of the instruments of violence. The later was more forcefully demonstrated in December 1999 when federal troops razed the central Niger Delta town of Odi to the ground, after some government soldiers were ambushed and killed. For these technical reasons, the incentive for a constructive and enduring engagement on both sides has remained hard to come by.

MILITANT INSURGENCY: TOWARD "ETHNO-NATIONALISM"

The source of ethnic militancy in Nigeria cannot be blamed on the Cold War politics (1945–1989); they are deeply rooted in the history and character of state formation, power and in the trajectory of political development, especially in the formative years of Nigeria's independence. While it can also partly be attributed to the perceived failure of federalism in the country; it did not evolve as a challenge to the ideal of federalism per se, but as a repudiation of its failures to address enduring issues of governance and distributive politics. As various groups advocate for a "true federalism," but the real issue remains as to what "true" federalism means, at least when the quest is juxtaposed with the multiple and often disparate demands made by militants in the region. But if the real grain behind the call for "true" federalism is a demand to redesign the structural allocation of power and representation in the country, then the state's response so far may have fallen short.

In an effort to redistribute wealth, oil-producing states now receive 13 percent allocation of oil revenues in line with the derivation formula contained in federal budget guidelines. But how much of this filter to the local people who really need it has remained anybody's guess. According to a 2007 Human Rights Watch Report, "the Rivers State government had a budget of $1.3 billion in 2006—but which included transportation fees of $65,000 a day for the governor's office; $10 million for catering, entertainment, gifts and souvenirs; and $38 million for two helicopters; while the budget for health services only amounted to a paltry sum of $22 million."[12] The Niger-Delta Development Commission (NDDC) was also created during the Obasanjo administration as a way of addressing the developmental problems of the region, but its practical impact remains quite limited. Though belated, the government has also sought to tighten the regulatory requirements for environmental impact statements regarding oil exploration and drilling. The current vice president of Nigeria Goodluck Jonathan, who was a former governor of Bayelsa state, was chosen to run under the platform of the ruling PDP, partly as way of calming tensions as well as restoring a feeling of inclusion among the people of the Delta region.

On their own part, some of the "oil companies have tried to develop and implement several community development programmes (roads, hospitals, and schools); as part of their strategies for managing the grievances of the local people and to dissuade them from engaging in violence."[13] While the "Shell Petroleum Development Corporation (SPDC) claims that it spends $100 million each year on social and health programs in the Niger Delta; Exxon stated that it had set aside $21 million for similar projects in 2007, and that it had built 95 percent of the road network in the town of Eket,"[14] Akwa Ibom state—again shifting government's responsibility to an extra-constitutional agency that lacks the sovereign and enforcement authority to ensure that these projects are properly accounted for. In a rather ironic way, these community projects create political and economic incentives that grant the major oil corporations access and undue influence in the evolving pattern of local politics in ways that, more often than not, become detrimental to the broader interests of the very communities they seek to help. Nonetheless, suffice it to say that "the oil companies now find themselves in an uneasy position, stuck in a crisis that they, on the one hand, helped to create";[15] and on the other, must see resolved in other to remain safe and operational. But as the anarchy endures, militant activities have become more brazen and widespread.

The region now has various militant organizations such as the Niger Delta People's Volunteer Force (NDPVF) led by Alhaji Mujahid Asari Dokubo, Tom Ateke's Niger Delta Vigilante (NDV), the Movement for the Emancipation of the Niger Delta (MEND) led by Godswill Tamuno, the Ijaw Youth Movement, the Egbesu Boys, and scores of others. Since oil exploration began in Nigeria following the drilling of the first well in Oloibiri (Niger Delta) in 1956, the nine states that constitute the Niger Delta have been sites of intense violence. The current eruption began during the Ogoni (MOSOP) uprisings in the early 1990s; "but from 1997, while Warri (the capital of Delta State) was the center of violence, it shifted to various communities in the Rivers state in 2003."[16] "Although the violence has manifested in different forms—in Warri it is seen as a conflict between Ijaw and Itshekiri ethnic militias, in Rivers state as a battle between rival Ijaw groups—it is, on the one hand, a fight for control of oil wealth and government resources,"[17] and on the other, a fight directed at the state and the oil corporations. While there have been various skirmishes or clashes with federal law enforcement and the army, yet the violence has generally been contained within the region as opposed to a broad based nationwide insurgency. But the various manifestations of the crisis portend a rather ominous prospect both for region and country.

Since 2006, "armed rebel gangs have blown up oil pipelines, disabled pumping stations, and kidnapped over 150 oil workers to the extent that many of the oil corporations now confine their employees to heavily fortified compounds, allowing them to travel only by armored vehicles, helicopter, or security escorts."[18] Botched rescue attempts by federal soldiers have, oftentimes, led to the deaths of hostages and innocent civilians caught in the crossfire. For instance, on February 18, 2006, several boatloads of MEND fighters attacked Shell's gigantic Forcados oil export terminal on the Escravos River (about three hundred kilometers from Lagos); and in the ensuing gun battle with navy troops, they set fire to the tanker loading platform. They also stormed a pipeline-laying barge that was operated for Shell by the U.S. engineering firm Wilbros and kidnapped nine foreign workers. By the time it was over, they had killed five government soldiers (four army troops and one paramilitary policeman).

In the following May, militants from MEND attacked a convoy bringing provisions to Agip, a subsidiary of Italian oil company Eni; nine out of eleven soldiers escorting the convoy were killed. The same type of attack occurred in October 2006 when militants in fast-moving speed boats attacked federal troops escorting a Shell barge in the Cawthorne area of Rivers state; five soldiers were killed and nine were declared missing. Amid all the bombings, kidnappings, and taking of hostages for ransom, several criminal gangs have also followed suit; thus making hostage taking, especially of foreign oil workers and expatriates a "lucrative" enterprise.

Because there are many different ethnic groups that make up the Niger-Delta region, some of whom have mutually vexing problems, and have fought against each other for decades over issues ranging from land ownership, mineral rights, farmlands, majority-minority status, state and local government issues; it would be difficult, if not impossible, to develop the kind of collective, culturally driven ethno-nationalism needed to inspire a sustained and vibrant revolution. While this is not to say that a consensus could not be achieved on important political issues, but then much of this would first have to go through the different cultural filters before they are validated. Also, it can be observed that essentially all of the major advocacy organizations as well as militant groups have evolved along ethnic and cultural foundations; and for many of them, their primary objective is focused on how the various issues of contention would impact their own land and people. Some of them have fought and continue to fight against each other over illegal oil revenues, territorial turfs, or as enforcers for political patrons during elections.

For instance, the intra-Ijaw clashes between Mujahid Asari Dokubo's NDPVF (Niger Delta People's Volunteer Force) and Tom Ateke's NDV (Niger Delta Vigilante) in 2003–2004 alone "resulted in the deaths of hundreds of young Ijaw fighters, the killing of dozens of largely Ijaw local people and the destruction of several Ijaw villages." Of more strategic import as well as concern is that the Ijaws, who comprise the largest minority group in the Niger Delta with a population of about 7 million; also has the largest number of powerful militant groups. These militant groups have, over the years, acquired effective training and mastery in the tactics, logistics, maneuvers, and weapon systems of insurgency warfare. Hence, and despite existing interethnic political and communal conflicts, a rising Ijaw nationalist fervor could inspire a renewed historical ambition for extra-territorial conquest across the Niger Delta against other ethnic-minority groups of the region. Unless properly addressed, the multiple problems of the region would continue to offer fertile breeding grounds for inexhaustible conflict.

NEGOTIATING POWER AND ECONOMICS

The ongoing crisis in the Niger Delta should not be seen in isolation from the larger political history of Nigeria within which minority aspirations for representation in the national power equation has always been a crucial factor. The cover article of the *African Concord* of April 24, 1989, aptly titled "The Rising Power of Minorities," offers an insightful testimony to the enduring character of minority struggles in Nigeria. There is a pragmatic recognition that "ethnic minority" does not necessarily equate to "political minority," and the historic role of having played second fiddle in the nation's political firmament may have come to a screeching end. A couple of things made this possible: first was that the series of state creation exercises which began on May 12, 1967, when the country was split into twelve states, initiated a political and economic transformation of the minorities—a process that has intensified in many ways over the years. The crisis in the Niger Delta remains a central part of this transformation.

Because the initial and later acts of state creation extended development to most areas of the minority states, it also guaranteed them greater representation in the federal government. Today, there are collectively more minority states in the country than was the case in 1967. Under the current federal system where each of the states have "relative" equality (in lieu of the "federal character" principle) in the number of representatives in the national legislature as well as in executive appointments, one could, in fact, argue that the minorities run the Nigerian government. While "the emergence of petroleum as the mainstay of Nigeria's economy has also conferred greater economic importance on the minorities as a group; the considerable presence of the Middle Belters in the top ranks of the armed forces also points to the powerful leverage of minorities in that most critical sector."[19]

But the Niger Delta issue is both a "process" and at the same time a "process-in-transformation." And consistent with the natural instincts of human beings, it is a process driven by the singular quest for power and control. Oftentimes this quest has been advanced as a campaign for "self-determination"—a reference that for obvious reasons, rarely seats well with most Nigerians. Nonetheless, it is rather misleading when we try to equate the idea of self-determination with an unreserved quest for absolute political independence or sovereignty. This is far from the truth, and to the extent that common references to self-determination could be misconstrued as a negative advocacy, it can be blamed on the cavalier and generalized way in which it has oftentimes been used in circumstances that are essentially unalike.

The point is that "self-determination" need not necessarily mean full sovereignty, and as such, to recognize a right to self-determination does not in itself commit us to affirming that every group to which the principle applies must of necessity uphold the view of secession as an end-game doctrine. My hypothesis has always been that the moral appeal of the principle of self-determination depends precisely on its vagueness. It is a kind of placeholder for a range of possible accommodations that could specify various forms of authorities and relationships, as well as other more basic corporate (constitutional) and cultural values that might be amenable to a particular geopolitical context. Once these basic values are identified, it should thus be possible to dispense largely a common framework that would guarantee all the contending parties a mutually rewarding political space for all their aspirations within a common political community, hence making the clamor for full sovereignty either unnecessary or inarguable.

THE MORAL OF PROPERTY RIGHTS

It would certainly be an understatement to view the crisis in the Niger Delta as solely an issue of "relative deprivation" and "environmental degradation." It is much more than that. Because the underlying issues of contention are essentially matters of property rights and legitimate authority; the evolving nexus between state power and a conflict economy means that "the pervasiveness and intensity of ethnic politics and *conflict* would, in the final analysis, remain a measure of the ongoing contestation."[20] Several other issues that fuel and sustain the violence include "the manipulation of frustrated youth by political leaders, traditional elites, and organized crime syndicates involved in oil theft, unemployment, and the widespread availability of small arms and other lethal weapons."[21] But above all, a more robust explanation rests on key political and sociological foundations.

The Niger Delta crisis seems to be inspired by a cross-section of the educated regional political elite inside and outside of government. The gun-wielding militants are basically the foot soldiers; while the continued advocacy for "self-determination" is oftentimes used as a "wild-card" to strengthen their hand in the negotiation process. Their objective is, firstly, to seek a radical rewriting of the federal Constitution that would grant them increased political autonomy over the region. Secondly, they seek abrogation of federal decrees, particularly those that deal with property rights pertaining to ownership of land and mineral resources—the Petroleum Decree (1969), the Minerals Decree (1971), and the Land Use Decree (1978). Hence, satisfying these two central issues would grant them the sovereign (political and economic) autonomy to manage the oil resources drilled from their land and region.

They seek the political security a powerful Nigerian state offers; but the political autonomy to decide the nature and boundaries within which it must operate. As Eghosa Osaghae points out, "even with the rebellions in the region, the demands have continued to be for equity and justice within the Nigerian state rather than for separate sovereign states."[22] Because very dramatic solutions would be needed to resolve the key issues of political and economic autonomy (property rights), it has been very difficult for both sides to come to a compromise. While temporary stopgap measures can only assuage emotions from boiling over, they cannot offer long-lasting solutions. The "goal post" will continue to shift but only around the margins of the key issues in contention without creating enough momentum that could explode them prematurely. Even if the opportunity for some form of durable agreement remains remote, that in itself, should not provide enough justification for negating them. The mere fact that they are presented for deliberation has its own political benefit. And as long as the "cat has already been let out of the bag," it must not be allowed to go astray. The same circumstance should also apply in the state's disposition toward the Chief Ralph Uwazuruike led Movement for the Actualization of the Sovereign State of Biafra (MASSOB) in the Southeast, as well as Dr. Frederick Fasheun's Odua People's Congress (OPC) in the Southwest. To the extent that all parties bring crucial issues to the table, they should thus been seen as an integral part of the negotiation at finding a mutually acceptable solution.

The fluid nature of Nigerian politics and the often-tempestuous flashes that it generates should bear constant reminder that the possibility for a prolonged argument on the final nature of the state system remains very credible. But history has taught us that where sane minds operate, there will always be an angel listening. As long as one can adequately preserve life as well as safeguard what has already been achieved, and to the extent that it is avoidable without worsening the current condition, fundamental change need not be made by a preemptive recourse to force, but by a consistent and unwavering advocacy devoid of fear and personal self-interest.

NOTES

1. The Project for the Research of Islamic Movements (PRISM), "Nigerian Oil 'Total War," 6, at www.e-prism.org.

2. R. T. Akinyele, "States Creation in Nigeria: The Willink Report in Retrospect," *African Studies Review* 39, no. 2 (September 1996): 75.

3. Akinyele, "States Creation in Nigeria: The Willink Report in Retrospect," 75. The NCNC was later to become the National Council of Nigerian Citizens.

4. D. S. Rothchild, "Safeguarding Nigeria's Minorities," *Duquesne Review* 8 (Spring 1964): 38. Also summarized in R. T. Akinyele, "States Creation in Nigeria: The Willink Report in Retrospect," *African Studies Review* 39, no. 2 (September 1996): 75.

5. Akinyele, "States Creation in Nigeria: The Willink Report in Retrospect," 79.

6. Philip Efiong, *Nigeria and Biafra: My Story* (Princeton, N.J.: Sungai Books, 2003), 71.

7. Ima Niboro, "Blood Bath in the Delta," *Tell Magazine*, January 1999, 22.

8. PRISM, "Nigerian Oil 'Total War," 6.

9. PRISM, "Nigerian Oil 'Total War," 6.

10. Jan Willem Van Gelder and Joseph Moerkamp, "The Niger Delta: A Disrupted Ecology—The Role of Shell and Other Oil Companies," Discussion paper by Greenpeace Nederland. Also summarized in John Boye Ejobowah, "Who Owns the Oil? The Politics of Ethnicity in the Niger Delta of Nigeria," *Africa Today* (1999): 38.

11. *The Guardian*, January 4, 1999; as summarized in Ejobowah, "Who Owns the Oil?" 38.

12. Summarized in Jad Mouawad, "Growing Unrest Posing a Threat to Nigerian Oil," *New York Times*, April 21, 2007, at www.nytimes.com/2007/04/21/business/worldbusiness/21oil.html.

13. Kenneth Omeje, "Petrobusiness and Security Threats in the Niger Delta, Nigeria," *Current Sociology* 54, no. 3 (2006): 479.

14. Mouawad, "Growing Unrest Posing a Threat to Nigerian Oil," at www .nytimes.com/2007/04/21/business/worldbusiness/21oil.html.

15. Mouawad, "Growing Unrest Posing a Threat to Nigerian Oil," at www .nytimes.com/2007/04/21/business/worldbusiness/21oil.html.

16. Human Rights Watch, "Rivers and Blood: Guns, Oil and Power in Nigeria's Rivers State," February 2005, 3.

17. Human Rights Watch, "Rivers and Blood: Guns, Oil and Power in Nigeria's Rivers State," February 2005, 3–4. Also see Darren Kew and David L. Phillips, "Seeking Peace in the Niger Delta: Oil, Natural Gas, and Other Vital Resources," *New England Journal of Public Policy* 21, no. 2 (June 2007): 154–70.

18. Mouawad, "Growing Unrest Posing a Threat to Nigerian Oil," at www .nytimes.com/2007/04/21/business/worldbusiness/21oil.html.

19. "The Rising Power of Minorities," *African Concord* 3, no. 4 (24 April 1989), 15.

20. Eghosa E. Osaghae, "Explaining the Changing Patterns of Ethnic Politics in Nigeria," *Nationalism and Ethnic Politics* 9, no. 3 (Autumn 2003): 71.

21. Human Rights Watch, "Rivers and Blood: Guns, Oil and Power in Nigeria's Rivers State," February 2005, 2–3.

22. Osaghae, "Explaining the Changing Patterns of Ethnic Politics in Nigeria," 66.

11

—⁊⁊⁊—

Constitutionalism and Political Development

By offering specific rules and order that guide political action, Constitutions provide a structure in which governance activities follow (ought of follow) a regularized pattern or order that lend themselves to predictability. The "structure" of governance can take two forms: The first is that of institutional design and the functional relationships that connects the various units to each other; and the second is the method by which political actors communicate (transact) across all institutional levels in the process of carrying out their formal obligations. These obligations include law making, constituency representation, and overall responsibility for national welfare. In democratic polities as in most other forms of governmental systems, the Constitution provides the foundation as well as the mechanism for the distribution of power, authority, and incentives of citizenship. To the extent that governmental systems can be construed as processes driven by politics and circumstance, it therefore becomes incumbent on political leaders to ensure that the Constitution and other statutory laws of the state are made to adapt to these circumstances. History has shown that Constitutions or regimes that remain static over time or refuse to adapt to prevailing circumstances have been made inconsequential as key institutions of the state and rule of law are abandoned.

This is the situation facing the Nigerian state and its citizens at this critical juncture in its political development. A review of the Nigerian Constitution presents a surprising portrait of a project that was not well thought out in all its ramifications. One can see an inarticulate document ridden with contradictions and convoluted logic—all of which would indicate a brewing crisis of disarray in governance. It is, in fact, a very unusual document, especially for everyone that is engaged in the long drawn-out process of state-building. I have therefore made specific in-text commentaries relative to a series of contradictions and a seeming absence of logic that would justify some provisions in specific sections of the Constitution to the extent they impact on the issue of governance in a "shared" federal system (see appendix C). As I indicated earlier, there is nothing essentially wrong in the ideal of federalism, but it depends on how it is articulated and managed in specific geopolitical and cultural contexts. The real issue is whether the dynamics of the Nigerian political environment has outgrown the type of accommodation that federalism offers; and whether other models of governance could be more effectively adapted to it, in such a way that they are more properly aligned to the prevailing interests within a multiethnic system.

DEMOCRACY: INSTRUMENTAL BUT HOW FUNCTIONAL?

On a structural level, democracy is less a form of government as it is an "ideal" that guides the process of governance. In other words, it is a principle that regulates the relationship and interactions between political actors, institutions of government, and the citizens. It offers an essential framework within which political structures such as federalism, confederacy, or consociationalism could operate. In other to properly discuss the applicability of each of these political structures to the Nigerian context, I will explore, first, the broader implications of democracy as a guiding principle. Democracy is an ideal of governance that has been embraced by many societies and countries. But the irony is that while "liberal democracy may be more functional for a society that has already achieved a high degree of social equality and consensus concerning certain basic values; but for societies that are highly polarized along lines of social class, nationality, or religion, democracy can be a formula for stalemate and stagnation."[1] And to the extent that the "universalism and formality that characterizes the rule of law in liberal democracies does provide a level playing field on which people can compete, form, coalitions, and ultimately make compromises";[2] the ideal, nonetheless, could pose some problems in the way the political calculus of *majority rule* evolves, especially for multiethnic societies.

In a "multiethnic" society such as Nigeria, majority rule has a curious way of making democracy undemocratic. If one of the major ethnic groups has a majority, then it would be able to dominate the government (especially the legislature) on an almost permanent basis. The minority would be forced on a regular basis to compromise or build such coalitions in which its own interests would become secondary. The simple reason why minority legislators in the National Assembly, are oftentimes unable to deliver on their proposals is that they may not have the votes. In those rare circumstances when they are able to muster any form of loose coalition, they are forced to compromise away the core elements of their proposals in such a way that the original incentive for making such a proposal is lost. In the practical sense of the term, absolute "majority rule" within an absolute democracy are inimical to the political interests of "legislative" minorities and their constituencies.

GOVERNANCE: STRUCTURAL AND INSTITUTIONAL CONTEXTS

Federalism

Federalism is the division of powers between the national and state governments. Under this arrangement, the federal government and states derive authority from the people. But while the national government holds such powers as foreign, and economic policies; state governments hold power (often reserved) in various programmatic areas and policy implementation. There are also other areas where they share concurrent powers such as the power to tax, borrow money, and law enforcement. It is noteworthy that many segments of the Nigerian society have been advocating what is called "true" federalism. This could be a desirable option, that is, if the operational conditions clearly follow the normal conventions of a federal system.

In Nigeria, the long period of military government produced greater discontinuity between the two sets of federal arrangements (the First and Second Republics) than is ordinarily present when federal systems are altered.[3] The simple reality is that the national government cannot control or regulate the states without the power of resource control. If you add military (coercive) power, then the national government is naturally in a better position to back up its demands with force. But how willing is the national government to give up the power of resource control for the sake of "true" federalism? As long as state governments lack control of the resources within their territories, and as long as the national government controls law enforcement, the ultimate power of distributive and coercive politics will be concentrated at the center under a de facto "unitary" system. Hence whoever controls the federal government controls the purse strings of the nation as well as the authoritative allocation of values (distribution of public goods, political and economic rents, as well as opportunities for development). The centralization of oil resources breeds corruption at the political center, and corruption,[4] in turn, breeds bad governance. And all these militate against the securing of a "true" federal system. But there are three specific issues that ought to remain central in the ongoing debate about the nature of federalism in the country:

- Upward review of the derivative principle—an upward review or a proportional increase in the 13 percent derivation formula—a mid-range approach on the issue of resource control. This principle should be expanded to include other high yield minerals (tin, copper, iron, coal, etc.) and agricultural products like groundnuts (peanuts), cocoa, and palm produce.
- State law enforcement or police force—since "public safety" is an essential state prerogative in any federal system.
- Legal residency in any state—the right of all citizens of Nigeria to take up legal residency in any state of the federation for the purpose of voting, running for public office, employment, or as an inalienable right of citizenship. Every legal resident should be granted the same privileges and immunities as native-born citizens of the state.

Unless the above three stipulations are ceded back to the state governments, it is highly unlikely that the country would achieve a "true" federal system. In a multiethnic society, outright majority rule is highly problematic. What it means is that the ethnic group or geopolitical zone that has the largest majority would always be in a position to win major popular elections if they do not allow their votes to be split between two or more competing parties. They will practically rule the country and impose their arbitrary will on it forever. The only mitigating factor would be the creation of a minority veto power to check potential excesses of the majority. But Nigeria has tried to avoid this scenario by creating what it believes to be "broad based" national parties. But it would be very difficult to create a truly "broad based" national party in Nigeria because sooner or later, one finds that the party has become dominated by a particular ethnic group or geopolitical zone. The party becomes "regionalized" while co-opting elements from other geopolitical zones in an attempt to create a false image of national appeal and followership.

The contradiction in Nigeria's hybrid form of federalism is that it reflects a competing interest between presidential and a federal system of government. In a tug-of-war between the president and the legislature or any of the states, the president therefore would be inclined to resort to dictatorial tendencies to resolve issues of shared powers and authority. "It is sometimes argued that presidentialism is particularly appropriate for federal republics because the presidency can serve as a unifying symbol, especially in the absence of a monarchy, and can represent the nation as a totality in a way a parliament cannot."[5] However, the success of such an arrangement depends very much on the method of election chosen. A simple plurality in a single election, which might assure hegemony to the largest ethnic group, might not work. "Nigerians have attempted to deal with this problem in their constitution by dividing the country into relatively large, ethnically homogenous states and requiring that a presidential candidate gain at least 25 percent of the votes in two-thirds of the states of the federation to assure that he does not represent any particular ethnic group or narrow coalition."[6] The idea here is that a union of any two of the three largest groups behind a single candidate would not be sufficient support to reach the required threshold. But this formula has not worked in Nigeria simply because the idea itself works at cross-purposes to the six-region zonal formula for electing the president, or in the larger picture, other competing issues of the North-South divide.

Furthermore, because presidential systems are, more often than not, associated with weak, fractionalized, and clientelistic or personalistic parties, its various problems have also manifested themselves at the state level in Nigeria. The direct election of governors and their unipersonal authority is an indirect consequence of presidentialism. Such a system creates an inequality of representation because, in the case of multiple competitors for the office, it may deprive the majority of citizens of any chance to participate in the choice of the executive of the State; and that executive is in no direct way accountable to the state legislature.[7] This is the problem that Nigerians in general, have with most of their state governors—the inclination to personalize the state government and to use executive authority to enforce arbitrary rule. Hence, a presidential system within a democracy based on straight majority rule will not solve the enduring geopolitical conflicts in a multiethnic society such as Nigeria. In the long run, a structural realignment of the model and form of governance would serve the best interest of the country.

Confederacy

In the same vein, confederacy had its appeal when it was expedient to resolve the tensed situation in Nigeria in the 1960s. Confederacy is a type of governmental system in which the national government derives its powers from the states (units). In this case, essentially all the policy making and implementation authority belong to the states, and each state retains its independence and ultimate authority to govern within its territories. The national government is weak. But how does it fare today as an option for Nigerians? The danger is that many who prefer this option may still be doing so with a similar mindset as that of the 1960s. But there ought to be a recognition that the politics and the alignment of social forces in the 1960s is much different from what we have today in the twenty-first century. What confederacy offered then, pales in comparison to the political problems it would unravel today. While this is not an attempt to undermine continuing debate on the merits of confederacy, it is equally important to explore its dynamics as well as the specific contexts where its application would be mutually exclusive. Confederacy would not solve all of Nigeria's problems; and could, in fact, make them more complex and difficult to manage.

And the reason is very simple. Confederacy means that much of the controlling powers of the state would be given back to the constituent units. But in a political model where the units could literarily do or pass any law they deem necessary, noncitizens of other states (to the extent that they are spread out in all nooks and cranny of the country) could become the target. Each state would be in a position to impose its own vision of education on non-citizens living in their territory, declare exclusionary zones for certain types of businesses, would seek to regulate aspects of social and family life, the location of churches, mosques, synagogues, as well as invoke arbitrary laws with a specific intent to harm. The worst that noncitizens could face would be the loss of "property rights" in other states and an increased arbitrariness in the application of the principle of eminent domain. To an extent, while the federal constitution offers minimal individual protection regarding property rights; states, on the other hand, would have the discretion to decide for themselves how issues of this nature would be handled.

Confederacy is an option that should be considered with great care from the perspective of collective rights and from an economic point of view. Because many industrial activities, investments, and assets owned by citizens of other states are located outside their own territory, it would therefore be highly problematic if individual states have the exclusive authority and discretion to decide on such issues as property rights and ownership, legal residency rules, business certification and revocation, right to worship one's own religious preference, education policy, and other arbitrary regulations that may be targeted against the economic interests of non-indigenes. Even under the existing federal system, some states in Nigeria have engaged in arbitrary policies that have proven to be inimical to the political and economic interests of non-indigenes. What confederacy offered in the 1960s is quite different from the prospects of today. And when considered in light of current realities, it would harm the prospects of all Nigerians, particularly non-indigenes of states, more than it advances it.

But despite its seeming inadequacies, Nigerians could still secure the most important incentives of confederacy (devolution of power) while at the same time avoiding its negative consequences. Part of this would be state control of public safety, education policy (as long as it is nondiscriminatory), proportional increase in the derivative formula, economic development and intra-state commerce. There is a need to make specific mention of education policy. While many continue to advocate universal education for the country, it is important that states take on this responsibility so that each can develop at its own pace within its available human resources and skills. Hence a "universal" education that seeks to offer preferential treatment to specific sections of the country is not universal after all.

Consociationalism

Consociationalism is a subtype of democracy, but it differs from the ideal model as a result of its amenability to the problems of multiethnic societies as well as the protection of minority interests. It is relevant for "democracies with sub-cultural cleavages and with tendencies toward instability, but which are deliberately turned into more stable systems by the leaders of the major subcultures."[8] A fundamental assumption of consociational democracy is that "ethnic division need not result in conflict; and even if political mobilization is organized on ethnic lines, civil politics can be maintained if ethnic elites adhere to a power-sharing bargain that equitably protects all groups."[9] In the context of African political systems, this would explain a type of political system that is "willing to accommodate a variety of groups of divergent ideas in order to achieve the goal of unity. It is essentially a system of compromise and accommodation."[10] Such accommodation must also embrace the principle of proportional representation, opportunity for minority veto on important policy issues, and their representation in the context of grand coalitions.[11]

A unique feature of *consociational democracy* is not so much about any particular institutional design, but about the overarching cooperation at the elite level with the deliberate aim of counteracting disintegrative tendencies in the system. "One factor predisposing elites toward compromise may be the traumatic memory of past conflicts (i.e., a civil war), which may invariably, perpetuate their antagonisms, but which may also cause them to draw together."[12] Because the principle of "compromise and accommodation" were lacking in the First and Second Republics, the zero-sum nature of political contestation in both periods laid the groundwork for their eventual overthrow by force. *Consociational democracy* provides a platform for building the kind of broadly based *grand coalition* that would prevent attempts at regional or partisan domination of Nigeria's political center as well as federal policy. It offers the kind of consensus democracy that is characterized by sharing, limiting, and dispersing power than could be achieved in a straight and aggressive majority rule. And because of inherent inadequacies, a "true" federalism in Nigeria would still centralize too much power at the center and would institutionalize the kind of geopolitical hegemony that could lead to continued instability and civil war.

Alternatively, *consociational democracy* would accommodate the interests of all cultural segments within the framework of a "grand coalition" informed by elite consensus and the principle of proportional representation that also includes a mechanism for the distribution of the nation's resources. It embraces a universal premise that combines the collective rights of nationalities in the multinational and multicultural society, with the rights of individuals fully protected by the state.[13] As an example, the Colombian Liberal and Conservative parties agreed in 1958 to alternate in the presidency for a period of sixteen years, as part of a *consociational* design to avoid civil wars and dictatorships which had plagued the country. In Lebanon, *the National Pact* of 1943 stipulated that the two top executive posts would be shared by the two major religious groups: The president of the republic must be a Maronite and the president of the council a Sunni. Consensus democracy (which is advocated here) is characterized by sharing, limiting, and dispersing power, and is much more likely to achieve the objective of untrammeled representation than straight or absolute majority rule. In plural societies, consensus democracy means "defensive" democracy, and this should be less threatening to the cultural and ethnic diversity of a country than "aggressive" absolute majority rule.

In fact, the current six zonal structure in Nigeria is most conducive to a form of consociational design, despite the difficulty that may, sometimes, arise in maintaining grand coalitions. For instance, a consociational system could be used to administer or control those program areas that have always served the best interest of all. It would also allow for legislative votes to be done in the context of legislatures from the six existing geopolitical zones. The basic requirement would be that all legislative bills or policy making would take effect only by a qualified consensus vote of two-thirds among the legislators from each of the six geopolitical zones. Where this consensus is lacking in any one of them, then such legislation or policy would not take effect. While this may occasionally grant veto power to one of the geopolitical zones, but then, this would also encourage all the participants to seek a compromise. However, in those rare circumstance where a particular geopolitical zone would arbitrarily stalemate the legislative process by refusing to act in good faith, a *cloture* can be invoked by a three-fifth vote of all the legislators from the other geopolitical zones, where the number of those supporting a specific policy or program is four or above. A cloture allows legislation or a bill to be brought to a vote despite continued objections.

It should also be pointed out that while the model could be further refined, the idea is that it would allow a situation that avoids the seemingly detrimental effects of absolute majority rule which would sooner or later devolve into ethnic domination on the part of the group that has an overriding majority in the national legislature. This is also relevant in a presidential form of government. In fact, a major criticism of the presidential form of government is its strong inclination toward majoritarian democracy, especially in many countries where—because a natural consensus is lacking—a "consensual" instead of a majoritarian form of democracy is needed. These countries include not only those with deep ethnic, racial, and religious cleavages but also those with intense political differences stemming from a recent history of civil war or military dictatorship, huge socioeconomic inequalities, and so on.

I have had several occasions to discuss the evolving character of political development in Nigeria with the famed political scientist Robert A. Dahl, Sterling Professor Emeritus, Yale University. His view has always been that the true test of a democratic regime is when and how it overcomes its first crisis, including but not limited to the electoral processes used to decide which party would take over the reins of government. While he prefers a more gradualist approach toward democratic consolidation, he maintains the view that even in authoritarian regimes (a feature that has been most prevalent in Nigeria over the years), as a country grows in sustained economic development, it would slowly start to develop an active civil society, followed by a vibrant middle class formation, and a legal system as well as a supportive political culture that has the respect for the rule of law (see appendix B). But then, these would become more profound and robust overtime.

In a fairly similar vein, Sheri Berman acknowledges that just as "democracy developed in various ways and in various local contexts across Europe; it never came easily, peacefully, or in some straightforward, stage-like progression."[14] She points out that because a "stable democracy is something likely to develop over the long term only in fits and starts, and possibly with much turmoil";[15] it should hardly be surprising that many young democracies today are proving to be weak, ineffectual, illiberal, and often little more than arenas for extra-parliamentary and even violent contestation."[16] Citing the historical fact that many "contemporary democracies of today had trouble reaching a stable and mature democratic endpoint, she concludes that while problems and failures do not preclude the success of democracy; in retrospect, they ought to be seen as integral parts of the long-term processes through which nondemocratic institutions and culture are eliminated, and their democratic successors forged."[17] While this is not to suggest that every aspiring democracy must of necessity pass through these phases, the point is that conflict situations, in and of themselves, should not be the final arbiter of whether democracy succeeds or not. Rather the issue is how democratic principles and rule of law are made to function in light of its virtues and limitations in different geopolitical and cultural contexts.

NOTES

1. Francis Fukuyama, *The End of History and the Last Man* (New York: Free Press, 1992), 118.
2. Fukuyama, *The End of History and the Last Man*, 117.
3. Donald L. Horowitz, *Ethnic Groups in Conflict* (Berkeley: University of California Press, 2000), 603.
4. See Susan Rose-Ackerman, *Corruption and Government: Causes, Consequences, and Reform* (New York: Cambridge University Press, 1999).
5. Juan J. Linz and Arturo Valenzuela, eds., *The Failure of Presidential Democracy* (Baltimore: Johns Hopkins University Press, 1994), 42.
6. Juan J. Linz and Arturo Valenzuela, *The Failure of Presidential Democracy* (Baltimore: Johns Hopkins University Press, 1994), 44.
7. Linz and Valenzuela, *The Failure of Presidential Democracy*, 43.
8. Arend Lijphart, "Consociational Democracy," pp. 133–47 in *Comparative Politics: Notes and Readings*, ed. Roy C. Macridis and Bernard E. Brown. (Homewood, Ill.: The Dorsey Press, 1977), 136.
9. From Chaim Kaufman, "Possible and Impossible Solutions to Ethnic Civil Wars," *International Security* 20, no. 4 (1996): 136–75. Kaufman also presents four key components of the consociational model: (1) joint exercise of governmental power; (2) proportional distribution of government funds and jobs; (3) autonomy on ethnic issues; and (4) a minority veto on issues of vital importance to each group. While check could be put in to prevent reckless abuse of item 4, Kaufman points out that while power-sharing could avert potential ethnic conflicts or dampen mild ones; it remains to be seen whether it can bring peace under conditions of intense violence and extreme ethnic mobilization that are likely to motivate intervention. Also see Arend Lijphart, "The Power-Sharing Approach," pp. 491–509 in *Conflict and Peacemaking in Multiethnic Societies*, ed. Joseph V. Montville (Lexington, Mass.: Lexington Books, 1990).
10. David E. Apter, *The Political Kingdom in Uganda: A Study in Bureaucratic Nationalism* (Princeton, N.J.: Princeton University Press, 1961).
11. See Donald Horowitz, "The Cracked Foundations of the Right to Secede," *Journal of Democracy* 14, no. 2 (April 2003): 14–16.
12. Lijphart, "Consociational Democracy," 134.
13. Juan J. Linz and Alfred Stepan, *Problems of Democratic Transition and Consolidation: Southern Europe, South American, and Post-Communist Europe* (Baltimore: Johns Hopkins University Press, 1996), 33–34.
14. Sheri Berman, "How Democracies Emerge: Lessons from Europe," *Journal of Democracy* 18, no. 1 (January 2007): 37.

15. Berman, "How Democracies Emerge: Lessons from Europe," 39.

16. Berman, "How Democracies Emerge: Lessons from Europe," 38–39.

17. Berman, "How Democracies Emerge: Lessons from Europe," 38. Her historical account discusses the turbulent history in the development of democracy in England—(the intensely violent period of the English Civil War, 1642–1651); Oliver Cromwell's republican but dictatorial Commonwealth (1649–1653), and the Protectorate (1653–1659)—a period of overt one-man rule first by Cromwell and then by his son Richard, whose May 1659 resignation set the stage for the restoration of the Stuart monarchy in 1660. Europe had seen a violently turbulent period through the period 1798 to 1914, and even beyond. And then there was the United States for whom it took a bloody civil war (1861–1865) to put it on the path of true democracy—and then another century for its national state to bring democratic rights and freedoms to the entire population.

12

—⁓—

Embedding African Democracy and Development

The Imperative of Institutional Capital

To the extent that this chapter focuses on Africa broadly construed, it will certainly touch on various aspects of the Nigerian experience.[1] Contemporary experience indicates that everywhere in Africa, the history of democracy and economic development has mostly been based on a history of disappointments. In the same vein, conventional analyses or study of these experiences have generally been built around a theory of criticisms with less alternative voice granted to the fundamental issues inherent in the African context.[2] To address this epistemological anomaly, I begin by elaborating four central themes: the dialectics of African democracy, the resiliency of primary conditions, the challenge of post-modern liberalism, and the case for the primacy of *institutional capital*. By building on the central thesis of Parsonian structural-functionalism and its implication for contemporary institutional analysis, I advance a central thesis that the lack of stable democracies in Africa is due mainly to the weakness or absence of institutions rather than the "state" per se. The purpose of institutions is to create the basis for collective action, while the basis for "states" is the integration of action in such a way that it serves a purposeful and legitimate end. A failure in the first obligation makes success in the latter more difficult or impossible.

EVOLVING MECHANISMS OF DEMOCRACY

When viewed as a desirable end for which all societies ought to aspire, democracy takes on the semblance of a universal norm. This also goes with the presumption that if it can work in a particular country, it should also work in others. But once exposed to the dynamics of different geo-political and cultural contexts, democracy offers quite unique variations both in its substantive merit as well as in its rhetorical appeal. It is in this light that we can view democratic failures in Africa as both a structural and cultural issue. As Amartya Sen argues,[3] "a country does not have to be deemed fit *for* democracy, rather it has to become fit *through* democracy." What matters most is not a preemptive assumption on the universality of democracy's promise, but rather on how specific cultural processes engender the conditions that make democracy an indispensable choice for political consensus and governance. When seen in this light, we are then in a better position to properly assess democracy's assumed virtues which includes, "the intrinsic importance of political participation and freedom in human life; the instrumental importance of political incentives in keeping governments responsible and accountable; and the constructive role of democracy in the formation of values and in the understanding of needs, rights, and duties."[4]

But the irony of democracy is that while it makes it possible for issues and policies to be contested, genuine victory is only possible if all actors agree to abide by the rules of the game. But where fundamental institutions are lacking or where they are easily changed and replaced according to the political wind, it becomes very difficult to establish a permanent placeholder or an institutional anchor upon which these rules of the game can be constituted and legitimized. Effective democracy, therefore, requires both an institutional and procedural legitimacy based on mutual consensus among competing actors. Where this consensus is lacking and the pressures for democratization are placed on the political society, premature democratization occurs in such a way that it could enable competing groups to strike out on their own on the basis of a zero-sum calculation. This condition is akin to what Jürgen Habermas[5] refers to as "the *fundamental contradiction*' of a social formation when its organizational principle necessitates that individuals and groups repeatedly confront one another with claims and intentions that are, in the long run, incompatible." But as "soon as incompatibility becomes conscious, conflict becomes manifest, and irreconcilable interests are recognized as antagonistic interests."[6] By defining group interests in terms of their conflict with one another, thereby excluding the idea of an interest of society as a whole, the resultant of the group pressure (conflict) would thus become the only determinant of the course of government policy.[7] This phenomenon seems to embrace many of Africa's contemporary experiments in democracy.

THE DIALECTICS OF AFRICAN DEMOCRACY

At the prodding of the World Bank, the IMF, the United States and major European powers such as Britain and France, African countries like Kenya, Nigeria, Tanzania, Niger, Ivory Coast, Ghana, Mali, and others were forced into engaging in what would be considered premature liberalization of their economies and politics. Nonetheless, the process of democratic transition requires a passage of two phases, liberalization and democratization. Linz and Stepan[8] point out that in a nondemocratic setting, *liberalization* may entail a mix of policy and social changes, such as less censorship of the media, somewhat greater space for the organization of autonomous working-class activities, the introduction of some legal safeguards for individuals such as habeas corpus, the releasing of most political prisoners, the return of exiles, perhaps measures for improving the distribution of income, and most important, the toleration of opposition. On the other hand, *democratization* entails liberalization but is a wider and more specifically political concept. Democratization requires open contestation over the right to win control of the government, and this in turn requires free competitive elections, the results of which determine who governs. But though these ideals may be generally acceptable, democracy requires a preliminary consensus among competing interests that specific electoral procedures would be recognized, that electoral results would be upheld, and that the institutions charged with expending such collective responsibilities be granted legal and popular legitimacy.

However, the level of openness and political permissiveness that liberalization entails, oftentimes generates its own contradiction. Political liberalization has the tendency to resurface critical issues of poverty, resource redistribution, property rights, and power relations as the cornerstone of political contestation. When broad political interests diverge and become factionalized, they present breeding grounds for factional conflict and political dissent. Various social forces and reactionary elements arise to challenge the legitimacy of those in control of state power; and economic opportunists, both internal and external, move in to take advantage of the evolving state of uncertainty. The ensuing crisis of legitimacy, struggle for state power, and economic uncertainty reproduces itself into a state of anarchy that quickly brings the liberalization process to an abrupt end. The first stage (liberalization) in the process of democratic consolidation is thus aborted, as the regime in power cracks down and scuttles most of the liberties granted at the beginning of the liberalization process.

Test cases abound in the African context. In November 1987, Kenya's Daniel Arap Moi closed the Nairobi University and had several student leaders arrested following demonstrations and protests critical of his government. Consequent attempts to liberalize the economy as well as institute governmental accountability ran head on to the interests of the entrenched political elite. As the Kenyan business elite (mainly the European and Asian middle class) teamed up to resist the seemingly state-centric economic policies of the Kenyan government, President Arap Moi felt a conspiracy against his control of state power and he clamped down on the opposition. Nonetheless, "it was the repressive methods employed by President Jomo Kenyatta (earlier) and Moi (later) that helped to contain dissident elements, including tribal and ethnic separatist movements."[9]

The same approach to *containment* policy can be said of Ghana. When Flight Lieutenant Jerry Rawlings first took over the reins of power in Ghana as leader of the Provisional National Defense Council, his first economic program was no more than a hurried flirtation with some crude form of centralized planning. He started out on a Marxist-Socialist economic framework, but quickly backtracked as Ghana's economic realities set in. Ghana needed the infusion of foreign direct investment, and to secure that, it would have to liberalize its economy, dispose of moribund state enterprises, and reduce the size of the labor force in the public sector. Rawlings's subsequent rapprochement with the IMF and the World Bank and the imposed liberalization policies earned Ghana the enviable fame as a test model on how a structural adjustment program could work for many African countries. But in quick succession, a combination of high inflation and a fall in cocoa prices derailed much of the early economic successes and Ghana once again fell into political turmoil and economic stagnation. With stagnating economic conditions, increasing internal opposition, and widespread political discontent, Rawlings had to clamp down on the opposition in order to stay in power. Again, the road toward market liberalization and democratic consolidation was aborted.

Nigeria's case with periodic abrogation of the democratic process has become legendary. The country offers, "within a single case, characteristics that identify Africa."[10] "Forces of both integration and dissolution have been evident throughout the country's independent history, with one or the other being most prevalent at any moment. These opposing forces are rooted in the constant struggle between authoritarian and democratic governance, the push for development and the persistence of underdevelopment, the burden of public corruption and the pressure for accountability."[11] Nonetheless, there remain many glaring cases of state anarchy and official malfeasance. In June 1993, the then military head of state General Ibrahim Babangida nullified the presidential election that would have ushered in a democratically elected Third Republic. This very act created both a constitutional and political crisis that eventually paved the way for another military takeover by General Sani

Abacha on November 17, 1993. Over a three-month period between July 1994 and September 1994, the oil union workers and the Nigerian Labor Congress went on strike in protest of the military regime of Sani Abacha on its arrest of M. K. O. Abiola (considered by many as having won the June 12 presidential election) and other leaders of the democracy movement. The military responded by arresting the most vocal leaders of the pro-democracy movement, shutting down universities and media houses, and expanded its surveillance of groups and other avenues of civic expression. The basis for the emergence of civil society came to an abrupt end. "Nigeria today remains essentially an *unfinished state* characterized by instabilities and uncertainties."[12]

There was a time when Cote D'Ivoire was celebrated as a leading "island" of political and economic stability in Sub-Saharan Africa, but ironically that was when the country was under the nepotic rule of Felix Houphouet-Boigny (1960–1993) and could hardly be characterized as a "democratic" polity, at least by western standards. The political exit of Houphouet-Boigny ushered in the short-lived administration of Henri Konan Bedie in 1993. Within two years, amid a series of political machinations and subterfuges between elements of the various political and ethnic elites, the military, for the first time in the history of the country took over the reins of government. Since then, there have been two more military insurrections or coups in the country and the political crisis seem to have unearthed deep-rooted ethnic and religious divisions that were hitherto subdued by the overbearing leadership of Houphouet-Boigny. As with most African countries, once they are set on the path of political conquest by the military, they rarely recover the true instincts for the democratic process. This state of affairs is akin to what Li and Thompson call the *contagion effect*[13]—a term that suggests that "once the military intervenes against civilian leaders, military leaders become much more confident and willing to pursue similar actions in the future."[14] Once a coup occurs in a country, there exists a greater possibility of successive coups occurring within the same country.

The same situation applies very much to miniscule Gambia, in which the old guard had retained political and economic power under the presidency of Dawda Jawara (1965–1994), until he was overthrown by Captain Yahya Jammeh in 1994. Since then, various elements within the military continued to plot against Captain Jammeh. Since Samuel Doe overthrew the government of William Tolbert in 1980, Liberia has seen no peace. Today, both Liberia and Sierra Leone (its adjacent neighbor) are still relatively on fire, one more intense than the other. And what do these two countries have in common? The seething tension between the indigenous population and the returnees from early American and British slave trade ushered in a class system and cronyism that eventually manifested itself in the struggle for control of political power. Unlike many other African countries, Liberia and Sierra Leone were never colonized and so did not have to seek independence from the colonial powers. Whereas the "quest for independence" did not provide a political foundation for the expression of nationalism as a unifying force; it meant that class, ethnicity, and cultural divisions became more pronounced (an in fact, consequential) in all matters of national political discourse.

When Rhodesia (now Zimbabwe) secured its independence from the white minority government of Ian Smith in 1980, Robert Mugabe became its first president. It was hoped that racial harmony, economic stability, and democracy would prevail. After more than twenty-seven years in power, Robert Mugabe has no intention of relinquishing political power, either by the ballot or by other means. But instead, an economic warfare ensued between the government and agricultural landowners who were mostly white Zimbabweans; political opposition has literarily been subdued; and the economy has since fallen into disarray. The African context exposes a series of intriguing dilemmas: why is political leadership viewed more as an entitlement rather than as a privilege to serve? James S. Coleman[15] touches on this particular issue when he stipulates that "one of the factors nudging several African leaders toward greater authoritarianism, is the constant threat (real or imaginary) that dissident tribal, ethnic, or regional groups pose to the integrity of new states." Though he points to the cases of Sudan, Ghana, and Guinea; one would also add to the list such authoritarian-oligarchic regimes as that of then Idi Amin of Uganda, Nigeria under Sani Abacha, Jean-Bedel Bokassa of Central African Republic, Mobutu of Zaire, Blaise Compaore of Burkina Faso, Arap Moi of Kenya, Mengistu Haile Mariam of Ethiopia, and the list is endless. In abject disregard for formal institutional checks and balances, "leaders intent on silencing outspoken elements of civil society depended on loyal military troops and police forces that were both willing and able to enforce presidential directives."[16] As a result, the creation and rapid expansion of a coercive apparatus, comprising a wide variety of security forces, served as a critical component of the concentration of state power,"[17]—a legacy not lost on the fact that the "coercive nature of colonial police and military forces may have contributed to the creation of an authoritarian environment that carried over into the post-independent era."[18]

In their seminal work on democratic experiments in Africa, Bratton and Van de Walle[19] contend that "the efforts of African citizens to hold their leaders accountable for providing the common good are, at heart, a quest for democracy," but it remains to be seen how many African countries measure up to this standard. Yet, they argue of the necessity "to view recent African political developments as a useful point of comparison both within the continent and to other world regions."[20] By adopting a minimalist orientation in their study, they seem in a way, to understate the driving parameters of African democracy. By preferring an "approach that captures *basic* elements as most useful in distinguishing political regimes, especially in situations where democratization has only just begun,"[21] they essentially limit the argument to specific cases of stalemated transitions to democracy (in which initial promising processes seem to have bogged down). Though the study encompassed the period from 1990–1994, it is important to look at what obtained prior to the study and what was observed at the end. A study of "authoritarian reversals" does not ipso facto offer enough explanation or knowledge concerning the lack of democratic consolidation among African states. And neither do increasing trends on indicators like political protests, political liberty, competitive elections, or *attempts* at multipartyism suggest democratic consolidation in the absolute sense. They only reflect episodic and strategic shifts in regime transitions rather than a genuine indicator of trends toward democratic consolidation. Table 12.1 provides a characterization of various African regimes in terms of specific political orientations. Notwithstanding whether the elections were free and fair, popular or imposed, it shows that only five countries can be assumed to have met one crucial requirement of democracy: competitive party systems (at least two or more parties).

Table 12.1.   Modal Regimes by Country, Sub-Saharan Africa, 1989

Plebiscitary One-Party Systems (n=16)	Military Oligarchies (n=11)	Competitive One-Party Systems (n=13)	Settler Oligarchies (n=2)	Multiparty Systems (n=5)
Angola	Burkina Faso	Cameroon	Namibia	Botswana
Benin	Burundi	CAR	South Africa	Gambia
Cape Verde	Chad	Cote d'Ivoire		Mauritania
Comoros	Ghana	Madagascar		Senegal
Congo	Guinea	Mali		Zimbabwe
Djibouti	Lesotho	Malawi		
Eq. Guinea	Liberia	Rwanda		
Ethiopia	Mauritania	Sao Tome		
Gabon	Nigeria	Seychelles		
Kenya	Uganda	Sierra Leone		
Mozambique		Tanzania		
Niger		Togo		
Somalia		Zambia		
Swaziland				
Zaire				

Source: Michael Bratton and Nicolas Van De Walle, *Democratic Experiments in Africa* (New York: Cambridge University Press, 1997), p. 79.

But a closer look at table 12.2 indicates that the same political dynamics remain essentially in place, and in most cases even worse. Many of the countries indicated as undergoing democratic transitions (the Congo, Cape Verde, Madagascar, Mozambique, Sao Tome, Zambia, Mali, Central African Republic, Niger) have all fallen back into tremendous chaos and anarchy, that is, assuming that there was ever an initial movement toward democratic transition. If we are concerned about attempted transitions to democracy, then the answer should be obvious. But if we are more interested as to why these attempted transitions did not consolidate or take hold, then it behooves us to look elsewhere, perhaps at the *institutional* and *structural* foundations of the typical African state.

The missing link in the Bratton and Van de Walle thesis was their inability to address the "why" question. Rather they point to the fact that "most nations in the developing world, especially sub-Saharan Africa, retain in *modified* form many of the characteristics of patrimonial rule, and as such should be construed as *neopatrimonial*—those hybrid political systems in which the customs and patterns of patrimonialism co-exist with, and suffuse, rational-legal institutions";[22] but nonetheless, reflect a networked form of personal or patriarchal rule. Nonetheless, there are structural conditions that set African polities apart from others in the quest for democratic consolidation.

Table 12.2.   Transition Outcomes, Sub-Saharan Africa, 1994 (as of December 31, 1994)

Precluded Transitions (2)	Blocked Transitions (12)	Flawed Transitions (12)	Democratic Transitions (16)
Liberia	Angola	Burkina Faso	Benin
Sudan	Burundi	Cameroon	Cape Verde
	Chad	Comoros	Central Africa Republic
	Ethiopia	Cote d'Ivoire	Congo
	Guinea	Djibouti	Guinea-Bissau
	Nigeria	Eq. Guinea	Lesotho
	Rwanda	Gabon	Madagascar
	Sierra Leone	Ghana	Malawi
	Somalia	Kenya	Mali
	Tanzania	Mauritania	Mozambique
	Uganda	Swaziland	Namibia
	Zaire	Togo	Niger
			Sao Tome
			Seychelles
			South Africa
			Zambia

Source: Michael Bratton and Nicolas van De Walle, *Democratic Experiments in Africa* (New York: Cambridge University Press, 1997), p. 120.

THE RESILIENCY OF PRIMARY CONDITIONS

The introduction of colonial rule in Africa ran head on to the paternalistic indigenous institutions of traditional authority. The customs, symbolisms, cultural mysticisms, and belief systems came under enormous stress. To adapt to the challenges of the new political regime as well as the necessities of the emergent cosmopolitan society, the indigenous social structure had to change. The growth of industrialization, the establishment of railroads, the commercialization of the economy, advancement in education, the emergence of a rudimentary civil serve system, and the need for manual labor created a migration of people from the rural areas to the urban centers. As people of different ethno-linguistic backgrounds who could barely understand each other's local vernaculars found themselves as *strangers* in the big townships, the only mechanism for ensuring cultural homogeneity was to create tribal or ethnic associations as a basis "for continued expression of loyalty and obligation to the kinship group, town, or village where the lineage is localized."[23] Ironically, while this "general ferment produced forces which tended to break down tribal barriers on the one hand; yet the kinship ties remained obdurate by asserting itself in the tribal associations."[24]

By providing a medium for the perpetuation of different aspects of the traditional culture among the increasing urban population, the tribal associations can equally be said to have retarded the process of cultural integration, at least in the formative stages of national political development. The issue of cultural integration is very important as a way of bridging the ethno-linguistic, economic, and the rural-urban cleavages that have tended to undermine a genuine sense of universal loyalty to the state, as opposed to the ethnic group. Furthermore, a central administrative authority controlled by the colonial regime, was in many cases, "forced to co-exist with widely differing local authorities each of which derived some powers from its imperial masters and some from the traditional loyalty shown by its people."[25] The concept of *indirect rule* in Northern Nigeria during the period of colonial administration of the country is a good case in point. To the extent that colonial authority is coercive and traditional authority is paternalistic, the historical method of resolving fundamental issues in African politics has generally involved either of the two types of authority; and has only marginally (if not recently) embraced the virtues of consensus and compromise—two crucial elements of the democratic process.

In *Democracy and Development*, Alex Hadenius[26] points out that while political democracy *sensu stricto* signifies that people should *control* the activities of the state, it requires that citizens are able, in various respects, to function as free and equal rulers. But the possibility of *control* can naturally also depend on the nature of the object of influence; hence governments may differ in the extent to which they are amenable to democratic control. For instance, "the establishment of a large state in an economically weakly developed society makes it particularly difficult to apply the democratic form of the division of labor. Since public positions in these societies represent essentially the only way to social and economic improvement, the control of government becomes crucial. When so much is at stake in political life, there is no scope for the tolerance and peaceful competition which democracy requires. For the fact that the difference of result between gain and loss is too great, politics instead assumes the nature of a relentless zero-sum game."[27]

Suffice it then to state that Africa's peculiar conditions encumber not so much about transitions to democracy as the consolidation of enduring democracies. Not surprisingly, Richard Sandbrook[28] asks a very fundamental question: "Can liberal democracies emerge and survive in Africa?" He argues that with the waning of the Cold war, geopolitical considerations are no longer as compelling (as formerly) in the capitals of the major global powers. France, the United States, and Russia are no longer willing to support "their" African strongmen against all challenges. Moreover, Western liberal democracies and the international institutions they dominate are now freer to pursue their natural preferences for electoral democracies. He concludes that just as the cultural, historical, political, and socioeconomic conditions of Africa have not been fertile ground for nourishing strong developmental states; they are generally unfavorable to democracy, hence Africa (Sub-Saharan Africa in particular) is unlikely soon to yield many stable democracies.

THE CHALLENGE OF POSTMODERN LIBERALISM

As indicated by Michael Chege,[29] the case for African democracy rests on entirely different premises: after the collapse of colonialism and communism, popularly elected governance and the rule of law ought to be demanded as human values in their own right, irrespective of whether or not they promote economic growth. "The truth is that generalizations about economic conditions in sub-Saharan Africa (or Africa in general) hide a great deal of intercountry variation and should be approached with considerable circumspection. The optimal long-term development policy options for African states may, in fact, be more country-specific than the African development crisis debate suggests."[30] Priority should be given to deep-seated structural reforms such as diversification of the agricultural monoculture, cuts in defense spending, investments in education, in human capital skills, and in an efficient and technically oriented bureaucratic system. Even as we look at the "tenuous statistical relationship between growth and democracy in Africa, as well as the abundant evidence of spectacular economic growth under authoritarian governments in the Asian NICs, Chile under Pinochet, and Brazil under the military, it may be unrealistic to place too much stress on the link between democracy and Africa's economic recovery."[31]

As Malawi's Thandika Mkandawire has argued, "the case for liberal economic reforms in Africa is erected on contestable factual premises."[32] Even so, the above assumption remains problematic: how to create a viable indigenous capital class that is genuinely linked to the productive and financial sectors of the economy? In most African countries, the classic dichotomy between macroeconomic and microeconomic policies is very fuzzy at best, and the reason is not far-fetched. The corporate interest that binds the entrepreneurial and the political class means that access to capital is limited and not widespread. The state is the primary source of private capital accumulation, and this is due more to the entrenched patron-client relationships embedded in the domestic economy as opposed to wealth generated in the standard production process. In order to obtain credit from such multilateral lending institutions as the IMF and the World Bank, many African countries have had very little problem engaging in the process of economic liberalization, especially as it entails privatization, debt reduction, and streamlining the public sector. Privatization of public utilities means that only those who have money can bid for such facilities. While the majority of the citizens are poor and uneducated, they will not be able to bid or buy shares in such public utilities.

Furthermore, a typical approach to debt reduction has always been to reschedule old loans that invariably pass enormous credit obligations to future generations—a perfect recipe for continued economic paralysis. On the other hand, streamlining the public sector means that poor low-level workers will be laid off while the economic interests of the political-entrepreneurial alliance are well protected. Elite economic interests have sustained a hegemonic influence, thus creating policy disequilibrium in which only powerful and well-connected actors benefit more from maintaining the status quo than from risking policy uncertainty in the name of liberalization. And so, one finds that in many African countries liberalization programs rarely spread the wealth or improve the lot of the average citizen; they only protect and solidify the chokehold of the political-entrepreneurial alliance on the domestic economy.

In the advanced economies of the West, the middle class is generally viewed as a crucial element in the market economy. This is essentially correct because not only are there more people in this category, it also forms the cornerstone of capitalist consumerism as well as the foundation of most national economic policies. In many African countries, especially

Nigeria, Kenya, and Ghana where perhaps there were some rudimentary formations of the middle class, such economic classifications have since evaporated at the onslaught of wrenching economic mismanagement, predatory governance, and institutionalized corruption. There is no vibrant middle class: you are either rich or you are poor, hence any economic model prefaced on the conventional macroeconomic classification is bound to fail. Elsewhere, it has been argued that increased infusion of foreign direct investment in the African economy will lead to increased economic development. But first, African countries must achieve sustained political stability under popular democratic governance. The irony of this argument is that the massive poverty in many of the African countries has remained a source of factional crisis, death, deprivation, and political instability as the general clamor for resource redistribution is directed at the political center. In the same way that foreign direct investment can thrive in an atmosphere of political stability, it can also create conditions that make political stability possible, by creating jobs and providing opportunity for economic prosperity.

In their study of the relationship between democracy and economic development, Adam Przeworski et al.[33] point out that "one way poverty binds is that when a society is poor, so is the state, and when the state is poor it cannot extract resources and provide public services required for development." "Poverty breeds frustration, and frustration frequently breeds aggression, both domestic and external";[34] hence "even if democracies do occasionally spring up in poor countries, they are extremely fragile when facing poverty; whereas in wealthy countries they are impregnable."[35] "Barriers to development are often more subtle than the current emphasis on 'good governance' in debtor countries suggest."[36] So the idea of using political stability as a precondition for increase in foreign direct investment in Africa negates the alternative possibility that foreign direct investment can also provide the incentive for creating political stability in the first place.

DO INSTITUTIONS MATTER?
A CASE FOR INSTITUTIONAL CAPITAL

According to John Ikenberry,[37] to the extent that they can help overcome and integrate diverse and competing interests, institutions matter. He was quite marveled at the fact that policy makers in twentieth-century America have sustained a genuine assumption that institutions (in this case international institutions) limit the scope and severity of conflicts, and states that agree to participate in such institutions are, in effect, joining a political process that shapes, constrain, and channel their actions.

The same assumption holds true for nation-states since much of the fundamentals that drive international relations can be localized to the level of internal (indigenous) political actors. The dynamics of political power and dominance at the international level is very much replicated within the typical nation-state. In the same way that the separation of powers, checks and balances, and other constitutional devices were created as ways to limit power;[38] "institutions construct actors and define their available modes of action; they constrain behavior, but they also empower it."[39] Hence, the *structure* of political systems, such as the state, matters.[40]

A fundamental prerequisite for the democratic process is that critical institutions should be in place, so as to enable the assimilation of the core values of democracy. While democracy creates value, institutions enable democratic values to be assimilated and sustained within society. Where such institutions are not present, the democratization process either stalemates or is rejected outright by opposing forces. There is a primary need for institutions such as educational facilities—to expose citizens to the essential virtues, imperatives, and limitations of democracy; agricultural infrastructure—to prevent hunger and reduce the level of social frustration generally associated with poverty; health care—to live a better and quality life; and of course, an independent judicial system—to safeguard the fundamental rights and liberties that democracy provides.

The conventional argument has been that *democracy* will enable functional institutions to be created, but it remains to be seen how democratic virtues could begin to permeate society without the initial conditions provided by institutions. If we accept the fact that "the flowering of any type of regime requires the mature development of a system of inter-locking political institutions and sets of widely shared political values,"[41] and to the extent that "all sustained development must rest on this assumption; development cannot take place in the absence of stable, reliable institutions,"[42] that reinforces the will of the governed. While knowledge of events and their value are connected to previous understandings, to the understandings of other people, and to social linkages of friendship and trust;[43] "it takes political institutions to organize these interactions in ways that shape interpretations and preferences."[44]

While early institutionalists[45] view institutions as the structural embodiment of different sets of a functional and normative order; contemporary advocates of institutional theory[46] seek to re-establish the importance of normative frameworks and rule systems in guiding, constraining, and empowering social and political behavior. Talcott Parsons' structural-institutional model strikes a deeper note here. As in most of his writings,[47] Parsons stressed the subjective dimension of institutions, whereby individual actors internalize shared norms so that they become the basis for the individual's action. But in his analysis of organizations,

Parsons shifts attention to the objective dimension: a system of norms defining what the relations of individuals ought to be. He argues that "these wider normative structures serve to legitimate the existence of organizations (institutions) but, more specifically, they legitimate the main functional patterns of operation which are necessary to implement the values."[48] "As organizations (institutions) become infused with value, they are no longer regarded as expendable tools; and participants want to see that they are preserved. By embodying a distinctive set of values, an institution acquires a characteristic structure—a distinctive identity. Maintaining the organization is no longer simply an instrumental matter of keeping the machinery working; it becomes a struggle to preserve a set of unique values."[49]

Traditional and recognized institutions engender a stabilizing effect, and reduce the burden of decisional analysis involved in the process of seeking immediate remedies for seemingly intractable social and political problems. In the same way that interest groups reinforce democratic pluralism, institutions provide the legitimate infrastructure that makes popular democracy possible, or even efficacious. In countries like Nigeria, where institutional decay has reached incomprehensible proportions, the sun may already be setting on its nascent democracy. As the process jolts and sputters, key institutions of law enforcement have practically been abdicated. The public safety system has been overtaken by extra-judicial vigilante groups; while the court system and *justice* itself, has been deeply politicized and compromised. The mission of the bureaucratic institutions has equally been coopted to serve such interests that are unconnected to their original mandates. The army, with its own sets of rules and doctrine, has overtaken law enforcement now conflated under the guise of national security. The result is, more than two hundred civilians shot dead by army personnel after they were sent in late October 2001 to the Benue state of Nigeria to contain ethnic and religious strife between three ethnic groups.

While institutions help to maintain consistency, and perhaps, predictability in the behavior of political actors, but even when performance fails to meet expectations, they provide a natural basis in the search for new solutions. "When individuals enter an institution and encounter a new situation, they try to associate it with a situation for which the rules already exist. Through rules and a *logic of appropriateness*, political institutions realize order, stability, and predictability on the one hand, and flexibility and adaptiveness on the other."[50] In the same way that institutions enhance democratic competition, they also mitigate the chances of personalizing administrative issues into political conflicts. Hence, "a major activity of political institutions is educating individuals into knowledgeable citizens."[51] A knowledgeable citizen is one who is familiar with the rules of appropriate behavior and with the moral and intellectual virtues of the polity, and who thus knows the institutional reasons for behaviors, and can justify them by reference to the requirements of a larger order.[52] Institutional durability and legitimacy is enhanced the more an institution is widely integrated into a larger political order in such a way that changes in one institution will necessitate reciprocal changes in others.

EMPOWERING INSTITUTIONS

Though collective action dilemmas generally lead to the creation of institutions to solve them, "institutions, on the other hand, provide the means by which cooperation dividends are captured; and nothing inherent in the logic of these approaches makes them antithetical."[53] "By shaping change to make it more consistent with existing procedures and practices, institutions maintain stability in the face of pressure to change."[54] But the concept of institutions as utilized here goes beyond the structural and functional characteristics. It includes such elements as the rule of law, traditions and customs, etiquette, obeying traffic conventions, press freedom, systems of bureaucratic accountability, untrammeled electoral participation, political responsiveness, independent judiciary, impersonality of office, self-sanction and restraint, and other normative considerations in public and private life. The African political culture must also cultivate a new behavioral norm among the citizenry. The average citizen must come to accept the necessity and importance of critical institutions, and by obeying the rules that govern the existence of these institutions, he or she invariably gives it legitimacy. But when traffic conventions are violated because there is no police officer around the corner; when speed limits are constantly abridged; and when public officials are bribed to do that which they are already being paid for by the government, then the people become reluctant accessories to the decay and ineptitude confronting institutions in Africa. More often than not, the law itself becomes the victim.

When simple rules of social conduct are adjudicated outside the laws of the land, and without any credible challenge to this kind of behavior, there is the tendency that the people will eventually come to accept and internalize this as a standard practice. Without regard to the conventions that stipulate the nature and scope of relationship between the government and the governed, between individual citizens and others, it would be very difficult to create a favorable environment where rule of law would enable the process of democratic consolidation. In his work *Democracy and Development in Africa*,[55] Claude Ake bemoaned the fact that "there was little concern about how the political structures and practices, the administrative system, or even the social institutions of a country might affect its possibility of development. He concludes that while the institutional environment in Africa has become so complicated and so important in determining how people behave, any development paradigm that takes this environment for granted will not be a useful tool for the pursuit of development." In the developmental process, even "the traditional institutions, often castigated as 'outmoded,' can be very useful."⁵⁶

In this chapter, three fundamental issues have been addressed. First, is that Africa's democracy does have its peculiar conditions which are rarely recognized; and second, that the failure of democracy in Africa is not due to the decay or absence of the "state" system but is simply due to the weakness of institutions; and third, that democracy as an objective is generally possible within African states, but the approach to its attainment needs to be redefined and redirected from what currently obtains. "While Western democracies, especially France and the United States, and the Soviet Union were notorious for their willingness to buttress 'friendly' African dictators during the heyday of the Cold War,"⁵⁷ "the retreat from Africa by these former cold war patrons, may have therefore unleashed internally disruptive rather than democratic politics."⁵⁸ Adapting the structural-functionalist theme of early socioanthropologists and the neoinstitutional thesis of contemporary institutionalists, it is argued that the development of *institutional capital* must be given precedent if the democratic impulse in Africa is to be successful. By institutional capital is meant the acquisition of such instrumental and normative objectives as efficient academic institutions, health care agencies, robust political parties, effective judicial systems, independent press agencies, effective civil service and banking systems, recognition of traditional and cultural power hierarchies, constitutional law and order, discipline and service, private and public civility, and other critical elements of sociopolitical development.

Institutions provide integrative norms and sanctions that affect the ways in which individuals and groups become activated within and outside established rules of appropriate behavior; "the level of trust among citizens and leaders, the common aspirations of a political community, the shared language, understanding, and norms of the community, and the meaning of concepts like democracy, justice, liberty, and equality."⁵⁹ The contemporary orientation to nation building and state consolidation, which tends to focus change at the top should be reevaluated in favor of a more horizontal and society-based approach. There should be a redirection of focus on institution building rather than nation building. Effective institutions will, in turn, yield effective nation-states. A most acceptable framework for the democratic experience is that it has to be constitutive, consensual, and reciprocal. To the extent that a "satisfactory institutional solution must cope with the need for exchange, the problem of enforcing deals, the problem of extending the life of deals, and the necessity for making deals robust to unanticipated events";[60] what Africa needs most are *functional* institutions. In the structural-functional tradition, *institutions* create *structure*, and *structure* creates *function*. This seems, in very fundamental ways, to reflect the immediate and long-term challenge to Africa's democracy and development.

NOTES

1. This chapter is a revised version of my article that was first published as "Embedding African Democracy and Development: The Imperative of Institutional Capital," *International Review of Administrative Sciences* 70, no. 3 (2004): 527–45.

2. For a detailed account of contemporary democratic and economic experiences in Africa, consult the following sources: Jennifer Widner, ed. *Economic Change and Political Liberalization in Sub-Saharan Africa* (Baltimore: Johns Hopkins University Press, 1994); Richard Sandbrook, *The Politics of Africa's Economic Recovery* (New York: Cambridge University Press, 1993); Christopher Clapham, *Africa and the International System: The Politics of State Survival* (New York: Cambridge University Press, 1996); George B. N. Ayittey, *Africa in Chaos* (New York: St. Martin's Press, 1998); Robert H. Bates, *Markets and States in Tropical Africa: The Political Basis of Agricultural Policies* (Berkeley: University of California Press, 1981); Michael Bratton and Nicolas Van de Walle, *Democratic Experiments in Africa: Regime Transitions in Comparative Perspective* (New York: Cambridge University Press, 1997); Jeffery Herbst, *States and Power in Africa: Comparative Lessons in Authority And Control* (Princeton, N.J.: Princeton University Press, 2000).

3. Amartya Sen, "Democracy as a Universal Value," *Journal of Democracy* 10, no. 3 (1999): 3–17.

4. Sen, "Democracy as a Universal Value," 7.

5. Jürgen Habermas, *Legitimation Crisis* (Boston: Beacon Press, 1973), 27.

6. Habermas, *Legitimation Crisis*, 27.

7. Arthur F. Bently, *The Process of Government* (Evanston, Ill.: Principia Press, 1949).

8. Juan J. Linz and Alfred Stepan, *Problems of Democratic Transition and Consolidation: Southern Europe, South America, and Post-Communist Europe* (Baltimore: Johns Hopkins University Press, 1996), 3.

9. Kenneth Ingham, *Politics in Modern Africa: The Uneven Tribal Dimension* (London: Routledge, 1990): 113–14.

10. Richard A. Joseph, Peter Lewis, Darren Kew, and Scott Taylor, "The Making of the Modern Nigerian State," in *Introduction to Comparative Politics: Political Challenges and Changing Agendas*, ed. Mark Kesselman, Joel Krieger, and William A. Joseph, 2nd ed. (New York: Houghton-Mifflin, 2000), 545–606.

11. Joseph, Lewis, Kew, and Taylor, "The Making of the Modern Nigerian State," 547.

12. Joseph, Lewis, Kew, and Taylor, "The Making of the Modern Nigerian State," 547.

13. Richard P. Y. Li and William R. Thompson, "The Coup Contagion Hypothesis," *Journal of Conflict Resolution* 19, no. 1 (1975): 63–88.

14. Peter J. Schraeder, *African Politics and Society: A Mosaic in Transformation* (New York: Bedford/St. Martin's, 2000), 247–48.

15. James S. Coleman, *Nationalism and Development in Africa: Selected Essays* (Berkeley: University of California Press, 1994), 98.

16. Schraeder, *African Politics and Society: A Mosaic in Transformation*, 225.

17. Schraeder, *African Politics and Society: A Mosaic in Transformation*, 225.

18. Schraeder, *African Politics and Society: A Mosaic in Transformation*, 105.

19. Michael Bratton and Nicolas Van de Walle, *Democratic Experiments in Africa: Regime Transitions in Comparative Perspective* (New York: Cambridge University Press, 1997), 10.

20. Bratton and Van de Walle, *Democratic Experiments in Africa*, 10.

21. Bratton and Van de Walle, *Democratic Experiments in Africa*, 12.

22. Bratton and Van de Walle, *Democratic Experiments in Africa*, 62.

23. Coleman, *Nationalism and Development in Africa*, 15.

24. Coleman, *Nationalism and Development in Africa*, 16.

25. Ingham, *Politics in Modern Africa*, 3.

26. Alex Hadenius, *Democracy and Development* (New York: Cambridge University Press, 1992), 133–34 .

27. Hadenius, *Democracy and Development*, 136.

28. Richard Sandbrook, *The Politics of Africa's Economic Recovery* (New York: Cambridge University Press, 1993), 87.

29. Michael Chege, "Sub-Saharan Africa: Underdevelopment's Last Stand," in *Global Change, Regional Response: The New International Context of Development*, ed. Barbara Stallings (New York: Cambridge University Press, 1995), 309–45.

30. Chege, "Sub-Saharan Africa: Underdevelopment's Last Stand," 314.

31. Chege, "Sub-Saharan Africa: Underdevelopment's Last Stand," 324.

32. Chege, "Sub-Saharan Africa: Underdevelopment's Last Stand," 313.

33. Adam Przeworski, Michael E. Alvarez, Jose Antonio Cheibub, and Fernando Limongi, *Democracy and Development: Political Institutions and Well-Being in the World, 1950–1990* (New York: Cambridge University Press, 2000), 270.

34. Olusegun Obansanjo, "Democracy and Development in Africa," Speech delivered at Harvard University's ARCO Forum for Public Affairs, Kennedy School of Government, October 30, 1999.

35. Przeworski, Alvarez, Cheibub, and Limongi, *Democracy and Development*, 269.

36. Jeffrey Sachs, "Helping the World's Poorest," *The Economist*, August 14, 1999.

37. John Ikenberry, "Why Export Democracy?" *Wilson Quarterly* 23, no. 3 (1999): 56–65.

38. Ikenberry, "Why Export Democracy?" 56–65.

39. Richard W. Scott, *Institutions and Organizations*, 2nd ed. (Thousand Oaks, Calif.: Sage Publications, 2001), 34.

40. Theda Skocpol, "Bringing the State Back In: Strategies of Analysis in Current Research," in *Bringing the State Back In*, ed. Peter B. Evans, Dietrich

Rueschemeyer, and Theda Skocpol (Cambridge: Cambridge University Press, 1985), 3–37.

41. Bratton and Van de Walle, *Democratic Experiments in Africa*, 12.

42. Carole Henderson Tyson and Mary K. Graber, "The Future of U.S. Policy toward Africa," *Focus*. Washington, D.C.: Joint Center for Political and Economic Studies, 2001, 6.

43. Richard L. Daft and Karl E. Weick, "Toward a Model of Organizations as Interpretation Systems," *Academy of Management Review* 9 (1984): 284–95.

44. James G. March and Johan P. Olsen, "The New Institutionalism: Organizational Factors in Political Life," *American Political Science Review* 78 (1984): 734–49.

45. For a review of some of the early institutionalists, see Max Weber, *The Theory of Social and Economic Organization*, trans. and ed. A. M. Henderson and Talcott Parsons (New York: Oxford University Press, 1947); Emile Durkheim, *Division of Labor in Society* (Glencoe, Ill.: Free Press, 1949); Karl Marx, "Economic and Philosophical Manuscripts: Selections," in *The Marx-Engels Reader*, ed. Robert C. Tucker (1844; New York: Norton, 1972), 52–106; Talcott Parsons, "A Sociological Approach to the Theory of Organizations," in *Structure and Processes in Modern Societies*, ed. Talcott Parsons (Glencoe, Ill.: Free Press, 1956), 16–58; Kingsley Davis, *Human Society* (New York: Macmillan, 1949).

46. For a review of some of the literature on contemporary institutional theory, see James G. March and Johan P. Olsen, "The New Institutionalism: Organizational Factors in Political Life," *American Political Science Review* 78 (1984): 734–49; James G. March and Johan P. Olsen, *Rediscovering Institutions: The Organizational Basis of Politics* (New York: Free Press, 1989); Stephen D. Krasner, "Sovereignty: An Institutional Perspective," *Comparative Political Studies* 21 (1988): 66–94; Peter Hall, *Governing the Economy: The Politics of State Intervention in Britain and France* (Cambridge: Polity Press, 1986); Theda Skocpol, "Bringing the State Back In: Strategies of Analysis in Current Research," in *Bringing the State Back In*, ed. Peter B. Evans, Dietrich Rueschemeyer, and Theda Skocpol (Cambridge: Cambridge University Press, 1985), 3–37; John Zysman, *Governments, Markets, and Growth: Finance and the Politics of Industrial Change* (Ithaca, N.Y.: Cornell University Press, 1983); Barry R. Weingast, "The Political Institutions of Representative Government," Working Paper in Political Science P-89-14, Hoover Institution, Stanford University, 1989; Kenneth A. Shepsle, "Studying Institutions: Lessons from the Rational Choice Approach," *Journal of Theoretical Politics* 1 (1989): 131–47; Robert O. Keohane, ed., *International Institutions and State Power: Essays in International Relations Theory* (Boulder, Colo.: Westview Press, 1989); Oliver E. Williamson, *The Economic Institutions of Capitalism* (New York: Free Press, 1985); Terry M. Moe, "Political Institutions: The Neglected Side of the Story," *Journal of Law, Economics, and Organizations* 6 (1990): 213–53; and Douglas C. North, *Institutions, Institutional Change, and Economic Performance* (Cambridge: Cambridge University Press, 1990).

47. See Talcott Parsons, *The Structure of Social Action* (New York: McGraw-Hill, 1937); Talcott Parsons, "A Sociological Approach to the Theory of Organizations," in *Structure and Processes in Modern Societies*, ed. Talcott Parsons (Glencoe, Ill.: Free Press, 1956), 16–58. Also see Richard W. Scott, *Institutions and Organizations*, 2nd ed. (Thousand Oaks, Calif.: Sage Publications, 2001), 25–26.

48. Talcott Parsons, *The Structure of Social Action* (New York: McGraw-Hill, 1937); Talcott Parsons, "A Sociological Approach to the Theory of Organizations," in *Structure and Processes in Modern Societies*, ed. Talcott Parsons (Glencoe, Ill.: Free Press, 1956), 27.

49. Scott, *Institutions and Organizations*, 24.

50. James G. March and Johan P. Olsen, *Rediscovering Institutions: The Organizational Basis of Politics* (New York: The Free Press, 1989), 160.

51. March and Olsen, *Rediscovering Institutions*, 161.

52. Alasdair MacIntyre, *Whose Justice? Which Rationality?* (Notre Dame, Ind.: University of Notre Dame Press, 1988).

53. Kenneth A. Shepsle and Barry R. Weingast, "Positive Theories of Congressional Institutions," in *Positive Theories of Congressional Institutions*, ed. Kenneth A. Shepsle and Barry R. Weingast (Ann Arbor: University of Michigan Press, 1995), 22.

54. March and Olsen, *Rediscovering Institutions*, 63.

55. Claude Ake, *Democracy and Development in Africa* (Washington, D.C.: Brookings Institution Press, 1996), 13–14.

56. George B. N. Ayittey, *Africa in Chaos* (New York: St. Martin's Press, 1998), 312.

57. Sandbrook, *The Politics of Africa's Economic Recovery*, 99.

58. Chege, "Sub-Saharan Africa: Underdevelopment's Last Stand," 329.

59. March and Olsen, *Rediscovering Institutions*, 164.

60. Shepsle and Weingast, "Positive Theories of Congressional Institutions," 11.

Appendix A

*Role Call and Votes on
2007 Presidential Elections*

Table A1.1. Results of Nigerian Presidential Election and Candidates, April 21, 2007. As announced by the _Independent National Election Commission_ (INEC) on April 23, 2007

Position	Presidential Candidate	Vice-Presidential Candidate	Political Party	Votes	% of Total
1	Alhaji Umaru Musa Yar'Adua	Goodluck Jonathan	People's Democratic Party (PDP)	24,638,063	69.604
2	Maj. Gen. Muhammadu Buhari (Rtd)	Hon. Edwin Ume-Ezeoke	All Nigeria Peoples Party (ANPP)	6,605,299	18.660
3	Alhaji Atiku Abubakar	Sen. Peter Obi	Action Congress (AC)	2,637,848	7.452
4	Orji Uzor Kalu	Inuwa Abdulkadir	Progressive Peoples Alliance (PPA)		
5	Alhaji Attahiru Dalhatu Bafarawa	Ebere Udeogu	Democratic Peoples Party (DPP)	289,224	0.817
6	Dim Chukwuemeka Odumegwu Ojukwu	Alhaji Habib Ibrahim Gajo	All Progressive Grand Alliance (APGA)	155,947	0.441
7	Chief Christopher Pere Ajuwa (replacing late Chief Adefarati)	Alhaji Mahmud Danjuma Sani	Alliance for Democracy (AD)	89,241	0.252
8	Rev. Chris O. Okotie	Fela Akinola Binutu	Fresh Democratic Party (FRESH)	74,049	0.209
9	Prof. Patrick O. Utomi	Ibrahim Musa	African Democratic Congress (ADC)	50,849	0.144
10	Dr. Brimmy Asekharuagbom Olaghere	Mrs. Zainab Goggo Bayero	Nigerian Peoples Congress (NPC)	33,771	0.095
11	Chief Ambrose Owuru	Alhaji Ibrahim Danjuma	Hope Democratic Party (HDP)	28,519	0.081
12	Arthur Nwankwo	Mohammed Abdullahi	Peoples Mandate Party (PMP)	24,164	0.068

13	Chief Emmanuel Osita Okereke	Hajiya Asabe Mauna	African Labor Party (ALP)	22,677	0.064
14	Sir. Lawrence Famakinde Adedoyin	Alhaji Ali Abacha	African Political System (APS)	22,409	0.063
15	Alhaji Aliyu Habu-Fari	Prince Chudi Charles Chukwuani	National Democratic Party (NDP)	21,974	0.062
16	Galtima Baboyi Liman	Abiti Onoyom Ndok	New Nigeria Peoples Party (NNPP)	21,665	0.061
17	Maxi Okwu	Hajiya Rabia Yasat Affah (CENGIS)	Citizens Popular Party (CPP)	14,027	0.040
18	Chief Sonny Joseph Odogwu	Hajia Larai Umaru	Republican Party of Nigeria (RPN)	13,566	0.038
19	Dr. Iheanyichukwu Godswill Nnaji	Adamu Musa	Better Nigeria Progressive Party (BNPP)	11,705	0.033
20	Dr. Osagie O. Obayuwama	Yunusa S. Tanko	National Conscience Party (NCP)	8,229	0.023
21	Dr. Olapade Agoro	Mrs. Eghenayheore Dele Ayi	National Action Council (NAC)	5,752	0.016
22	Dr. Akpone Solomon	Alhaji Abdullahi S. Abdullahi	National Majority Democratic Party (NMDP)	5,664	0.016
23	Prof. Isa Odidi	Oluwafolajimi Akeem-Bello	New Democrats (ND)	5,408	0.015
24	Major Mojisola Adekunle Obasanjo (Rtd)	Mohammed Mohammed Abdullahi	Masses Movement of Nigeria	4,309	0.012
25	Mallam Aminu Garbarti Abubakar	Kingsley Onye-Eze Ibe	National Unity Party (NUP)	4,355	0.012
TOTALS				35,397,517	99.998

Appendix B

Note from Robert A. Dahl,
Renowned Political Scientist
of the Twenty-first Century

Yale University

DEPARTMENT OF POLITICAL SCIENCE
P.O. Box 208301
New Haven, Connecticut 06520-8301

ROBERT A. DAHL
Sterling Professor Emeritus of Political Science

Telephone: 203 432-5767
Fax: 203 432-6196

9/30/98

Dear Kalu,

Reflecting on our interesting conversation last Monday, I realize that my view on a slow transition toward elections, following upon the introduction of the other main institutions of "polyarchy," may require special conditions that don't and won't exist in Nigeria. South Korea and Taiwan were both strong states, highly homogeneous ethnically, with a relatively (it's always relative) uncorrupted political elite of military leaders who were committed to, and did bring about, rapid modernization and economic development in their countries. Thus by the time they permitted or even facilitated full democratization, with free and fair elections, the society was already pretty ready for democracy.

From your description of Nigeria, that kind of leadership can't be counted on. Quite the contrary, perhaps: military rule evidently is likely to result in a corrupt "kleptocracy" that exploits its power for personal gain and domination. If so, it's conceivable that elections have to *precede* the fuller development of the social and economic institutions that would help to give stability to democratic political institutions. And therefore perhaps only a rather brief period may be possible during which the other main democratic political institutions would be introduced: access to independent sources of information, freedom of expression, existence of independent political organizations, and the creation of a constitutional system.

Insofar as I understand it, I like your idea of searching for a form of constitutional decentralization—confederacy or whatever. That strikes me as essential.

Good luck!

Sincerely yours,

Bob

Appendix C

Basic Pitfalls of the 1999 Nigerian Constitution: A Commentary on Selected Sections [as Abbreviated]

CHAPTER 1

Part I: General Provisions

1. (1) This Constitution is supreme and its provisions shall have binding force on the authorities and persons throughout the Federal Republic of Nigeria.

(2) The Federal Republic of Nigeria shall not be governed, nor shall any persons or group of persons take control of the Government of Nigeria or any part thereof, except in accordance with the provisions of this Constitution.

Commentary

But if the military takes over political power and nullifies the existing Constitution, the above provision thus becomes inconsequential. Then what happens? There should be a specification within the Constitution that such actions (arbitrary usurpation of the political power of the Government) shall be construed as treason, hence illegitimate and punishable by applicable laws in place at the time of commission of such acts. Arbitrary usurpation of political authority shall not in itself constitute a legitimate abrogation of the Constitution to the extent that the Constitution, in itself, makes an a priori provision that such acts are illegal and represents a contravention of the supreme laws of the land.

(3) If any other law *(in the land)* is inconsistent with the provisions of this Constitution, this Constitution shall prevail, and that other law shall, to the extent of the inconsistency, be void.

Commentary

The above provision is problematic. The idea of "to the extent of the inconsistency" is ambiguous, and yet quite political. Who decides "the extent of inconsistency of the two laws? This offers a lot of interpretations which may not be founded on legal but political and arbitrary grounds.

2. (1) Nigeria is one indivisible and indissoluble sovereign state to be known by the name of the Federal Republic of Nigeria.

Commentary

Technically, "indivisible" and "indissoluble" are one and the same thing. In what way would it not be "indivisible"? It should be specified as to whether what is implied here is about state creation, regionalization, or a break up into sovereign entities. Otherwise, this provision essentially precludes the authority to create more states. Also such a provision should not be a necessary condition for association in any form of political society, because it does not allow those who may be aggrieved by the system the choice of alternative means of association consistent with changes in political fortunes and aspirations. Is there any condition under which Nigeria can be dissolved?

(2) Nigeria shall be a Federation consisting of States and a Federal Capital Territory.

Commentary

If Nigeria is a federation, then who decides if and when it ought to be dissolved? Should this not be the role of the federating units to do so either collectively, or in a duly constituted framework constituted for the expressed purpose of determining the fate of the federation.

3. (1) There shall be 36 states in Nigeria, that is to say, Abia, Adamawa, Akwa Ibom, Anambra, Bauchi, Bayelsa, Benue, Borno, Cross River, Delta, Ebonyi, Edo, Ekiti, Enugu, Gombe, Imo, Jigawa, Kaduna, Kano, Katsina, Kebbi, Kogi, Kwara, Lagos, Nasarawa, Niger, Ogun, Ondo, Osun, Oyo, Plateau, Rivers, Sokoto, Taraba, Yobe and Zamfara.

(2) Each state of Nigeria, named in the first column of Part I of the First Schedule to this Constitution, shall consist of the area shown opposite thereto in the second column of that Schedule.

(3) The headquarters of the Governor of each State shall be known as the Capital City of that State as shown in the third column of the said Part I of the First Schedule opposite the State named in the first column thereof.

(4) The Federal Capital Territory, Abuja, shall be as defined in Part II of the First Scheduled to this Constitution.

(5) The provisions of this Constitution in Part I of Chapter VIII hereof shall in relation to the Federal Capital Territory, Abuja, have effect in the manner set out thereunder.

(6) There shall be 768 Local Government Areas in Nigeria as shown in the second column of Part I of the First Schedule to this Constitution and six area councils as shown in Part II of that Schedule.

Commentary

Much of the provisions in (3) above should not be part of any Constitution. First, it permanently pegs the number of states to 36, with defined capital cities, and also in the number of local governments. It should be noted that there could be a need for the creation of more states and local governments as the population and residential demographics change over time. But this would mean that in order to create more states, to spin off a new state from an adjoining state, or to create more local governments to address issues of local politics and advocacy, there would first need to be a "constitutional amendment." Even if a constitutional amendment is desired, the Constitution itself should be able to specify the circumstances (or process) by which such an amendment would be approved and upheld as a new law. So far, the current Constitution is silent on that.

Part II: Powers of the Federal Republic of Nigeria

4. (1) The legislative powers of the Federal Republic of Nigeria shall be vested in a National Assembly for the Federation, which shall consist of a Senate and a House of Representatives.

(2) The National Assembly shall have power to make laws for the peace, order and good government of the Federation or any part thereof with respect to any matter included in the Exclusive Legislative List set out in Part I of the Second Schedule to this Constitution.

Commentary

The power to make laws for peace, order, and good government is too ambiguous and does not provide any specific power to the National Assembly. The legal-moralistic approach offered here is too obvious and simplistic because such values have always been (ought to be) the raison d'etre of any good government. The Constitution should specify exactly what type of laws and in what areas (juris-dictions) the National Assembly should have the power to make laws, i.e., power to coin money, power to provide for national security, power to collect taxes. (I think these are also meant for "peace, order, and good government," but yet they provide the concrete steps needed to achieve the aforementioned values).

(3) The power of the National Assembly to make laws for the peace, order and good government of the Federation with respect to any matter included in the Exclusive Legislative List shall, save as otherwise provided in this Constitution, be to the exclusion of the Houses of Assembly of States.

Commentary

The provision in (3) above is unnecessary and is already provided for in (2) above. It should also specify the scope of jurisdiction to which the laws of the National Assembly ought to apply.

(4) In addition and without prejudice to the powers conferred by subsection (2) of this section, the National Assembly shall have power to make laws with respect to the following matters, that is to say:-

(a) any matter in the Concurrent Legislative List set out in the first column of Part II of the Second Schedule to this Constitution to the extent prescribed in the second column opposite thereto; and

Commentary

In what ways do the following "unspecified" powers prejudice subsection (2) of this section? Taking the reader somewhere to find these "powers" is tactless, rather the provision (powers) should be indicated under the section where they are mentioned (under "a" above).

(b) any other matter with respect to which it is empowered to make laws in accordance with the provisions of this Constitution.

(5) If any Law enacted by the House of Assembly of a State is inconsistent with any law validly made by the National Assembly, the law made by

the National Assembly shall prevail, and that other Law shall, to the extent of the inconsistency, be void.

Commentary

But who decides "the extent to which the inconsistency is inconsistent"?

(6) The legislative powers of a State of the Federation shall be vested in the House of Assembly of the State.

(7) The House of Assembly of a State shall have power to make laws for the peace, order and good government of the State or any part thereof with respect to the following matters, that is to say:—

(a) any matter not included in the Exclusive Legislative List set out in Part I of the Second Schedule to this Constitution.

(b) any matter included in the Concurrent Legislative List set out in the first column of Part II of the Second Schedule to this Constitution to the extent prescribed in the second column opposite thereto; and

(c) any other matter with respect to which it is empowered to make laws in accordance with the provisions of this Constitution.

Commentary

This is too vacuous. If the states have any power assigned to them in the Constitution, it should be stated in this column, not referenced somewhere else. I would prefer that states have no explicit power in the federal Constitution, but should have "residual powers" prefaced on due process and equal citizenship rights. I would recommend that states have their own Constitutions, but in the federal Constitution, there should be an Article known as the "Supremacy Clause" in which the federal law would override state laws in areas of conflict. Although this is already indicated in Part 1, subsection (3), yet there is a need to also have a provision within the federal Constitution that stipulates "equal treatment under the law." In this way, some states would be "federally and legally" prevented from engaging in imposing arbitrary statutes that harm the interest and privileges of their non-indigene residents.

(8) Save as otherwise provided by this Constitution, the exercise of legislative powers by the National Assembly or by a House of Assembly shall be subject to the jurisdiction of courts of law and of judicial tribunals established by law, and accordingly, the National Assembly or a House

of Assembly shall not enact any law, that ousts or purports to oust the jurisdiction of a court of law or of a judicial tribunal established by law.

Commentary

This provision is too wordy and contorted. Since the national legislature makes laws, why should it not have the power to make "corrective laws" if the old law (or a system of justice) is found to be prejudicial to any particular interest in the country. In fact, this provision may allow too much subjectivity and politics to influence judicial proceedings. The Constitution should be the basis for providing for the structure and power of the lower courts or judicial tribunals, not the legislature. The legislature can make laws that guide their operations, as long as they follow constitutional guidelines and such laws are not retroactive or made without reasonable cause.

(9) Notwithstanding the foregoing provisions of this section, the National Assembly or a House of Assembly shall not, in relation to any criminal offence whatsoever, have power to make any law which shall have retrospective effect.

Commentary

This should also include "civil laws."

5. (1) Subject to the provisions of this Constitution, the executive powers of the Federation:

(a) shall be vested in the President and may subject as aforesaid and to the provisions of any law made by the National Assembly, be exercised by him either directly or through the Vice-President and Ministers of the Government of the Federation or officers in the public service of the Federation; and

Commentary

This is the source of much confusion as to the scope of executive authority. I think it would be necessary to specify what those "executive powers are."

(b) shall extend to the execution and maintenance of this Constitution, all laws made by the National Assembly and to all matters with respect to which the National Assembly has, for the time being, power to make laws.

(2) Subject to the provisions of this Constitution, the executive powers of a State:

(a) shall be vested in the Governor of that State and may, subject as aforesaid and to the provisions of any Law made by a House of Assembly, be exercised by him either directly or through the Deputy Governor and Commissioners of the Government of that State or officers in the public service of the State; and

(b) shall extend to the execution and maintenance of this Constitution, all laws made by the *House of Assembly of the State* and to all matters with respect to which the *House of Assembly* has for the time being power to make laws.

Commentary

On reflection and consequent to the earlier provisions in 2 (a) above, the provision in 2 (b) should read "by the National legislature" and to all matters with respect to which the "national Legislature" has for the time being power to make laws. This is because the first sentence in this section makes reference to "shall extend to the execution and maintenance of this (federal) Constitution."

(3) The executive powers vested in a State under subsection (2) of this section shall be so exercised as not to:—

Commentary

"Executive powers" cannot be vested in a "State," otherwise it would be construed as being vested in all citizens of the "State" to the extent that they are owners of the "State." Rather "executive powers" are vested in an "Office" (not the State) such as that of a Governor or Lt. Governor.

(a) impede or prejudice the exercise of the executive powers of the Federation;

(b) endanger any asset or investment of the Government of the Federation in that State; or

(c) endanger the continuance of a Federal Government in Nigeria.

Commentary

How do we know and what specific acts would constitute endangerment of and /or prejudice to the exercise of executive powers of the Federation? What specific actions constitute endangerment, and who determines when such has occurred? By "executive powers" is meant presidential powers, and this particular provision is really meant to protect the power of the Executive, not the national Government which would necessarily include the (legislature, the executive, and the judiciary). Is this really what was meant by this stipulation?

(4) Notwithstanding the foregoing provisions of this section:—

(a) the President shall not declare a state of war between the Federation and another country except with the sanction of a resolution of both Houses of the National Assembly, sitting in a joint session; and

Commentary

How many votes would be needed to pass such a resolution in either chamber of the National Assembly or in a joint session?

(b) except with the prior approval of the Senate, no member of the armed forces of the Federation shall be deployed on combat duty outside Nigeria.

Commentary

By how many votes in the Senate? The conditions for this resolution (if any) should be explicitly indicated in the Constitution.

(5) Notwithstanding the provisions of subsection (4) of this section, the President, in consultation with the National Defense Council, may deploy members of the armed forces of the Federation on a limited combat duty outside Nigeria if he is satisfied that the national security is under imminent threat or danger:

Commentary

This is too much of a blank check. Under what conditions should the President unilaterally nullify the provisions of 5 (subsection 4) above? Either you have (4) above or you don't have it? It seems that the Constitution is mixing the power to "declare war" with another provision that might be construed as a "War Powers Act." Both of them are highly contradictory and such a contradiction cannot be obviated by a simple statement such as "Notwithstanding the provisions of subsection (4) of this section." In fact, such a statement completely nullifies the whole of (4) subsections (a and b) above. I think the provision in (5) above should not be part of the Constitution, but can be prefaced as a separate legislation in another federal statute or Act.

Provided that the President shall, within seven days of actual combat engagement, seek the consent of the Senate and the Senate shall thereafter give or refuse the said consent within 14 days.

Commentary

Then what happens either way, or if the Senate refuses?

6. (1) The judicial powers of the Federation shall be vested in the courts to which this section relates, being courts established for the Federation.

(2) The judicial powers of a State shall be vested in the courts to which this section relates, being courts established, subject as provided by this Constitution, for a State.

(3) The courts to which this section relates, established by this Constitution for the Federation and for the States, specified in subsection (5) (a) to (1) of this section, shall be the only superior courts of record in Nigeria; and save as otherwise prescribed by the National Assembly or by the House of Assembly of a State, each court shall have all the powers of a superior court of record.

Commentary

Would these be known as "federal" or "state" courts? Either way, they need to be explicitly stated.

(4) Nothing in the foregoing provisions of this section shall be construed as precluding:—

(a) the National Assembly or *any* House of Assembly from establishing courts, other than those to which this section relates, with subordinate jurisdiction to that of a High Court;

Commentary

What this means is that the "Senate" or the "House" can unilaterally establish a court on its own without the conventional legislative consent in the two chambers. Why should the national legislature or either of the chambers have the power to establish subordinate or parallel judicial systems, when in fact, we have ones already performing these functions? Does this pertain to federal or state courts?

(b) the National Assembly or any House of Assembly, which does not require it, from abolishing any court which it has power to establish or which it has brought into being.

Commentary

This particular provision contradicts the provision in Part II, section 4 (subsection 8).

(5) This section relates to:—

(a) the Supreme Court of Nigeria;

(b) the Court of Appeal;

(c) the Federal High Court;

(d) the High Court of the Federal Capital Territory, Abuja;

(e) a High Court of a State

(f) the Sharia Court of Appeal of the Federal Capital Territory, Abuja;

(g) a Sharia Court of Appeal of a State;

(h) the Customary Court of Appeal of the Federal Capital Territory, Abuja;

(i) a Customary Court of Appeal of a State;

(j) such other courts as may be authorized by law to exercise jurisdiction on matters with respect to which the National Assembly may make laws; and

(k) such other court as may be authorised by law to exercise jurisdiction at first instance or on appeal on matters with respect to which a House of Assembly may make laws.

Commentary

Which House of Assembly? State or National?

(6) The judicial powers vested in accordance with the foregoing provisions of this section—

(a) shall extend, notwithstanding anything to the contrary government or authority and to any persons in Nigeria, and to all actions and proceedings relating thereto, for the determination of any question as to the *civil rights* and *obligations* of that persons;

Commentary

What's the difference between an individual's "civil rights" and "obligation?" These should be explicitly specified as to what they are.

(c) shall not except as otherwise provided by this Constitution, extend to any issue or question as to whether any act of omission by any authority or person or as to whether any law or any judicial decision is in conformity with the Fundamental Objectives and Directive Principles of State Policy set out in Chapter II of this Constitution;

Commentary

This is quite surprising. Technically, what this means is that the government and its agencies have the power to "self-police" themselves, and can break the law (willing or unwillingly), yet would not be made to answer for it. The courts are now limited in terms of the scope of their authority, and certain exceptions in the laws are already made a priori to the commission of a particular offense. This provision exonerates all government and public officials for any legal infraction of the law as well as culpability. It should be removed. In fact, the courts should have the power of "judicial review" that would allow it to question and to adjudicate official and private acts in accordance with the law and the principle of due process.

(d) shall not, as from date when this section comes into force, *extend* to *any action* or *proceedings* relating to any existing law made on or after 15th January, 1966 for determining any issue or question as to the competence of any authority or person to make any such law.

Commentary

Then, this provision could be used to argue in favor of the January 15, 1966 military coup, the so-called Unification Decree, or in fact, the July 1966 counter-coup. Otherwise, what's the real purpose here of this provision?

(7). (1) The system of local government by democratically elected local government councils is under this Constitution guaranteed; and accordingly, the Government of every State shall, subject to section 8 of this

Constitution, ensure their existence under a Law which provides for the establishment, structure, composition, finance and functions of such councils.

(2) The person authorized by law to prescribe the area over which a local government council may exercise authority shall-

(a) define such area as clearly as practicable; and

(b) ensure, to the extent to which it may be reasonably justifiable that in defining such area regard is paid to—

(i) the common interest of the community in the area;

(ii) traditional association of the community; and

(iii) administrative convenience.

Commentary

This is too much power to be given to a "person." Rather it should be given to a committee. Local representatives from the affected areas (local government area) should also be members of this committee. The committee's recommendation should also be approved by the state legislature, in consideration of the provisions of the federal constitution.

(3) it shall be the duty of a local government council within the State to participate in economic planning and development of the area referred to in subsection (2) of this section and to this end an economic planning board shall be established by a Law enacted by the House of Assembly of the State.

(4) The Government of a State shall ensure that every person who is entitled to vote or be voted for at an election to House of Assembly shall have the right to vote or be voted for at an election to a local government council.

Commentary

What entitles a person to "vote"? I would believe that the condition should be "national citizenship." Otherwise, the "right to vote" and the conditions for such vote should be explicitly specified in the Constitution. States should not be allowed to arbitrary decide the conditions that entitle the "right to vote." It should be protected as a right of universal suffrage and citizenship, irrespective of state of origin.

(5) The functions to be conferred by Law upon local government council shall include those set out in the Fourth Schedule to this Constitution.

(6) Subject to the provisions of this Constitution—

(a) the National Assembly shall make provisions for statutory allocation of public revenue to local government councils in the Federation; and

(b) the House of Assembly of a State shall make provisions for statutory allocation of public revenue to local government councils within the State.

Commentary

But this should be done consistent with the general stipulations of the National Assembly, and the Constitution of the federal government. There should be a uniform formula in the mechanism for the allocation of public revenue to local governments throughout the federation.

(8). (1) An Act of the National Assembly for the purpose of creating a new State shall only be passed if—

(a) a request, supported by at least two-thirds majority of members (representing the area demanding the creation of the new State) in each of the following, namely—

(i) the Senate and the House of Representatives,

(ii) the House of Assembly in respect of the area, and

(iii) the local government councils in respect of the area,

is received by the National Assembly;

(b) a proposal for the creation of the State is thereafter approved in a referendum by at least two-thirds majority of the people of the area where the demand for creation of the State originated;

(c) the result of the referendum is then approved by a simple majority of all the States of the Federation supported by a simple majority of members of the Houses of Assembly; and

(d) the proposal is approved by a resolution passed by two-thirds majority of members of each House of the National Assembly.

Commentary

This is too tedious and cumbersome a process. The federal constitution already indicated in Part 1 (Section 3) that there shall be only 36 states in the federation, hence any change in this number must be prefaced by a "constitutional amendment." Even if the procedures specified above is correct, the mandate for initiating such a process in the first place must be derived through a constitutional amendment, otherwise it would not be legitimate. The alternative then would be to change the provisions in Part 1 (Section 3) in such a way that it allows the possibility for the creation of more states in the future. But that again, in itself, would require a constitutional amendment. What is required here should be a simple local plebiscite, a vote in the state legislature, and a final ratification in the national legislature.

(2) An Act of the National Assembly for the purpose of boundary adjustment of any existing State shall only be passed if—

(a) a request for the boundary adjustment, supported by two-thirds majority of members (representing the area demanding *and the area affected by the boundary adjustment*) in each of the following, namely-

(i) the Senate and the House of Representatives,

(ii) the House of Assembly in respect of the area, and

(iii) the local government councils in respect of the area.

is received by the National Assembly; and

(b) a proposal for the boundary adjustment is approved by—

(i) a simple majority of members of each House of the National Assembly, and

(ii) a simple majority of members of the House of Assembly in respect of the area concerned.

Commentary

This is too tedious and problematic. The provision actually defeats the same purpose and rights which it purports to uphold. The killer words here are "and the area af-

fected by the boundary adjustment." *Of course no area wants its land mass and population to be reduced or balkanized, so those who are favored by the status quo would always vote against such a move at boundary adjustment. This provision is quite deceitful and dishonest to the extent that it superficially offers what it cannot provide. Simply put, there will be no opportunity for "boundary adjustment" unless the key words* "and the area affected by the boundary adjustment" *is removed. I will also like to ask whether the approval or vote of the then Imo State people was sought for before the "boundary adjustment" that led to the cession of Obigbo to the Rivers State was made? Certainly Imo State must have been well affected.*

(3) A bill for a Law of a House of Assembly for the purpose of creating a new local government area shall only be passed if—

(a) a request supported by at least two-thirds majority of members (representing the area demanding the creation of the new local government area) in each of the following, namely—

(i) the House of Assembly in respect of the area, and

(ii) the local government councils in respect of the area,

is received by the House of Assembly.

(b) a proposal for the creation of the local government area is thereafter approved in a referendum by at least two-thirds majority of the people of the local government area where the demand for the proposed local government area originated;

(c) the result of the referendum is then approved by a simple majority of the members in each local government council in a majority of all the local government councils in the State; and

(d) the result of the referendum is approved by a resolution passed by two-thirds majority of members of the House of Assembly.

Commentary

Again, this cannot be done without first passing a constitutional amendment that rectifies the provision in Part 1, (Section 3, Subsection 6) concerning local governments.

(4) A bill for a Law of House of Assembly for the purpose of boundary adjustment of any existing local government area shall only be passed if—

(a) a request for the boundary adjustment is supported by two-thirds majority of members (representing the area demanding and the area affected by the boundary adjustment) in each of the following, namely—

(i) the House of Assembly in respect of the area, and

(ii) the local government council in respect of the area, is received by the House of Assembly; and

(b) a proposal for the boundary adjustment is approved by a simple majority of members of the House of Assembly in respect of the area concerned.

Commentary

The above is too wordy. It would need to be simplified and the procedure pruned down.

(5) An Act of the National Assembly passed in accordance with this section shall make consequential provisions with respect to the names and headquarters of State or Local government areas as provided in section 3 of this Constitution and in Parts I and II of the First Schedule to this Constitution.

(6) For the purpose of enabling the National Assembly to exercise the powers conferred upon it by subsection (5) of this section, each House of Assembly shall, after the creation of more local government areas pursuant to subsection (3) of this section, make adequate returns to each House of the National Assembly

Commentary

What constitutes "adequate" returns, and in what form?

9. (1) The National Assembly may, subject to the provision of this section, alter any of the provisions of this Constitution.

(2) An Act of the National Assembly for the alteration of this Constitution, not being an Act to which section 8 of this Constitution applies, shall not be passed in either House of the National Assembly unless the proposal is supported by the votes of not less than two-thirds majority of all the members of that House and approved by resolution of the Houses of Assembly of not less than two-thirds of all the States.

(3) An Act of the National Assembly for the purpose of altering the provisions of this section, section 8 or Chapter IV of this Constitution shall not be passed by either House of the National Assembly unless the proposal is approved by the votes of not less than four-fifths majority of all the members of each House, and also approved by resolution of the House of Assembly of not less than two-third of all States.

Commentary

Section 9 (Subsections 1 and 2) above are redundant and unnecessary. In fact, Subsection (1) overrides (defeats) sub-sections (2) and (3) because it grants the National Assembly the power to alter any of the provisions of this Constitution. This, in itself, is an unlimited power that can allow the National Assembly to override many of the powers of the Executive and the Courts. And yet, these are also powers to which the National Assembly had been precluded in various sections and references in the Constitution. Also in sub-section (2), it qualifies such authority by basing it on a two-third vote of the state legislatures. This whole area is full of chaos and contradiction and it makes for a very messy system of governance (for lack of a better term). I think that Section 9 (sub-sections 1 and 3) should be deleted. Subsection 2 should be left in place because I think it technically covers what was meant here.

(4) For the purposes of section 8 of this Constitution and of subsections (2) and (3) of this section, the number of members of each House of the National Assembly shall, notwithstanding any vacancy, be deemed to be the number of members specified in sections 48 and 49 of this Constitution.

Prohibition of State Religion.

10. The Government of the Federation or of a State shall not adopt any religion as State Religion.

Commentary

How true is this, and what are the sanctions for infraction?

11. (1) The National Assembly may make laws for the Federation or any part therefore with respect to the maintenance and securing of public safety and public order and providing, maintaining and securing of such supplies and service as may be designed by the National Assembly as essential supplies and services.

Commentary

This means that the National Assembly could make (any) law or laws for the states? This also confers "emergency or martial powers to the National Assembly" rather than the President. But as typical with most federal units, such martial and emergency powers are always the prerogative of the Executive. So how is this?

(2) Nothing in this section shall preclude a House of Assembly from making laws with respect to the matter referred to in this section, including the provision for maintenance and securing of such supplies and services as may be designated by the National Assembly as essential supplies and services.

(3) During any period when the Federation is at war the National Assembly may make such laws for the peace, order and good government of the Federation or any part therefore with respect to matters not included in the Exclusive Legislative List as may appear to it to be necessary or expedient for the defence of the Federation.

Commentary

How is this provision any different from the constitutional powers of the National Assembly as provided in Part II, Section 4 (Sub-section 1 and 2)?

(4) At any time when any House of Assembly of a State is unable to perform its functions by reason of the situation prevailing in that State, the National Assembly may make such laws for the peace, order and good government of that State with respect to matters on which a House of Assembly may make laws as may appear to the National Assembly to be necessary or expedient until such time as the House of Assembly is able to resume its functions; and any such laws enacted by the National Assembly pursuant to this section shall have effect as if they were laws enacted by the House of Assembly of the State:

Provided that nothing in this section shall be construed as conferring on the National Assembly power to remove the Governor or the Deputy Governor of the State from office.

Commentary

So why has the Executive been allowed to perform such roles, particularly regarding the Anambra state crisis?

(5) For the purposes of subsection (4) of this section, a House of Assembly shall not be deemed to be unable to perform its functions so long as the House of Assembly can hold a meeting and transact business.

Commentary

Does this refer to a House of Assembly at the federal or state level? This technically means that the House of Assembly can be judged to be performing its duties as long as it can hold meetings. But it does not matter whether the outcome of such meetings results in addressing fundamental issues of substance or whether it benefits the interests of a particular constituency. Is this what was really intended here?

12. (1) No treaty between the Federation and any other country shall have the force of law to the extent to which any such treaty has been enacted into law by the National Assembly.

Commentary

What then does this stand for? If a treaty has been enacted into law by the National Assembly, why should it not have the force of law?

(2) The National Assembly may make laws for the Federation or any part thereof with respect to matters not included in the Exclusive Legislative List for the purpose of implementing a treaty.

Commentary

This is too broad a provision. What specific laws are meant here and under what circumstances? In fact this also means that the National Assembly can, of its own volition, make laws governing the states, with or without a particular state's consent. But yet, to what extent is this type of excess allowed in a federal system? The National Assembly can literarily do anything.

(3) A bill for an Act of the National Assembly passed pursuant to the provisions of subsection (2) of this section shall not be presented to the President for assent, and shall not be enacted unless it is ratified by a majority of all the House of Assembly in the Federation.

Commentary

Does "House of Assembly" refer to all the 36 states? If so, this point should be clarified? But if such a bill has already been ratified (encoded in law) by the

Houses of Assembly, why is the President's assent necessary or imperative after-the-fact? Is the President to be just a rubber-stamp? What is the import of this provision? What of if the President is opposed to such a bill and he refuses to give his acquiescence? Then what happens?

CHAPTER V: THE LEGISLATURE

Part I: National Assembly:
Composition and Staff of National Assembly

47. There shall be a National Assembly for the Federation which shall consist of a Senate and a House of Representatives.

48. The Senate shall consist of three Senators from each State and one from the Federal Capital Territory, Abuja.

49. Subject to the provisions of this Constitution, the House of Representatives shall consist of three hundred and sixty members representing constituencies of nearly equal population as far as possible, provided that no constituency shall fall within more than one State.

50. (1) There shall be:—

(a) a President and a Deputy President of the Senate, who shall be elected by the members of that House from among themselves; and

(b) a Speaker and a Deputy Speaker of the House of Representatives, who shall be elected by the members of that House from among themselves.

(2) The President or Deputy President of the Senate or the Speaker or Deputy Speaker of the House of Representatives shall vacate his office—

(a) if he ceases to be a member of the Senate or of the House of Representatives, as the case may be, otherwise than by reason of a dissolution of the Senate or the House of Representatives; or

(b) when the House of which he was a member first sits after any dissolution of that House; or

(c) if he is removed from office by a resolution of the Senate or of the House of Representatives, as the case may be, by the votes of not less than two-thirds majority of the members of that House.

51. There shall be a Clerk to the National Assembly and such other staff as may be prescribed by an Act of the National Assembly, and the method of appointment of the Clerk and other staff of the National Assembly shall be as prescribed by that tab.

Procedure for Summoning and Dissolution of National Assembly

52. (1) Every member of the Senate or the House of Representatives shall, before taking his seat, declare his assets and liabilities as prescribed in this Constitution and subsequently take and subscribe to the Oath of Allegiance and the oath of membership as prescribed in the Seventh Schedule to this Constitution before the President of the Senate or, as the case may be, the Speaker of the House of Representatives, but a member may before taking the oaths take part in the election of a President and a Deputy President of the Senate, as the case may be, or a Speaker and a Deputy Speaker of the House of Representatives.

Commentary

They should also be required to declare their assets and file their tax returns every year for the duration of their tenure. Those who have been found to be derelict in the proper maintenance of their financial records and in making timely payments against their financial obligations to the state (paying their due taxes) would be disqualified for running for public office.

(2) The President and Deputy President of the Senate and the Speaker and the Deputy Speaker of the House of Representatives shall declare their assets and liabilities as prescribed in this Constitution and subsequently take and subscribe to the Oath of Allegiance and the oath of membership prescribed as aforesaid before the Clerk of the National Assembly.

Commentary

Same as above should apply.

53. (1) At any sitting of the National Assembly—

(a) in the case of the Senate, the President of the Senate shall preside, and in his absence the Deputy President shall preside; and

(b) in the case of the House of Representatives, the Speaker of that House shall preside, and in his absence the Deputy Speaker shall preside.

(2) At any joint sitting of the Senate and House of Representatives—

(a) the President of Senate shall preside, and in his absence the Speaker of the House of Representatives shall preside; and

(b) in the absence of the persons mentioned in paragraph (a) of this subsection, the Deputy President of the Senate shall preside, and in his absence the Deputy Speaker of the House of Representatives shall preside.

(3) In the absence of the persons mentioned in the foregoing provisions of this section, such member of the Senate or the House of Representatives or of the joint sitting, as the case may be, as the Senate or the House of Representatives or the joint sitting may elect for that purpose shall preside.

54. (1) The quorum of the Senate or of the House of Representatives shall be one-third of all the members of the Legislative House concerned.

(2) The quorum of a joint sitting of both the Senate or of the House of Representatives shall be one-third of all the members of both Houses.

(3) If objection is taken by any member of the Senate or the House of Representatives present that there are present in the House of which he is a member besides the person presiding fewer than one-third of all the members of that House and that it is not competent for the House to transact business, and after such interval as may be prescribed in the rules of procedure of the House, the person presiding ascertains that the number of members present is still less than one-third of all the members of the House he shall adjourn the House.

Commentary

This should simply indicate that there should be no Senate or House resolutions passed on businesses conducted without the required quorum.

(4) The foregoing provisions of this section shall apply in relation to a joint sitting of both Houses of the National Assembly as they apply in relation to a House of the National Assembly as it references to the Senate or the House of Representatives and a member of either Houses are references to both Houses and to any member of the National Assembly, respectively.

Commentary

What does the above mean? Anybody would be lost trying to make much sense out of this. So convoluted.

55. The business of the National Assembly shall be conducted in English, and in Hausa, Ibo and Yoruba when adequate arrangements have been made therefore.

Commentary

Will the outcome of the proceedings also be recorded in all the above languages? The problem with this provision is that different language usages might lead to different interpretations and meanings beyond what was originally intended.

56. (1) Except as otherwise provided by this Constitution any question proposed for decision in the Senate or the House of Representatives shall be determined by the required majority or the members present and voting; and the person presiding shall cast a vote whenever necessary to avoid an equality of votes but shall not vote in any other case.

(2) Except as otherwise provided by this Constitution, the required majority for the purpose of determining any question shall be a simple majority.

(3) The Senate or the House of Representatives shall by its rules provide—

(a) that a member of the House shall declare any direct pecuniary interest he may have in any matter coming before the House for deliberation;

(b) that the House may by resolution decide whether or not such member may vote, or participate in its deliberations, on such matter;

(c) the penalty, if any, which the House may impose for failure to declare any direct pecuniary interest such member may have; and

(d) for such other matters pertaining to the foregoing as the House may think necessary, but nothing in the foregoing provisions shall enable any rules to be made to require any member, who signifies his intention not to vote on or participate in such matter, and who does not so vote or participate, to declare any such interest.

57. Any person who sits or votes in the Senate or the House of Representatives knowing or having reasonable grounds for knowing that he is not entitled to do so commits an offence and is liable on conviction to such punishment as shall be prescribed by an Act of the National Assembly.

58. (1) The power of the National Assembly to make laws shall be exercised by bills passed by both the Senate and the House of Representatives

and, except as otherwise provided by subsection (5) of this section, assented to by the President.

Commentary

Can the National Assembly make laws on its own initiative without recourse to any proposal or submission from the President? Either way, it must be clarified.

(2) A bill may originate in either the Senate or the House of Representatives and shall not become law unless it has been passed and, except as otherwise provided by this section and section 59 of this Constitution, assented to in accordance with the provisions of this section.

(3) Where a bill has been passed by the House in which it originated, it shall be sent to the other House, and it shall be presented to the President for assent when it has been passed by that other House and agreement has been reached between the two Houses on any amendment made on it.

Commentary

This should state specifically, "Unless it has been passed by both chambers, and signed into law by the President; or where the House and the Senate override a President's veto by 2/3 vote in both chambers." Also a conference committee of both Houses must have reconciled the two versions of the bill—a compromise resolution—before it is sent to the President for his signature or veto.

(4) Where a bill is presented to the President for assent, he shall within thirty days thereof signify that he assents or that he withholds assent.

(5) Where the President withholds his assent and the bill is again passed by each House by two-thirds majority, the bill shall become law and the assent of the President shall not be required.

Commentary

Same as above. This section may be deleted since it duplicates above.

59. (1) The provisions of this section shall apply to:

(a) an appropriation bill or a supplementary appropriation bill, including any other bill for the payment, issue or withdrawal from the Consolidated Revenue Fund or any other public fund of the Federation of any money charged thereon or any alteration in the amount of such a payment, issue or withdrawal; and

(b) a bill for the imposition of or increase in any tax, duty or fee or any reduction, withdrawal or cancellation thereof.

(2) Where a bill to which this section applies is passed by one of the Houses of the National Assembly but is not passed by the other House within a period of two months from the commencement of a financial year, the President of the Senate shall within fourteen days thereafter arrange for and convene a meeting of the joint finance committee to examine the bill with a view to resolving the differences between the two Houses.

(3) Where the joint finance committee fails to resolve such differences, then the bill shall be presented to the National Assembly sitting at a joint meeting, and if the bill is passed at such joint meeting, it shall be presented to the President for assent.

(4) Where the President, within thirty days after the presentation of the bill to him, fails to signify his assent or where he withholds assent, then the bill shall again be presented to the National Assembly sitting at a joint meeting, and if passed by two-thirds majority of members of both houses at such joint meeting, the bill shall become law and the assent of the President shall not be required.

(5) In this section, "joint finance committee" refers to the joint committee of the National Assembly on finance established pursuant to section 62(3) of this Constitution.

60. Subject to the provisions of this Constitution, the Senate or the House of Representatives shall have power to regulate its own procedure, including the procedure for summoning and recess of the House.

61. The Senate or the House of Representatives may act notwithstanding any vacancy in its membership, and the presence or participation of any person not entitled to be present at or to participate in the proceedings of the House shall not invalidate those proceedings.

62. (1) The Senate or the House of Representatives may appoint a committee of its members for such special or general purpose as in its opinion would be better regulated and managed by means of such a committee, and may by resolution, regulation or otherwise, as it thinks fit, delegate any functions exercisable by it to any such committee.

Commentary

*This should be clearly indicated as an Ad Hoc Committee and the terms of refer-
ence, scope, and duration specifically indicated. This distinction is necessary as a
way of differentiating the activity from that of a Standing Committee.*

(2) The number of members of a committee appointed under this section,
their terms of office and quorum shall be fixed by the House appointing it.

(3) The Senate and the House of Representatives shall appoint a joint committee on finance consisting of an equal number of persons appointed by
each House and may appoint any other joint committee under the provisions of this section.

(4) Nothing in this section shall be construed as authorizing such House
to delegate to a committee the power to decide whether a bill shall be
passed into law or to determine any matter which it is empowered to determine by resolution under the provisions of this Constitution, but the
committee may be authorized to make recommendations to the House
on any such matter.

63. The Senate and the House of Representatives shall each sit for a period
of not less than one hundred and eighty-one days in a year.

64. (1) The Senate and the House of Representatives shall each stand dissolved at the expiration of a period of four years commencing from the
date of the first sitting of the House.

(2) If the Federation is at war in which the territory of Nigeria is physically involved and the President considers that it is not practicable to hold
elections, the National Assembly may by resolution extend the period of
four years mentioned in subsection (1) of this section from time to time
but not beyond a period of six months at any one time.

(3) Subject to the provisions of this Constitution, the person elected as the
President shall have power to issue a proclamation for the holding of the
first session of the National Assembly immediately after his being sworn
in, or for its dissolution as provided in this section.

Commentary

*This should be specified in the Constitution as a neutral, but not at the discretion
or whim of the President. This process should be an established Constitutional
protocol, but not as an executive or presidential prerogative.*

Qualifications for Membership of National Assembly and Right of Attendance

65. (1) Subject to the provisions of section 66 of this Constitution, a person shall be qualified for election as a member of: (a) the Senate, if he is a citizen of Nigeria and has attained the age of 35 years; and

(b) the House of Representatives, if he is a citizen of Nigeria and has attained the age of 30 years;

(2) A person shall be qualified for election under subsection (1) of this section if:

(a) he has been educated up to at least School Certificate level or its equivalent; and

(b) he is a member of a political party and is sponsored by that party.

66. (1) No person shall be qualified for election to the Senate or the House of Representatives if:

Commentary

What about those who have chosen to be independents?

(a) subject to the provisions of section 28 of this Constitution, he has voluntarily acquired the citizenship of a country other than Nigeria or, except in such cases as may be prescribed by the National Assembly, has made a declaration of allegiance to such a country;

Commentary

There should be a specification here that "those holding dual citizenship status are not affected by the aforementioned provision, and will retain full entitlement to Nigerian citizenship."

(b) under any law in force in any part of Nigeria, he is adjudged to be a lunatic or otherwise declared to be of unsound mind;

Commentary

This section would need to be clarified. The law cannot adjudge anyone regarding whether such person is or is not a lunatic. The mental state of a person has to be determined through medical means. This section should reflect such "if the person has been medically adjudged by a doctor or a licensed medically competent person."

(c) he is under a sentence of death imposed on him by any competent court of law or tribunal in Nigeria or a sentence of imprisonment or fine for an offence involving dishonesty or fraud (by whatever name called) or any other offence imposed on him by such a court or tribunal or substituted by a competent authority for any other sentence imposed on him by such a court;

Commentary

This needs to specify whether it applies exclusively to criminal or civil offences, or both?

(d) within a period of less than 10 years before the date of an election to a legislative house, he has been convicted and sentenced for an offence involving dishonesty or he has been found guilty of a contravention of the Code of Conduct;

Commentary

How do you convict someone of being dishonest? It is important to specify the particular types of dishonesty implied here.

(e) he is an undischarged bankrupt, having been adjudged or otherwise declared bankrupt under any law in force in any part of Nigeria;

Commentary

This is unnecessary. A person's citizenship rights and obligation should not be nullified simply by virtue of having been bankrupt. Bankruptcy is not a criminal or moral offense.

(f) he is a person employed in the public service of the Federation or of any State and has not resigned, withdrawn or retired from such employment 30 days before the date of election;

(g) he is a member of a secret society;

(h) he has been indicted for embezzlement or fraud by Judicial Commission of Inquiry or an Administrative Panel of Inquiry or a Tribunal set up under the Tribunals of Inquiry Act, a Tribunals of Inquiry Law or any other law by the Federal or State Government which indictment has been accepted by the Federal or State Governments respectively; or.

Commentary

There is a need to include "civil or criminal" courts.

(1) he has presented a forged certificate to the Independence National Electoral Commission.

(2) Where in respect of any person who has been—

(a) adjudged to be a lunatic;

(b) declared to be of unsound mind;

(c) sentenced to death or imprisonment; or

(d) adjudged or declared bankrupt,

Commentary

Items 2(a) and 2(b) must be prefaced by a duly authorized medical certification. What does "unsound mind" mean, and who determines whether an individual has an "unsound mind," and under what criterion?

any appeal against the decision is pending in any court of law in accordance with any law in force in Nigeria, subsection (1) of the section shall not apply during a period beginning from the date when such appeal is lodged and ending on the date when the appeal is finally determined or, as the case may be, the appeal lapses or is abandoned, whichever is earlier.

(3) For the purposes of subsection (2) of this section "appeal" includes any application for an injunction or an order certiorari, *mandamus*, prohibition or habeas corpus, or any appeal from any such application.

67. (1) The President may attend any joint meeting of the National Assembly or any meeting of either House of the National Assembly, either to deliver an address on national affairs including fiscal measures, or to make such statement on the policy of government as he considers to be of national importance.

Commentary

The president should not have the power to attend any meeting of the national legislature. There could be some joint meetings that may not require the presence of the President. The idea of separation of powers also allows each unit of the national government some measure of exclusivity.

(2) A Minister of the Government of the Federation attend either House of the National Assembly if invited to express to the House the conduct of his Ministry, and in particular when the affairs of that Ministry are under discussion.

(3) Nothing in this section shall enable any person who is not a member of the Senate or of the House of Representatives to vote in that House or in any of its committees.

68. (1) A member of the Senate or of the House of Representatives shall vacate his seat in the House of which he is a member if—

(a) he becomes a member of another legislative house;

(b) any other circumstances arise that, if he were not a member of the Senate or the House of Representatives, would cause him to be disqualified for election as a member;

Commentary

What would those circumstances be? They would need to be specified here.

(c) he ceases to be a citizen of Nigeria;

Commentary

What about those who hold dual citizenships?

(d) he becomes President, Vice-President, Governor, Deputy Governor or a Minister of the Government of the Federation or a Commissioner of the Government of a State or a Special Adviser;

(e) save as otherwise prescribed by this Constitution, he becomes a member of a commission or other body established by this Constitution or by any other law;

(f) without just cause he is absent from meetings of the House of which he is a member for a period amounting in the aggregate to more than one-third of the total number of days during which the House meets in any one year;

(g) being a person whose election to the House was sponsored by a political party, he becomes a member of another political party before the expiration of the period for which that House was elected;

Provided that his membership of the latter political party is not as a result of a division in the political party of which he was previously a member or of a merger of two or more political parties or factions by one of which he was previously sponsored; or

Commentary

This is an extra-constitutional measure. The National Assembly should not be legislating about political parties unless as part of its regulatory power over interest groups (if any). Besides, this raises an issue of conflict of interest since members of the National Assembly are also members of various political parties. The majority party in the National Assembly will have the opportunity to manipulate the process in its favor.

(h) the President of the Senate or, as the case may be, the Speaker of the House of Representatives receives a certificate under the hand of the Chairman of the Independent National Electoral Commission stating that the provisions of section 69 of this Constitution have been complied with in respect of the recall of that member.

(2) The President of the Senate or the Speaker of the House of Representatives, as the case may be, shall give effect to the provisions of subsection (1) of this section, so however that the President of the Senate or the Speaker of the House of Representatives or a member shall first present evidence satisfactory to the House concerned that any of the provisions of that subsection has become applicable in respect of that member.

(3) A member of the Senate or of the House of Representatives shall be deemed to be absent without just cause from a meeting of the House of which he is a member, unless the person presiding certifies in writing that he is satisfied that the absence of the member from the meeting was for a just cause.

Commentary

What constitutes "just cause"? Some specific examples need to be indicated in order to avoid any ambiguity.

69. A member of the Senate or of the House Representatives may be re-called as such a member if—

(a) there is presented to the Chairman of the Independent National Electoral Commission a petition in that behalf signed by more than one-half of the persons registered to vote in that member's constituency alleging their loss of confidence in that member; and

(b) the petition is thereafter, in a referendum conducted by the Independent National Electoral Commission within ninety days of the date of receipt of the petition, approved by a simple majority of the votes of the persons registered to vote in that member's constituency.

Commentary

This could be prejudicial to the member concerned. In a society where money is a central instrument of politics, how are we to determine that such recall referendum are not being conducted as a result of financial inducement, rather than other objective factors of misconduct or dereliction of duty?

70. A member of the Senate or of the House of Representatives shall receive such salary and other allowances as Revenue Mobilisation Allocation and Fiscal Commission may determine

Commentary

There should be a standard salary and "allowance" structure that would be limited only to official duties. Allowances that do not directly facilitate a legislator's job as stipulated should not be allowed either in law or in practice.

D: Elections to National Assembly

71. Subject to the provisions of section 72 of this Constitution, the Independent National Electoral Commission shall—

(a) divide each State of the Federation into three Senatorial districts for purposes of elections to the Senate; and

Commentary

It may also be more cost-effective (and politically more beneficial for Ndigbo) to have only two Senatorial districts in each state. For the simple fact that the North claims to have 19 states, it means that a situation in which we have 3 senatorial

districts will certainly grant the North an absolute majority in the Senate in all matters of political discourse that come into the chamber. As an approximation, that would give the North about 57 senatorial votes as opposed to the whole of the Southeast having 15 senatorial votes. The 15 senatorial votes for the Southeast certainly does not square very well with its population in the federation. By this number alone, the role of the Southeast in the Senate becomes inconsequential. Do the math!

(b) subject to the provisions of section 49 of this Constitution, divide the Federation into three hundred and sixty Federal constituencies for purposes of elections to the House of Representatives.

72. No Senatorial district or Federal constituency shall fall within more than one State, and the boundaries of each district or constituency shall be as contiguous as possible and be such that the number of inhabitants thereof is as nearly equal to the population quota as is reasonably practicable.

73. (1) The Independent National Electoral Commission shall review the division of States and of the Federation into Senatorial districts and Federal constituencies at intervals of not less than ten years, and may alter the districts or constituencies in accordance with the provisions of this section to such extent as it may consider desirable in the light of the review.

(2) Notwithstanding subsection (1) of this section, the Independent National Electoral Commission may at any time carry out such a review and alter the districts or constituencies in accordance with the provisions of this section to such extent as it considers necessary, in consequence of any amendment to section 8 of this Constitution or any provision replacing that section, or by reason of the holding of a census of the population, or pursuant to an Act of the National Assembly.

Commentary

It is a rather dangerous precedent to grant and "Executive" Commission specific powers within the Constitution. It could become a permanent and "legal" political tool in the hands of an overly activist president.

74. Where the boundaries of any Senatorial district or Federal constituency established under section 71 of this Constitution are altered in accordance with the provisions section 73 hereof, the alteration shall come into effect after it has been approved by each House of the National Assembly and after the current life of the Senate (in the case of an alteration to the boundaries of a Senatorial district) or the House (in the case of an alteration to the boundaries of a Federal constituency).

75. For the purposes of section 72 of this Constitution, the number of inhabitants of Nigeria or any part thereof shall be ascertained by reference to the 1991 census of the population of Nigeria or the latest census held in pursuance of an Act of the National Assembly after the coming into force of the provisions of this Part of this Chapter of this Constitution.

76. (1) Elections to each House of the National Assembly shall be held on a date to be appointed by the Independent National Electoral Commission.

(2) The date mentioned in subsection (1) of this section shall not be earlier than sixty days before and not later than the date on which the House stands dissolved, or where the election to fill a vacancy occurring more than three months before such date; not later than one month after the vacancy occurred.

77. (1) Subject to the provisions of this Constitution, every Senatorial district or Federal constituency established in accordance with the provisions of this Part of this Chapter shall return a member who shall be directly elected to the Senate or the House of Representatives in such a manner as may be prescribed by an act of the National Assembly.

(2) Every citizen of Nigeria, who has attained the age of eighteen years residing in Nigeria at the time of the registration of voters for purposes of election to a legislative house, shall be entitled to be registered as a voter for that election.

78. The registration of voters and the conduct of elections shall be subject to the direction and supervision of Independent National Electoral Commission.

79. The National Assembly shall make provisions in respects to—

(a) persons who may apply to an election tribunal for determination of any question as to whether—

(i) any person has been validly elected as a member of the Senate or of the House of Representatives,

(ii) the term of office of any person has ceased, or

(iii) the seat in the Senate or in the House of Representatives of a member of that House has become vacant;

(b) circumstances and manner in which, and the conditions upon which, such application may be made; and

(c) powers, practice and procedure of the election tribunal in relation to any such application.

Powers and Control over Public Funds:

80. (1) All revenues or other moneys raised or received by the Federation (not being revenues or other moneys payable under this Constitution or any Act of the National Assembly into any other public fund of the Federation established for a specific purpose) shall be paid into and form one Consolidated Revenue Fund of the Federation.

Commentary

The provision for creating "Special Fund Accounts" should not be included in a Constitution. Rather, and if necessary, it should be part of an existing administrative law. As it is, it creates a potential loophole for fraud, especially since many of these special fund accounts are difficult to account for both in terms of their administration or expenditures. Who decides which funds go into a special account and why, is a question that would need to be fully addressed, not by legislative fiat but as a matter of genuine administrative efficacy and expediency.

(2) No moneys shall be withdrawn from the Consolidated Revenue Fund of the Federation except to meet expenditure that is charged upon the fund by this Constitution or where the issue of those moneys has been authorized by an Appropriation Act, Supplementary Appropriation Act or an Act passed in pursuance of section 81 of this Constitution.

(3) No moneys shall be withdrawn from any public fund of the Federation, other than the Consolidated Revenue Fund of the Federation, unless the issue of those moneys has been authorized by an Act of the National Assembly.

(4) No moneys shall be withdrawn from the Consolidated Revenue Fund or any other public fund of the Federation, except in the manner prescribed by the National Assembly.

81. (1) The President shall cause to be prepared and laid before each House of the National Assembly at any time in each financial year estimates of the revenues and expenditure of the Federation for the next following financial year.

(2) The heads of expenditure contained in the estimates (other than expenditure charged upon the Consolidated Revenue Fund of the Federation by this Constitution) shall be included in a bill, to be known as an Appropriation Bill, providing for the issue from the Consolidated Revenue Fund of the sums necessary to meet that expenditure and the appropriation of those sums for the purposes specified therein.

(3) Any amount standing to the credit of the judiciary in the Consolidated Revenue Fund of the Federation shall be paid directly to the National Judicial Council for disbursement to the heads of the courts established for the Federation and the State under section 6 of this Constitution.

(4) If in respect of any financial year it is found that—

(a) the amount appropriated by the Appropriation Act for any purpose is insufficient; or

(b) a need has arisen for expenditure for a purpose for which no amount has been appropriated by the Act, a supplementary estimate showing the sums required shall be laid before each House of the National Assembly and the heads of any such expenditure shall be included in a Supplementary Appropriation Bill.

82. If the Appropriation Bill in respect of any financial year has not been passed into law by the beginning of the financial year, the President may authorise the withdrawal of moneys in the Consolidated Revenue Fund of the Federation for the purpose of meeting expenditure necessary to carry on the services of the Government of the Federation for a period not exceeding months or until the coming into operation of the Appropriate Act, whichever is the earlier:

Commentary

This should be authorized in three-month intervals and renewable only once, pending final or formal appropriation of funds as stipulated in this constitution.

Provided that the withdrawal in respect of any such period shall not exceed the amount authorized to be withdrawn from the Consolidated Revenue Fund of the Federation under the provisions of the Appropriation Act passed by the National Assembly for the corresponding period in the immediately preceding financial year, being an amount proportionate to the total amount so authorized for the immediately preceding financial year.

83. (1) The National Assembly may by law make provisions for the establishment of a Contingencies Fund for the Federation and for authorizing the President, if satisfied that there has arisen an urgent and unforeseen need for expenditure for which no other provision exists, to make advances from the Fund to meet the need.

(2) Where any advance is made in accordance with the provisions of this section, a Supplementary Estimate shall be presented and a Supplementary Appropriation Bill shall be introduced as soon as possible for the purpose of replacing the amount so advanced.

Commentary

The provisions in Section 83, subsections (1) and (2) should be reconsidered. It offers a "legal" loophole for the siphoning away of government funds. All appropriations should go through the normal appropriation process. Supplementary appropriations cannot be a priorily authorized by law, when there is already a standing provision for regular appropriations.

84. (1) There shall be paid to the holders of the offices mentioned in this section such remuneration, salaries and allowances as may be prescribed by the National Assembly, but not exceeding the amount as shall have been determined by the Revenue Mobilisation Allocation and Fiscal Commission.

(2) The remuneration, salaries and allowances payable to the holders of the offices so mentioned shall be a charge upon the Consolidated Revenue Fund of the Federation.

(3) The remuneration and salaries payable to the holders of the said offices and their conditions of service, other than allowances, shall not be altered to their disadvantage after their appointment.

(4) The offices aforesaid are the offices of President, Vice-President, Chief Justice of Nigeria, Justice of the Supreme Court, President of the Court of Appeal, Justice of the Court of Appeal, Chief Judge of the Federal High Court, Judge of the Federal High Court, Chief Judge and Judge of the High Court of the Federal Capital Territory, Abuja, Chief Judge of a State, Judge of the High Court of a State, Grand *Kadi* of the Sharia Court of Appeal of the Federal Capital Territory, Abuja, President and Judge of the Customary Court of Appeal of the Federal Capital Territory, Abuja, Grand *Kadi* and *Kadi* of the Sharia Court of Appeal of a State, President and Judge of the Customary Court of Appeal of a State,

the Auditor-General for the Federation and the Chairmen and members of the following executive bodies, namely, the Code of Conduct Bureau, the Federal Civil Service Commission, the Independent National Electoral Commission, the National Judicial Council, the Federal Judicial Service Commission, the Judicial Service Committee of the Federal Capital Territory, Abuja, the Federal Character Commission, the Code of Conduct Tribunal, the National Population Commission, the Revenue Mobilisation Allocation and Fiscal Commission, the Nigeria Police Council and the Police Service Commission.

(5) Any person who has held office as President or Vice-President shall be entitled to pension for life at a rate equivalent to the annual salary of the incumbent President or Vice-President:

Provided that such a person was not removed from office by the process of impeachment or for breach of any provisions of this Constitution.

(6) Any pension granted by virtue of subsection (5) of this section shall be a charge upon the Consolidated Revenue Fund of the Federation.

(7) The recurrent expenditure of judicial offices in the Federation (in addition to salaries and allowances of the judicial officers mentioned in subsection (4) of this section) shall be a charge upon the Consolidated Revenue Fund of the Federation.

85. (1) There shall be an Auditor-General for the Federation who shall be appointed in accordance with the provisions of section 86 of this Constitution.

(2) The public accounts of the Federation and of all offices and courts of the Federation shall be audited and reported on to the Auditor-General who shall submit his reports to the National Assembly; and for that purpose, the Auditor-General or any person authorized by him in that behalf shall have access to all the books, records, returns and other documents relating to those accounts.

(3) Nothing in subsection (2) of this section shall be construed as authorizing the Auditor-General to audit the accounts of or appoint auditors for government statutory corporations, commissions, authorities, agencies, including all persons and bodies established by an Act of the National Assembly, but the Auditor-General shall—

(a) provide such bodies with—

(i) a list of auditors qualified to be appointed by them as external auditors and from which the bodies shall appoint their external auditors, and

(ii) guidelines on the level of fees to be paid to external auditors; and

(b) comment on their annual accounts and auditor's reports thereon.

(4) The Auditor-General shall have power to conduct checks of all government statutory corporations, commissions, authorities, agencies, including all persons and bodies established by an Act of the National Assembly.

(5) The Auditor-General shall, within ninety days of receipt of the Accountant-General's financial statement, submit his reports under this section to each House of the National Assembly and each House shall cause the reports to be considered by a committee of the House of the National Assembly responsible for public accounts.

(6) In the exercise of his functions under this Constitution, the Auditor-General shall not be subject to the direction or control of any other authority or person.

86. (1) The Auditor-General for the Federation shall be appointed by the President on the recommendation of the Federal Civil Service Commission subject to confirmation by the Senate.

(2) The power to appoint persons to act in the office of the Auditor-General shall vest in the President.

(3) Except with the sanction of a resolution of the Senate, no person shall act in the office of the Auditor-General for a period exceeding six months.

87. (1) A person holding the office of the Auditor-General for the Federation shall be removed from office by the President acting on an address supported by two-thirds majority of the Senate praying that he be so removed for inability to discharge the functions of his-office (whether arising from infirmity of mind or body or any other cause) or for misconduct.

(2) The Auditor-General shall not be removed from office before such retiring age as may be prescribed by law, save in accordance with the provisions of this section.

88. (1) Subject to the provisions of this Constitution, each House of the National Assembly shall have power by resolution published in its journal

or in the Official Gazette of the Government of the Federation to direct or cause to be directed investigation into—

(a) any matter or thing with respect to which it has power to make laws, and

(b) the conduct of affairs of any person, authority, ministry or government department charged, or intended to be charged, with the duty of or responsibility for—

(i) executing or administering laws enacted by National Assembly, and

(ii) disbursing or administering moneys appropriated or to be appropriated by the National Assembly.

(2) The powers conferred on the National Assembly under the provisions of this section are exercisable only for the purpose of enabling it to—

(a) make laws with respect to any matter within its legislative competence and correct any defects in existing laws; and

(b) expose corruption, inefficiency or waste in the execution or administration of laws within its legislative competence and in the disbursement or administration of funds appropriated by it.

Commentary

Why are all the above provisions included under the legislative section? Particularly for Section 2(b), who determines and exposes "corruption" or "waste" by legislators? Who exercises oversight?

89. (1) For the purposes of any investigation under section 88 of this Constitutional and subject to the provisions thereof, the Senate or the House of Representatives or a committee appointed in accordance with section 62 of this Constitution shall have power to—

(a) procure all such evidence, written or oral, direct or circumstantial, as it may think necessary or desirable, and examine all persons as witnesses whose evidence may be material or relevant to the subject matter;

(b) require such evidence to be given on oath;

(c) summon any person in Nigeria to give evidence at any place or produce any document or other thing in his possession or under his control, and examine him as a witness and require him to produce any document or other thing in his possession or under his control, subject to all just exceptions; and

Commentary

Also needs to have the power to summon people "outside" of Nigeria to the extent they represent potential witnesses to criminal, civil, or treasonable cases.

(d) issue a warrant to compel the attendance of any person who, after having been summoned to attend, fails, refuses or neglects to do so and does not excuse such failure, refusal or neglect to the satisfaction of the House or the committee in question, and order him to pay all costs which may have been occasioned in compelling his attendance or by reason of his failure, refusal or neglect to obey the summons, and also to impose such fine as may be prescribed for any such failure, refused or neglect; and any fine so imposed shall be recoverable in the same manner as a fine imposed by a court of law.

(2) A summons or warrant issued under this section may be served or executed by any member of the Nigeria Police Force or by any person authorized in that behalf by the President of the Senate or the Speaker of the House of Representatives, as the case may require.

Commentary

If the president of the Senate or the Speaker of the House can authorize summons or a warrant against any citizen, then what would be the role of the courts and/or judges? The president of the Senate or the Speaker of the House should not able to authorize any summons or warrants. They are not the "courts" or the "law." However if there is ever a case of "contempt of National Assembly/Congress," then the normal legislative procedure should determine as well as provide the guidelines for action.

Part II: House of Assembly of a State

A. Composition and Staff of House of Assembly:

90. There shall be a House of Assembly for each of the States of the Federation.

91. Subject to the provisions of this Constitution, a House of Assembly of a State shall consist of three or four times the number of seats which that

State has in the House of Representatives divided in a way to reflect, as far as possible nearly equal population:

Commentary

This is a primary source of conflict. The terms and conditions should be specific and clearly indicated. It should be made clear whether it would be either three or four times (seats), nothing here should be left to individual or group discretion.

Provided that a House of Assembly of a State shall consist of not less than twenty-four and not more than forty members.

92. (1) There shall be a Speaker and a Deputy Speaker of a House of Assembly who shall be elected by the members of the House from among themselves.

(2) The Speaker or Deputy Speaker of the House of Assembly shall vacate his office—

(a) if he ceases to be a member of the House of Assembly otherwise than by reason of the dissolution of the House;

(b) When the House first sits after dissolution of the previous House; or

(c) if he is removed from office by a resolution of House of Assembly by the votes of not less than two-third majority of the members of the House.

93. There shall be a Clerk to a House of Assembly and such other staff as may be prescribed by a Law enacted by the House of Assembly, and the method of appointment of the Clerk and other staff of the House shall be as prescribed by that Law.

Procedure for Summoning and Dissolution of a House of Assembly

94. (1) Every person elected to a House of Assembly shall before taking his seat in that House, declare his assets and liabilities in the manner prescribed in this Constitution and subsequently take and subscribe before the Speaker of the House, the Oath of Allegiance and oath of membership prescribed in the Seventh Schedule to this Constitution, but a member may, before taking the oaths, take part in the election of the Speaker and Deputy Speaker of the House of Assembly.

(2) The Speaker and Deputy Speaker of a House of Assembly shall declare their assets and liabilities in the manner prescribed by this Constitution

and subsequently take and subscribe to the Oath of Allegiance and the oath of membership prescribed as aforesaid before the Clerk of the House of Assembly.

95. (1) At any sitting of a House of Assembly, the Speaker of that House shall preside, and in his absence the Deputy Speaker shall preside.

(2) In the absence of the Speaker and Deputy Speaker of the House, such member of the House as the House may elect for a purpose shall preside.

96. (1) The quorum of a House of Assembly shall be one-third of all the members of the House.

(2) If objection is taken by any member of a House of Assembly present that there are present in that House (besides the person presiding) fewer than one-third of all the members of that House and that it is not competent for the House to transact business, and after such interval as may be prescribed in the rules of procedure of the House, the person presiding ascertains that the number of members present is still less than one-third of all the members of the House, he shall adjourn the House.

97. The business of a House of Assembly shall be conducted in English, but the House may in addition to English conduct the business of the House in one or more other languages spoken in the State as the House may by resolution approve.

98. (1) Except as otherwise provided by this Constitution, any question proposed for decision in a House of Assembly shall be determined by the required majority of the members present and voting; and the person presiding shall cast a vote whenever necessary to avoid an equality of votes but shall not vote in any other case.

Commentary

What number qualifies as "required" majority? It should be stated here.

(2) Except as otherwise provided by this Constitution, the required majority for the purpose of determining any question shall be a simple majority.

(3) A House of Assembly shall by its rules provide—

(a) that a member of the House shall declare any direct pecuniary interest he may have in any matter coming before the House for deliberation;

Commentary

Memberships of the Senate or the House should be "gender-neutral," that is, "he or she."

(b) that the House may by resolution decide whether or not such member may vote or participate in its deliberations, on such matter;

(c) the penalty, if any, which the House may impose for failure to declare any direct pecuniary interest such member may have; and

(d) for such other matters pertaining to the foregoing as the House may think necessary, but nothing in this subsection shall enable any rules to be made to require any member, who signifies his intention not to vote on or participate in such matter, and who does not so vote or participate, to declare any such interest.

99. Any person who sits or votes in a House of Assembly of a State knowing or having reasonable grounds for knowing that he is not entitled to do so commits an offence and is liable on conviction to such punishment as shall be prescribed by a Law of the House of Assembly.

100. (1) The power of a House of Assembly to make laws shall be exercised by bills passed by the House of Assembly and, except as otherwise provided by this section, assented to by the Governor.

Commentary

Lawmaking is a joint obligation between the House and the Senate. It should be so indicated for clarification; and the specific role of each chamber delineated.

(2) A bill shall not become Law unless it has been duly passed and, subject to subsection (1) of this section, assented to in accordance with the provisions of this section.

(3) Where a bill has been passed by the House of Assembly it shall be presented to the Governor for assent.

(4) Where a bill is presented to the Governor for assent he shall within thirty days thereof signify that he assents or that he withholds assent.

(5) Where the Governor withholds assent and the bill is again passed by the House of Assembly by two-thirds majority, the bill shall become law and the assent of the Governor shall not be required.

101. Subject to the provisions of this Constitution, a House of Assembly shall have power to regulate its own procedure, including the procedure for summoning and recess of the House.

102. A House of Assembly may act notwithstanding any vacancy in its membership, and the presence or participation of any person not entitled to be present at or to participate in the proceedings of the House shall not invalidate such proceedings.

103. (1) A House of Assembly may appoint a committee of its members for any special or general purpose as in its opinion would be better regulated and managed by means of such a committee, and may by resolution, regulation or otherwise as it thinks fit delegate any functions exercisable by it to any such committee.

(2) The number of members of a committee appointed under this section, their term of office and quorum shall be fixed by the House of Assembly.

(3) Nothing in this section shall be construed as authorizing a House of Assembly to delegate to a committee the power to decide whether a bill shall be passed into Law or to determine any matter which it is empowered to determine by resolution under the provisions of this Constitution, but such a committee of the House may be authorized to make recommendations to the House on any such matter.

Commentary

What this technically means is that all bills must be decided on the House floor, and the Committees are inconsequential when it comes to which bills becomes law and which do not. This is wrong. The Committees (especially the Standing Committees) should have the power to vote "up or down," to approve (vote out of committee) or kill any bill presented to it for consideration. The Committee system should remain the "work-horse" of the legislature. In that way, it would help to reduce much of the rancor and bitter political battles that occur on the House and Senate floors.

104. A House of Assembly shall sit for a period of not less than one hundred and eighty-one days in a year.

105. (1) A House of Assembly shall stand dissolved at the expiration of a period of four years commencing from the date of the first sitting of the House.

(2) If the Federation is at war in which the territory of Nigeria is physically involved and the President considers that it is not practicable to hold

elections, the National Assembly may by resolution extend the period of four years mentioned in subsection (1) of this section from time to time but not beyond a period of six months at any one time.

(3) Subject to the provisions of this Constitution, the person elected as the Governor of a State shall have power to issue a proclamation for the holding of the first session of the House of Assembly of the State concerned immediately after his being sworn in, or for its dissolution as provided in this section.

C: Qualification for Membership of House of Assembly and Right of Attendance

106. Subject to the provisions of section 107 of this Constitution, a person shall be qualified for election as a member of a House of Assembly if—

(a) he is a citizen of Nigeria;

(b) he has attained the age of thirty years;

(c) he has been educated up to at least the School Certificate level or its equivalent; and

(d) he is a member of a political party and is sponsored by that party.

Commentary

This would lead to the development of "party bosses," and invariably to "boss" politics. The party is not really a Constitutional part of the government; rather it is an interest group seeking to control the power of the government by electing its members to public office. Any qualified citizen should be opportuned to aspire for public office, to sponsor himself or herself, or be sponsored by other types of legitimate interest groups. What the above provision does is that it essentially excludes those who are independents (belong to no political party). Simply put, the party system should not be the only and most prominent avenue for seeking and securing public office, to the extent that the individual intent and commitment is genuine.

107. (1) No person shall be qualified for election to a House of Assembly if—

(a) subject to the provisions of Section 28 of this Constitution, he has voluntarily acquired the citizenship of a country other than Nigeria or, except in such cases as may be prescribed by the National Assembly, has made a declaration of allegiance to such a country;

(b) under any law in force in any part of Nigeria, he is adjudged to be a lunatic or otherwise declared to be of unsound mind;

(c) he is under a sentence of death imposed on him by any competent court of law or tribunal in Nigeria or a sentence of imprisonment or fine for an offence involving dishonesty or fraud (by whatever name called) or any other offence imposed on him by such a court or tribunal substituted by a competent authority for any other sentence imposed on him by such a court or tribunal;

(d) within a period of less than ten years before the date of an election to the House of Assembly, he has been convicted and sentenced for an offence involving dishonesty or he has been found guilty of a contravention of the Code of Conduct;

(e) he is an undischarged bankrupt, having been adjudged or otherwise declared bankrupt under any law in force in any part of Nigeria;

(f) he is a person employed in the public service of the Federation or of any State and he has not resigned, withdrawn or retired from such employment thirty days before the date of election;

(g) he is a member of any secret society;

(h) he has been indicted for embezzlement or fraud by a Judicial Commission of Inquiry or an Administrative Panel of Inquiry or a Tribunal set up under the Tribunals of Inquiry Act, a Tribunals of Inquiry Law or any other law by the Federal and State Government which indictment has been accepted by the Federal or State Government, respectively; or

(i) he has presented a forged certificate to the Independent National Electoral Commission.

(2) Where in respect of any person who has been—

(a) adjudged to be a lunatic;

(b) declared to be of unsound mind;

(c) sentenced to death or imprisonment; or

(d) adjudged or declared bankrupt,

any appeal against the decision is pending in any court of law in accordance with any law in force in Nigeria, subsection (1) of this section shall not apply during a period beginning from the date when such appeal is lodged and ending on the date when the appeal is finally determined or, as the case may be, the appeal lapses or is abandoned, whichever is earlier.

(3) For the purposes of subsection (2) of this section, an "appeal" includes any application for an injunction or an order of certiorari, mandamus, prohibition or habeas corpus, or any appeal from any such application.

108. (1) The Governor of a State may attend a meeting of a House of Assembly of the State either to deliver an address on State affairs or to make such statement on the policy of government as he may consider being of importance to the State.

Commentary

This should be carefully thought out. The Governor should not have a blanket warrant to attend any/or all meetings of the House of Assembly. The specific cases where this might be allowed should be so indicated. The idea of separation of powers should be maintained.

(2) A Commissioner of the Government of a State shall attend the House of Assembly of the State if invited to explain to the House of Assembly the conduct of his Ministry, and in particular when the affairs of that Ministry are under discussion.

Commentary

The power of "legislative oversight" should be exercised with reasonable cause and purpose.

(3) Nothing in this section shall enable any person who is not a member of a House of Assembly to vote in that House or in any of its committees.

109. (1) A member of a House of Assembly shall vacate his seat in the House if—

(a) he becomes a member of another legislative house;

(b) any other circumstances arise that, if he were not a member of that House, would cause him to be disqualified for election as such a member;

(c) he ceases to be a citizen of Nigeria;

(d) he becomes President, Vice-President, Governor, Deputy Governor or a Minister of the Government of the Federation or a Commissioner of the Government of a State or a Special Adviser;

(e) save as otherwise prescribed by this Constitution, he becomes a member of a commission or other body established by this Constitution or by any other law;

(f) without just cause he is absent from meetings of the House of Assembly for a period amounting in the aggregate to more than one-third of the total number of days during which the House meets in any one year;

(g) being a person whose election to the House of Assembly was sponsored by a political party, he becomes a member of another political party before the expiration of the period for which that House was elected:

Provided that his membership of the latter political party is not as a result of a division in the political party of which he was previously a member or of a merger of two or more political parties or factions by one of which he was previously sponsored; or

(h) the Speaker of the House of Assembly receives a certificate under the hand of the Chairman of the Independent National Electoral Commission stating that the provisions of section 110 of this Constitution have been complied with in respect of the recall of the member.

(2) The Speaker of the House of Assembly shall give effect to subsection (1) of this section, so however that the Speaker or a member shall first present evidence satisfactory to the House that any of the provisions of that subsection has become applicable in respect of the member.

(3) A member of a House of Assembly shall be deemed to be absent without just cause from a meeting of the House of Assembly unless the person presiding certifies in writing that he is satisfied that the absence of the member from the meeting was for a just cause.

110. A member of the House of Assembly may be recalled as such a member if—

(a) there is presented to the Chairman of the Independent National Electoral Commission a petition in that behalf signed by more than one-half of the persons registered to vote in that member's constituency alleging their loss of confidence in that member; and

(b) the petition is thereafter, in a referendum conducted by the Independent National Electoral Commission within ninety days of the date of the receipt of the petition, approved by a simple majority of the votes of the persons registered to vote in that member's constituency.

111. A member of the House of Assembly shall receive such salary and other allowances as the Revenue Mobilisation Allocation and Fiscal Commission may determine.

D: Elections to a House of Assembly:

112. Subject to the provisions of sections 91 and 113 of this Constitution, the Independent National Electoral Commission shall divide every state in the federation into such number of state constituencies as is equal to three or four times the number of Federal constituencies within that state.

113. The boundaries of each State constituency shall be such that the number of inhabitants thereof is as nearly equal to the population quota as is reasonably practicable.

114. (1) The Independent National Electoral Commission shall review the division of every State into constituencies at intervals of not less than ten years, and may alter such constituencies in accordance with the provisions of this section to such extent as it may consider desirable in the light of the review.

(2) The Independent National Electoral Commission may at any time carry out such a review and alter the constituencies in accordance with the provisions of this section to such extent as it considers necessary in consequence of any alteration of the boundaries of the State or by reason of the holding of a census of the population of Nigeria in pursuance of an Act of the National Assembly.

115. Where the boundaries of any State constituency established under section 112 of this Constitution are altered in accordance with the provisions of section 114 of this Constitution, that alteration shall come into effect after it has been approved by the National Assembly and after the current life of the House of Assembly.

116. (1) Elections to a House of Assembly shall be held on a date to be appointed by the Independent National Electoral Commission.

(2) The date mentioned in subsection (1) of this section shall not be earlier than sixty days before and not later than the date on which the House of Assembly stands dissolved, or where the election is to fill a vacancy occurring more than three months before such date, not later than one month after the vacancy occurred.

117. (1) Subject to the provisions of this Constitution, every State constituency established in accordance with the provisions of this part of this Chapter shall return one member who shall be directly elected to a House of Assembly in such manner as may be prescribed by an Act of the National Assembly.

(2) Every citizen of Nigeria, who has attained the age of eighteen years residing in Nigeria at the time of the registration of voters for purposes of election to any legislative house, shall be entitled to be registered as a voter for that election.

118. The registration of voters and the conduct of elections shall be subject to the direction and supervision of the Independent National Electoral Commission.

119. The National Assembly shall make provisions in respect to—

(a) persons who may apply to an election tribunal for the determination of any question as to whether—

(i) any person has been validly elected as a member of a House of Assembly,

(ii) the term of office of any person has ceased, or

(iii) the seat in a House of Assembly of a member of that House has become vacant;

(b) circumstances and manner in which, and the conditions upon which, such application may be made; and

(c) powers, practice and procedure of the election tribunal in relation to any such application.

E: Powers and Control over Public Funds

120. (1) All revenues or other moneys raised or received by a State (not being revenues or other moneys payable under this Constitution or any Law

of a House of Assembly into any other public fund of the State established for a specific purpose) shall be paid into and form one Consolidated Revenue Fund of the State.

(2) No moneys shall be withdrawn from the Consolidated Revenue Fund of the State except to meet expenditure that is charged upon the Fund by this Constitution or where the issue of those moneys has been authorized by an Appropriation Law, Supplementary Appropriation Law or Law passed in pursuance of section 121 of this Constitution.

(3) No moneys shall be withdrawn from any public fund of the State, other than the Consolidated Revenue Fund of the State, unless the issue of those moneys has been authorized by a Law of the House of Assembly of the State.

(4) No moneys shall be withdrawn from the Consolidated Revenue Fund of the State or any other public fund of the State except in the manner prescribed by the House of Assembly.

121. (1) The Governor shall cause to be prepared and laid before the House of Assembly at any time before the commencement of each financial year estimates of the revenues and expenditure of the State for the next following financial year.

(2) The heads of expenditure contained in the estimates, other than expenditure charged upon the Consolidated Revenue Fund of the State by this Constitution, shall be included in a bill, to be known as an Appropriation Bill, providing for the issue from the Consolidated Revenue Fund of the State of the sums necessary to meet that expenditure and the appropriation of those sums for the purposes specified therein.

(3) Any amount standing to the credit of the judiciary in the Consolidated Revenue Fund of the State shall be paid directly to the heads of the courts concerned.

(4) If in respect of any financial year, it is found that—

(a) the amount appropriated by the Appropriation Law for any purpose is insufficient; or

(b) a need has arisen for expenditure for a purpose for which no amount has been appropriated by the Law, a supplementary estimate showing the sums required shall be laid before the House of Assembly and the heads of any such expenditure shall be included in a Supplementary Appropriation Bill.

122. If the Appropriation Bill in respect of any financial year has not been passed into Law by the beginning of the financial year, the Governor may authorise the withdrawal of moneys from the Consolidated Revenue Fund of the State for the purpose of meeting expenditure necessary to carry on the services of the government for a period not exceeding six months or until the coming into operation of the Law, whichever is the earlier:

Provided that the withdrawal in respect of any such period shall not exceed the amount authorized to be withdrawn from the Consolidated Revenue Fund of the State under the provisions of the Appropriation Law passed by the House of Assembly for the corresponding period in the immediately preceding financial year, being an amount proportionate to the total amount so authorized for the immediately preceding financial year.

123. (1) A House of Assembly may by Law make provisions for the establishment of a Contingencies Fund for the State and for authorizing the Governor, if satisfied that there has arisen an urgent and unforeseen need for expenditure for which no other provision exists, to make advances from the Fund to meet that need.

(2) Where any advance is made in accordance with the provisions of this section, a Supplementary Estimate shall be presented and a Supplementary Appropriation Bill shall be introduced as soon as possible for the purpose of replacing the amount so advanced.

124. (1) There shall be paid to the holders of the offices mentioned in this section such remuneration and salaries as may be prescribed by a House of Assembly, but not exceeding the amount as shall have been determined by the Revenue Mobilisation Allocation and Fiscal Commission.

(2) The remuneration, salaries and allowances payable to the holders of the offices so mentioned shall be charged upon the Consolidated Revenue Fund of the State.

(3) The remuneration and salaries payable to the holders of the said offices and their conditions of service, other than allowances, shall not be altered to their disadvantage after their appointment.

(4) The offices aforesaid are the offices of Governor, Deputy Governor, Auditor-General for a State and the Chairman and members of the following

bodies, that is to say, the State Civil Service Commission, the State Independent Electoral Commission and the State Judicial Service Commission.

(5) Provisions may be made by a Law of a House of Assembly for the grant of a pension or gratuity to or in respect of a person who had held office as Governor or Deputy Governor and was not removed from office as a result of impeachment; and any pension granted by virtue of any provisions made in pursuance of this subsection shall be a charge upon the Consolidated Revenue Fund of the State.

125. (1) There shall be an Auditor-General for each State who shall be appointed in accordance with the provisions of section 126 of this Constitution.

(2) The public accounts of a State and of all offices and courts of the State shall be audited by the Auditor-General for the State who shall submit his reports to the House of Assembly of the State concerned, and for that purpose the Auditor-General or any person authorized by him in that behalf shall have access to all the books, records, returns and other documents relating to those accounts.

(3) Nothing in subsection (2) of this section shall be construed as authorizing the Auditor-General to audit the accounts of or appoint auditors for government statutory corporations, commissions, authorities, agencies, including all persons and bodies established by Law by the Auditor-General shall—

(a) provide such bodies with—

(i) a list of auditors qualified to be appointed by them as external auditors and from which the bodies shall appoint their external auditors, and

(ii) a guideline on the level of fees to be paid to external auditors; and

(b) comment on their annual accounts and auditor's report thereon.

(4) The Auditor-General for the State shall have power to conduct periodic checks of all government statutory corporations, commissions, authorities, agencies, including all persons and bodies established by a law of the House of Assembly of the State.

(5) The Auditor-General for a State shall, within ninety days of receipt of the Accountant-General's financial statement and annual accounts of

the State, submit his report to the House of Assembly of the State and the House shall cause the report to be considered by a committee of the House responsible for public accounts.

(6) In the exercise of his functions under this Constitution, the Auditor-General for a State shall not be subject to the direction or control of any other authority or person.

126. (1) The Auditor-General for a State shall be appointed by the Governor of the State on the recommendation of the State Civil Service Commission subject to confirmation by the House of Assembly of the State.

(2) The power to appoint persons to act in the office of the Auditor-General for a State shall vest in the Governor.

(3) Except with the sanction of a resolution of the House of Assembly of a State, no person shall act in the office of the Auditor-General for a State for a period exceeding six months.

127. (1) A person holding the office of Auditor-General under section 126 (1) of this Constitution shall be removed from office by the Governor of the State acting on an address supported by two-thirds majority of the House of Assembly praying that he be so removed for inability to discharge the functions of his office (whether arising from infirmity of mind or body or any other cause) or for misconduct.

(2) An Auditor-General shall not been removed from office before such retiring age as may be prescribed by Law, save in accordance with the provisions of this section.

128. (1) Subject to the provisions of this Constitution, a House of Assembly shall have power by resolution published in its journal or in the Office Gazette of the Government of the State to direct or cause to be directed an inquiry or investigation into—

(a) any matter or thing with respect to which it has power to make laws; and

(b) the conduct of affairs of any person, authority, ministry or government department charged, or intended to be charged, with the duty of or responsibility for—

(i) executing or administering laws enacted by that House of Assembly, and

(ii) disbursing or administering moneys appropriated or to be appropriated by such House.

(2) The powers conferred on a House of Assembly under the provisions of this section are exercisable only for the purpose of enabling the House to—

(a) make laws with respect to any matter within its legislative competence and correct any defects in existing laws; and

(b) expose corruption, inefficiency of waste in the execution or administration of laws within its legislative competence and in the disbursement or administration of funds appropriated by it.

129. (1) For the purposes of any investigation under section 128 of this Constitution, and subject to the provisions thereof, a House of Assembly or a committee appointed in accordance with section 103 of this Constitution shall have power to—

(a) procure all such evidence, written or oral, direct or circumstantial, as it may think necessary or desirable, and examine all persons as witnesses whose evidence may be material or relevant to the subject matter;

(b) require such evidence to be given on oath;

(c) summon any person in Nigeria to give evidence at any place or produce any document or other thing in his possession or under his control, and examine him as a witness and require him to produce any document or other thing in his possession or under his control, subject to all just exceptions; and

(d) issue a warrant to compel the attendance of any person who, after having been summoned to attend, fails, refuses or neglects to do so and does not excuse such failure, refusal or neglect to the satisfaction of the House of Assembly or the committee, and order him to pay all costs which may have been occasioned in compelling his attendance or by reason of his failure, refusal or neglect to obey the summons and also to impose such fines as may be prescribed for any such failure, refusal or neglect; and any fine so imposed shall be recoverable in the same manner as a fine imposed by a court of law.

(2) A summons or warrant issued under this section may be served or executed by any member of the Nigeria Police Force or by any person authorized in that behalf by the Speaker of the House of Assembly of the State.

CHAPTER VI: THE EXECUTIVE

Part I: Federal Executive

A: The President of the Federation

130. (1) There shall be for the Federation a President.

(2) The President shall be the Head of State, the Chief Executive of the Federation and Commander-in-Chief of the Armed Forces of the Federation.

Commentary

As Commander-in-Chief, the President should not hold another executive portfolio or a ministerial appointment within the Executive branch.

131. A person shall be qualified for election to the office of the President if—

(a) he is a citizen of Nigeria by birth;

(b) he has attained the age of forty years;

(c) he is a member of a political party and is sponsored by that political party; and

(d) he has been educated up to at least School Certificate level or its equivalent.

Bibliography

Aborishade, Oladimeji, and Robert J. Mundt. *Politics in Nigeria*. 2nd ed. New York: Longman Publishers, 2002.

Acuna, Carlos A., and Catalina Smulovitz. "Adjusting the Armed Forces to Democracy: Success, Failures, and Ambiguities in the Southern Cone." Pp. 13–38 in *Constructing Democracy: Human Rights, Citizenship, and Society in Latin America*, edited by Elizabeth Jelin and Eric Hershberg. Boulder, Colo.: Westview Press, 1996.

Adamolekun, Ladipo. "Introduction: Federalism in Nigeria." *Publius: The Journal of Federalism* 21, no. 4 (1991): 1–11.

Adekanye, J. Bayo. "Military Occupation and Social Stratification." An inaugural lecture delivered at the University of Ibadan, Nigeria, November 25, 1993, pp. 1–56.

Ademoyega, Adewale. *Why We Struck: The Story of the First Nigerian Coup*. Ibadan, Nigeria: Evans Brothers Publishers Limited, 1981.

African Concord. "The Rising Power of Minorities," April 24, 1989, 15.

African Guardian. "A Savage Carnage," June 1, 1992, 22.

Aguda, Oluwadare. "The Nigerian Approach to Politics." African Studies Seminar Papers, 2, Sudan Research Unit, University of Khartoum, Sudan, 1969.

Ajayi, J. F. A., and R. Smith. *Yoruba Warfare in the Nineteenth Century*. Cambridge: 1964.

Ake, Claude. "Is Africa Democratizing?" Text from the 1993 Guardian Lecture, Nigerian Institute of International Affairs, Lagos, Nigeria, December 11, 1993.

———. *Democracy and Development in Africa*. Washington, D.C.: Brookings Institution Press, 1996.

Akinjogbin, I. A. "The Oyo Empire in the Eighteenth Century: A Reassessment." *Journal of the Historical Society of Nigeria* 3, no. 3 (December 1966): 449–60.

Akinola, Anthony. "Phases of Nigerian Democracy." *West Africa*, July 9–15, 2001, 11–12.

Akinrinade, Sola. "Constitutionalism and the Resolution of Conflicts in Nigeria." *Round Table* 368, no. 1 (2003): 41–52.

Akintoye, S. A. *Revolution and Power Politics in Yorubaland, 1840–1893.* London: Longman, 1971.

Akinyele, R. T. "States Creation in Nigeria: The Willink Report in Retrospect." *African Studies Review* 39, no. 2 (September 1996): 71–94.

———. "Ethnicity, Religion and Politics in Nigeria." Pp. 123–47 in *The Amalgamation and Its Enemies: An Interpretive History of Modern Nigeria,* edited by Richard A. Olaniyan. Ile-Ife, Nigeria: Obafemi Awolowo University Press, 2003.

Albert, Isaac Olawale. "Ife-Modakeke Crisis." Pp. 142–83 in *Community Conflicts in Nigeria: Management, Resolution and Transformation,* edited by Onigu Otite and Isaac Olawale Albert. Ibadan, Nigeria: Spectrum Books Limited, 1999.

Amuwo, Kunle, and Bayo Okunade. "Political Democracy and Economic Dictatorship: Notes of Paradoxes and Illogicalities of a Transiting Neo-Colonial State." In *Toward the Survival of the Third Republic,* edited by A. T. Gana and S. G. Tyoden. Jos, Nigeria: Department of Political Science, University of Jos, 1990.

Anderson, Benedict. *Imagined Communities: Reflections on the Origin and Spread of Nationalism.* London: Verso, 1991.

Apter, David E. *The Political Kingdom in Uganda: A Study in Bureaucratic Nationalism.* Princeton, N.J.: Princeton University Press, 1961.

Arendt, Hannah. *On Violence.* New York: Harcourt, Brace & World, 1970.

———. *Crises of the Republic.* New York: Harcourt Brace Jovanovich, 1972.

Ayittey, George B. N. *Africa in Chaos.* New York: St. Martin's Press, 1998.

Babatope, Ebenezer. *The Abacha Regime and the June 12 Crisis: A Struggle for Democracy.* Lagos, Nigeria: Ebino Topsy, 1995.

Badru, Padre. *Imperialism and Ethnic Politics in Nigeria, 1960–1966.* Trenton, N.J.: Africa World Press, 1998.

Bagudu, Nankin. *Identity, Political Religiosity and Communal Violence in Nigeria: Implications.* Jos, Nigeria: League for Human Rights, 2003.

Balogun, Ola. *The Tragic Years: Nigeria in Crisis.* Benin, Nigeria: Ethiope Publishing, 1973.

———. *Markets and States in Tropical Africa: The Political Basis of Agricultural Policies.* Berkeley: University of California Press, 1981.

Bates, Robert, ed. *Toward a Political Economy of Development: A Rational Choice Perspective.* Berkeley: University of California Press, 1988.

Beblawi, Hazem, and Giacomo Luciani. *The Rentier State, Volume II.* London: Croom Helm, 1987.

Bently, Arthur F. *The Process of Government.* Evanston, Ill.: Principia Press, 1949.

Berman, Sheri. "How Democracies Emerge: Lessons from Europe." *Journal of Democracy* 18, no. 1 (January 2007): 28–41.

Best, Shedrack Gaya, Alamveabee Efhiraim Idyorough, and Zainab Bayero Shehu. "Communal Conflicts and the Possibilities of Conflict Resolution in Nigeria: A Case Study of the Tiv-Jukun Conflicts in Wukari Local Government Area of Taraba State." Pp. 82–117 in *Community Conflicts in Nigeria: Management, Resolution and Transformation,* edited by Onigu Otite and Isaac Olawale Albert. Ibadan, Nigeria: Spectrum Books, 1999.

Bienen, Henry. "Military Rule and Political Process: Nigerian Examples." *Comparative Politics* 10, no. 2 (1978): 205–25.

Bigsten, Arne, and Karl Ove Moene. "Growth and Rent Dispensation: The Case of Kenya." *Journal of African Economics* 5 (1996): 177–98.

Boyd, Carolyn P. *Praetorian Politics in Liberal Spain*. Chapel Hill: University of North Carolina Press, 1979.

Brass, Paul R. *Ethnicity and Nationalism: Theory and Comparison*. Newbury Park, Calif.: Sage Publications, 1991.

Bratton, Michael, and Nicolas Van de Walle. *Democratic Experiments in Africa: Regime Transitions in Comparative Perspective*. New York: Cambridge University Press, 1997.

Bridges, Thomas. *The Culture of Citizenship: Inventing Postmodern Civic Culture*. Albany: State University of New York, 1994.

Burrell, Gibson, and Gareth Morgan. *Sociological Paradigms and Organizational Analysis*. Burlington, Vt.: Ashgate, 2000.

Cameroon, Sir Donald. "Memorandum on Native Administration," July 13, 1934, para. 5.

Carens, Joseph H. *Culture, Citizenship, and Community: A Contextual Exploration of Justice as Evenhandedness*. New York: Oxford University Press, 2000.

Chazan, Naomi, Robert Mortimer, John Ravenhill, and Donald Rothchild. *Politics and Society in Contemporary Africa*. Boulder, Colo.: Lynne Rienner Publishers, 1992.

Chege, Michael. "Sub-Saharan Africa: Underdevelopment's Last Stand." Pp. 309–45 in *Global Change, Regional Response: The New International Context of Development*, edited by Barbara Stallings. New York: Cambridge University Press, 1995.

Chehabi, H. E., and Juan J. Linz, ed. *Sultanistic Regimes*. Baltimore: Johns Hopkins University Press, 1998.

———. "A Theory of Sultanism 1." Pp. 3–47 in *Sultanistic Regimes*, edited by H. E. Chehabi and Juan J. Linz, Baltimore: Johns Hopkins University Press, 1998.

Clapham, Christopher. *Africa and the International System: The Politics of State Survival*. New York: Cambridge University Press, 1996.

Coleman, James S. *Nationalism and Development in Africa: Selected Essays*. Berkeley: University of California Press, 1994.

Collier, Paul, and Anke Hoeffler. "Greed and Grievance in Civil War, Policy Research Paper 2355." Washington, D.C.: World Bank, 2000.

The Comet. "The Making of Kaduna Sharia War," June 30, 2000.

Crowther, Michael. *The Story of Nigeria*. London: Faber and Faber, 1962.

Crozier, Michael, Samuel P. Huntington, and Joji Watanuki. *The Crisis of Democracy: Report on the Governability of Democracies to The Trilateral Commission*. New York: University Press, 1975.

Daft, Richard L., and Karl E. Weick. "Toward a Model of Organizations as Interpretation Systems." *Academy of Management Review* 9 (1984): 284–95.

Davis, Kingsley, *Human Society*. New York: Macmillan, 1949.

Diamond, Larry. *Class, Ethnicity, and Democracy in Nigeria*. Syracuse, N.Y.: Syracuse University Press, 1988.

——. "Nigeria: Pluralism, Statism, and the Struggle for Democracy." Pp. 351–409 in *Politics in Developing Countries: Comparing Experiences with Democracy*, edited by Larry Diamond, Juan J. Linz, and Seymour Martin Lipset. Boulder, Colo.: Lynne Rienner Publishers, 1990.

Diamond, Larry, Anthony Kirk-Green, and Oyeleye Oyediran, eds. *Transition Without End: Nigerian Politics and Civil Society Under Babangida*. Boulder, Colo.: Lynne Rienner Publishers, 1997.

Dollar, David, and Jakob Svensson, "What Explains the Success or Failure of Structural Adjustment Programs?" Policy Research Working Paper 1938. The World Bank Macroeconomics and Growth, Development Research Group, Washington, D.C., 1998, 1–36.

Durkheim, Emile. *Division of Labor in Society*. Glencoe, Ill.: Free Press, 1949.

Duvall, Raymond, and John Freeman. "The State and Dependent Capitalism." *International Studies Quarterly* 25, no. 1 (1981): 106.

The Economist. "A Blacklist to Bolster Democracy," February 17, 2007.

Efiong, Philip. *Nigeria and Biafra: My Story*. Princeton, N.J.: Sungai Books, 2003.

Ejobowah, John Boye. "Who Owns the Oil? The Politics of Ethnicity in the Niger Delta of Nigeria." *Africa Today* (1999): 29–47.

Ekeocha, Okey. "The Scramble for Oil." *African Guardian*, March 5, 1990, 18.

——. "A Hardy Perennial." *African Guardian*, June 1, 1992, 27.

Fatton, R. *Predatory Rule: The State and Civil Society in Africa*. Boulder, Colo.: Lynne Rienner Publishers, 1992.

Fearon James D., and David D. Laitin. "A Cross-Sectional Study of Large-Scale Ethnic Violence in the Postwar Period." Unpublished Draft Paper, Department of Political Science, University of Chicago, September 30, 1997, 1–39.

——. "Ethnicity, Insurgency and Civil War." *American Political Science Review* 97 (February 2003): 75–90.

Friedman, Thomas L. "The First Law of Petropolitics." May/June 2006. www .foreignpolicy.com/story/cms.php?story_id=3426&print=1.

Fukuyama, Francis. *The End of History and the Last Man*. New York: Free Press, 1992.

——. *State-Building: Governance and World Order in the 21st Century*. Ithaca, N.Y.: Cornell University Press, 2004.

Ganji, Akbar. "The Struggle Against Sultanism." *Journal of Democracy* 6, no. 4 (October 2005): 35–51.

Garba, Joseph. "The Military Regime and the Nigerian Society." Address to a Seminar on Nigeria in Transition, September 11, 1979.

Geertz, Clifford. *The Interpretation of Cultures [Selected Essays]*. New York: Basic Books, 1973.

Gelb, Alan et al. *Oil Windfalls: Blessing or Curse?* New York: Oxford University Press, 1988.

George, Alexander. "Case Studies and Theory Development: The Method of Structured, Focused Comparison." In *Diplomacy: New Approaches in History, Theory, and Policy*, edited by Paul Lauren. New York: Free Press, 1979.

Gilpin, Robert. *U.S. Power and the Multinational Corporation: The Political Economy of Foreign Direct Investment*. New York: Basic Books, 1975.

———. *The Political Economy of International Relations*. Princeton, N.J.: Princeton University Press, 1987.

———. *Global Political Economy: Understanding the International Economic Order*. Princeton, N.J.: Princeton University Press, 2001.

Gowon, Yakubu. "Federalism and Nigerian Unity: Problems and Prospects." Pp. 23–28 in *Federalism and Nation-Building in Nigeria: The Challenges of the 21st Century*, edited by J. Isawa Elaigwu, P. C. Logams, and H. S. Galadima. Nigeria: National Council on Intergovernmental Relations, 1994.

Graf, William D. *The Nigerian State*. Portsmouth, NH: Heinemann, 1988.

Guardian. January 4, 1999

Guardian 16, no. 7667, November 10, 1999.

Guardian Newspaper, "AC, ANPP Protest Yar'Adua's Victory," April 24, 2007. www.guardiannewsngr.com/news/article01.

———. "A Causal Model of Civil Strife: A Comparative Analysis Using New Indices." *American Political Science Review* 62 (1968): 1104–24.

Gurr, Ted Robert. *Why Men Rebel*. Princeton, N.J.: Princeton University Press, 1970.

Habermas, Jürgen. *Legitimation Crisis*. Boston: Beacon Press, 1973.

Hadenius, Alex. *Democracy and Development*. New York: Cambridge University Press, 1992.

Haggard, Stephen, and Sylvia Maxfield. "The Political Economy of Financial Internationalization in the Developing World." *International Organization* 50, no. 1 (1996): 35–68.

Hall, Peter. *Governing the Economy: The Politics of State Intervention in Britain and France*. Cambridge: Polity Press, 1986.

Lasswell, Harold D. "Sino-Japanese Crisis: The Garrison State versus the Civilian State." *China Quarterly* 2 (1937): 643–49.

———. "The Garrison State." *American Journal of Sociology* 46, no. 4 (1941): 455–68.

Herbst, Jeffrey. *States and Power in Africa: Comparative Lessons in Authority and Control*. Princeton, N.J.: Princeton University Press, 2000.

Herskovitz, Jean. "Nigeria's Rigged Democracy." *Foreign Affairs* (July/August, 2007): 115–30.

Horowitz, Donald L. *Ethnic Groups in Conflict*. 2nd ed. Berkeley: University of California Press, 2000.

———. "The Cracked Foundations of the Right to Secede." *Journal of Democracy* 14, no. 2 (April 2003): 5–17.

Human Rights Watch. "The 'Miss World Riots': Continued Impunity for Killings in Kaduna" July 2003, 1–32. www.hrw.org.

———. "Rivers and Blood: Guns, Oil and Power in Nigeria's Rivers State," February 2005.

Huntington, Samuel P. *The Soldier and the State: The Theory and Politics of Civil-Military Relations*. New York: Vintage Books, 1957.

———. *Political Order in Changing Societies*. New Haven, Conn.: Yale University Press, 1968.

———. "Reforming Civil-Military Relations." Pp. 3–11 in *Civil-Military Relations and Democracy*, edited by Larry Diamond and Marc F. Plattner. Baltimore: Johns Hopkins University Press, 1996.

Hwang, Edward K. "Simulation of Political Development, Political Conflict, and Regulation Policies." *Journal of Political and Military Sociology* 25 (Winter 1997): 249–78.

Ihonvbere, Julius O. "Beyond Governance: The State and Democratization in Sub-Saharan Africa." *Journal of Asian and African Studies* 5 (1995): 154.

———. "Are Things Falling Apart? The Military and the Crisis of Democratization in Nigeria." *Journal of Modern African Studies* 34, no. 2 (June 1996): 193–225.

Ikem, Augustine, and Comfort Briggs-Anigboh. *Oil and Fiscal Federalism in Nigeria.* Aldershot, Eng.: Ashgate, 1998.

Ikime, Obaro. *Niger Delta Rivalry: Itshekiri-Urhobo Relations and the European Presence 1884–1936.* Harlow, UK: Longmans, 1969.

Ikenberry, John. "Why Export Democracy?" *Wilson Quarterly* 23, no. 3 (1999): 56–65.

Imobighe, T. A. "Warri Crisis in Historical and Contemporary Perspectives." Pp. 36–52 in *Conflict and Instability in the Niger Delta: The Warri Case,* edited by T. A. Imobighe, Celestine O. Bassey, and Judith Burdin Asuni. Abuja, Nigeria: Spectrum Books, 2002.

Ingham, Kenneth. *Politics in Modern Africa: The Uneven Tribal Dimension.* London: Routledge, 1990.

Ivison, Duncan. "Modus Vivendi Citizenship." Pp. 123–143 in *The Demands of Citizenship,* edited by Catriona McKinnon and Ian Hampsher-Monk. London: Continuum, 2003.

Janowitz, Morris. *The Military in the Political Development of New States.* Chicago: University of Chicago Press, 1964.

Jelin, Elizabeth. "Citizenship Revisited: Solidarity, Responsibility, and Rights." In *Constructing Democracy: Human Rights, Citizenship, and Society in Latin America,* edited by Elizabeth Jelin and Eric Hershberg. Boulder, Colo.: Westview Press, 1996.

Joseph, Richard A. *Democracy and Prebendal Politics in Nigeria: The Rise and Fall of the Second Republic.* New York: Cambridge University Press, 1987.

Joseph, Richard A., Peter Lewis, Darren Kew, and Scott Taylor. "The Making of the Modern Nigerian State." Pp. 545–606 in *Introduction to Comparative Politics: Political Challenges and Changing Agendas,* 2nd ed., edited by Mark Kesselman, Joel Krieger, and William A. Joseph. New York: Houghton-Mifflin, 2000.

Kalu, Kalu N. "The Praetorian Orthodoxy: Crisis of the Nigerian Military State." *Journal of Political and Military Sociology* 28 (Winter 2000): 271–92.

———. "Embedding African Democracy and Development: The Imperative of Institutional Capital." *International Review of Administrative Sciences* 70, no. 3 (2004): 527–45.

———. "Development and Identity: Framing the South-South Dialogue." Pp. 149–62 in *Vision and Policy in Nigerian Economics: The Legacy of Pius Okigbo,* edited by Jane I. Guyer and LaRay Denzer. Ibadan, Nigeria: Ibadan University Press, 2005.

Kalu, Ogbu. "Harsh Flutes: The Religious Dimension of the Legitimacy Crisis in Nigeria, 1993–1998." Lecture delivered at the Center for the Study of World Religions, Harvard University, February 24, 1999.

Kastfelt, Niels. *Religion and Politics in Nigeria: A Study in Middle Belt Christianity.* London: British Academic Press, 1994.

Kaufman, Chaim. "Possible and Impossible Solutions to Ethnic Civil Wars." *International Security* 20, no. 4 (1996): 136–75.

Keohane, Robert O., ed. *International Institutions and State Power: Essays in International Relations Theory*. Boulder, Colo.: Westview Press, 1989.

Kew, Darren, and Peter Lewis. "The Making of the Modern Nigerian State." Pp. 240–95 in *Introduction to Politics of the Developing World*, edited by William A. Joseph, Mark Kesselman, and Joel Krieger. Boston: Houghton-Mifflin Co, 2007.

Kew, Darren, and David L. Phillips. "Seeking Peace in the Niger Delta: Oil, Natural Gas, and Other Vital Resources." *The New England Journal of Public Policy* 21, no. 2 (June 2007): 154–70.

Key, V. O. *Politics, Parties, and Pressure Groups*. New York: Thomas Y. Cromwell, 1964.

Kirk-Green, Anthony, and Douglas Rimmer. *Nigeria Since 1970: A Political and Economic Outline*. London: Hodder and Stoughton, 1981.

Kirk-Green, A. H. M. *Lugard and the Amalgamation of Nigeria: A Documentary Record*. London: Frank Cass & Company Ltd, 1968.

———. *Crisis and Conflict in Nigeria: 1967–1970*. Vol. 2. London: Oxford University Press, 1971.

Krasner, Stephen D. "Sovereignty: An Institutional Perspective." *Comparative Political Studies* 21 (1988): 66–94.

Kriesberg, Louis, ed. *Constructive Conflicts: From Escalation to Resolution*. Lanham, Md.: Rowman & Littlefield, 2003.

Krueger, Anne O. "The Political Economy of a Rent-Seeking Society." *American Economic Review* 64: 291–303.

Kukah, Mathew Hassan, and Toyin Falola. *Religious Militancy and Self-Assertion: Islam and Politics in Nigeria*. Aldershot, Eng.: Avebury, 1996.

Lake, David A. "Beneath the Commerce of Nations: A Theory of International Economic Structures." *International Studies Quarterly* 28 (1984): 143–70.

Lapalombara, Joseph. *Politics Within Nations*. Englewood Cliffs, N.J.: Prentice Hall, 1974.

Lapalombara, Joseph, and Jeffrey Anderson. "Political Parties." Pp. 393–412 in *Encyclopedia of Government and Politics*, vol. 1, edited by Mary Hawkesworth and Maurice Kogan. New York: Routledge, 1992.

Li, Richard P. Y., and William R. Thompson. "The Coup Contagion Hypothesis." *Journal of Conflict Resolution* 19, no. 1 (1975): 63–88.

Lijphart, Arend. "Consociational Democracy." Pp. 133–47 in *Comparative Politics: Notes and Readings*, edited by Roy C. Macridis and Bernard E. Brown. Homewood, Ill: The Dorsey Press, 1977.

———. "The Power-Sharing Approach." Pp. 491–509 in *Conflict and Peacemaking in Multiethnic Societies*, edited by Joseph V. Montville. Lexington, Mass.: Lexington Books, 1990.

Linz, Juan J., and Alfred Stepan. *Problems of Democratic Transition and Consolidation: Southern Europe, South American, and Post-Communist Europe*. Baltimore: The Johns Hopkins University Press, 1996.

Linz, Juan J., and Arturo Valenzuela, eds. *The Failure of Presidential Democracy*. Baltimore: Johns Hopkins University Press, 1994.

Luciani, Giacomo. "Oil and Political Economy in the International Relations of the Middle East." Pp. 79–104 in *International Relations of the Middle East*, edited by Louise Fawcett. New York: Oxford University Press, 2005.

Luckham, A. R. *The Nigerian Military: A Sociological Analysis of Authority & Revolt 1967–1970*. London: Cambridge University Press, 1971.

Machiavelli, Niccolo. *Discourses on Livy*. New York: Barnes and Noble Publishing, 2005.

MacIntyre, Alasdair. *Whose Justice? Which Rationality?* Notre Dame, Ind.: University of Notre Dame Press, 1988.

MacIver, Robert M. "The Myth of Authority." Pp. 263–99 in *Comparative Politics: Notes and Readings*, edited by Roy C. Macridis and Bernard Brown. Homewood, Ill.: The Dorsey Press, 1977.

Macridis, Roy C., and Bernard E. Brown. "The Political Process." Pp. 237–62 in *Comparative Politics: Notes and Readings*, edited by Roy C. Macridis and Bernard Brown. Homewood, Ill.: The Dorsey Press, 1977.

Mahdavy, Hossein. "The Pattern and Problems of Economic Development in Rentier States: The Case of Iran." Pp. 428–67 in *Studies in the Economic History of the Middle East*, edited by M. A. Cook. Oxford: Oxford University Press, 1970.

Maier, Karl. *This House Has Fallen: Midnight in Nigeria*. New York: Public Affairs, 2000.

Mamdani, Mahmood. *Citizen and Subject: Contemporary Africa and the Legacy of Late Colonialism*. Princeton, N.J.: Princeton University Press, 1996.

March, James G., and Johan P. Olsen. "The New Institutionalism: Organizational Factors in Political Life." *American Political Science Review* 78 (1984): 734–49.

———. *Rediscovering Institutions: The Organizational Basis of Politics*. New York: Free Press, 1989.

Marx, Karl, "Economic and Philosophical Manuscripts: Selections." Pp. 52–106 in *The Marx-Engels Reader*, edited by Robert C. Tucker. New York: Norton, 1972 [1844]).

Mayer, Lawrence, John Burnett, and Susan Ogden. *Comparative Politics: Nations and Theories in a Changing World*. Upper Saddle River, N.J.: Prentice Hall, 1996.

Mbachu, Ndulue. "Nigeria's Military Purge Seen as Timely." *Reuters Ltd*, June 11, 1999.

Meagher, Kate. "Social Capital, Social Liabilities, and Political Capital: Social Networks and Informal Manufacturing in Nigeria." *African Affairs* 105/421 (2006): 553–82.

Migdal, Joel S. *Strong Societies and Weak States: State-Society Relations and State Capabilities in the Third World*. Princeton, N.J.: Princeton University Press, 1988.

Midgal, Joel S., Atul Kohli, and Vivienne Shue. *State Power and Social Forces: Domination and Transformation in the Third World*. New York: Cambridge University Press, 1994.

Moe, Terry M. "Political Institutions: The Neglected Side of the Story." Special Issue, *Journal of Law, Economics, and Organization* 6 (1990).

Morris, William, ed. *The American Heritage Dictionary of the English Language*. Boston: Houghton Mifflin, 1976.

Mouawad, Jad. "Growing Unrest Posing a Threat to Nigerian Oil." *New York Times*, April 21, 2007. www.nytimes.com/2007/04/21/business/worldbusiness/21oil.html.

Mueller, John. "The Banality of 'Ethnic' War." *International Security* 25, no. 1 (Summer 2000): 42–70.

Nafziger, E. Wayne. *The Economics of Political Instability: The Nigerian-Biafran War.* Boulder, Colo.: Westview Press, 1983.

Nelson, Harold D., ed. *Nigeria: A Country Study.* Washington, D.C.: American University, 1982.

Nelson, Joan M. "The Politics of Economic Transformation: Is the Third World Experience Relevant in Eastern Europe?" *World Politics* 45, no. 3 (April 1993): 433–63.

The News. "The Leader of the Leader," December 18, 2000, 17.

Nibor, Ima. "Blood Bath in the Delta." *Tell Magazine*, no. 3 (January 1999).

Nkemdirim, Benjamin. *Social Change and Political Violence in Colonial Nigeria.* Devon, UK: Arthur H. Stockwell, 1975.

Nnoli, Okwudiba. *Ethnic Politics in Nigeria.* Enugu, Nigeria: Fourth Dimension Publishers, 1978.

Nordlinger, Eric A. *Soldiers in Politics: Military Coups and Governments.* Englewood Cliffs, N.J.: Prentice Hall, 1977.

North, Douglas C. *Institutions, Institutional Change, and Economic Performance.* Cambridge: Cambridge University Press, 1990.

Northern Regional Government. *Report on the Kano Disturbances.* Nigeria: Government Printer, 1953.

Nwankwo, Agwuncha Arthur. *The Military Option to Democracy: Class, Power, and Violence in Nigerian Politics.* Enugu, Nigeria: Fourth Dimension Publishers, 1984.

———. *Nigerians As Outsiders: Military Dictatorship and Nigeria's Destiny.* Enugu, Nigeria: Fourth Dimension Press, 1996.

Nzimiro, Ikenna. "British-Fulani Conquests Weakened National Unity." *Nigeria Marches On* (1985): 9–14.

Obasanjo, Olusegun. "Democracy and Development in Africa." Speech delivered at Harvard University's ARCO Forum for Public Affairs, Kennedy School of Government, October 30, 1999.

Oche, O. "Low Intensity Conflicts, National Security and Democratic Sustenance." Pp. 108–23 in *Nigeria Under Democratic Rule, 1993–2003*, vol. 2, edited by Hassan A. Saliu. Ibadan, Nigeria: University Press PLC, 2005.

Oderemi, Kunle. "2007 Presidency: Arewa vs. Ohanaeze No Retreat, No Surrender," *Sunday Punch*, May 16, 2004.

Okeke, Okechukwu. *Hausa-Fulani Hegemony: The Dominance of the Muslim North in Contemporary Nigerian Politics.* Enugu, Nigeria: Arena Press, 1992.

Okonta, Ike. "Nigeria: Chronicle of a Dying State." Pp. 213–217 in *World Politics*, 27th ed., edited by Helen E. Purkit. Dubuque, Ia.: McGraw-Hill, 2007.

Omeje, Kenneth. "Petrobusiness and Security Threats in the Niger Delta, Nigeria." *Current Sociology* 54, no. 3 (2006): 477–99.

———. "The Rentier State: Oil-Related Legislation and Conflict in the Niger Delta, Nigeria." *Conflict, Security and Development* 6, no. 2 (June 2006): 211–30.

———. "Oil Conflict and Accumulation Politics in Nigeria." Report from Africa: Population, Health, Environment, and Conflict, *ECSP Report* 12 (2007): 44–49.

Osaghae, Eghosa E. "Regulating Conflicts in Nigeria." *Peace Review* 14, no. 2 (June 2002): 217–24.

————. "Explaining the Changing Patterns of Ethnic Politics in Nigeria." *National-ism and Ethnic Politics* 9, no. 3 (Autumn 2003): 54–73.

Oyediran, Oyeleye, eds. *Survey of Nigerian Affairs, 1978–1979.* Lagos, Nigeria: Ni-gerian Institute of International Affairs, 1988.

Parsons, Talcott. *The Structure of Social Action.* New York: McGraw-Hill, 1937.

————. "A Sociological Approach to the Theory of Organizations." Pp. 16–58 in *Structure and Processes in Modern Societies*, edited by Talcott Parsons. Glencoe, Ill.: Free Press, 1956.

Perlmutter, Amos. "The Praetorian State and the Praetorian Army: Toward a Tax-onomy of Civil-Military Relations in Developing Polities." *Comparative Politics* 1, no. 3 (1969): 382–404.

Peters, Enrique Dussel, and Mathew A. Verghis. "The State, Market, and Devel-opment: A Rapporteurs Report." Working Paper 196, summary of conference papers and discussion held at the Kellog Institute, June 1993, 1–14. kellogg .nd.edu/publications/workingpapers/WPS/196.pdf.

Pham, J. Peter. "Nigeria: Crisis of Legitimacy." *The National Interest Online*, April 24, 2007. www.nationalinterest.org.

The Project for the Research of Islamic Movements (PRISM). "Nigerian Oil 'Total War.'" Herzilya, Israel. www.e-prism.org.

Przeworski, Adam, Michael E. Alvarez, Jose Antonio Cheibub, and Fernando Limongi, *Democracy and Development: Political Institutions and Well-Being in the World, 1950–1990.* New York: Cambridge University Press, 2000.

Putnam, Robert D. *The Comparative Study of Political Elites.* Englewood Cliffs, N.J.: Prentice Hall, 1976.

————. *Making Democracy Work: Civic Traditions in Modern Italy.* Princeton, N.J.: Princeton University Press, 1993.

————. "Turning In, Turning Out: The Strange Disappearance of Social Capital in America." *Political Science & Politics* 28 (1995): 664–83.

Rabushka, Alvin, and Kenneth A. Shepsle. *Politics in Plural Societies: A Theory of Democratic Instability.* Columbus, Ohio: Charles E. Merrill, 1972.

Reis, Fabio Wanderley. "The State, the Market, and Democratic Citizenship." Pp. 121–37 in *Constructing Democracy: Human Rights, Citizenship, and Society in Latin America*, edited by Elizabeth Jelin and Eric Hershberg. Boulder, Colo.: Westview Press, 1996.

Rial, Juan. "Armies and Civil Society in Latin America." In *Civil-Military Relations and Democracy*, edited by Larry Diamond and Marc F. Plattner. Baltimore: Johns Hopkins University Press, 1996.

Rose-Ackerman, Susan. *Corruption and Government: Causes, Consequences, and Re-form.* New York: Cambridge University Press, 1999.

Rosenbluth, Frances McCall. *Financial Politics in Contemporary Japan.* Ithaca, N.Y.: Cornell University Press, 1989.

Roth, Guenther, and Claus Wittich, ed. *Max Weber: Economy and Society: An Outline of Interpretive Sociology.* Vol. 1. Berkeley: University of California Press, 1978.

Rothchild, D. S. "Safeguarding Nigeria's Minorities." *Duquesne Review* 8 (Spring 1964): 34–51.

Rotberg, Robert I. "Failed States in a World of Terror." Pp. 131–37 in *Global Poli-tics in a Changing World*, 3rd ed., edited by Richard W. Mansbach and Edward Rhodes. Boston: Houghton Mifflin, 2006.

Ruggie, John Gerard. "International Regimes, Transactions, and Change: Embedded Liberalism in the Post-War Economic Order." *International Organization* 36, no. 2 (1982): 379–415.

Rustow, Dankwart A. "Transitions to Democracy: Toward a Dynamic Model." *Comparative Politics* 2, no. 3 (April 1970): 337–60.

Sachs, Jeffrey. "Helping the World's Poorest." *The Economist*, August 14, 1999.

Sachs, Jeffrey, and Andrew M. Warner. "Natural Resource Abundance and Economic Growth." *Development Discussion Paper* 517a. Cambridge, Mass.: Harvard Institute for International Development, October 1995.

Sandbrook, Richard. *The Politics of Africa's Economic Recovery*. New York: Cambridge University Press, 1993.

Sarkesian, Sam C. "Military Professionalism and Civil-Military Relations in the West." *International Political Science Review* 2, no. 3 (1981): 283–97.

Sartori, Giovanni. "Concept Misinformation in Comparative Politics." Pp. 24–49 in *Comparative Politics: Notes and Readings*, edited by Roy C. Macridis and Bernard Brown. Homewood, Ill.: The Dorsey Press, 1977.

Schon, Donald A., and Martin Rein. *Frame Reflection: Toward the Resolution of Intractable Policy Controversies*. New York: Basic Books, 1994.

Schraeder, Peter J. *African Politics and Society: A Mosaic in Transformation*. New York: Bedford/St. Martin's, 2000.

Scott, Richard W. *Institutions and Organizations*. 2nd ed. Thousand Oaks, Calif.: Sage Publications, 2001.

Scrutiny. "The Missing Billions," July 1998, 1.

Sen, Amartya. "Democracy as a Universal Value." *Journal of Democracy* 10, no. 3 (1999): 3–17.

Serageldin, Ismail. Foreword to "Social Capital and Poverty," by Paul Collier. Working Paper 4, World Bank's Social Capital Initiative, Washington, D.C., November 1998.

Shain, Yossi, and Juan J. Linz. *Between States: Interim Governments and Democratic Transitions*. New York: Cambridge University Press, 1995.

Shepsle, Kenneth A, "Studying Institutions: Lessons from the Rational Choice Approach." *Journal of Theoretical Politics* 1 (1989): 131–47.

Shepsle, Kenneth A., and Barry R. Weingast. "Positive Theories of Congressional Institutions." Pp. 5–35 in *Positive Theories of Congressional Institutions*, ed. Kenneth A. Shepsle and Barry R. Weingast. Ann Arbor: University of Michigan Press, 1995.

Shoemaker, Pamela, James W. Tankard, and Dominic L. Lasorsa. *How to Build Social Science Theories*. Thousand Oaks, Calif.: Sage Publications, 2004.

Singh, Ajit. "Openness and Market-Friendly Approach to Development: Learning the Right Lessons from Development Experience." *World Development Report* 22, no. 12 (1994): 1811–23.

Skocpol, Theda. *States and Social Revolutions: A Comparative Analysis of France, Russia, and China*. New York: Cambridge University Press, 1979.

———. "Bringing the State Back In: Strategies of Analysis in Current Research." Pp. 3–37 in *Bringing the State Back In*, edited by Peter B. Evans, Dietrich Rueschemeyer, and Theda Skocpol. Cambridge: Cambridge University Press, 1985.

Snyder, Richard. "Paths Out of Sultanistic Regimes: Combining Structural and Voluntarist Perspectives." Pp. 49–81 in *Sultanistic Regimes*, edited by H. E. Chehabi and Juan J. Linz. Baltimore: Johns Hopkins University Press, 1998.

Somerekun, Kayode. *Perspectives on the Nigerian Oil Industry*. Lagos, Nigeria: Amkra Books, 1995.

Stepan, Alfred. *The Military in Politics: Changing Patterns in Brazil*. Princeton, N.J.: Princeton University Press, 1971.

———. "The New Professionalism of Internal Warfare and Military Role-Expansion," in *Authoritarian Brazil*, ed. Alfred Stepan. New Haven, Conn.: University Press, 1973.

———. *The State and Society: Peru in Comparative Perspective*. Princeton, N.J.: Princeton University Press, 1978.

———. *Rethinking Military Politics: Brazil and the Southern Cone*. Princeton, N.J.: Princeton University Press, 1988.

Stever, James A. "The Glass Firewall Between Military and Civil Administration." *Administration and Society* 31, no. 1 (1999): 43.

Streeten, Paul. "Markets and States: Against Minimalism." *World Development Report* 21, no. 8 (1993): 1281–98.

Suberu, Rotimi T. *Federalism and Ethnic Conflict in Nigeria*. Washington, D.C.: United States Institute of Peace, 2001.

Tarrow, Sidney. "Inside Insurgencies: Politics and Violence in an Age of Civil War." *American Political Science Review* 5, no. 3 (2007): 587–600.

Tell Magazine. "Plundering and Looting Unlimited," August 24, 1998, 12–32.

Timberg, Craig. "Christians Turn on Muslims in Nigeria, More Than 30 Die." *Washington Post Foreign Service*, February 23, 2006.

Tyson, Carole Henderson, and Mary K. Graber. "The Future of U.S. Policy Toward Africa." *Focus*. Washington, D.C.: Joint Center for Political and Economic Studies, 2001.

Ujo, A. A. *Citizenship in Nigeria*. Kaduna, Nigeria: Passmark International, 1994.

Ukiwo, Ukoha. "The Study of Ethnicity in Nigeria." *Oxford Development Studies* 33, no. 1 (March 2005): 7–23.

U.S. Energy Information Administration. *Nigeria: Country Analysis Briefs*, Department of Energy, International Energy Annual, April 2007. www.eia.doe.gov.

U.S. State Department. "Nigeria: Country Report on Human Rights Practices for 1996." Bureau of Democracy, Human Rights, and Labor, January 30, 1997.

Van Gelder, Jan Willem, and Joseph Moerkamp. "The Niger Delta: A Disrupted Ecology—The Role of Shell and Other Oil Companies." A Discussion paper by Greenpeace Nederland.

Vaughan, Olufemi. *Nigerian Chiefs: Traditional Power in Modern Politics, 1890s–1990s*. Rochester, N.Y.: University of Rochester Press, 2000.

Wade, Robert. "East Asia's Economic Success: Conflicting Perspectives, Partial Insights, Shaky Evidence." *World Politics* 44 (January 1992): 270–320.

Weber, Max, *The Theory of Social and Economic Organization*. Translated and edited by A M. Henderson and Talcott Parsons. New York: Oxford University Press, 1947.

Weick, Karl. *The Social Psychology of Organizing*. 2nd ed. New York: McGraw-Hill Inc, 1979.

Weingast, Barry R. "The Political Institutions of Representative Government," Working Paper in Political Science P-89-14. Hoover Institution, Stanford University, 1989.

West Africa. "Zik Starts a Debate." March 27, 1965, 333.

———. "Nigeria After the War: Lubricating the Economy with Oil." Saturday, 24 1970, 99.

Widner, Jennifer, ed. *Economic Change and Political Liberalization in Sub-Saharan Africa*. Baltimore: Johns Hopkins University Press, 1994.

Williamson, Oliver E. *The Economic Institutions of Capitalism*. New York: Free Press, 1985.

Wright, Stephen. *Nigeria: Struggle for Stability and Status*. Boulder, Colo.: Westview Press, 1998.

Yates, Douglas. *The Rentier State in Africa: Oil Rent Dependency and Neocolonialism in the Republic of Gabon*. Trenton, N.J.: Africa World Press, Inc, 1996.

Zakaria, Fareed. *From Wealth to Power: The Unusual Origins of America's World Role*. Princeton, N.J.: Princeton University Press, 1998.

Zysman, John. *Governments, Markets, and Growth: Finance and the Politics of Industrial Change*. Ithaca, N.Y.: Cornell University, 1983.

Index

Ironsi, 73, 93. *See also* Aguiyi-Ironsi, J.
   T. U.
Islamic religion, 42
Isoko, 174
Itshekiri, 66, 174; Itshekiri-Urhobo
   relations, 66–69
Iwu, Maurice, 165

Jammeh, Yahya, 203
Janowitz, Morris, 90
Japan, 23
Jasawa, 58
Jawara, Dawda, 203
Jibo, Mvendaga, 117n17
Jibril, Aliyu, 78
Jimeta, 58
Joint Action Committee of Nigeria,
   102
Joint Development Zone (JDZ), 135
Jonathan, Goodluck, 180
Jos, 73
Jukun ethnic groups, 58

Kaduna, 81; Christian population in,
   83–84; crisis, 58; killings in, 83;
   mayhem in, 83; mafia, 95; Sharia in,
   83, 84
Kafanchan riots, 80
Kampala, Uganda, 108
Kano, 73, 81; census in, 70; economic
   hegemony in, 70; riots of May 1953,
   70–71
Kasuwan Maganis riot (1984), 80
Katat people, 79
Kataf Youth Development Association
   (KYDA), 78
Katsina State, 162
Kebbi, 81
Kenya, 161, 162
Kenyatta, Jomo, 202
Key, V. O., 167
Kiama Declaration, 178
Kibaki, Mwai, 161
Kingibe, Bana, 106
Kirk-Green, A. H. M., 39
Kolade, Christopher, 149
Kyari, Abba, 91

Lagos, xvii; colony of, 36; Lagos-
   Ibadan axis, xviii
laissez-faire market individualism, 16
Land Use Decree of 1978, 184
Langtang gang, 95
Lapalombara, Joseph, 111
Largema, Abogo, 116n11
Lasswell, Harold, 146
latency effect, 153
Latin America, 137, 139
legal-institutional-descriptive
   approach, 15
legal-rational legitimation, 26
legal residency rules, 192
legislative hegemony, 38
legislative supremacy, 38
legitimacy, xv; crisis, 96
liberal democracy, 3, 113, 188;
   economic doctrine, 21
liberalization, 201
Liberia, 203, 204
Linz, Juan, 152
logic of appropriateness, 212
Lord Lugard's Amalgamation of, 55
Luckham, A. R., 90
Lugard, Sir Frederick, 34, 36
Lyttleton Cosntitution of 1954, 57

Macaulay, Herbert, 39
Machiavellian statecraft, 9
MacMillan Center for International
   and Area Studies, xv, xix
Macpherson Constitution of 1951, 38, 74
Madagascar, 206
mafiocracy, 167
Mahdavi, Hossein, 123
Maiduguri, 58; riots, 84
Maimalari, Zakariya, 116n11
Maitatsine religious riots, 57;
   followers, 77; sect, 77
majority rule, 188, 190
Malaysia, 23
Mariam, Mengistu Haile, 204
Marcos, 26
marginalization, 170
market economy, 209
market failures, 7

Organization of African Unity, 108
Organization of Petroleum Exporting
    Countries (OPEC), 137, 139
organized amateurism, 130–31
Orkar, Gideon, 95
Orok, 116n12
orthodoxy, 89–120
Osaghae, Eghosa E., 184
Osogbo, 68
Osun state, 68
over-arching agency, 12
Oyo refugees, 68–69

Pahlavi, Shah Reza, 123
Pam, Yakubu, 116n11
Pandora's Box, 90
parallel distortions, 124
parochial objectives, 111
Parsonian structural-functionalism, 199
party democracy, xviii
patrimonialism, 24, 104; tendencies, 24
patron-client arrangements, 25;
    relationship, 25
People's Democratic Party, 17, 131,
    162, 165, 166
Perlmutter, 4, 100
Perlmutter, Amos, 99, 150
petro-authoritarianism, 141
Petroleum and Natural Gas Senior
    Staff Association of Nigeria
    (PENGASSAN), 136
Petroleum Decree 1969, 126, 184
Petroleum Trust Fund, 105
petrolist states, 140
Plateau state, 59, 60, 81
policy controversies, 19
policy disequilibrium, 209
political activism, xvi; anarchy, 98;
    assassinations, 1; authority, 89;
    brinkmanship, 76; citizenship, 147;
    contestation, 1; corruption, 45;
    culture, xvi, 115, 195; development,
    xv, 4, 7, 33, 39, 89, 187; disunity,
    77; dynamics, 1; economy, 6, 7,
    21; education, 115; engagement,
    148; godfatherism, 45; identity, 53;
    impasse, 96; impenetrability, 42;
    indoctrination, 111, 115; instability,

1, 22, 24; institutions, 211;
    integration, 3, 56; knowledge, 113;
    legitimacy, 51; liberalization, 22,
    157; mobilization, 76; opportunity,
    61; participation, 7, 24, 62; parties,
    35; power, 114; prisoners, 102;
    profiteering, 92, 115; recruitment,
    111; solidarity, 16; space, xviii;
    subjugation, 3; system, 49, 113;
    tycoons, 128
political-diplomatic approach, 45
Political Memorandum no. 9 of 1918, 48
political mining, 128
*Politics and Society in Contemporary
    Africa* (Chazan et al.), 2
politics of personality, 111
popular consensus, xvi
postcolonial regime, 14
postmodern liberalism, 199, 206
poverty, 210
practical realism, 111
praetorian guards, 89, 158;
    guardians, 101; military state,
    146; praetorianism, 99; praetorian
    society, 99
prebendalism, 6, 25; prebends, 24
prebendal politics, 25
Presidential Election Petition Tribunal,
    164
presidentialism, 8, 190
Presidential Policy Advisory
    Committee (PPAC), 150
presidential system, 1891
presultanistic oligarchies, 27
primordial politics, 47; attachments, 99
principle of derivation, 52
privatization, 105
Privy Council, 46
procedural legitimacy, 200
pro-democracy activist, 102, 106
pro-democracy organizations, 19
production sharing contracts (PSCs),
    132
productive entrepreneurship, 125
professional code, 90; education, 113
progressive administration, 109
property rights, 192, 201
Prophet Mohammed, 82, 84

About the Author

Kalu N. Kalu is an associate professor of political science at Auburn University–Montgomery (AUM). He has been a research affiliate at the Council on African Studies/The Macmillan Center for International and Area Studies, Yale University. He also teaches courses on national security and intelligence policy—Globalization and Governance, and International Conflict Processes: War & Peace—in the AUM's Air University Graduate Program in International Relations offered at Maxwell Air Force Base. His research emphasis is in the areas of institutional development and organizational change, citizenship and administrative theory, IT-leadership interface, complex adaptive systems, civil-military relations, national security and intelligence policy, and health care politics and policies. Dr. Kalu is widely published, with articles appearing in leading peer-reviewed journals and handbooks such as *Journal of Political and Military Sociology, Administrative Theory & Praxis, Public Administration Review, Administration & Society, International Review of Administrative Sciences, American Review of Public Administration, Social Science Computer Review, Handbook of Research on Public Information Technology, Homeland Security Handbook, the Yale Political Quarterly*, and others. He has participated in several international learned conferences and traveled extensively to many parts of the world including Canada, Germany, Sweden, Denmark, Italy, Israel, United Arab Emirates, Singapore, and Malaysia. Correspondence may be sent to kkalu@aum.edu.